Spectacle Culture and American Identity

Spectacle Culture and American Identity

1815–1940

Susan Tenneriello

First published in 2013 by
PALGRAVE MACMILLAN®
in the United States—a division of St. Martin's Press LLC,
175 Fifth Avenue, New York, NY 10010.

Where this book is distributed in the UK, Europe and the rest of the world,
this is by Palgrave Macmillan, a division of Macmillan Publishers Limited,
registered in England, company number 785998, of Houndmills,
Basingstoke, Hampshire RG21 6XS.

Palgrave Macmillan is the global academic imprint of the above companies
and has companies and representatives throughout the world.

Palgrave® and Macmillan® are registered trademarks in the United States,
the United Kingdom, Europe and other countries.

ISBN: 978–1–137–36061–8

Library of Congress Cataloging-in-Publication Data

Tenneriello, Susan.
    Spectacle culture and American identity, 1815–1940 / by Susan
Tenneriello.
        pages cm
    Includes bibliographical references and index.
    ISBN 978–1–137–36061–8 (alk. paper)
        1. Popular culture—United States—History. 2. National
characteristics, American. 3. Spectacular, The. I. Title.

E169.1.T4635 2013
306.0973—dc23   2013024011

A catalogue record of the book is available from the British Library.

Design by Newgen Knowledge Works (P) Ltd., Chennai, India.

First edition: December 2013

10 9 8 7 6 5 4 3 2 1

To Peter

Star Rock Seacoast

Contents

Figures

Acknowledgments

Writing this book has taken me down a long, winding road. I began soon after graduating from the PhD Program in Theatre at the CUNY Graduate Center. Many people pass through its pages directly and indirectly. My roots at the CUNY Graduate Center continue to nourish any path I'm on. First, I must thank Judith Milhous, Daniel Gerould, Marvin Carlson, and Jean Graham-Jones for their vitality, wit, encouragement, and advice, which accompany all my endeavors.

Without the institutional support I have received, the wide-ranging research necessary could not have been accomplished. Three Performing Arts Research Grants from PSC-CUNY between 2008 and 2012 allowed me to travel and complete sections of the manuscript. Two Whiting mini-Grants from 2009 to 2011 also provided timely research support. I thank the Office of the Provost and Dean Jeffrey Peck of the Weissman School of Arts and Sciences at Baruch College for travel funding to numerous conferences while I was working on chapters. In addition, this study benefits from research assistance provided by the Baruch Honors Program and its Director Nancy Aries.

I extend warm thanks to David Savran and James Wilson, co-editors of *The Journal of American Drama and Theatre*, for allowing me to reprint an article on Imre Kiralfy, which forms part of chapter 3. Numerous research collections, curators, and librarians have aided me with illustrative materials and documents. I'm indebted to Jason Jurgena from the US Department of the Interior Museum. Thanks to AnnaLee Pauls and Charles Greene at Princeton University Library for their gracious assistance. I also want to express my appreciation to the Minnesota Historical Society, Cornell University Library, Yale University's Beinecke Rare Book and Manuscript Library, History Colorado, and the Smithsonian American Art Museum.

Palgrave Macmillan's continued interest since the early stages of the manuscript has been a constant source of encouragement. My gratitude to this commitment runs deep. Special thanks to associate editor Robyn Curtis for steering me through. I also thank editorial assistant Erica Buchman for all her help. My appreciation extends to the indispensable Daniel Gundlach for preparing the index. Through many revisions reshaping the manuscript, the perceptive feedback from blind readers has enriched the whole. Their considerable attention, critical insights, and specific recommendations are most appreciated. Remaining flaws are mine.

I'm fortunate for friends and colleagues that have given me unstinting advice and clarity. Barbara Lewis emboldened my thinking overall, especially on panoramic space. Mimi D'Aponte sharpened some of my ideas on the theme. Conversations with Marla Carlson, Rose Malague, and Bruce Kirle provoked me forward. I can't forget Jill Dolan's generous counsel. My wonderful colleagues in the Fine and Performing Arts Department and across Baruch College sustained me through every phase. I'm thankful for the enthusiastic and steady guidance from colleagues Terry Berkowitz, Karen Shelby, and Katherine Behar. Office Manger Skip Dietrich's nimble assistance is deeply appreciated. Jana O'Keefe Bazzoni, Paula Berggren, and Suzanne Epstein, I thank for their foresight.

Walking every step of the way with me is my family. Loving thanks to Patti and Joe Hewitt, Geraldine Tenneriello, and Sara and Brian Darby for keeping me grounded, patiently enduring my neglect, giving me unconditional support, and making me pasta. Understanding and humor make me grateful for friends Elise Engler, Leslie Atherholt, Manolo Tejeda, Donna Mitchell, Laura Kidder, and Roz Koenen. All my love to Peter Golfinopoulos, the beacon in my life.

Introduction: Setting the Scene

Spectacle is ubiquitous and agile; it leaps and burrows throughout virtual, live, and static mediums. Although spectacle is a constant presence today, my interest led back in time to sift out its span in modern cultural production. What set of practices contribute to its indelible, yet shape shifting propensities? The pursuit of this question is the foundation of this book: to investigate the emerging industries of spectacle as a permeable tradition, one that admits and yields interdisciplinary methods. I concentrate my analysis on the immersive sensibilities of spectacle in nineteenth- and early twentieth-century American mass culture. Competing influences converge in spectacle practices that are tightly coupled to the explosive growth of the culture industry in the United States.[1] In particular, two aspects of this circulation hold significance for me. One is the billowing attraction of scenic spectacles that wind through an experiential "American" landscape. The sites and landscape subjects popularized in scenic spectacles pour into painted installation panoramas, multimedia performances, exhibition settings, and artfully staged museum dioramas. Related to these trends are the flourishing technologies of sensory media that scenic spectacles absorb and reflect. Production processes assemble cross-disciplinary methods that ingest vision technology, theatricality, and environmental interaction. Incorporating art historical and media treatments of immersive techniques, I accent the changing American landscape as a fluid "scene space" in order to foreground the networked ways in which spectacle mediums shaped, and were shaped by, the larger social, economic, and political forces of the day.

In respect to landscape dynamics, my focus on scenic spectacles pursues an underlining question. How does the territorial acquisition of land, as a scenic economy of "American" history, flow in tandem back and forth along the landscape spectrum of physical sites? Perhaps you have visited the Grand Canyon or walked across the Brooklyn Bridge?

.In the nineteenth century, these iconic forces of "nature," physical and technical, claims of wrested territorial possession and engineering superiority, stirred a porous scenic status of poetry and actuality. Panoramic and multimedia spectacles of the Grand Canyon and the Brooklyn Bridge joined stages of sensation filled "scenic views" in nineteenth-century entertainments that play reverberating roles in designating landscape "American." Scenic spectacles, in particular, offer immersive vantage points into the recessive spaces, immediacy, violence, and ephemeral sensorium embedded in the socioeconomic agency of a perpetually moving horizon line of nationhood.

A terrain of landscape subjects, geographical locations, and site-specific environments most concerns me. Its array of scenic phenomena on and beyond the stage leeches into a staple ingredient of mass entertainments, a quest for novelty—the immediacy of something new or unusual. Walt Whitman, in the first edition of *Leaves of Grass*, attributed the natural dynamism of the country to a "live nation," taking creative agency to frame freedom in the spiritual substance of a multifarious landscape.[2] Creative engagement with "live" scenic models distributed a societal lexicon suggesting an ongoing discourse with landscape. By elaboration, scenic spectacles interact with segments of a competitive culture industry, and so articulate ways cutting-edge technology rejuvenates the sentient motion of the national landscape. In a shorthand way, scenic spectacles locate sites of novelty; broadly speaking, they bring into perspective "a new scene."

I apply a cross-disciplinary orientation to the historical research in order to stretch performance analysis over wider contexts in which art history and media histories encourage theatrical applications. The vast collection of stationary painted panoramas, theatrical moving panoramas, site-specific performances, government-sponsored fairs, and museum dioramic displays have received broad historical treatment. Richard D. Altick's foundational study of nineteenth-century urban culture and popular entertainments in England, *The Shows of London* (1978), surveys the spread of panoramas, dioramas, and exhibitions. For decades, more nuanced and specialized studies continue to distinguish nationalized and global components in various genres of cultural display.[3] Studies of American activities remain fragmented in historical and theoretical examinations of separate genres.[4] By contrast, I collate a select matrix of scenic models that have not received wide critical examination side by side in order to bundle a set of case studies that directly animate landscape on historical platforms of sensory media.

Central to this study is blending comparative studies from art history and visual culture with commercial and institutional spectacle productions. Deliberations of new media often address aesthetic technology in respect to scenic frames, editing, and perceptional illusion important to contemporary modalities of virtual spaces.[5] In contrast to this work, I take a different approach in order to explore sensory enactment. I confine my scope primarily to commercial and administrative applications of spectacle mediums that serve to actualize or dramatize scenes of wonder and enterprise. Revisiting icons of wonder and enterprise highlight landmarks of a scenic heritage founded in economic ideography that abounded in physical nature and human ingenuity. Diverse systems of live and static media presence flow along these trajectories. This activity spans a time frame from 1815 to 1915, and reaches to the 1940s. Its range corresponds to the Federal period's departure from agrarian social states, past industrialization, and through different avenues of corporate globalism.

Core genres of scenic spectacles I cover are installation panoramas, multimedia performance, site-specific spectacles, exhibition attractions, and educational media. Each form carries sight lines beyond fixed frames. These sight lines radiate perplexing fragmentation and density across scenic routes that contemporaneously transmit a variable national landscape. They branch into different facets of immersive practices that arguably course through other forms of popular entertainment. Of significance is how scenic spectacles pass back and forth fitfully from the physical phenomena of the land to mythology, fantasy, illusion, or reality, depending on the political, individual, or institutional authority defining the meaning of the word "America." Further, I believe they complement a larger, more deeply examined historical field of pre-twentieth-first century spectacle culture that my specific focus here omits: community pageants, public demonstrations, and popular entertainments, such as circus, melodrama, minstrelsy, burlesque, or Wild West Shows. The significance of spectacle I tug at theorizes its properties in practical processes of production. By examining acting vocabularies of visual technology, theatricality, and environmental staging in concurrent types of sensory media, I investigate a branch of infrastructure in the culture industry interlocking scenic distribution of an economic "nature." In addition, spectacle's autonomous regeneration opens contexts for the examination of how creative democracy is a transgressive part of civilian dialog. This creative and practical topography raises questions relative to the imprecise definitions of national belonging and borders.

Changing American Landscapes in Scenic Spectacles

Panoramic spectacles or "scenic shows" become popular in America by the early 1800s. American artists quickly transformed this novel form of vision technology into installation mediums that tapped into the scenic features of the North American landscape: Niagara Falls, the Hudson and Mississippi Rivers, and the Western Rockies. Reformulations of "native" subject matter appeared in touring scenic excursions among swirling debates of identity and ideas of nationhood. Theatrical moving panoramas on the popular stage demonstrate a wide variety of multimedia storytelling. These performance panoramas broadcast different viewpoints engaging social discourse. Their divergence from each other offer insight into how individual positions reinvent, reaffirm, or dissent in formally constituted principles of nationalism and citizenship as ongoing, all embracing, and predestined, assuming totality is an illusion. Borrowing a phrase from Daphne A. Brooks's examination of escaped slave Henry Box Brown's radical abolition panorama *Mirror of Slavery*, performers "enter the landscape."[6] Brooks brings attention to spectacle as strategies of intervention to disorient perceptions of race in political activism and performance in *Bodies in Dissent: Spectacular Performances of Race and Freedom, 1850–1910*. My examination reaches into developing industries and methods of fabrication. Early scenic spectacles distribute embodied, experiential energies that express critical viewpoints, competitive tactics, and aesthetic strategies amplifying divisions and transitions in social democracy. Among the first mass sightings of the internal geography of the United States in European capitols were scenic shows touring Niagara Falls, the Mississippi River, Indian ethnographies, and slave narratives.

Experimental practices, variations of storytelling, and disparity over the "American" experience are some of the characteristics of scenic spectacles over the antebellum era. During postbellum reconstruction and beyond, commercial and institutional ambitions elicit social interaction. Large-scale industrialization activated large-scale scenic spectacles. Over the last decades of the nineteenth century and into the twentieth century, historical dramas, world's fairs, and museum dioramas spread new configurations of spatial interaction in step with local, regional, national, and global expansion. Site-specific attractions transpose notions of heritage and historiography in social settings. Theatre spectacles grasp the momentum of trade networks filling stages with scenes of industrial aggrandizement. Machinery, transportation systems, material products, and domestic architecture craft material prosperity into sites of economic advance and national heritage. Land conversation and historic preservation recover natural landmarks in the establishment of national parks as scenic "reserves." In the modern era, museum culture resets social dimensions in the scenic frames of heritage displays.

US scenic heritage harbors significant agency in light of Barbara Kirshenblatt-Gimblett's serial examination of museum display as an "economy of showing." Assessing the politics of heritage in the produced agency of display, she writes,

> The processes whereby errors become archaisms, objects become ethnographic, and ways of life become heritage test the alienability of what was found at the source. They also test the limits, even the violations, of a second life as heritage, particularly in the presence of the not yet dead. While exhibition may capitalize on visual interest, these processes are driven by a political economy whose stakes lie elsewhere—in foreclosures and inalienablities.[7]

The processes of transmitting cultural iconography are equally troubled by the violence and genocides at the source of US economic heritage. Land values allocate marketplace designs in "commemorative" monuments and ethnicities. Ceremonial affirmation of historical myths obscure the operations of commercial and institutional infrastructure jockeying for a political stake in phasing in economic (re) development. The territorial quest for continental possession triggering internal conflicts over social and economic expansion coupled itself to a creative quest as well. My research draws on government policies and debates in the contested political economy of aggressively moving continental borders. Containment policies, geographical extension, exploration of natural resources, transportation networks, settlement, and industrial growth resonate in scenic spectacles. Internal disparities over definitions of nationalism demonstrate conflicted stages recurring in debates over sectional rights and systematic multinational underpinning that suggest democratic principles are components of a visionary artifice.

Complicating the function of scenic spectacles and their boundless transgressions, I concentrate on the transactions of spectacle novelty in relation to shifting politics of economic policy. American scenic spectacles canvass landscape narratives that enter cultural and multinational communication alongside the active conditions of instability. The violence of war serving the politics of land acquisition, territorial incursions, and advancing colonization is often overwritten in fabled scenic lore of a majestic "natural" genesis. Geographical transgression entwines itself in an unfolding iconographic heritage that buries in heroic reminisces what Drew Gilpin Faust describes as "the good death." [8] Scenic transformations communicate with geopolitical momentum, dismantling the past in the forward edge of novelty. The scenic economy often plays into and pushes off a visionary phase-in of futurity, directing movement to a new destination. Scenic spectacles *appear* in one shape and remerge in another. They conceal; they radicalize; they distribute erroneous and real-time perspectives of landscape reproducing history. They remain fluid and discursive even when acting in concert with hallmarks of large-scale desires and aspirations: home, community, and country.

How spectatorship participates in evoking or revoking citizenship as "natural" is part of an interchanging performed syntax in scenic spectacles. Spectatorship optimizes unrestrained exploration of sensation and effect, vantage points, mobility, physical immediacy, and proximity to relational experiences to which economic "actors" respond. Attentive to subversive, radical, and protest narratives entangling the presence or erasure of racial and ethnic embodiment in scenic spectacles, I confront the interpretive hurdle of reissuing mythological origin tales, the "mistakes" of genealogy explored by Tavia Nyong'o in *The Amalgamation Waltz: Race, Performance, and the Ruses of Memory*. His interrogation of "biopolitical" tradition in which the hybrid treatment of race history simultaneous compounds overcoming white supremacy and achieving integration, calls into question the aspirational order underpinning Americanism. The challenge he presents, "Americanism, that is to say, becomes its own remedy. But such a position is helplessly in thrall to the empty tautologies of the national Thing. It accommodates hybridity to an official teleology that is forever reducing the many to the one. Such a politics hardly inspires hope for hybridity's subversive potential." [9] Nyong'o's instructive insights append itself to the numerous pitfalls of reconsidering political-economics in scenic lineage. This awareness significantly infiltrates critical discussion over what scenic spectacles pull in and push out.

My questions revolve around the tactics, strategies, organizational methods, immersive techniques, and administrative aims geared to *attract*—not necessarily succeed—broad social movement to new stages of political-economic growth. For guidance, I turn to economic theory. Douglass C. North defines the base challenge economic processes involve is the manner in which change is confronted: by reducing uncertainty into certainty or converting uncertainty into risk. "Adaptive efficiency" is a model of productive creativity he argues is necessary in a dynamic environment of changing circumstances to invent a "novel and new world."[10] In outlining US efficiency, he holds to institutional governance, formal rules by which safe conditions constrain uncertainty: "the maintenance of order over long periods of time and the rapid reestablishment of order when a society undertakes radical change have distinguished societies like the United States from most of those in world history. The key is the establishment of institutions of impersonal exchange that constrain the players and limit political rule making."[11] Where political myths inter one from many, the spatial quest to move boundaries of commercial and institutional traffic aid opportunity to decentralize, even upend economic order given unexpected waves of creative agency. Political tensions configuring social democracy in the nineteenth century are sometimes stabilized. However, the economic urgency of its actors to adapt to change—inventing new landscapes—show the default may well reside in the instabilities of economic transformations. Scenic spectacles, in this way, express the adaptive efficiency to create new spaces to occupy.

Landscape, Panorama, and Immersion

I take a direct approach to different strategies of constructing spatial sensation, elaborating changes in shifting patterns of perspective interpretation from a stable horizon line used in early panoramas to the interactive artifice of multidimensional perspectives. Useful to outline here is a bird's eye view of landscape painting and immersive techniques drawn on throughout this book.

Landscape painting was a relatively young genre in Western art. Nonfigurative picturesque motifs become independent subject matter in the seventeenth and early eighteenth century. In the fantasy style of Italian mannerist painting, landscape subjects typically stabilized spatial perspective environmentally with a high vantage point, rocky mountainous terrain, and a far distant river or seacoast. This spatial orientation entered the naturalized treatment of topographical views. Painted "panoramic views," appeared in Northern Europe in the late sixteenth century. Exemplified by Peter Brueghel the Elder, panorama techniques characteristically used sweeping bands of color to suggest spatial recession.[12] Combining a high vantage point and often a low horizon line, perspective space kept the eye descending down into a valley or winding river. In Breughel's use of panoramic perspective, his own satirical pessimism on the human condition shapes the point of view over the scenic ingredients. The viewer usually looks down on the foreground and any human activity occurring in the frame. As an interpretive medium, the panoramic mode employs technical patterns to induce the spatial illusion of depth and movement; it is a form that provides great elasticity to the ideological slant and vision of the individual artist or stylistic school.

Early stationary panoramic painting created by white, academically trained artists applied established conventions of perspective illusion found in canvas painting since the Italian Renaissance. One-point perspective conditioned the spectator to accept a symbolic point of view toward nature as stable and unchanging. With the introduction of aerial perspective in the Baroque era, the viewer was released from the hierarchical structure of linear perspective. The ability to experience the sensations of atmospheric effects dissolved physical boundaries, allowing for a more subjective exploration of space. In turn, panoramic space encircled the spectator. It oriented the viewer to experience a composite site from within a 360-degree representation of a spatial illusion. One charmed visitor to an exhibit admitted, "It is very easy to forget that we are viewing a painting, when we can look on every side and see the continuous works of nature and art blending in the distant horizon."[13] Rather than view the painterly affects of a scene from outside its frame, as a separate static object, suddenly the viewer moved around the scene. Robert Barker's panorama *A View of London from the Roof of the Albion Mills* transposed the overview of scenic landscape to modern landmarks, mapping new urban symbols in architecture and industry. The *View of London* raised the spectator to a new altitude, perched by the chimneys of a flour mill above the Thames with a "complete view of the cities of London, Westminster, and the Borough of Southwark" that reached "as far as sight extends."[14] The boundary of the canvas edges were removed and replaced by a "bird's eye view," giving the viewer a mobile vantage point both overlooking the landscape scenery and the public scene of the exhibition.

A set distance and leveling a platform to position the viewer's eye in line with the painted horizon was critical to create the sensation of *being* "on the spot."[15] This environmental framework actually masks the physical structure of the installation environment. The spectator's field of vision controlled the framing mechanisms to take in the whole or focus on parts. Although the painting was stationary, the spectator could not contemplate it fully without turning to experience sections of the whole. Once the viewer began turning in the space, individual perspectives of the illusion were not only shaped by apprehending portions of the scenic composition but by the three-dimensional physical presence of other visitors entering the viewer's visual frame. Alison Griffiths's recounts the experiential gasp of a viewer who felt "shivers down the spine" at a panorama installation.[16] The immediacy of the illusionism reoriented the spectator's sensory equilibrium to the coexistence of actual and imaginary circumstances. Within the experiential space of panoramic installations, the immersive production values encouraged the self-selecting design of individual *viewpoints* in a systematic presentational environment.

Stephan Oettermann locates the term panorama in a hybrid of Greek roots, invented, coined, and patented in the late eighteenth century to designate a technical form of creating a 360-degree landscape painting.[17] Nineteenth-century panoramic environments are one type of vision technology. "Immersion" is the descriptor Oliver Grau uses to detail various historic forms of image space that use visualization or illusion techniques to produce perceptional sensation. He characterizes immersion by its perceptional capacity of "diminishing critical distance to what is shown and increasing emotional involvement to what is happening."[18] What Grau intimates is that the felt immediacy of the production values aligns cognition with somatic experiences, a site of inquiry into sensate understanding widely addressed in aesthetic theories of the eighteenth century.[19] Among historic systems of immersion are representational forms of perspective space; integration techniques that unify the observer in an illusion space; projection into alternate spaces that open illusion to sensual interplay; static pictorial "windows" that extend into a different reality. Working out of Grau's concept of image spaces to explore scenic spaces, thematic threads examined are industry systems of immersion, dramatic techniques activating sensory space, and experimental and standardized methods of designing environmental space. Modern panoramic mediums dispersed ways of animating presence that held currency in visual culture and quickly crossed into entertainment practices, embracing mechanical science and manufacturing procedures. The changing styles of fabrication in commercial and institutional output diversify the organizational methods of producing scene spaces to shape different purposes and contents. Developments in spatial immersion also lean forward into twentieth-century media spectacles.

Spectacle and Sensory Media

The concept of spectacle may evoke the theoretical position of the Situationist International widely known through Guy Debord's *Society of the Spectacle*, and less through his 1998 update *Comments on the Society of the Spectacle* in which he adjusts the abstract commodity symbol of capital control to consumption, media, and technology. In his later work, Debord revises former binary definitions of spectacle: the "concentrated" and "diffuse," derived from cold war polarities of totalitarian regimes and democratic power structures. Where the concentrated spectacle condenses control around authoritarian restraint, diffuse systems enable seductive governance within commodity choice. Specifying a US superstructure diffusing productive consumption globally, Debord adds a third model. He defines the "integrated" spectacle, a combined dictatorship of desire falsifying "all reality," including government's ability to "falsify the whole production of perception."[20] Debord's stake in identifying commodity aesthetics in the semiotics of appearance conceives spectacle as a product of capital conglomeration emerging in the nineteenth century, but not how production strategies also unarm the conceptual realm of "integration."

The deconstruction of Debord's spectacle dimension is receiving new critical attention in media theory. Spectacle and media are now linked in popular and theoretical discussion of contemporary culture to the degree of distinguishing politicized models of "techno spectacle," "mega spectacle," and "interactive spectacle" in Douglas Kellner's and Steven Best's updated analysis.[21] Kellner builds on Debord's concept of societal media organized around the production and consumption of images, commodities, and staged events. He argues that media spectacles are those phenomena of media culture that "embody contemporary society's basic values, serve to initiate individuals into its way of life, and dramatize its controversies and struggles, as well as its modes of conflict resolution."[22] The shift in orientation accents counteractions in social activity that challenges integration. More to the point, such a pronounced emphasis on performed mediums of societal force and counter force suggest that spectacles intercede on an oscillating realm of destabilizing practices. It flushes out syntaxes that reach deep into theatrical spheres of history.

Facets of spectacle treated in performance histories involve visual technologies, environmental staging, multidimensional pageantry, narrative, and interactive scale. In the *Poetics*, Aristotle characterized the production values or spectacle of Greek Tragedy with sentient distinction, "as emotionally potent." The word he uses is "appearance" (ὄψις), which means not only visual effects but also visionary sensibility, apart from the cognitive realm (poetry) of performance.[23] Twentieth-century studies of spectacle locate a performed set of practices. They provide ideological distinctions in branches that enact the public sphere. The abstract properties of spectacle can be further disbanded in relation to art historical developments in illusion and perspective techniques by drawing on the politics of spectacle from particular paths, such as imperial Roman triumphal parades and Renaissance royal entries.[24]

A Cross Section of Scenic Models

A multipart format generates, shall I say, a panoramic cross section of scenic spectacles that demonstrate a constellation of sensory media. The five chapters are not strictly chronological but show sometimes concurrent yet diversified activity. The first chapters address static and dynamic forms of visual immersion and multimedia applications in the antebellum period, while the latter chapters extend into live interactive formats. Examples of entertainment environments, exhibition spaces, and educational settings stretch from the post-Civil War climate through the modern era. An epilogue teases out how twenty-first-century off shoots found in the precedents and prototypes of scenic spectacles live on in installation, entertainment, and exhibitionary culture.

Chapter 1 elaborates the industry outgrowth of visual media in the antebellum period. Tracing the introduction of installation panoramas in cultural and political spaces, the visibility of scenic discourse enhances ways in which landscape and history exchange meaning. I develop the scenic landscape at intersections in geoeconomic transitions to a free market economy after the War of 1812. Close examination is given to the narrative treatment of scenic spectacles in relation to the production of actual, illusionary, and ideal landscapes. Media aesthetics and art historical studies of perspective logic and panoramic technology line my approach to exposing how scenic immersion converses with American vernaculars and monumental narratives that cast divisive vantage points over sentiments of progress, liberty, and individual prosperity.

A series of moving river panoramas featuring pan-Mississippi scenic routes is the subject of chapter 2. This outlet of theatrical panoramas join state-of-the-art entertainment trends in multimedia performance. I examine the ways these touring scenic spectacles asserted a self-determining power in cultural production between 1846 and 1850. They fomented social discourse in real-time and mechanized-time that accelerate the "transappearance" of Midwest development.[25] These touring shows spread dramatic narratives of life along the Mississippi River that competed for perceptional sway, as well as commercial survival for the artists who produced them. Early river panoramas express the medium's dramatic formula: immersive sensation, episodic action, and live storytelling. These entertainment vehicles are intercepted by protest narratives in abolition panoramas that reroute the fictional tracks. At the same time, Western panoramas augment commercial maturity using techniques of abridgment, visual montage, and special effects. I take an in-depth look at multiplying genres, regional styles, artistic motivation, and faster manufacturing methods widening experimental methods of multimedia performance.

Chapter 3 sets in motion transitions to the industrial era and beyond. I juxtapose site-specific attractions that parallel large-scale transformation to multinational networks. One of the leading spectacle producers of the period is Imre Kiralfy. His grand historical site-specific spectacles, in particular, are significant for several reasons. He threads corporate commerce and large-scale industrialization into a blockbuster brand of entertainment that celebrated democratizing virtues of modernization in patriotic stories. I accent how his social philosophy validates competitive meritocracy and draw out connections with the propaganda function of early Roman political spectacles. Kiralfy swept the energy of industrial modernity into wonderlands of immersive storytelling in two site-specific historical productions on Staten Island, *The Fall of Babylon* and *Nero, or The Destruction of Rome*. In contrast to urban splendors, the Western Plains assert natural magnitude. Government actions in coordination with corporate interests established the first National Park. I juxtapose the city and the country, as the natural wonderland of Yellowstone Park is "reserved" for scenic tourism and as national heritage. Because Kiralfy enlarged a conglomeration of partnerships in step with corporate entertainment practices, the coincidence of administrative involvement in destination attractions allows me to investigate distinctive "American" scenic brands, or what Maurya Wickstrom terms "brandscapes" of corporate globalism.[26] Technology, transportation, and marketing were harnessed into a Kiralfy brand of entertainment with wide application across genres of dance, circus, and cinema. He eventually turned to designing exposition grounds in Europe placing him at intersections of global practices. This outgrowth of commercial "specs" seeds the next chapter in relationship to government-sponsored expositions from 1851 to 1915.

Looking at the adaptive efficiency of the institutional apparatus, I inquire into the ways administrative strategies adjudicate a participatory presence in globalization in chapter 4. I draw attention to US entrance into competitive multinational trade networks taking shape between 1876 and 1915 in relationship to exhibition environments. Exhibition administrations in the United States can be viewed as situational models, facilitating aspirant geopolitical pluralism in transnational and international commerce. The 1876 Philadelphia World's Fair underscores a shift from single building exhibition sites, such as the initial universal exposition held in New York that was modeled after London's Crystal Palace (1851), to a surrounding spatial perspective in which visitors move through and around separate buildings in an ever-changing landscape. The administrative agenda of the Philadelphia Centennial is emphasized in respect to the design themes of site planning. For contrast, other exhibition plans are folded in, including the New Orleans Cotton Centennial Exposition (1885) and San Francisco International Panama-Pacific Exposition (1915). Later exhibition grounds dramatize diversified, regional aims of economic habitation in the multifaceted "nature" of wealth creation. I approach exhibition production following Shmuel N. Eisenstadt's framework of "multiple modernities" that dismantle the orthodoxy of Westernization as a uniform cultural context of secular industrial progress.[27] US exhibition practices demonstrate different management models. The *in situ* occupation of landscape mirrors the widening grip of corporate and private enterprise agitating for governing powers.

The last chapter furthers the institutional narratives of scenic spectacle as educational media. US museums in the modern era interact with policies of national reform. Centralized attempts toward managing labor and political dissent through economic integration reared debate beyond the war years. Popular instructional models found in heritage exhibits and museum display conjoin educational and government reforms. Scenic dioramas, specifically the use of painted panoramas and three-dimensional staged models, are featured in US government and state institutions. I consider the perceptional agency encountered in diorama formats a type of pseudospectacle. The preservation of nature and history coincide with nostalgia expounded by Frederick Jackson Turner's "frontier" myth of the Great West. Rebecca Schneider's illumination of the "remains" of historical reenactment assists. Particularly significant to me is raising the notion of a "lack of memory" that "America is innocent of battle and ignorant of loss." [28] In reframing heritage, these miniature scenic spectacles suspend while opening the voids of history that Schneider revives. Troubling this landscape is how wilderness conservation and historical preservation performed a curatorial role in codifying an indigenous "American" heritage, reburying Indian genocide in the ethnographic aesthetics of natural reserves and regional lore.

Scenic spectacles collapse borders of graphic and visual arts, multimedia technology, spectatorship, and physical architecture. I leave current scenes to an epilogue but worth mentioning here—and elaborated on later—is a 2011 state-of-the-art show at the National Museum of American History in Washington, DC, *America on the Move*. With principle sponsorship by General Motors Corporation, the exhibition immersed visitors in the "sights, sounds, and sensations of rail and road transportation in the United States from 1876 to 1999." [29] Life-size multimedia dioramas formed a network of travel by rail and road routing visitors through actual trains, cars, subways, and shipping containers. Its exit point launched the visitor through space exploration. This type of somatic interactivity is now largely familiar to twenty-first century audiences. Then as now, scenic spectacles contribute hybrid distribution systems of cross-genre formats, narrative openings, sensory play, and spatial extensions that fabricate spontaneous interaction. Furthermore, the movement through a fragmented geopolitical terrain cued to lifestyle commerce along a transportation landscape updates signposts of earlier scenic spectacles that we are visiting.

Immersive Scenes: Visual Media, Painted Panoramas, and Landscape Narratives

Among the history paintings and statuary displayed in the Rotunda of the US Capitol in Washington, DC, resides a panorama of 19 panels dramatizing episodes in American history. Painted in fresco with a neutral palate of white and brown to emulate the effect of classical sculptural relief, The *Frieze of American History* wraps around the belt of the Rotunda's walls 58 ft from the floor. Each panel (8 × 4 ft) depicts a different scene in the contentious terrain of nation building. The popular narrative begins with Columbus stepping onto "American" soil and leads clockwise to the Wright brothers' 1903 *Flyer* lifting off into the sky. The storied movement preserves a "natural" expansion across the continent through the Spanish conquests of North America to the growth of American industry.[1] Constantino Brumidi, who also painted *The Apotheosis of Washington* on the canopy of Thomas Walter's iconic dome, made the first sketch for the panorama in 1859.[2] Yet, it took nearly a century to complete it. Over time, commissioned artists made incremental amendments to the painted panels while consolidating any stylistic variations to maintain a unified design.[3] Frame by frame the scenic text, like the creation of the panorama itself, convey a never-ending campaign to fashion the diverse character of the people and the prosperity of the land into the perpetual motion of nationhood.

The *Frieze of American History* raises a panoramic motif in early nineteenth-century scenic spectacles, that of landscape and history. Two distinct vistas: one manifesting values of nature, shaping imaginative sensations, the other linked to politics, shaping narrative meanings, embroider scenic modes of exchange in the antebellum period. In various ways, American landscape panoramas harbor historic scenic content, paralleling geographical movement through landlocked battles: civil rights, sectional politics, Indian authority, territorial boundaries, and material progress. The entrance of visual media in the form of installation panoramas wrap landscape narratives around the internal struggle over the direction of the country's destiny after the War of 1812. Balancing federal policies of Western expansion and states' interests persisted as a competing logic in national survival in the postwar climate.[4] The 1820 Missouri Comprise, allowing Missouri to enter the Union as a slave state and Maine as a free state, temporarily held together a delicate balance of free and slave states in Congress. American scenic landscapes reflect a branch of "panoramania" sweeping Western European cities that coincide with the splintering attributes of domestic politics.[5] In tandem with economic energies jolting political schisms, cultural communities brewed the styles, subjects, and vocabularies of domestic traditions. Rosemarie K. Bank conceives a spatial history in antebellum theatre culture constitutive of "multiple, simultaneous relationships."[6] Scene spaces conjoin Bank's spatial realm through mediums of spectacle immersion. Featured here, the popular visual media of installation panoramas. Scenic panoramas emit differing landscape narratives as the infrastructure of a culture industry takes economic shape. I weave the wayward story of the Capitol panorama with early appearances of the Niagara landscape to air the ebb and flow among the actual environment, illusion, and public ideals that cycle throughout this study. These political and cultural scenes instill sensory vernaculars of the "American" landscape that complicate memes of progress, opportunity, and independence in regional topography, wilderness, Indian cultures, and race inequalities. The variant and overarching vantage points appearing in panoramic scenes of wonder and enterprise provide a glimpse into synchronic disparities of historical discourse.

Contrary Landscape Narratives

The story of the Capitol panorama begins in concert with a rapidly accelerating political economy. Static principles of "progress" that underpin nation building respond to active conditions of violence and uncertainty undermining national survival. The *Frieze of American History* negotiates this interior spectrum of volatility by amending territorial acquisition into a binding stasis. At the start point of the panorama's creation federal consolidation shattered single party politics wide apart. Thomas O'Brien explains that polarizing fissures in the antebellum political climate splintered the Republican Party over how government conceptualizes "a shared social basis."[7] Older traditions, advocated by slave-holding states of a newly formed Whig Party, took measure to conserve a social contract of mutual interests free from government interference. The nativist agenda sought internal expansion of agricultural wealth creation by sustaining the economic institution of slavery. Modern tradition, championed by the National Republican Party, required a step forward to unify the people as the state: "insisting that, unless one could define the people by a catalog of social habits, economic institutions, racial characteristics, and religious customs, there was no legitimate sanction for a state."[8] The so-called progressives promoted market economics.

In his second inaugural address (1833), President Andrew Jackson called for a "sprit of liberal concession and compromise" of states under a "Federal Union" to preserve order and liberty.[9] His leadership of the Democratic Party endorsed a centrist line of "popular sovereignty."[10] Jackson's expansion of executive powers agitated the protracted debate over the country's direction. Institutional processes, in one analysis, recover the stagecraft of state power. The Capitol panorama sanctions an artifice of continental "emancipation" in this administrative design. In practice, partisan systems of political economy: nuanced among conservative, liberal, and centrist positions, modulated indeterminate shares in social liberty. These fractures work with and against the autonomous energies of business and cultural practices disbanding the limitations imposed by the privileged freedoms of legal and economic systems. In communication with political culture's contentious sensibilities, landscape themes were among the first genres of installation panoramas to broach commercial and independent interaction with economic narratives.

Niagara landscapes raise alternative vocabularies of historical ideography that communicate the instabilities of political economy. In different ways, the fearsome "power" of the Niagara landscape underscores the transgressive spaces of "natural" order reflected in the Capitol panorama. Romantic filtrations of the sublime entering treatments of landscape subjects portend supersensual tensions of awe and terror, where destruction, repression, disorder, and exclusion are constituent to progress, prosperity, and consensus. The currency of America landscape imparts immersive presence in the "natural" equivocation of freedom. Actual landscape sites, such as Niagara Falls, negotiate "monumental" narratives of the country's historical destiny. Geographical spaces communicate dynamic circumstances where landscape and spectacle forge a dialogic medium of visual narrative.

Questions of mediation posed by landscape theorists enumerate various approaches to "ways of seeing."[11] This functioning premise was set forth by Denis E. Cosgrove in his influential *Social Formation and Symbolic Landscape*. Cosgrove emphasized perceptional strategies in landscape art as a methodology to decode societal discourse.[12] One particular line of inquiry hinges the economies of land and culture to the commercial production of early nineteenth-century installation panoramas. W. J. Thomas Mitchell voices a Marxist orientation to the ideological functions of landscape in terms of valuations. He defines landscape not as a genre of art but as a "medium of cultural expression" that is a "representation of something that is already a representation in its own right."[13] This concept is especially significant given the desecration of Indian cultures by legalized force. Panoramic vision layers additional mediation on landscape narratives. Discrepancies in particular strategies of manufacture, market forces, and ideological functions pressure visibility in a new media autonomy. Three oscillating perspectives among commercial, political, and independent viewpoints serve to ply land values and land myths as an immersive medium, one that I attempt to demonstrate transfers the actions of history to a visionary space.

The Industry of Visual Media: Methods of Production

Inaugurating a scenic sensorium in the early decades of the nineteenth century, circular painted panoramas play a role in enlarging permanent circuitry of a permeable immersive medium. An industry of technical media proliferated with rapid diversification. Stephan Oettermann claims an unintentional side effect in the manufacture of stationary panoramas created a new and more "democratic perspective."[14] He grounds this theory in the technical possibilities of unifying many viewing points into one all-encompassing painted perspective, which in turn enables observers to indiscriminately engage different viewpoints in the painting without distortion. His formal appraisal strains to defend a fuzzy pluralism. The "effect"—by which

I mean the virtuosity of the technical medium—of this democratizing apparatus is worth fleshing out. Sensory technologies couple a distinct system of interactive production values. The all-encompassing views of panoramic installations posit scenic immersion partner to inhabiting spatial illusion and dramatic storytelling.

Landscape genres catapulted from a picturesque form of painting to specially designed display spaces. The concept of creating a circular painted panorama is credited to Irish artist Robert Barker in 1785. While living in Scotland, Barker had the notion of drawing everything he could see from the top of a high hill in Edinburgh on four sheets of paper. He then transferred the sections of drawings to a large canvas that he suspended in a wooden shed. The resulting scene space surrounded the spectator, who had a vantage point on top of a hill looking down into a city and out over a rustic countryside. Rather than view the painterly affects of a scene from outside its frame, as a separate static object, suddenly the viewer moved around the scene. Barker first called his exhibition "nature at a glance" (*la nature à coup d'œil*).[15] In order to distinguish his display from traditional forms of painting, by 1791, he coined the term *panorama* ("all sight" or "all seeing") in the advertising for a London exhibit of his *Panorama of Edinburgh*.[16] The branding of panorama technology resides in the manufacturing science behind the novelty of displaying a circular painted 360-degree topographical "view." The painted scene was a magnification of a landscape, recomposed from on-site renderings. A mathematical grid overlaid on the canvas enabled the separate sections to be blended into a composite wrap-around view.

Oettermann considers panoramic space a departure from the idealized perspective of classical art.[17] However, the scene painting was stabilized with a curving horizon line to establish a diminishing perspective in relation to the spectator's centralized (ideal) position. Furthermore, painting techniques were quite conventional and aligned the spectator within a stable—though hidden—framing mechanism. Panoramic space depended on aesthetic consistency to attract belief in the illusion. Barker detailed his method. The painter must "fix his station and delineate connectedly every object that presents itself to his view as he turns around, concluding his drawing by a connection with where he began."[18] The resulting "bird's eye of view" enlivened the physical mobility of spectatorship within a system of standardized production values. The enveloping scene conveyed a resonating scroll admired for its literacy. One "struck" visitor to a *Panorama of Jerusalem* remarked "though I have never seen that ancient city,

I have read so much about, and studied its geography so much, that I am quite confident of its correctness."[19]

Panoramic typology inexhaustibly transmitted world affairs, current events, and historiography to the commonplace. Barker's second panorama, A View of London from the Roof of the Albion Mills, raising spectators above London to overlook urban markings of industrialization in architecture and manufacturing, popularized cityscapes. New subjects had the potential to reflect trending political and economic empowerment, as well as colonial allies or desired territorial destinations. The Empire view from England's panoramic oeuvre between 1813 and 1815 offered a Grand Tour: Florence, Berlin, Moscow, Lisbon, Venice, Paris, and London.[20] Installation art, in one sense, mirrored interest in travel, exoticism, and nostalgia. On the other hand, it disseminated blueprints of nationalism, cultural mythologies, ethnographic stereotypes, and historical legend. Ralph Hyde notes, "the value of the panorama as an educational experience was dependent on its success in conveying visual information about the real world."[21] Advertising and exhibition pamphlets available to visitors authenticated the factual precision of the paintings. Curatorial labels employed anecdote, scientific, and accredited information affixing standardized scripts to global distribution. Information was often sourced directly from travel or historical literature. Robert Burford's panorama of the Falls of Niagara (1837) adapted details from Joseph Wentworth Ingraham's detailed 1834 visitor's guide. Burford's program parroted Ingraham's self-proclaimed discovery of a cavern behind the central falls coined the "Cave of the Winds" for its "sights and sounds."[22] Textual notations distributed nomenclature to fill in relational context, but the scenic presence contrived a felt interaction with an illusionary site.

Barker's main innovation is the commercial venture of launching a public art installation. The technical feat of Barker's panorama was its integration into the architectural space it was displayed in, a design he patented in 1787, and which continues to be used in constructing panorama displays to this day.[23] His plans called for a circular building, a rotunda. The architectural space intensified natural shape rather than geometrical construction; the building supplied the physical "framing," according to Barker, "on which this drawing or painting may be performed."[24] A central viewing platform, with distance of approximately 10 ft between viewers and painting, enclosed the spectators and kept them from approaching too close to the painting. Visitors entered from below so that a doorway would not pierce through the painting itself. The painting was suspended around the inner circumference of the structure. The top and bottom of the unframed canvas were masked to project only the scenic illusion. The use of top lighting illuminated the painting, so that the image seemed to emanate from the only source of light in the viewing room. A skylight reduced the risk of shadows ruining the illusion.[25] The overhead lighting was invisible to the visitor who stood in the dark, shut off from the outside world. Invisible framework aggregated spatial containment and scenic exploration that felt a natural extension into "the continuous works of nature and art blending in the distant horizon."[26] With the addition of central platforms, the subject position to the exterior world was momentarily disrupted in the sensible circumstance of *being* "on the spot."[27]

With architect Robert Mitchell, Barker built a two-storied permanent rotunda in Leicester Square, London. The Leicester Square Panorama was an immediate and lasting success; it survived 70 years.[28] Barker's rotunda separated the "fine art" of painting from private patronage and the academic authority of institutional committees. The ensuing popularity of panoramas, which eventually gained acceptance by both the Royal Academy of England and the prestigious Institut de France, brought the privileged sphere of high culture to a profit-driven market venue.[29] The rotunda industry established transnational distribution networks capable of sustaining itself by catering to changing public tastes. Visual media's widespread legibility funneled its own regeneration toward continuous modernization; its commercial roots required an ongoing repertory of new imports or exports to remain competitive. Lecturers assumed the role of expert, providing an auditory layer as narrator to the immersive situation.

Oliver Grau's definition of the type of immersion deployed in stationary panoramas distinguishes it from among "historic spaces of illusion": ritual forms of Roman mosaic, private environments, and decorative illusions found in Baroque ceiling panoramas.[30] The iterative function of the panorama in his estimation is the "representation of nature in the service of an illusion."[31] It conjoins verisimilitude to the sensory mechanics of integration in visual effect strategies. A by-product of verisimilitude is the spectator's hypersensitivity to the production values of the illusion. Panoramic immersion produces a felt discontinuity with the unities of time and place. The effects are wound in the sensations of novelty. Edmund Burke called novelty the simplest emotion, "curiosity": "whatever desire we have for, or whatever pleasure we take in novelty."[32] Part of the attraction to panoramas was feeling comfortably displaced. Degrees of sensual reflex could trigger a delicious delirium. One visitor to an exhibit marveled over the "innumerable conflicting sensations that crowd upon the mind in the course of an hour" that "leave the spectator in a mazy dream."[33] The quality of artistic "deception" adjusted the framing formula in order to revive sensate immediacy. Scenic environments often received praise for awakening feelings of actuality, where "everything appears natural"[34] While the experiential sensations of the painting activated the spectator's relational presence, the visual display materialized out of an "artifactual" landscape. Theodor Adorno's theory poses the aesthetic object hood of nature out of the violation of natural conditions. The panoramas artifactual status perpetuated intoxication in an aesthetic circumstance that simultaneously destroys external circumstances.[35] By reciprocal turns, the invented landscape voids the site it was made from. The artifactual notion of immersive integration sensitizes relational awareness to factual distortions. The spectator was not necessarily assimilated into the illusion but attracted to its pleasurable sensory disorganization. Artifactual spaces entertain complicit interaction with disintegration. Inhabiting novel feelings is fleeting; immersive spontaneity maintains sensory presence with technological improvements. The spectator's identification with the scenic commonplace remains in flux with a destabilizing environment of change.

The artifactual world of commercial panoramas expressed technical virtuosity. Patterns in aesthetic standards depended on whether an individual artist or, as the industry grew, collaborative teams produced the panorama. Increasingly, teams of genre specialists and fine-art students were employed to manufacture the painting.[36] Mainstream popularity ultimately loosened aesthetic epistemologies of elite art enabling auteur styles and assembly by manufacturing processes. The sensory installation convenes an interior sociological sphere that blurs boundaries of aesthetic distance through interactive mediation. This form of multidimensional spectacle houses inhabitants in the scenic life of an occupied space, one that accelerates along with global economies.

Methods of producing panoramas relied on conventional aesthetic systems that extend back to classical principles of perspective construction while advancing forward into graphic design. Barker's innovation was aided by optical technology and scientific developments related to the camera obscura—used in geographical cartography— amalgamated to systems of perspective.[37] Jonathan Crary likens the subject-effect of the projection device to a "metaphysic of interiority, teasing out its formal proximity to moving images."[38] "It must be stressed," he writes, "that the camera obscura defines the position of an interiorized observer to an exterior world, not just a two-dimensional representation, as is the case with perspective."[39] Idioms of romantic technique absorbed the viewer in continuity with spatial extension beyond the pictorial frame. Richard D. Altick points out two features of romantic influence from visual art on spectacle scene design. The chief characteristic was the amplified scale of scenic panorama. Another feature was the appeal of landscape subjects in contrast to more traditional fare of classical or topical material.[40] Graphic media added different framing devices: cropping, juxtaposition, close ups, multiple viewpoints, and recognizable circumstance.[41] In Barker's view of Edinburgh, there are multiple entry points into the scene.[42] Sheep graze in the foreground, figures on a ridge send the eye over a mountain ridge, or a mother and child stroll on the embankment. The viewer's mobility, whether standing still or turning in space, enables perceptional framing to explore scenes. Movement along one path leads along a road to discover a horse and carriage; another lane winds into town. Installation panoramas obscure the ideological construct by freeing the sentient gaze to assimilate multiple points of view and to habituate the senses to feel contiguous spaces beyond the boundaries of painted material. Visibility is edited to maximize a composite assembly of near and far simultaneity. Motifs of agriculture, architecture, mills, as well as the coexistence of rural rolling hills and urbanization emulsify a leisurely visitation in landscape themed panoramas. The compressed delineation and reorganization of land references in immersive design mediate a disposition to containment in a terrestrial play of neutral values.

Scenic formulas propelled a market for visual narrative capable of repetitive variations that agile intervention could reprogram. The mechanics of manipulating perspective angles to extend movement around the scene increased variations on visual media that included multiperspective pleoramas, kaleidoscopic myrioramas, magnified cosmoramas, and three-dimensional dioramas and pan-stereoramas to name a few. With roaming sight lines, spectators controlled the narrative experience by moving their position or by widening or focusing their gaze. Rather than a representation of nature, interaction energized a tangible scenic drama. The byplay of immersion involved the spectator in the dramatics of a live empirical experience.

At the same time, panoramic propensities construct (mis)conceptual models, the ephemeral attachment to public taste and biases speeded up a changing repertory of social habitats. Scenic panoramas yielded dynamic interaction in the execution of a painting occupying the spectator in a *staged* space. The emulsion of painted design and viability of the illusion earn mention in reviews of panoramas. A Philadelphia visitor to a *Panorama of Mexico* marveled curiously at "the skill and faithfulness of the artist" who "rendered the canvas almost illusive."[43] Temporal content was both actual, extending the e/motions of spatial expanse, and sensible, optimizing the imaginative fabrication of a conversion to simultaneity. Michel Foucault's concept of the panoptic, encompassing the self-consuming power of cultural ownership, coincides with the rise of static panoramas generally.[44] The "sovereign gaze" Foucault assigns to the visionary domination of the European bourgeois speaks, in part, to the global infiltration of panoramic spectacle. Arguably, an inversion of structure occurs with immersion. It seals the gaze in the idiosyncrasies of an imaginative disorder. Apart from notable mesmerizing *trompe l'oeil* effects, commercial panoramas economize landscape in the intimacy of illusion. The vortex of artifactual presence generates a slippery optical agency. In scripting an interactive place, a place that violates the external phenomena it describes, the designed circumstance confers engagement with the spectator's perceptional strategies to fill in unseen space.

Scenic Histories in American Panoramic Production

The introduction of stationary panoramas in Eastern cities in the first decades of the nineteenth century found a narrow audience. Preferences among the largely Protestant governing classes in America inclined toward European art, literature, and drama. The majority of panoramas displayed in affluent American cities, such as New York, Philadelphia, and Boston in the late eighteenth and early nineteenth century were duplicates by English artists of popular displays in London. Patronage dictated risk and reward. A panorama of Jerusalem was first shown in Philadelphia in 1790.[45] Artist, playwright, and theatre manager William Dunlap credits his home state New York with the inaugural appearance of a panorama in America in 1794.[46] It was a copy of Barker's view of *A View of London* by

English portraitist and landscape painter William Winstanley. Often housed in makeshift galleries, prolonged exhibitions could be quite profitable. In Boston, a touring *Panorama of Athens* earned receipts of one hundred dollars a week.[47] Admission prices fell over time, encouraging the social value of making available elite "culture" to the middle and working classes. The manufactured reproduction of profitable travel narratives spread standardization quickly. Increasing patronage of panorama spectacles by a white, privileged segment of American society opened the door for struggling artists to join in a potentially lucrative enterprise. In the same year as Winstanley displayed his *View of London* (1795), American artist Edward Savage exhibited the same subject in Philadelphia.[48] Winstanley soon exhibited a copy of the picturesque South Carolina city of *Charleston*, measuring 100 ft long and 20 ft high, in New York a couple of years later.[49] It may be the first panorama of an American city. The itinerant life of these touring "exhibits" remained characteristic of the form. However, the wear and tear on the canvases left few examples behind.[50] The display was set up in a private residence on Greenwich Street along with engravings, "fine artworks," and other luxury items for sale with an exclusive admission price of 45 cents for adults and 25 cents for children.[51] By the 1820s, new revenue-generating opportunities mobilized private investment in the panorama industry. Grau observes, "In the beginning, the rotundas were built in various forms but increasing institutionalization—later, buildings only housed panoramas with standardized measurements."[52] In turn, canvas's size was regulated for ready installation.

One of the first commercial rotundas built by an American was by artist John Vanderlyn.[53] Born in Kingston, New York, Vanderlyn gained entry to establishment circles through the patronage of New York Senator Aaron Burr. He seized on the panorama craze for reasons that remain cloudy. Vanderlyn traveled abroad to train at the prestigious French Academy under Francois-André Vincent. In Paris, Robert Fulton's successful rotunda in the Boulevard Montmartre may have garnered his awareness of the panorama's potential for reaching a large audience.[54] History painting was held as the highest achievement in fine art among academic circles. When associates frowned on the project as a debasement of fine art, Vanderlyn defended himself. He insisted that his purpose was to bring European historical painting to an American public. Plans for a two-story rotunda in New York included displaying his *Panoramic View of the Palace and Gardens of Versailles* (1818–1819) on the second floor, his history paintings, and old master paintings from his personal collection in a first floor gallery.[55] Visitors to the rotunda, promotions noted, can visit Paris to "catch the manners living as they rise, and with them catch the means to promote a taste for the fine arts."[56] With municipal backing and private funding from 142 subscribers, including then Governor of New York DeWitt Clinton, he built a brick, domed rotunda modeled after the Parthenon in Rome on the corner of City Hall Park.[57] This strategic location was across the street from the fashionable Park Theatre.[58] Whether the venture stemmed, in part, from commercial motives, or self-serving publicity, the panorama subtly blends political circumstance with picturesque fantasy.

Vanderlyn's *Versailles* is a rare surviving example of an early nineteenth-century American stationary painted panorama.[59] It highlights the Northeastern taste for a return to "universal space."[60] Observed by Bank, universal space holds onto a recessive Euro-American realm that withholds progress even as it pronounces it. Originally 19 ft high, the panorama opened on June 29, 1819. The scenic environment surrounds one with a view of the palace and water-park on one side and the gardens, grand alley, and great canal opposite.[61] From the center of the installation, one gains the full impact of strolling among the well-dressed figures on the grounds. The painted treatment employs rigorous perspective drawing to create a visual narrative. Vanderlyn began sketches for his panorama during the Napoleonic era. At the time, Versailles was a public garden and museum. He incorporated the restoration of the Bourbon monarchy into the finished work, which occurred after he left France. King Louis XVIII, as if to reassert political sovereignty, appears in the painting on the balcony of the palace. In another section, sovereigns from the allied nations to France mingle in a group, while the artist himself is seen with a companion pointing them out. Its monarchal associations were not lost on one reviewer, who noted the effect was "calculated to awaken political recollections.[62] Vanderlyn promoted his panorama as a vehicle to enrich all classes of society.[63] Yet, his portrayal of the French republic did not substantially resonate with the urban public to sustain the venture. His fixation on aristocratic power in European circumstances suggests his own displacement with cross-sectional audiences disbanding a unitary representational heritage.[64]

Rapid development and unstable monetary policies followed the aftermath of the War of 1812, culminating in the 1819 bank panic. The panic awakened public anxiety to the "boom and bust" hardship of capitalism and left the country fracturing under social and political divisions.[65] In the widening domestic market of the entertainment economy where elite and popular stages collided for patronage, the dynamics of race, class, and nationalism unfolded. Antebellum theatre navigated social agency and conflict molding mainstream, popular, and alternative cultural production. Creative entrepreneurs and talent from African-American and immigrant communities, urban centers, and rural towns laid the ground floor of a manifold, yet profit-minded entertainment industry.[66] Vanderlyn's rotunda never saw a profit. In the first year, he earned $1,200, a sum that did not even cover the expenses of the painting. Shortly after, he began touring the panorama in cities from New Orleans to Montreal, while leasing the rotunda to other exhibitors. Although his personal aspirations were dashed, the venture did contribute to a swelling visual art tradition of public galleries and touring exhibitions. Vanderlyn's new bottle filled with old allegiances straddled the shores of change. Clearly, the landscape of Republican history was only slightly modified in early panorama exhibits. Another set of framing mechanisms unfolded in government practices.

Monumental Embellishments in the Capitol

Establishment artists, who trained primarily in England, perpetuated white cultural hierarchies by shaping American subjects according to neoclassical conventions. These standards informed the institutional dominance of Eastern academies as well as heavy competition for government projects. Vanderlyn's attempt to popularize historical painting intensified a contentious relationship with fellow members of The Academy of Fine Arts. The first president of the academy, John Trumbull was one of his fiercest rivals. They competed for portrait, municipal, and government commissions, including the first federally sponsored "historical memorials" designated in the reconstruction of the US Capitol.[67]

From its inception, the ongoing artwork commissioned for the US Capitol was conceived and executed by artists trained in an established European tradition of academic painting, sculpture, and architecture. The first American academies, such as The American Academy of Fine Arts (1817) and its rival, the National Academy of Design (1826), were styled after European schools of fine art.[68] The "intellectual foundation of the US Capitol, writes Dell Upton, "was thoroughly neoclassical."[69] The architectural expression of these principles involved ordering nature according to reason. Geometrical shapes: spheres, circles, cubes, and triangles were employed as compositional properties toward regulating direct empirical experience of the natural world according to classical values of beauty. These principles corresponded to measured proportion and harmonious balance. William Thorton's original design of the Capitol buildings was composed of a central cube with a hemispherical dome, flanked by the two rectangular legislative wings. After the British burned this structure in 1814, numerous modifications to the architectural design were made to the Capitol's reconstruction.[70] One change was Benjamin Latrobe's plan for a circular Rotunda, again modeled after Rome's Pantheon. Its completion under the direction of Charles Bulfinch in 1830 also fell in step with the wide-spread use of rotundas as permanent exhibit spaces throughout Europe and North America.

In March 1817, Kent Ahrens relates that John Trumbull was commissioned by the Acting Secretary of State John Rush to paint four large paintings for the Rotunda on a theme selected by then President James Madison. The final works, such as *Declaration of Independence, Surrender of Lord Cornwallis at Yorktown, Surrender of General Burgoyne at Saratoga*, and *George Washington Resigning his Commission*, attached American scenes to monuments of defeated enemies and constitutional triumphs. Executed to position the viewer within the frame of events, they were conceived to visually project across the circular span of the Rotunda.[71] More than a decade later Congress began deliberations to "ornament" a blank wall opposite Trumbull's work with four complementary memorial paintings."[72] Patriarchal divisions flared between Eurocentric Northern tastes and Southern anti-European sentiment. New Massachusetts representative John Quincy Adams led the debate, asking whether four American artists "could be found who were fully competent to the execution of the task to be assigned to them."[73] Adams rival in the House, Virginia representative Henry Alexander Wise, rebutted in his belief that this country is "richer now in native talents in the fine arts than any country on the globe."[74] Selection of subject matter, approval of artists' submissions, whether events from after the Revolutionary War should be included, and even if the phrase "colonial history" should be stricken from consideration was regulated by often fruitless Congressional bickering until a joint committee was appointed in 1836 to contract "one or more competent artists" to execute four historical pictures.[75] The chosen subjects included the discovery of

America, colonization, the revolution, and the constitution. These institutional motifs of "natural" progress are refreshed in the Capitol panorama. As the colonial era dimmed from living memory, preservation of recorded memory came to be authorized by a collective compromise carried through institutional negotiation over the visibility and formal narrative of a founding history.

Phantom History: The Progress Narrative

The Capitol panorama is a permanent national example of the political adoption of a visual narrative in the early nineteenth century. Its historical function sets it apart from more dominant military and battle genres favored in England and France that absorbed social and political attention with immersive stories of recent wars.[76] The genre made up almost one-third of productions over the medium's history. It spawned a specialized international industry of European scenic artists producing war reenactments.[77] Commercial production of US battle panoramas came into vogue after the Civil War with brutal monuments of triumph and negation. American productions of war largely remained in the hands of enterprising artists. John Stevens's Midwestern tour of his *Sioux War Panorama* justified the military massacre of the Sioux uprising (1862) in Minnesota. Frontier conflicts, John Bell observes in his account of Stevens's biased version of events, functioned as "epic performance propaganda."[78] Lesser known is the independent producer William Wehner, who has yet to be fully examined. The Wisconsin painter owned the Wehner Panorama Studio in Milwaukee. His *Battles of Chattanooga* (1886) employed a team of studio artists to study documentation, reports, and actual uniforms of Union and Confederate soldiers in rendering the warfare.[79]

The most patronized battle panorama in the United States was Paul Philippoteaux's state-of-the art *The Battle of Gettysburg* (1883), recreating the third day of conflict on the afternoon of July 3, 1863. Drew Gilpin Faust writes of the Civil War that the magnitude of death and suffering in the months and years following the intensity of the war saw "vengeance came to play an ever more important role, joining principles of duty and self-defense in legitimizing violence."[80] Fitted with electric lighting effects and three-dimensional dioramic *faux terrain* in front of the scene, one reporter captured the altered sense of landscape: "it gives the perfect impression of a sweeping summer landscape made terrible by war."[81] The panorama envisioned events for maximum empathy among Northern audiences. The spectator's point of view was on the battlefield "in the center of the positions occupied by the troops of the North."[82] The panorama's continued popularity vivified public memory of the war years. After opening in Chicago--where it was shown for ten years—three additional versions toured Boston, Philadelphia, and New York. War song concerts were held during the second year of the panorama's run in New York that "proved quite a hit."[83]

Military panoramas also accelerated the graphic tempo of state propaganda. Napoleon immediately recognized the attraction of panoramas as a means to publicize his political legacy during the Napoleonic Wars. Shortly after the first rotunda opened in Paris, the emperor commissioned architect Jacques Cellerier to build seven rotundas on the square of the Champs-Elysées devoted to his major military battles of the Revolution. In effect, he devised a centralized broadcast of his own monolithic narrative in real time. In contrast, the Capitol panorama sidesteps the actual violence of institutional slavery and territorial aggression to elevate patriotic feeling by "a compromise between history and mythology."[84] It is not only deliberately decorative but also civic oriented. Military, political, and heroic themes melt into a figurative procession of "revolutionary" events that relived a scenic historiography of continental "emancipation."

This processional narrative reissues the festive royal progresses to territorial domains beginning in sixteenth-century Europe.[85] Renaissance royal tours to foreign colonies actualized the presence of the ruling monarch with monumental celebrations of power. Roy Strong details the rites of monarchal progresses that renovated a "phantom of universal empire," casting absolute power in a genealogy of classical imperialism.[86] The idealism of Renaissance art adorned decorative structures brandished with imperial arms or allegorical figures created by local artists and craftspeople. State visits granted prestige to the host city, giving street pageantry and ceremonial embellishments an atmosphere of patriotic grandeur. Elaborate temporary and permanent triumphal arches, ornamented with portrait statuary and figurative tableaux, framed an allegorical gateway to the territorial kingdom of the arriving sovereign. The Capitol panorama, I believe, also functions as a decorative gateway but one that monumentalizes an internal pageant of "progresses," East to West, North to South, embellishing traumas of war and aggressive wealth creation into a phantom history.

The monumental narrative that the Capitol panorama institutes exhibits the administrative logic of dehumanizing proportions. Regional identity interlocks with national unification in a spatial transept from the Northeast to the West. In the report presented to Congress in 1855 by the controversial superintendent of the Capitol extension Captain Montgomery Cunningham Meigs, the subject of the frieze would be the "history of America" shown in "the gradual progress of a continent from the depths of barbarism to the height of civilization."[87] An officer in the United States Army Corps of Engineers, Captain Meigs, was appointed by President Franklin Pierce to supervise the construction of new wings and rotunda. One of his charges was to commission painters and sculptures to decorate the buildings. Meigs's oversight of the federally funded project ignited protracted tensions among established and unknown artists over delineations of "native" culture during the building's enlargement in the 1850s. In contrast to earlier Congressional decisions, Meigs was in charge of the selection of artists and subject matter. His preference was for high Renaissance classicism, draped with American details. His willingness to overlook American-born artists in order to achieve monuments of "artistic distinction" according to Russell F. Weigly, made him willing to employ European talent "in a pinch."[88] Brumidi trained at the Academia di San Luca in Rome and helped with restorations in the Vatican Palace of a wall dedicated to Pope Gregory XVI in the third Loggia. The Italian political refugee fled Italy in 1848 during the Republican revolution after being imprisoned by Cardinal Jacques Antonelli, the papal secretary of state, for his association with a group of revolutionaries.[89] His skill at painting in fresco earned him employment.

The Capitol panorama includes numerous filters, all geared to express poetry and grandeur, "capable of appealing to the feeling of all classes."[90] Meigs construct of American history reiterated the perpetuated narrative founded on belief in "the struggle between the civilized man and the savage, between the cultivated and the wild nature."[91] Its republican root harmonizes the revolutionary *nature* of the country's founding principle: *e pluribus unum* (one from many), in a creation myth. Unlike conventional circular panoramas, it is a serial form. Episodes, rather than a blended composite, unify a temporal sequence of scenes. This serial order stabilizes the narrative of political integration, a collective unity encoded with states' rights and white supremacy. Initially, a frieze of sculpture was planned and submitted to Congress in 1855 by Meigs. The concept was modified to a painted fresco of 15 panels for reasons that remain unclear.[92] Even with adjustments, the design is a monument to virulent bias:

> The rude and barbarous civilization of some of the Ante-Columbian tribes; the contests of the Aztecs with their less civilized predecessors; their own conquest by the Spanish race; the wilder state of the hunter tribes of our own regions; the discovery, settlement, wars, treatises; the gradual advance of the white, and retreat of the red races; our own revolutionary and other struggles, with the illustration of the higher achievements of our present civilization, will afford a richness and variety of costume, character, and incident.[93]

Egregious shades legitimize a traditional narrative rooted in colonial history, exposing the other side of a violent *nature*. Civil cords of a heroic "poetry" bolstered the formalities of political culture; yet the navigational instruments of political policy employed lethal practices: military force and legal exclusion. Inquiring into the "nature" publicized in this political conscience flags a fraught terrain. Heather S. Nathans pierces the visible adornment in the dramatic discourse on abolition that pries open sympathies in the "clash between a broadly inclusive *sentimental* democracy and a narrowly defined *legal* democracy in contention over the legitimate rights of freedom.[94] Several patterns encrusted in the visionary sentiment of the whitened landscape, however, mold a representative fabric of national heritage. Tropes appearing in this panorama revive in later commercial and institutional scene spaces. First, the environment is subservient to economic development. Indigenous cultures are dehumanized into environmental forces to be eliminated or absorbed into markings of white power. Violence and struggle bind individuals in a shared experience. Finally, regional typology, settlement, and lifestyle privatize the "character" of the land as cultural possession. These four redactions emboss Indian genocide in the edification of moral and military victories of continental conquest.

Indian icons are figuratively conceptualized in elegiac and heroic trophies of defeated enemies and allies. Tecumseh, Shawnee ally of the British and French in the War of 1812, is memorialized on one panel: "The Death of Tecumseh."[95] His emblem renders him passive, burying his formidable stature as resistance leader of the Shawnee Confederacy. Vivien Green Fryd argues the iconography of ethnicities among the artwork of the Capitol reflect propaganda tools behind state expansionist policies during Indian removal. Assimilation theory merely repeats eradication of Indian identity. Legal repression was well underway when the panorama was introduced. By 1825, Indian removal was defined legally. Sanctioned government policy involved bringing "the tribes so completely under American control that they could be pushed from their ancestral lands."[96] The process of legally removing tribes from ancestral lands was carefully monitored by military negotiators to avoid antagonizing them, quelling any discontent, or reduce the ability of assorted tribes to band together against white pioneers. The sustained legal denial of citizenship feigned justification to arbitrate treaty negotiations or engage combat with a foreign enemy. Stuart Banner demonstrates that the process of colonization in American Indian Affairs exposes a larger by-product of legalized power. White mercantile assumptions about value of the land operated on a much broader institutional platform in two ways: to secure "favorable conditions" for trade routes, agriculture, and industrial expansion and to contain the disenfranchised. With the country's development, territorial borders were successively reassigned or renegotiated. The long-term goal of Western expansion was not in question. How to realize the economic and political functions of American/ness were debated. The memorial iconography of Indian "artifacts" included in the panorama shroud, in one way, commemorative symbols of legal and military victories. Its installation in the public hall of the Capitol politically broadcast internally and abroad the decorative laurels of winning the "war" by a "united" federation of power.

In another way, the self-reflexive fantasy of inhabiting Indian identity regurgitates acts of retribution by displaying a creation myth that disembodies Indian culture a second time. Consider the Capitol panorama a gateway into the allegorical idealism of the state's constitution *e pluribus unum*. The motto is inscribed on the canopy of the Rotunda as well as on pedestal of Thomas Crawford's Statue of Freedom that stands atop Walter's monumental cast-iron dome. The sculpture is poised on a rocky cliff, not a classically rendered pedestal found in European tradition. Codes of sectional party politics, Roman military imperialism, and American nativism converge in the statues helmet. Crawford's initial design, authorized in 1855, included a liberty cap. It was objected to by Jefferson Davis, Secretary of War, for its association with freed slaves. Crawford instead used the symbol of the ancient republic. The crested helmet is encircled with stars, an eagle's head, and talons. Indian feathers are tucked in as well. Tucked into representational strategies of "native" origins is regulating anything foreign, including the "savage" irrational forces in human nature, to habituate citizenship to competitive battle and risk. The narrative is an artifice, filling collective authority in phantom metaphors.

Shifting back and forth between national origins and commonality is the byplay among rational order, "alien" sensuality, and fluid momentum. The confluence occurs in the first panel of the Capitol panorama, located over the West entrance door (Figure 1.1). On it the classical female figure of Freedom stands, wearing the revolutionary cap of liberty. She holds a spear in her right hand and a shield of 13 states in her left. At her feet, an eagle grasps the fasces, symbolizing the authority of government. Under Freedom's right hand, the hand of conquest, sits a bare-chested Indian woman holding a bow and arrow, representing the untamed American continent—the original design of the panorama did not include this figure on the panel.[97] Under her left hand, the hand of democracy, sits another classically draped figure, representing history. She holds a stone tablet to record events as they occur. The figures symbolize America. What does this emblematic triumvirate portend about the cultural landscape? I want to suggest that they govern a cogent hybrid of past, present, and future ingrained in the visionary spaces of the political project, one in which

Figure 1.1 America and History.

Source: Panel from *Frieze of American History*, Constantino Brumidi, Rotunda, US Capitol, Architect of the Capitol.

transgression through space propels the sense of *movement* toward a share in shaping future destiny.

Return to the first panel of the Capitol panorama. A captive "native," the seminude Indian woman, yields the sensual body of the (alien) land to the liberties of nation. The blank slate of history mirrors the ongoing, erratic enterprise of transformation into a *representational* democracy. The ideal is not static but fosters changing environmental stages of violation, occupation, and wealth creation. The political institution, itself a conflicted system of negotiation and compromise, massages patriotic sentiment by neutralizing a citizen body to sublimate self-sacrifice—tucking a feather in one's cap. Visible differences shore up regenerative circuits perpetuating amendment across a more sublime nature, a space to be filled in. The creative origins of US history are here preserved in an emotional coexistence with sublime effects of awe and terror—a conceit that inclusively embraces ambiguities: hope, fear, optimism, and horror. Correlating awe is estrangement: "in which the mind feels itself set in motion" when touched by an experience without limits or boundaries.[98] Edmund Burke premises the sublime in the reactive condition to the *appearance* of suffering and death found in terror. "For fear being an apprehension of pain or death, it operates in a manner that resembles actual pain. Whatever therefore is terrible, with regard to sight, is sublime too."[99] He uses examples of scenes that stir psychophysical responses: a dog about to be beaten; the ocean. Burke's conservative theorem avoids actual punishment by indulging intense emotions in the *illusionary*. The actions of this accomplice to estrangement are lashed to actual pain and suffering. Its preservative function monumentalizes transformative acts of violence by simultaneous disintegration. Having an unwritten narrative of the future on a blank slate secures destiny is never achieved. It projects out of another space, the appearance of a new scene on the horizon.

The strange protracted distemper of the Capitol panorama has its own blank slate. Its installation spans the active design of history in the nineteenth century as well as the conservation of its "progress" narrative into the cold war period. Brumidi labored 25 years for $8.00 a day on the design from 1859 until his death in 1879 at the age of 72 in the belief his work was to "make beautiful the Capitol of the one country on earth in which there is liberty."[100] The classically trained artist, later daubed the Michelangelo of the Capitol, had barely started the *in situ* installation of the 15 panel design when he died. It was decades before his successor Filippo Costagini finished the last eight panels in 1918. However, Costagini miscalculated his measurements leaving a 31 ft gap. Reportedly, updated designs he proposed to Congress: driving the golden spike at the junction of the Union and Pacific railroad and President Cleveland opening the Chicago World's Fair, were met with howls, and swiftly rejected as unsatisfactory.[101] The empty space remained until 1950, at which time the unfinished "eyesore" was completed by Congressional resolution up to the beginning of the twentieth century with three "monumental" events marking strides in corporate nationalism: the end of the Civil War; the Spanish-American war, and the birth of aviation.[102] The progress narrative pays tribute to an artifactual history. In the ongoing institutional design, the blank space admits creative mobility. The visionary void yields a scenic renewal that is simultaneously static, perpetual, cohesive, and incomplete.

The Market Revolution in the Panorama Industry

"The postwar boom," writes Charles Sellers "ignited a generation of conflict over the republic's destiny."[103] National restructuring by the Fourteenth Congress (1815) established legal, financial credit, and transportation infrastructure enabling transition to a capital market economy.[104] In its wake, dissension in the National Republican party flared over the economic means of internal expansion and trade policies. One project undertaken was building the Erie Canal, which interconnected rural Western New York to downstate commercial ports. A new field of battle engaged ideological camps toward the path of national development. Conservative forces of private land-based wealth entered political competition with moderates supporting interlinking economic opportunity through mobilizing capital resources to increase internal commercial trade. Attitudes sustained by landowning gentry chafed at federal advocacy, associating nationalized development to British sovereignty of the revolutionary era. Capital backers wanted to reform the perceived aristocratic stranglehold mandating a confederated domestic economy. Reactionary allegiance to strict constitutional adherence privileging sectional expansion of a slave-based wealth creation vied fiercely with the enterprising energy of an aggressive free market democracy. Widening ripples of elite and egalitarian principles protracted into discursive power struggles. Andrew Jackson's election to the presidency in 1829 stirred the discourse.

Majority rule formed the basis of his democratic philosophy; he believed in "popular virtue—and in himself as its embodiment," remarks Daniel Walker Howe.[105] Historians view Jackson's economic policies triggering a progressive transformation to "the market revolution."[106] In his two terms as President, Jackson endorsed free market trade, opposed a national banking system, promised fiscal restraint, aggressively pursued continental expansion, and protected institutional slavery. Adept at managing partisan interests, Jackson forged a political dialog of negotiation, compromise, and by extension set off the creative mobility of capital empowerment. Social energies and business interests soon rooted out commercial systems of cultural exchange in an adaptive economic environment.

The National Republican Party supported unregulated opportunity afforded by the creation of economic infrastructure. Northern urban centers inaugurated a swelling international industry around mounting panorama installations.[107] English topographical painter Frederick Catherwood's successful Exhibition Gallery in New York both imported and manufactured panoramas by the 1830s.[108] The rotunda stood on the corner of Prince Street and Broadway in lower Manhattan among a growing theatre district running up Broadway.[109] Catherwood also partnered in Boston with a rotunda fittingly called, The Panorama. Increasingly immersive strategies diverged from a singular elite standard of historical painting. Catherwood's forte was exotic forays into comparative histories. A popular view of *Rome, Ancient and Modern* traded on political nostalgia of republican lore: "back to the times that captivated our earliest attention." A vision of terrestrial paradise in *The Bay of Islands, New Zealand* contained "the project of colonizing and improving" the islands shipping port important to the whaling industry.[110] Biblical and epic travelogs glazed landscapes with religious and trade histories.

One of Catherwood's most profitable exhibits was a "faithful" travelog to a Christian landscape in the *Panorama of Jerusalem*, mentioned earlier, that arrived in New York directly from a windfall run in London at the Leicester Square Rotunda.[111] Catherwood collaborated with Robert Burford on the panorama by supplying drawings made during a visit in 1834.[112] Catherwood used a camera lucidi for drawing on his field expeditions. The optical mirror was attached at an angle to the drawing pad so that the artist could trace a superimposed image of the terrain accurately. A precursor to photography, the device achieved greater illustrative realism in drawing technique. It was one of the several optical technologies: the panograph and

diagraph are others, used to map landscape in sections for easy
insertion into a panorama.[113] The Catherwood-Burford painting
employed multipoint perspective so that the spectator could roam in
any direction over the estimated 120 ft long and 20 ft wide scene. In
contrast to Vanerderlyn's painterly approach, Catherwood's graphic
technique replicated the "holy city" in such larger than life detail,
one patron exclaimed, "you can hardly bring yourself to believe
that what you see, are not real persons, buildings, walls, vales, and
hills."[114] The scenic pilgrimage laid out biblical sites in the life of
Jesus: Mount Olive and the ascension, Bethlehem, and the Church
of the Holy Sepulchre. Mosques and worshipping Muslims contrived
local "color" typical of Catherwood's work. Collapsing temporal
boundaries of distance, the visual architecture mounted imaginary
transference. Believing in the graphic veracity of the panorama confirmed contact with personal memories of visiting Jerusalem for one
reporter, who reconstructed his journey through the narrow streets
in detail. It churned up illogical, indecipherable paths of felt beliefs.
Such empathetic interaction in the visual dramatization curtailed
freedom of worship to Christian fellowship.

In addition, independently produced panoramas tapered landscape
ingredients to establish historical perspectives over industrial enterprise. New England's highly competitive maritime trade industry
turned out writers and artists from returning sailors, most famously
Herman Melville. Mythological seafaring also inspired whaling panoramas.[115] The first, in 1849, by Celeb Purrington and Benjamin
Russell made a three-year tour.[116] Maritime panoramas injected a
voyage around the world in heroic, hunting adventures. The watery
excursion rendered critical economic networks and supply of domestic
products to distant ports in the South Pacific. It charted the technical
methods used in the trade, nocturnal vistas of tranquil shores, and the
routes of the vessels. The "hardy" labor of faceless whalers dramatized the metaphorical human trials of bloody seafaring battle.[117] The
exotic aura surfing the actual dangers and hardship of the occupation
supplied emotional appeal. "This painting must produce vivid reminiscences" for those engage in the "exciting strife"; while to others
it must almost seem like making for themselves a voyage around the
world," exclaimed *The Boston Atlas*.[118] These landscapes of religion
and trade intimate religious and labor vernaculars transmitting visual
histories. They dramatize narratives that temporarily monumental-
izing broad societal beliefs and economic virtues by excluding aber-
rations to the design. Their "exciting" comfort invited complacent

differences. Commercial panoramas opined distraction, attraction, or "cheap intellectual pleasure."[119] They probe what Roland Barthes points out as a reversal with text.[120] Speaking of the connotative influence of the photographic message, Barthes turns over how graphic power renders words "parasitic" on the image; "the image no longer illustrates the words."[121] The impact of perceptional inferences becomes particularly striking in respect to the precarious effects of Niagara landscapes.

Niagara Landscapes: Heroic, Wilderness, Fugitive, and Expressive

A "Wonder of the World" proclaimed the cover of Ingraham's popular tourism guide. The synergy of national typography and natural vernaculars bonded at the site of Niagara Falls (Figure 1.2). Its landmark status monumentalized different tonalities to accumulating power. In the ascendancy of capital restructuring, the hard driving competitive energies laying infrastructure spread marginalized and disenfranchised inequalities. The legendary appearance of Niagara Falls not only uplifted the gaze to the immeasurable grandeur of the land's

Figure 1.2   Niagara Falls from Goat Island. Terrapin Tower in Moonlight.

Source: Print. Currier & Ives, 1856–1873. Popular Graphic Arts, Library of Congress, Prints and Photographs Division.

natural wealth but also confronted the senses with the sights, sounds, and physical presence of elemental ferocity.

An early voice on American environmental studies, J. Brinckerhoff Jackson argued that geological vernaculars transmitted iconographic significance. A lingering romantic ambiguity underpins the mythic natural "ruins" he inscribes on American landscape.[122] Niagara looms over the sensorium of divergent awareness. It embraced more than one myth, and great peril. Variant shades of scenic immersion shadow what Patrick McGreevy calls "accumulations" of meanings in the historic modalities in Niagara landscape.[123] Among them, Robert Burford's touring commercial panorama of Niagara. Its travel from London to Boston and New York in the 1830s matched a spiking tourism to the region after the opening of the Erie Canal. Daguerreotypist James Presley Ball and painter Robert Duncanson both photographed and painted Niagara landscapes that remain lost.[124] In 1855, their anti-slavery panorama, *Splendid Mammoth Pictorial Tour of the United States: Comprising Views of the African Slave Trade of Northern and Southern Cities; of Cotton and Sugar Plantations; of the Mississippi, Ohio and Susquehanna Rivers, Niagara Falls, etc*, agitated against the Fugitive Slave Act (1850). This work falls in step with a series of Mississippi River moving panoramas, examined separately. For now, I want to highlight the abolition narrative in Ball's and Duncanson's Niagara landscape. From the Hudson River School of landscape artists, Frederic Church's panoramic view of *Niagara* (1857), spread the lore of a national "type."[125] These three vantage points articulate landscape vernaculars rearing different "American" narratives. The early prestige of history painting receded in the physical presence of the Niagara vista.

Among the first views of Niagara Falls are illustrative studies (1801–1827) by Vanderlyn. His well-connected rival John Trumbull attempted in 1808 to exhibit a panorama of Niagara in London without success.[126] Trumbull may have run up against anti-American backlash in London before the war. Typical themes in these early scenes are origin tales. One convention elevated isolated white figures surveying the gloried mountain, while Indians were passively consumed into the scenery among the organic wild atmosphere of the land. Trumbull's mock up for his panorama stages it as a foundational myth. In the far corner of the landscape appears the *natural encounter* of a white man peacefully approaching an Indian family huddled beside a tepee that is encased by thick forest. Panoptic symbols of organic nobility stretch to the Capitol panorama as well. The fateful folktale of the "Indian princess" Pocahontas saving Captain John Smith from being clubbed to death in a Christian act of mercy follows the death of Spanish explorer De Soto in 1542, who discovered the Mississippi River. They are followed by the Landing of the Pilgrims. Her sacrifice presumes the inevitable cultivation of the indigenous land, a resource both "wild" and once subdued "sublime." Figurative narratives of wilderness, such as Trumbull's, restructure colonial motifs of paternalism and territorial wealth as a heroic sentiment of natural virtue.[127] Republican idealism embellishes sentiment in the organic possession of worth. This type of beneficent landscape conforms to rationale legislation—colonizing the wilderness. Democratic vigor fragmented the landscape with ethical dilemmas. Privatization, economic disenfranchisement, and racial violence altered environmental circumstances and found vocalization in other appearances of wild Niagara.

The building of the Erie Canal set in motion renovations to Upper New York State by the 1820s that occluded a region wrestling Indian authority out of the frame. Long the site of colonial invasion by British forces throughout the seventeenth and eighteenth centuries, American colonial forces courted the Seneca Confederacy to secure what was officially referred to as "the Niagara Frontier." The area comprised a strategic region bordering Canada on the East side of Buffalo and routing South to the Western territories between Lake Ontario and Lake Erie. The Seneca assumed leadership as "keepers of the Western door" among the league of Mohawk, Onondaga, Cayuga, and Tuscarora whose authority extended south into Pennsylvania and West into Ohio from New York State.[128]

One of the Confederacy's influential speaker's was Chief Red Jacket (Sagoyewatha). Red Jacket gained the Anglican name for wearing the British red coat during the revolutionary war; his was dogged by a tarnished reputation for maneuvering between British and American allegiances. Granville Ganter argues the recovery of Red Jacket's political discourse restores the cultural voice of Native authority.[129] His presence on stage during an 1828 "goodbye tour" in New York countered the rife theatrical circulation of Indian impersonations rolled out among the vogue for Indian romantic drama and Indian touring exhibitions, headed by Edwin Forrest's famed role as *Metamora*.[130] Known for his eloquence, Red Jacket spoke out against the sale of Indian lands, against encroachment of white's religion and culture, and in defense of Indian sovereignty.[131] When the 1789 treaty with the Six Nations was negotiated with American military representatives, he refused to see the treaty as binding. Five years later, he negotiated the Canandaigua Treaty, guarantying Indian sovereignty over four million acres in upstate New York.[132] When approached by a land speculator during a Buffalo Creek council in 1811, Red Jacket sent him away, saying, "We are determined not to sell our lands."[133] Pressure mounted in the nineteenth-century postwar transition to the market economy. After Red Jacket's death in 1838, the Buffalo Creek land was sold. Indian artifacts and the burial grounds of the Tuscarora and Seneca were desecrated by tourist trails. Skeletal "aboriginal remains" on Goat Island registered historic markings among the natural "ruins" of Niagara iconography.[134]

The Niagara Frontier was also the site of major battles between1812 and 1814. White settlements were left with property damage and community destruction during military occupation of public stores, hospital, and barracks.[135] Postwar claims by Niagara sufferers continued for seven years (1817–1824) in vain. One petition by Jasper Parish sought the exacting amount of $744.50 for compensation to repair his fencing. It seems the troops of Brigadier General Smyth, camping on the banks of the river in November 1812, made unauthorized used Parish's fences for firewood.[136] New York representative Churchill C. Cambreleng, on behalf of the petitioners, lobbied fellow House members to take action. He was stonewalled. An unidentified "distinguished" member remarked, "the right of petition (in relation to those claims at least) had become a privilege of having the petition rejected."[137] The message signaled possession of national liberty was its own advantage. Individual fate did not equate with bipartisan support to couple national *feeling* with national *interests* in "internal improvement."[138] A permanent appropriation fund from the sales of Public Lands and National Bank stock dividends was set up to increase internal trade and commerce by swift approval in 1824. House members argued for a "system" of roads and canals "connecting the distant parts of this widely extended republic; uniting and binding together by the strong ties of interest and intercourse."[139] The Niagara community was left to fend for itself.

Advantageous to connecting city and country was the machinery of industrial mobility: steam engines. River steamboat trade and travel routes developed faster than road and rail systems. Steamboat passage to the cataract of Niagara Falls harnessed technological power to the enterprise of freedom. In his cultural history of railways, Wolfgang Shivelbusch elaborates broad distinctions between the European and American experiences of industrial motion. Where Europeans experienced industrial transitions as destructive to nature: affecting material life and cultural tradition, the American experience garnered a means of gaining a new model of domestic life from wilderness—tourism and leisure. "In the United States," Shivelbusch remarks, the industrial revolution was seen as a natural development, not only because it appeared right at an early stage of American economic transformation but also because it happened first in agriculture and transportation."[140] The opening of rail and steamboat transportation granted ease of access to wilderness. Rail and steamer lines to Niagara were planned routes with tourism as a consideration. Steamers were running regular passenger ships from New York to Niagara by 1826.[141] Domestic and foreign travelers sailed up the Hudson to grasp the magnitude of the Falls in person. Travel up the Hudson River by steamboat to Buffalo personalized for passengers contact with new sights and sounds: different regional ways of life and local characteristics of geography. As river transportation increased, the scenic sentiments stirred the oratory of change. On vacation after his first season as a legitimate box office star, the actor Edwin Forrest traveled to Buffalo on the Erie Canal soon after it opened. In a letter to his mother from Buffalo, he wrote,

> I make this journey for the purpose of recreation, in viewing the romantic beautifies of our country, and the development of art and industry, which are so rapidly leading to wealth and happiness. I have passed through a series of flourishing towns ... all of which have given me delight.[142]

The mythic virility of Forrest's stage persona and robust oratorical skills came to be identified with the landmark. In the blossoming democratic language of "native" self-determination, he was seen as a "mountain of man" who's "roaring verbal cataracts" could flood a theatre like "the rushing waters of the Niagara."[143] Traveling by steamboat up the Hudson, the contiguous scale of sight and sense coexisted on the river. The cataract of Niagara Falls broadcast the first eponymous spectacle of natural wonder.

The vigorous beacon of the young democracy inspired visionary proximity to material growth, interconnecting countryside to city and the reverse—much like the revolving panorama excursions. In 1810, the population of Buffalo was roughly four hundred, according to a local historian.[144] By 1830, the city's economic recovery boasted close to nine-thousand inhabitants.[145] Regional growth connected city dwellers to the rural beauty of a fashionable Northeastern landscape. In turn, industrial and urban conceits open out from the city, becoming landscape.[146] Scenic vernaculars overlaid the attraction of economic prosperity and spatial freedom on idiomatic memories of historic survival and sacrifice. Travelers were assured comfort in rustic surroundings in no less than seven area hotels; foreigners could apprehend the democratic project of the classless Yankees share in wealth mobility.[147]

Painter and manager of the Leicester Square Rotunda Robert Burford exhibited his panorama of Niagara in 1833 made from drawings by Frederick Catherwood. However, different program editions of the panorama credit Burford as artist. It returned for a second showing the following year paired with a panorama of New York. Catherwood purchased this and two others for his New York Rotunda a few years before the exhibition structure burned down.[148] The rendering synthesizes the signs of economic prosperity entering the vast frame of the Niagara Falls. The upper section of the panorama is consumed with the falls, which cascade into the lower half. The spectator would be on the same ground plane with the depiction of visitors gazing up the vaporous rushing waters surrounding everything in sight. Well-dressed onlookers are seated or strolling near noted geographical features of the area, such as Table Rock overhang. The wild domain shows signs of architectural development; it is dotted with paths, bridges, and small accommodating hotels and guest houses. The nature setting is a *scenic wilderness* with visitors inhabiting a comfortable pastoral domain. Among the tiny figures "encroaching" on the scene is a party of Indians "barely perceptible amidst the grandeur of Falls in front and 'wilderness' around them."[149] Whether Burford had seen Trumbull's earlier version is not clear but his shadowy inhabitants are atmospheric figures, who guide the viewer back to the "foreign" occupiers milling about. Their immaterial presence is disassociated from the white circumstance. In contrast, the counter narrative to the panoramic views of scenic wilderness at Niagara confronts actual conditions. There hangs a brutal, more violent side over transitions to a capital economy that claimed progress but sustained reactionary policies.

Variations of the Niagara landscape after 1850 marked it a national landmark. Mass tourism to the preeminent wonder branded the falls a leisure destination. Hidden from public view, the pleasure site held different significance to abolitionists and fugitive slaves trying to reach freedom on the Underground Railroad. Antebellum African Americans subverted white objectification in a visual arts tradition that established their subjectivity in aesthetic practices.[150] Abolition art radicalized present circumstances, puncturing forced alienation and the segregated boundaries of denial. Over the decade of the 1850s, the recreation of slave narratives—appearing in print— and graphic details of the slave trade by fugitive slaves and abolitionist activists circulated widely in visual media. Ball opened a widely patronized fine art Gallery in downtown Cincinnati, Ohio, in 1849 that according to Joseph D. Ketner II engendered a vital, yet short-lived black art community.[151] Among the painters who worked with Ball was Duncanson. Known for their portraits and landscapes, they used a method of "coloring" photographs with oil paint that gave off painterly effects. The combination blended the exacting realism of a photographic print with the "artistic" brushwork of painting.[152] Wendy Jean Katz notes the deliberate discourse of refinement Ball adopted invested in the production and marketing of gentility, suggesting a strategy to promise greater civility in urban life.[153] Ball was active in the anti-slavery campaigns, and at the height of abolitionist fervor in the city he used the popular formula of the travel panorama to condemn the duplicities of the national ideal as the "land of the free and the home of the slave."[154] It is generally believed that Duncanson helped paint the lost 600 yard, 53-scene "mammoth" historical "landscape" of the United States.[155]

Ball's script details the economic functions of institutional slavery, disassembling the tranquil artifactual leisure landscape. His "tour" interrogates a system of trade, labor, and legislation without varnish as the hypocrisy of the national narrative, and confronts the public directly in the cause of abolition.[156] Like his contemporaries, Frederick Douglass and William Lloyd Garrison wielding free speech in abolition newspapers, opposition to the Fugitive Slave legislation runs throughout Ball's narrative.[157] Garrison's *The Liberator* ran weekly articles on the panorama when it was viewed in Amory Hall, Boston.[158] Ball drew on the slave narratives of William Wells Brown and Henry Box Brown to embody the deadly ramifications of the Fugitive Slave Act in the passage of scenes.

The dangers along the underground water and land routes from the Southern states to Canada linger at the popular tourist location of Niagara Falls as a paradox of American freedom. An annual estimate by the anti-slavery society of Canada reported in 1852 there were approximately thirty-thousand blacks in Western Canada. The figure rose to as many as seventy-five thousand in 1858.[159] Ball's commentary directs the viewer to ponder two sides of the falls. Shown from the US shore are grand views of the mighty waters, as well as the advantages of American progress, described in the engineering projects underway at the site. The last scene ponders the fate of fugitive slaves arriving on the Canadian side of the Niagara River.[160] In most Northern communities, Frank H. Severance explains, the special officers chasing the fugitives were "regarded with odium, and every possible obstacle put in the way of the discharge of their offensive duties."[161] The dangers of passage left those assisting anxious over the uncertain fate of fugitives. One letter to *The Liberator* asks after a man from Richmond who was sheltered in Milford overnight in route to Massachusetts: "I trust he has reached that soil which alone is free."[162]

Terror at Niagara stress correlations to the economic landscape. Awe and terror mask coercive and unbridled interactions swaying in the alienated sensations of despair and death at Niagara. It too attracted the stormy undercurrents of pathos as a site of death. In August 1852, a young woman walked to the cliff of the falls and "flung" herself into the whirlpool below.[163] Death by accident, by suicide, and for publicity stunts were regular occurrences.[164] Ball's final scene rests on the Canadian side of the Niagara River. Queenston was a terminus of the Underground Railroad. He too holds up the blank slate of history to expose the real and present horror of legalized violence occurring in the Niagara landscape. "The unwritten records of this enterprise would astonish the world with examples, of hazardous escapes, noble daring, and patient endurance of those engaged in 'running' slaves from the South." He relates the noble daring of one who made his way from Virginia with slave hunters on horseback on his heels as he ran to the river. Several carpenters working on a boat near him pulled him on board and rowed him to the other side. When he set his feet on the Canadian shore, "he threw his arms upward, exclaiming, 'Thank God I'm FREE!' Sunk upon the earth and died."

Ball's final vantage point clouds the mountain with uncertainty yet never relinquishes the right for self-empowerment. It is difficult to separate the hope and the actual. This tinge, like the technique of heightening photographic realism with oil paint, reverses the illusion effect to strip away gloss and arm resistance. The freedom to make one's own fate implied tangible paths of human destruction and protracted legal, political, and social battle. In juxtaposition, the intangible momentum to reach a new destination did not always blanket disillusion or adversity in visible signage of landmarks. The monument of Niagara channeled a transactive synergy of raw land onto which tonalities of crisis, despondency, inspiration, and spiritualism were projected into the physical space. Charles Dickens's journey to Niagara in 1842 left him feeling a profound life and death struggle at the falls, notes Natalie McKnight. He writes of the "mighty streams" of the falls dying in the descent to "unfathomable graves."[165] Landscape art from a generation extracting itself from European tradition found inspiration in the spiritual substance of the land itself, the yet "undefiled [by man] works" of "God, the creator."[166] The romantic impulse among these American artists favored the idiosyncrasies of natural subject matter. The Hudson River school of painting employed traditional panoramic techniques to shape the Eastern landscape into sublime expressions of natural poetry.

For a white generation coming into the "retrospective" age in Ralph Waldo Emerson words a theocracy of natural possession cast off bondage to Anglo-European lineage in the 1830s.[167] The rhapsodies of white nativism tendering the prospective sanctity of the American character exalted natural substance above all else. Among the Northeastern coterie of poets and painters adopting a romanticized transcendental gaze on the landscape, Emerson embellished nature worship with creative insight. In his 1836 book *Nature* Emerson waged, "Why should we not also enjoy an original relation to the universe? Why should we not have a poetry and philosophy of insight and not of tradition, and a religion by revelation to us, and not the history of theirs?"[168] Artist Thomas Cole, an influence on Duncanson's artistic development, viewed the majestic sweep of the land as the "sublimity of a shoreless ocean unislanded by the recorded deeds of man."[169] European soil was populated by man-made ruins; young America communed with the active tremors of history in the making. The land embodied "native" culture in Cole's oration. John O'Sullivan designated this self-perpetuating spirit "Manifest Destiny," envisioning for his readers a country "destined to be *the great nation of futurity*."[170] However, the promise and the experience thwarted the rhetoric of consensus. Tensions between wild nature and society's utilitarian destruction of it formed the basis of cultural preservation among the transcendentalists.[171] The critique of rampant materialism most famously appears in Cole's serial work *The Course of Empire* (1833–1836).

Frederic Edwin Church's pictorial panorama of *Niagara* (1857) exhorted the altered dimensions of the national mood. In a way, it siphoned off nature into a hallmark of the cultural landscape. "I believe an artist should paint what he sees," offered the reticent Church.[172]

His style of naturalism evoked the expressive artifact. The painting was exhibited at the commercial gallery of Williams, Stevens, and Williams in lower Manhattan for a month before touring major cities along the East coast. The owners paid Church 4,500 dollars for exclusive rights, and charged the public 25 cents for admission. Within two weeks, over one-hundred thousand visitors crowded the gallery, receiving for their payment a brochure extolling glowing commentaries.[173] The *New York Daily Times* hailed its splendid achievement due to the greatness of the Art itself and to the shining promise of its actual estate among us."[174] International success followed the US tour with shows from London to Glasgow, as well as an 1867 viewing at the Paris Universal Exhibition.

The painting measures 40 × 90.5 inches, allowing the spectator to enter its panoramic window. With no foreground, one reviewer remarked: "it is water to the base line, and water everywhere. The only land that appears is in two strips of shore in the distance; which, by the way, are most delicately and truthfully painted. Its grand character is given to the picture by the skillful presentation of the great mass of water; and the marvel of its treatment is the expression of mobility which every part of it conveys."[175] Much like the circular panorama, the scene had no edge, no visible frame. Unlike the static landscape of circular painted panoramas, Church's landscape came to life. The recessive expanse of the pictorial panorama floated the viewer within an imaginary 360-degree vantage point. In Church's scene space subjective immersion hovered on the brink of watery chaos. Its "sober truth" left one viewer feeling the "presence of the stupendous reality, with the abstraction of motion and sound."[176] An overhang of brooding clouds cap the sensory extension in the landscape's vacillating emotions. The horizon line disappears in the mingling of dusky sky and frothing waters; circulation vibrates in all directions.

Alfred Boime explores the interactive dimensions of harnessing destiny in the operations of visual composition by application of perspective in American pictorial panoramas. Its expression occurred on the heights, moving the visual trajectory to the landscape below:

> The experience on the heights and its literary and aesthetic translation became assimilated to popular culture and remained and continues to remain a fundamental component of the national dream. As such, it is inseparable from nationalist ideology. [T]here is an American viewpoint in landscape painting that can be identified with this characteristic line of vision [;] this peculiar gaze represents not only a visual line

of sight but an ideological one as well. [The] view from the summit metaphorically undercut the past and blazed a trail into the wilderness for the abodes of commerce and the seats of manufactures.[177]

Boime demarcates a stable historical perspective. But the horizon line moves, encouraging the reconsideration of scene space as a destabilizing practice. Church animates an alternate reality that stamped itself on the cultural imagination, adding to historical, industry, religious, abolitionist, and tourism panoramas. His Niagara animates spatial awareness of human erasure in civil and material progress, giving presence to estranged patterns in the poetic wilderness. Its aspirational turmoil enlivens empathies within the spectacle of conflicting domesticated sensibilities. Andrew Jackson's justification of territorial federalism warned: "Individuals must give up a share of liberty to preserve the rest."[178] His sentiment stirs an allusive agency, that of having a share in creating destiny. Its visionary ambiguity parallels the function of the America project, which remains the yet unwritten narrative of the future.

Scenic Discourse Unbound

The Rotunda with its soaring architectural space is considered the symbolic heart of the US Capitol; the panorama of history embedded in its walls is emblematic of the permanence of the phantom nature of America, which continues to emit contrary messages, continues to evade definition, and continues to attract or repel perspectives cast on it over what Tavia Nyong'o calls the "miscegenation of time."[179] The monumental design of its spectacle dimensions "reserves" the idea of democracy where the search for novelty, the unknown, the next frontier, simultaneously revives scenic space. In the formal culture of the Capitol, panoramic motifs amend territorial conquest and regional development to monumentalize the phantom memories of the country's ongoing destiny. Land acquisition manifested the rational of revolutionary independence, of free trade, of colonization, of states' rights, of legalized violence and oppression, and of continental unification; it endowed the institutional identity of a United States as a collective enterprise unencumbered by (European) historical precedent. The political landscape imported social alienation into landmarks of integration. It reified the myth of an organic identity, of a nation continuously rising out of the uncivilized wilderness. Hubert

Damisch elaborates the function of spatial perspective in painting constructs and harmonizes an idea of nature according to the dominant ideology. His theoretical insights offer a useful underpinning to the illusion of a monumental "America," evoked in the constitution of a *natural order*.[180] The enigmatic expressions of scenic discourse reciprocate an immersive vocabulary of decomposition.

The artifactual display of commercial panoramas suspended and embraced flux. Independent intersections voiced artistic interrogation of the representational economy. Landscape history is here preserved in a perpetual circulation of competing operations, shifting along the dynamics of actuality, illusion, ideals. The forward trajectory of this visionary principle advances through protracted negotiations of spatial boundaries. Scenic practices collaborate with the imperfect course of national design, transmitting the quest for reinvention and novelty. They preserve topographical patterns that move in all directions through progressive stages, through reactionary stages, and through radical protest, projecting out of and onto the physical phenomena a contrary landscape.

Stationary landscape panoramas intensified a spatial sense in visual media that was incidental and comprehensive, flexible and formulaic, and innovative and standardized. The increasing diversity of subject matter and commercial applications further fragment the idea of American/ness rather than chart a unified course. One binding medium remains constant in the unfolding national design—the land. Regional, political, and sociological distension dissolves or enlarges the visionary space of history with something new—with notions that can expand, contract, escape, misrepresent, or confront. Another branch of spectacle activity combined panoramic landscape with theatrical mechanics to move scenes allowing greater flexibility with temporal and spatial illusions. Moving panoramas experimented with multimedia technology, lighting effects, and performance elements. The multimedia application of visual and spatial extension (both experiential and symbolic) made environments appear and disappear; it deployed scene space as a changing medium of sensible occupation. Before the Civil War, moving panoramas of the Mississippi River access the economic lifeblood necessary to growing trade networks and Western expansion.

2

Moving Scenes: Multimedia Performance along the Mississippi River

One of the first theatrical treatments of the Niagara landscape in America included motion effects. It is not surprising that a genre of "trip" plays take advantage of the mechanics of moving panoramas on stage. Painter, playwright, and theatre manager William Dunlap wrote his last theatre piece *A Trip to Niagara; or, Travellers in America* (1828) for the popular Bowery Theatre. Dunlap's pro-American farce lampooned British manners at the height of anti-British fervor in New York. The play presents a party of English tourists traveling by steamship up the Hudson River. The journey's conceit is to "cure" one of the Englishmen of his prejudices of Yankees as uncouth and uncivil. Disembarking in the rural countryside, the city dwellers encounter assorted "self-defining American" stage types. A free black hotel servant Job Jennyson asserts "I am my own master," when mistaken for a slave by one of the visitors. A new stage character appears, the plain talking frontier man Leatherstocking from James Fenimore Cooper's novel *Pioneers*. Yet, Dunlap claimed his main intention "was to display scenery."[1] The "splendor" of the scene is what attracted attention.[2] During a sailing interlude between acts a reputed 25,000 ft of canvas attached on vertical rollers created the sensation of passing up the Hudson River to Niagara.[3] "The wonders and wonders of the Hudson" rolled by as storm and fog effects projected a changing atmosphere.[4] The theatrical landscape familiarized working-class urban audiences not only with country's regional customs and dialects but also with the natural architecture of nationhood. Such combination of technology, sprawling geography, and a spectrum of American characters affirmed for an urban crowd distant commonality, tying a sweeping scenic momentum to a collated national pride. "The external senses delight," one elated critic remarked, "by the magnificent view of *our* rivers and mountains" (my emphasis).[5]

Although Dunlap claimed notoriety for being among the first to use "moving scenery" in America, he appears to have jumped on a European trend. The French scenic spectacle *Paris and London* presented at the Arch Street Theatre treated Philadelphia audiences to a "moving panorama" of steamboat travel from Calais to Dover about the same time as *A Trip to Niagara* was running in New York City.[6] In the wake of painted panoramas, moving theatrical panoramas left the stationary circle of the rotunda. By the 1840s they developed into independent shows, often created by and performed by a single artist. Their features grew exponentially with technical machinery capable of rigging thousands of feet of canvas to roll horizontally between cylinders mounted on either side of the stage, making them easy to transport and install. The performance conventions of these multimedia shows incorporated production values of conventional theatre: music, melodramatic tableaux, dramatic action, lighting effects, and "acting" narrators that contributed to the sensory layers of sight, sound, and storytelling. Their appearance sparked one letter by Dewy Fay to the editors of the *Home Journal* rebuking the use of the term "panorama" for the new theatrical sensation that was not a static painting.[7]

John Bell relates moving panoramas to ancient and global traditions of "picture performance."[8] Characterized by juxtaposition of painted images and narrator, this form of storytelling added to the creation of epic, mythic histories. Nineteenth-century theatrical panoramas also intersect with the global business of entertainment imports and exports. Creeping into the restlessness of the 1850s is not only an episodic scope in these traveling shows, but recurrent scenic routes that are handled differently by individual artists. History, commerce, and amusement collide. Commercial systems of the new temporal media absorb state-of-the-art trends. Mushrooming genres, regional styles, artistic motivation, and faster manufacturing methods widened the narrative functions of immersive technology. The ideological spectrum mirrored any purpose from propaganda to fantasy. This forum of sociological discourse surmounted language barriers nationally and internationally. It situates literary, social, or entertainment trends in immersive practices. Genres sprang forth advocating educational instruction, social activism, tourism, science fiction, archaeological expedition, religious proselytizing, fantasy, and autobiography to name a few. The reach of performance panoramas widened pathways in cultural production for faith-based, conservative, liberal, and dissenting viewpoints. All of which converge in the timely popularity of moving river panoramas, particularly those canvassing the Mississippi River. These scenic spectacles transmit how economic migration West moved hand in hand with technological exploration.

Moving Along the Mississippi River

A series of moving theatrical river panoramas riveted attention on the Midwest with views of regional settlement and conflicts. These touring shows spread dramatic narratives of life along the Mississippi River that competed for perceptional sway, as well as commercial survival for the visual artists who produced them. Between 1846 and 1849 seven Mississippi panoramas ran in concert, crisscrossing American and European cities. Initially, the large-scale ingredients introduced in Mississippi River voyages were the creation of white artists whose aesthetic idealism and commercial awareness permeate conventions of this travel genre. Among the first was Samuel Adams Hudson's *12,000 ft. Grand Panoramic View of the Hudson River.*[9] Whether, in fact, Hudson's panorama spanned two miles is dubious. Shown in St. Louis in 1848, Hudson's stupendous ride "gratified crowds" to the point that admission fees were cut and reductions made for schools.[10] It embarked from New York Bay to the mouth of the Mohawk River or the reverse. Instead of rewinding the canvas, the direction of the cruise switched from one show to another show. Hudson's river voyage constructs the tour to simulate physical sensations of turning in space. His handling of scenic technology guided sight lines to *move* the viewer this way or that, leaving no pause within the temporal continuity. The tempo-based choreography allowed a multitude of impressions to coalesce in a cumulative awe. Alternating scenes panned back and forth from shoreline to shoreline maneuvering a side-to-side view of passing "cities, towns, and landings." Developing conventions of this type of scenic saturation permeates conscious immersion in media-based mobility.

Once riverscapes became trendy, everyone jumped in. In step with Hudson and his partner George W. Cassidy was the lasting success of John Banvard, a self-proclaimed self-taught artist, as well as

John Rowson Smith, an itinerant scene painter. For years, Banvard and Smith battled publically over who created the original and grandest Mississippi panorama. Artists from the Western hubs angled to add frontier currency, introducing recently opened regional territories. Theatrical painter, Samuel B. Stockwell, Henry Lewis, a carpenter and aspiring landscape painter, and decorative artist Leon Pomarède entered the market with Midwestern variations. The last was painted by John J. Egan. The work was commissioned by Dr. Montroville William Dickenson, a Professor at the Philadelphia College of Medicine and natural science enthusiast, to illustrate lectures on his 12-year archaeological expeditions to ancient Indian burial mounds throughout the Mississippi Valley. This rather idealized ethnographic treatment of Indian artifacts and history is the only one of which canvas fragments survive.[11]

Counter voices rejected the veiled hypocrisy of these entertainment vessels. Protest narratives by numerous African-American artists after 1850 challenged the sublime anthems of white nationalism underpinning river panoramas. Critical encounters disrupted picture-perfect storytelling allowing performers to "enter the landscape," as Daphne A. Brooks argues.[12] Scenes of flight, lynching, and brutality defrocked the neutered image by white artists of pan-Mississippi migration in the popular river panoramas. In addition to daguerreotypist James P. Ball's and painter Robert S. Duncanson's anti-slavery panorama, escaped slaves William Wells Brown, and Henry Box Brown redeployed the medium to upend the theatrical routes with testimonials of their own slave narratives. The faith-based panorama documented alternative religion and mainstream persecution. Carl Christian Anton Christensen began a "Mormon Panorama" in the 1850s to aid missionary work among Utah tribes (1878).[13] He created a second panorama documenting the violent harassment the Church of the Latter Day Saints endured across the country in its quest to establish the church. Discontinuities among so many individual works revises Angela Miller's claim that the river panoramas control a uniform representational screen of "historical movement."[14]

Miller and others sometimes encapsulate multimedia panoramas in proto-cinematic terms as "moving pictures," "newsreels," or even "arm chair travel."[15] The cinematic extension is part of the technology's outgrowth, yet can limit it to a two-dimensional screen of passive consumption. Brooks argues that the black aesthetics employed by abolitionist artists radically "intervened" in history by applying critical strategies to turn the standard patterns of the revolving panorama against itself.[16] Theatrical correspondence and precedents exist as well. Gwendolyn Waltz, for instance, elaborates increasing spatial byplay in multimedia staging and live performance in late nineteenth-century theatre.[17] Multimedia immersion extends into the popular realm, in part, from the "labyrinth" of production values devised for the Baroque staging of special effects.[18] Increasingly, attention is shifting to perceptional tactics at play in the immersive experience and the sensate effects of compressed acceleration in technological developments. Alison Griffiths's example of "cinema anthropology" flushes out the sensory envelopment of moving panoramas in relation to methods of fabricating "reenactments."[19] Her nuanced approach to the ways vision technology interacts with spectatorship accents how space, illusion, and presence materialize in "visual splendor."[20] Theatrical presence of media-reenactments complicates the splendor of sensory illusion further.

Paul Virilio's theory of "transappearance" carries spectacle mediation forward.[21] Virilio's philosophy of virtual architecture, or the science of speed and power operating in the logic of perspective screens, is a twentieth-century cultural critique of technological consciousness. The transappearance of simultaneity involves the malleable ways of "optical teleporting" in which the temporal acceleration of long distance transmission drives real-time perspective of tangible appearances that "outstrips the small-scale optics of *the perspective of real space*."[22] Virilio pursues modifications of the human relationship to the aesthetics of disappearance from the imaginary horizon line of classical convention to the electronic presence "where unity of time wins out over the unity of the place of encounter": the lost dimensions of spatial presence are transformed by technological dimensions. Moving back in time, technospatiality is quite significant in the transference of the pan-Mississippi landscape from "live" locations to manipulations of time-based technology in multimedia dramatizations. These coordinates occur in mechanized-time and real-time as the push for land acquisition and encroachment into uncharted Western territorial frontiers drew attention to interior regions of the continent. The multimedia performances of the river voyage animate embodied, experiential energies that telescope critical view points, competitive tactics, and historic mythology over real-time history in the making. River narratives, in this streaming circumstance, amplify the transappearances of media-generated perceptions.

Changing Territorial Boundaries: The Geography of River Views

A traveler on the newly opened National Road to Ohio exhorted: "Old America seems to be breaking up and moving westward."[23] Westward momentum shifted territorial boundaries indefinitely. In the often dangerous pan-Mississippi communities, the river solidified a network of interdependent economic systems. Three geographical areas were desirable to Eastern industrial entrepreneurs and settlers: natural vegetation suitable for farming fell North and South of the settled juncture of the Ohio and Mississippi Rivers; the forest belt of Southern Illinois and Indiana; the broad prairies of the Gulf Plains, especially Western Indiana and central Illinois, and the pine forests of Northern Michigan and Wisconsin.[24] Timber, mining, and agriculture connected pioneering efforts to regional avenues of commercial traffic from North to South, from Eastern states to settlement West of the Mississippi, and across the Atlantic. With the push to open territories in the Northwestern Lake Plains, the surge for unsettled lands by frontiersmen resulted in the "greatest population movement the nation had known."[25] The Eastern half of the continent was occupied by white settlement by 1850. States' rights advocates in the newly opened trans-Mississippi territories banded with Southern slave states to oppose banking regulation, trade tariffs, and abolition.

By 1846, the Mississippi panoramas entered head to head competition to be the first, the longest, and the latest excursion along the river beltways. River panoramas correspond to the rise of nautical genres in landscape painting, melodrama, and operetta.[26] In the long seafaring tradition of European nations, maritime themes branch into history, disasters at sea, and naval subjects; in the antebellum period, nautical fare infuses regionalism, tourism, and commerce with patriotic relish. Panoramas of the 1,000 mile lower Mississippi, from the confluence of the Ohio, appeared before even bigger panoramas incorporating the 1,300-mile long upper Mississippi into Illinois and Iowa. In comparison to the "majestic beauty" of the Hudson River, *Westward Ho* author James K. Pauling contemplated the "deep and profound" impact his first Mississippi journey yielded. "My imagination," he waxed, "was dwelling on its most interminable course."[27] The sentiment was not utopic but verified in the immediacy of apprehending territorial incursions in real time. Panoramic presence of the pan-Mississippi world conversed with nation building narratives, spreading the risks and instabilities navigating the fragile collective undertaking.

The passing shoreline often projected anything is possible even as the uneasy continental journey lurched on.

Riverscapes broadcast the farthest extent of the interior landscape alongside a rabid election campaign with Republicans and Democrats battling over protectionism, federal regulation, and slavery in the territories. Martin Van Buren lost his reelection bid in 1840. Labeled a champagne sipping (Eastern) elitist in what is considered the first modern publicity driven campaign, he was defeated by Whig ticket of William Henry Harrison, former Governor of the Indiana territories and his running mate Virginia Senator John Tyler. Harrison earned a reputation as frontier fighter during the war of 1812. The turning point of the War, the massacre of Indian coalition forces led by Chief Tecumseh, became known as the Battle of Tippecanoe River. Harrison served as General of the forces that shattered the British-Indian alliance and killed Tecumseh. The campaign slogan "Tippecanoe and Tyler Too" alluded to the packaging of Harrison as a log cabin republican—he was from wealthy Virginia family—plus a nod to protect Southern slave states.[28] Frontier lore conveyed graphic accounts of the internal conflicts. Mentioned earlier, John Stevens's *Sioux War Panorama*, commemorating a final battle of Indian resistance, was crafted for pioneer audiences in the culminating scene of the Sioux massacre. It would see five different versions between 1862 and 1878 during a regional tour through Minnesota, Iowa, Wisconsin, and Illinois.[29]

In opposition to the cultivated beauty of early Niagara landscapes the field of Western painting inaugurated scenic tales of wild beauty. Contrary to the rules and idealism of academic classicism, Western artists relied on empirical experiences to create archetypal scenes of "new country." Philadelphian George Catlin mused as he set off to Missouri to record the customs and ceremonies of the American Indian tribes West of the Mississippi, "I have long been of the opinion, that the wilderness of our country afforded models equal to those from which the Grecian sculptors transferred to the marble such inimitable grace and beauty."[30] So popular was Catlin's extensive gallery of paintings when he exhibited them in the East—before showing in London (1839) and Paris (1840)—that he turned to engravings, lithographs, and illustrated books to feed demand.[31] His rejection of the "fashionable" and "polished" models of beauty by Eastern artists rendered the "native" attitude of the American plains with free-spirited naturalistic impressions. The branding of the American West by aesthetic ethnographies encircled a period of segregation, displacement, and white occupation with the peculiarities of geoeconomic differences. Pan-Mississippi landscapes often evoked "beauty and grandeur," drafting home and country in the mantle of domestic industry and developing settlements while valorizing the strange regional terrain and distinct lifestyle of inhabitants. The dense forest, fertile valleys, towering bluffs, and rolling plains in scenic regionalism exerted a deceptive typography of borderless abundance. There is another aspect in this fabrication of scenic life that holds significance: the revitalization of creation mythos dispersing pioneer origins forged from the land. Regional heritage conjoined entertainment commodities that not only voiced a sectional American identity but also tossed aside old masters.

Catlin's brand of poetic license drawn from direct observation stood at the outset of the Western genre, which included moving theatrical panoramas. The outposts of the interior supplied fresh, homegrown subjects for aspiring artists, intent on capturing the self-styled poetry of new country. St. Louis, the Westernmost city in the country, before Iowa entered the Union (1846), rocketed from a population of six thousand to seventy-five thousand between 1830 and 1850. The city was the jumping off point to the far-Western trails, and an important link in river commerce and communication. The city's boom collected a patchwork of transient river workers and immigrant communities. In addition to a sizable German population, a small African-American community settled there. Dred Scott penned his historic petition for freedom from the city in 1846. Thomas Buchanan remarks that St. Louis whites had a reputation for being especially violent toward its black settlers and river workers.[32] St. Louis budded into an artistic enclave for itinerate scene painters, carpenters, decorative artists, printmakers, and landscape painters. Touring panoramas made their way from Missouri to New Orleans through the bustling river economies. Speaking of the racially mixed, striated audiences along the growing Southern theatrical circuits, James H. Dormon considers the riotous mood of regional playhouses a "popular resort for democracy."[33] The St. Louis Museum became a touring venue for copies of popular cosmoramas and panoramas under a succession of owner-directors.[34] It was starting point for the Mississippi river panoramas, which became a broadcast channel of the sociological spectacle occurring in the Midwest. Mark Twain recalled attending these moving panoramas shows in his youth eventually parodying them and their colorful performers in *Life on the Mississippi* (1883).[35]

The "moving pageant" of river panoramas tempered the geographical fluency of land mapping into an expeditionary entertainment. In Irit Rogoff's theory of cognitive mapping, geography becomes "a mode of location" in immersive mediation that embodies *in situ* histories.[36] The design of reenacting a pan-Mississippi voyage was unprecedented. Its execution required several steps. Cartographic methods were used by the panoramists similar to federalized topographic and geological survey teams, who hired artists to sketch terrain and vegetation on exploratory expeditions.[37] Banvard eventually coined the term "georama" to lend scientific credibility to his hyperbolic treatment of pan-Mississippi life. Visual artists employed open air techniques, sketching from boats and skiffs along the river to render detailed regional scenic maps of the Ohio and the Mississippi river system. The sketches were transferred into a fluid composition and then painted with water-based tempera on canvas or muslin between 6 and 12 ft high. Over time marketing strategies used printed testimonies to lure audiences, and intense competition led to individual artists to contract scene painters for studio manufacturing. Early river panoramas express the medium's dramatic formula: immersive sensation, scenic episodes, live storytelling; abolition panoramas reroute the fictional tracks; the Western genre augment commercial maturity using techniques of abridgment, visual montage, and special effects.

The Transappearance of Regional Myths

The first group of river panoramas executed by Hudson, Banvard, and Smith follow similar chronological design. They populate a navigational chart with sites of commerce, material comfort, and local "character" along the river banks. The Ohio River was an important commercial and transportation route on the lower Mississippi, linking Northeastern and Southern ports from Pittsburgh to the domestic and international levees of New Orleans. Each panorama shares numerous navigation landmarks used by ships along the rivers, eliding state boundaries in the "natural" course of geographical change. At the mouth of the confluence of the Ohio and Mississippi, a standard beacon was the city of Cairo, Illinois. Other mainstays were Natchez, Memphis, and Baton Rouge, Louisiana, on the lower Mississippi, as well as the treacherous sandbar littered with shipwrecks, known as Plump Point. Even though the first set of moving panoramas overlap emblems of the different states and territories, each artist composed a distinct dramatic trajectory in the selection, execution, and fabrication of scenic content. Hudson crafted a dazzling, leisurely two-hour river ride, "representing a country that would cost them [spectators] hundreds of dollars, and much time, and many dangers to visit." Banvard excelled at the heroic action-packed adventure. Smith fashioned the immigrant journey.

Hudson began executing a massive panorama of the Mississippi in 1838. Aided by his brothers and associate George W. Cassidy, he reputedly spent $25,000–$35,000 over ten years to complete a four-part work, portioning each "act" with the use of a different cylinder. Although Hudson's panorama appeared after Banvard's initial version, he completed three of four sections by 1848 laying claim to the "first and largest painting of the kind in the world." The river panoramists notoriously bloated the dimensions in advertising to trump competitors.[38] Advertised headlines trumpeted "mammoth," "leviathan," and "colossal" in announcing successive shows. The astounding, if accurate, 25,000 ft Great National Painting of the Ohio and Mississippi Rivers remained on tour for at least two years.[39] Whether in response or to gain an advantage, Banvard raised the profile boasting his panorama: the "largest painting in the world." However, when it appeared in New York, at the same time as Hudson's, it was not yet the "three mile" event of later fame.[40]

Hudson's work erases political strains and social tension from his profitable vision of pan-Mississippi life. His fanciful approach applied a heightened verisimilitude noted as "beautiful and life like."[41] The narrative accompanying the show outlines the 1,400 miles cruise over nine states from Pittsburgh to New Orleans. In April 1848, Hudson opened in Louisville, Kentucky, where the panorama was completed in a rented studio. It was destroyed by fire in a hall in Troy New York at the height of buzz during its first year touring, while a squad of eager competitors were scrambling to cash in on the new craze. Hudson, though, had made a copy, which his collaborator Cassidy sailed off to Europe with. It reappears in 1850 in Hamburg and Leipzig as the "Moving Giant Cyclorama of Cassidy & Co." The Hamburg performance was the city's first exposure to a moving panorama. Musical accompaniment was selected to mirror the tastes of the local audience. Spectators, who never traveled through the interior country firsthand, particularly in Germany, believed the "magically illuminated" landscape as fact. The rolling scenes astonished a first-time viewer from the Hamburger Nachrichten, who was deeply impressed by the passage of "trees, steamboats, and plantations."[42] For a first-time foreign audience the technopresence of natural, industrial, and agricultural scenic life suffused the abundance of America's limitless land wealth in the typology of wonder and enterprise.

A four day journey proceeded from old country to the inland features of new country, or the reverse depending on which direction the panorama starts. The scenery (as described in program material) swaddles cities and towns, with cross-cut scenes navigating past moonlit terrain and local landmarks. Transformation sequences common in theatrical spectacles and in diorama shows intensified impressions of temporal flow with transitional effects shifting day to night with in scenes that transitioned from sunlight to moonlight. Once past the Falls of Ohio, lush forests of cotton wood, sycamore, and ash on the shores of Missouri and Arkansas, gave way to tobacco plantations in Shawnee Town, Kansas. On passing a working plantation, one scene intermingles "a field of hemp, eight slaves at work, and Cave-in Rock." The scenic frame shapes segregation as part of the *natural* landscape. The dehumanized workforce lashes institutional slavery and agricultural commodities to regional production as topographical "landmarks."

The unusual character of vegetation and terrain from state to state stitch together a varied tapestry of references to geographical symbols and artifacts. Scenes of developing industries flagged the processes of accumulating power; the serene skyline of buildings perching over the river banks hailed a dreamy coexistence. Established signage became a storyline to reframe, overturn, delete, or reinvent. The confluence of commercial waterways was signposted by the low banks, prone to flooding, of Cairo, Illinois. A river bend passing the city of New Madrid, Missouri, ornamented with Spanish moss, may have held reminders of a series of earthquakes from 1811-1812, while the clay "Chalk Banks" of Kentucky transitioned into the agricultural region of the plantation industry. Historic Natchez, Mississippi, often passed by views of war hero Zachary Taylor's cotton plantation. In the Ball-Duncanson *Splendid Mammoth Pictorial Tour of the United States*, Ball's account took aim at reactionary sentiments to relate the criminal activity of the area and the lost identity of the Natchez, believed to have migrated from Mexico.[43] The cultures of Indian nations were more often translated into pre (American) historic sites of natural antiquities, such as the Wabash River past Evansville, Illinois, the city Natchez, and Tennessee Valley's elevated Chickasaw Bluffs, which form a natural levee against flooding. Commentary informed viewers that a scene along the Chickasaw Bluffs showed "an encampment of Indians on a visit to the graves of their fathers, as is their annual custom." The Chickasaw nation was removed from the valley during the Great Removal of the 1830s, joining the "trail of tears" alongside the Cherokee, Choctaw, Seminole, and Creek. Overwriting contested Indian conditions for scenic contours distributed popular historical logos. The violent uprisings of recent memory over Indian removal silenced indigenous cultural authority, further colonizing traditions in "preserved" scenic habitats or displays of ceremonial rituals.

The haste to claim the "gigantic idea" of the Mississippi panorama caused a great many public squabbles. Lewis at one point asserted that he had told Banvard of his Mississippi panorama concept, intimating that Banvard stole the idea. The intrepid Banvard eked out a living up and down the Mississippi with floating panorama shows before settling into painting (or duplicating, as he was suspect to do) large-scale moving panoramas.[44] He was in St. Louis about the same time Lewis was negotiating with local artists, including Stockwell and Pomarède to work with him on his panorama.[45] It is now apparent that the various artists were making preparations in St. Louis, Cincinnati, and Louisville by the 1840s.[46] Adding to the frantic mix, Smith exhibited a 200 ft panorama of the Mississippi and Ohio sometime between 1839 and 1840 in Boston. The first version of Banvard's river panorama of the *Mississippi from the Mouth of the Missouri to New Orleans* contained 39 scenes. It appears in 1846, prior to Hudson's and several years before the St. Louis contingent of Lewis, Stockwell, and Pomarède. Although Banvard may not have come up with the idea, he certainly made his fortune with the panorama.[47]

Banvard's initial showing—also in Louisville, Kentucky—was a failure. Unable to attract customers on the first day, he went out among the docks in the city and gave out free tickets to the boatmen. With their approval he gained word of mouth buzz. By the end of the first week, he was turning people away.[48] The show was seen in New Orleans then toured New York and Boston for over a year, Washington DC, and arrived at London's Egyptian Hall in 1849. By then, its legendary size held forth as the "largest picture ever executed by man"—depicting 12,000 miles of the river from the mouth of the Missouri to New Orleans.[49] He claimed earnings of $50,000 during the first seven months of its appearance in Boston at Amory Hall.[50] Variations of it remained on tour until at least 1863. Constantly adapting to his audiences and his competitors, at the outbreak of the

Civil War he presented in New York a four-part panorama, updated with a "War" sequence representing "naval and military operations" on the lower Mississippi.[51]

The initial 39 scenes tracked a long pan, transitioning from views of the Western shore above the mouth of the Ohio to views of the Eastern shore below it. Running two to three hours, Banvard's "imaginary passage of three June days" contained dynamic winding turns populated with dense uninhabited timberland that flows into bustling shipping lanes transporting goods and people on steamboats and flat boats. [52] Technically, Banvard applied conventional bird's eye views to the scene painting by raising the horizon line. Based on existing sketches, the perspective often comes from a high vantage point. Discrete human figures or natural terrain activate the foreground with close up details, leading the eye beyond the human activities up peaks or river banks or over flat lands. Beyond the foreground, the spatial vista has no edge. For one viewer, the scenic scale evoked the limitless terrain "where the shore is a boundless and pathless wilderness."[53] In other sections, the point of view looked down, straight forward, or was elevated above the subject, orienting the viewers' access to relational perceptions. It guides the felt interplay of standing on the fringe of an immense drama occurring. The dialog with attendees placed them at the extent of social habitation. Yet, the human dimension is usually featureless, present to enhance mood or suggest regional character. "Cheerful" slaves lounge on a grassy knoll beside a splendid plantation house. Military forts stand sentry on empty bluffs. Indian "villages" are sentimentalized in moonlit tranquility. This perspectivism masks a coercive field of expansionist rhetoric.

His recreational expedition on the "American" experience wetted the curiosity of Eastern audiences, many who, for the first time, were seeing evidence of frontier democracy—state by state—assembled in a unified design, as an unfolding *natural* order. Regional communities are boldly colored with emotional swells. The uninhabited stretches of woodlands and wilderness of the Northern Lake Plains portray danger, mystery, and excitement. The Central prairie grasslands juxtapose white settlement and Indian habitats. The Southern lowlands reflect wealthy agricultural economies and the shipping flotilla of domestic products: cotton, tobacco, timber, down the river. "A contrast is thus strongly forced upon the mind," commented a fan, "of the highest improvement and latest preeminent invention of art with the most lonely aspect of grand and desolate nature—the most striking and complete assemblage of splendor and comfort."[54]

The syncopated narrative is one of perils and triumph, of reassurance in the civil enterprise, of ethnicity and race segregated in exotic and dehumanizing caricature, and of rapidly improving comfort and convenience.

The enduring popular legacy of Banvard's work often stands in as representative of the genre. Its frontier romance operates in sync with a visionary pluralism by assimilating peripheral vantage points and consolidating reactionary *views* in mainstream social discourse. Banvard describes his calling to paint the "grandeur of the country" after reading a statement in a foreign journal that America had no artist adequate to accurately execute the natural beauties of the landscape.[55] Perhaps to distinguish his version from competitors, the panorama was touted as more than a painting, as promoted by the artist, it was "the soul of America."[56] Brooks finds the irony of the phenomenon of river panoramas is that the "idyllic and peaceful trope of national uniformity and expansionisms flourish in the midst of increasingly visible black abolitionist agitation."[57]

Commercial agency opened avenues for widening community and raising radical social platforms. Abolition panoramas pierced narratives of complacent slaves and servile river workers. Brooks illuminates the activist expressions countering leisure narratives in her study of fugitive slave Henry Box Brown's autobiographical recreation of his escape in his abolitionist moving panorama *Mirror of Slavery* (1852). The radical aesthetic throughout the African diaspora in Brooks theory dismantles oppressive constructs by "afro alienation acts."[58] Like Banvard, Box Brown's panorama is often held up as representative of political agitation. His work received a great deal of attention in the United States and abroad for which much evidence survives. William Wells Brown drew from his own popular autobiographical slave narrative and others to launch a panorama in England in 1850.[59] His *Original Panoramic Views of the Scenes in the Life of an American Slave, From His Birth in Slavery to His Death or His Escape to His First Home on British Soul* was modest in scale at 200–300 ft. It was based on sketches collected by Wells Brown and executed by London artists. Allan D. Austin notes that the lesser known works of Henry Brown and Box Brown's initial partner, J. C. A. Smith, are "as important as [Box] Brown's in this effort."[60] Ball and Duncanson laid out the violence occurring on the Mississippi, perhaps to directly counter the glossy influence of the leisure brand, in their 600 yard panorama. Their work remained in the United States, but surprisingly little evidence has come to light surrounding its reception on tour. J. N. Still executed a series of scenes from *Uncle Tom's Cabin* (1853), the same year a white Indiana painter Barton S. Hays did the same in a *Panorama of Slavery*. Hays worked as a portrait painter in Indiana, Ohio, and Minneapolis. He painted two panoramas related to *Uncle Tom's Cabin*. Plans were announced one version of them would appear in the East, but there the trail ends.[61]

In Banvard's panorama, slaves and free blacks are portrayed as isolated patches of docile contentment, reduced to decorative landscape metaphors. Wells Brown's *Panoramic Views*, as Sergio Costola uncovers, was a direct argument in response to Banvard's mild presentation of slavery. In creating it he wanted "to give a correct idea of the Peculiar Institution."[62] Consisting of 24 scenes, now lost, the performance was divided into two sections. The first half conversed over definitions and abusive conditions of slavery, commercial support by British trade interests, and the hypocrisy of American ideals; the second half narrated his autobiography, as well as stories of other escaped slaves. Ball's and Duncanson's work presented an account of human bondage from African villages, through the transatlantic voyage to Eastern ports, how the economic institution of the plantation system functions in the national economy, and the treacherous underground routes to freedom. Box Brown's panorama was in two parts. The first half traced the circum-Atlantic slave industry; the second half was structured around community, placing slave labor next to capitol institutions. Each of these panoramas aimed to awaken public scrutiny of slavery by challenging the standard formula of river panoramas to represent the "river" of human exploitation occurring daily. Box Brown's treatment inserted graphic scenes of the transatlantic slave trade, the auction block, beatings by slave owners, prisons, and lynching.[63] In asserting embodied control over white America's historical domination, the abolition panoramas used the apparatus of multimedia spectacle to turn the medium on itself and into political performance. They vocalize how economic heritage is submerged in history and replicated as fantasy. Praised among Northeastern hubs of abolitionist movements, Box Brown's panorama was generally received in Great Britain with sympathy, except for scathing resistance by the editor of *The Wolverhampton & Staffordshire Herald* (1852).[64] The English were jarred by the graphic "horrors" or took notice of the controversial "libel" on the American character.[65] Radical aesthetics disturb the vocabularies of techno-presence not only to decolonize the systemic "metaphorical assault" on African-American progress taking place, but rupture what Bertolt Brecht would call its "culinary" style.[66]

Employing six cylinders, Ball and Ducanson inverted the sentimentalized plantation codes to document the criminal acts legalized by institutional slavery in their *Splendid Mammoth Pictorial Tour of the United States*. Ball's discourse injected commentary on standard river scenes that broke the spell of ceaseless motion. His "tour" enumerated the economics of profit and labor on cotton and sugar plantations, fugitive life on the Mississippi, Ohio, and Susquehanna Rivers and vigilante mobs in slave states, exposing river panoramas fictional complicity in legal policies. [67] These works charged the political critique of American progress by openly calling for an end to slavery and agitating for inclusive civil rights. Box Brown's performance of the African Diaspora, exploitation, and disenfranchisement contested the media's controlling mechanisms of immersion. He subverted the usual temporal stream of rolling imagery by interrupting continual flow, to protest slavery as un-American. The employment of stop action and digressive techniques was not new. The devices were sometimes used in scenic moving panoramas to "either skip over a less interesting part of the journey or to depict landmarks that could not be seen clearly from traveler's vantage point."[68] Brown's interrogative modeling manipulated the performance values of the highly familiar river panorama to subvert the cultural context of black (face) performance and white assumptions about racial identity in America and England.[69] He reenacted on stage his escape by means of a wooden crate. His live recreation inserted an unmediated presence in the landscape that the white dialogic denied.

Banvard's upbeat stage persona came with a homespun Yankee twang (he was born in New York), jokes, and popular verse that delighted audiences. In his history of minstrel performance, Robert Toll observes, "before audiences defined blacks, in minstrelsy, they forged positive stage images of themselves."[70] The heroic mask of the "pioneer" artist, by which Banvard framed the performance, entwined the panoramic with a larger-than-life character in the tradition of white Yankee comedians. Thomas Wignell's wide eyed portrait of Brother Jonathan in Royall Tyler's *The Contrast* (1787) signaled the entrance of the Yankee on the American stage. The self-deprecating humor of the rural, white sunny character was honed by comedians, who reinvented the icon's performative framework. Banvard's stage contemporary Dan Marble turned out the regional dialect of the Western Yankee.[71] In Banvard's performance—poached from many sources—he emulsified the rough, struggling Western outposts, piquing the reading public's imagination. Threats to civil rule from extra-legal vigilantes and slave insurrections up and down the river are central to Banvard's treatment of river life.[72] He excelled at lavishing his audiences with heroic adventures on his river expeditions— likely lifted from stories he heard while working on the river— recounting days stranded on sand bars, facing starvation, or nearly dying from fever.[73] He survived wild storms; he escaped attacks by river bandits. The latter came at the hands of white outlaws, who attacked him in the dead of night and from whom he scraped by with his life.

A band of thieves Banvard intimates as the "murderous" Murrell gang had a very specific reputation on the Mississippi. The legend of John Murrell, believed to be a horse thief and counterfeiter, and his band of men entered folklore in 1835. He was accused of coordinating a mass slave rebellion and raid of the countryside.[74] The alleged conspiracy resulted in a coordinated mob lynching of white members of Murrells group along with a dozen slaves over several days in Madison County, Mississippi. Christopher Morris explains how the surrounding panic set in motion a united effort among communities countywide to organize and control potential threats from alleged criminals and slaves.[75] An elected committee of citizens, many wealthy land and slave owners, presided over the rule of "Judge Lynch" before the governor issued a proclamation to hand over suspects to "proper authorities."[76] Extra-legal vigilantism filled the vacuums of state policing along the Mississippi. Horse thieves, counterfeiters and slave stealers threatened white economic stability, playing off the financial insecurity of a flailing federal banking system, while violent outlaws accessed white anxieties of insurgency from abolition agitators and rebellions in slave states.

The panoramic instrument retracted sectionalism, abolitionists, and the banking depression to recoup a pastoral paternalistic order, an illusionary progress narrative reflecting Banvard's aspirations as much as it fabricates an "American" Grand Tour. Four thousand visitors in New York took in the wholesome novelty of the entertainment; an estimated two hundred and fifty thousand spectators saw the show in America. The scrappy showman wrapped his buoyant hero in optimism. He blunted the violence, the moral quagmire, economic instability, and civil anxieties jolting sectional differences. The coarse and brutal conditions of pioneering grew impressionistic and sentimental in expansionist mythology. Attributes of "native" talent, ingenuity, imagination, meritocracy, perseverance, and patriotism became the refrain around the persona of the show. "All the toil and danger, and exposure and moving accidents of this long and perilous voyage are hidden, however, from the inhabitants who contemplate the boats floating by their dwellings on beautiful spring mornings," Banvard told his audiences.[77] In doing so, his heroic "character" assumed white reproductive agency controlling the vantage point *over* defining history as economic progress. His transformative narrative channeled majority domination over minority interests by sensitizing spectator empathies to associate extremism as alien or savage force as uncultivated *raw nature*. By authenticating nonaggressive conquest, legalized order signified normalized conditions—in scenic beauty and civilized conditions. Irrational sensations—in the disproportions of natural phenomena—were sequestered to opaque neutral tones, thus taming radical "elements."

Banvard's "invention" earned notoriety for its diffusive narrative technology. Social dialog responded differently to performance media. Mainstream magazines: *Dwight's Family Magazine*, *The Eclectic Magazine of Foreign Literature*, *Littell's Living Age*, and the popular science journal *Scientific American* (Figure 2.1) all ran articles reiterating the exhilarating experience of being immersed in "life on the Mississippi." [78] Commentaries also engaged partisan views. William Lloyd Garrison's abolitionist *Liberator* took the opportunity to admire Banvard's panorama until the route passed Memphis—with its plantation scene of frolicking slaves. His reflections on actual atrocities taking place in the city ruptured the fanciful. He writes, "We could not help feeling sad to think that they were the headquarters of all that is polluted, oppressive, murderous ... we were painfully reminded of all the horrid scenes that have there occurred from time to time by the administration of Lynch Law."[79] Henry Wadsworth Longfellow's visit in Boston plucked poetry from the "boats and the sand-banks created with cottonwood and the bayous by moonlight."[80]The Baptist *Christian Watchman* drew attention to the floating world of steamer ships and river craft, but pronounced "the magnitude of the work is its greatest wonder."[81] Others lauded its "fidelity and truthfulness to nature."[82] In Boston, the panorama was viewed before a large and fashionable audience—reputed the largest in Boston's theatrical history—that included the Governor George N. Briggs, members of the Senate and House of Representations and municipal officials. [83] Endorsements by the Senate and the House in Washington, DC, allied the panorama with the spirit of national enterprise. The numerous scientific and government accolades Banvard achieved set him high

New Inventions.

Improved Iron Bedstead.

Mr. James Collins, of South Boston, Mass., is the inventor of a beautiful iron bedstead, which should command attention and come into general use. It is made of hollow taper iron tubes and the parts are attached to one another by peculiar dove-tail joints, so that the bedstead can be taken down and put up again in a few minutes. The same principle upon which these bedsteads are constructed can be applied to the manufacture of all kinds of furniture, which can be made plain or ornamental as desired. Owing to the parts being made hollow, the bedstead or other furniture can be made very light—much lighter than wood, for this form combines the greatest strength with the least weight of metal. There can be no doubt but iron bedsteads will yet supersede all others, as they should do, and Mr. Collins' (who is a machinist at Mr. Coney's) possesses merits which should arrest the attention of those desiring to invest money in a manufacture which will yet become very extensive.

Morris' Patent Combined Latch and Lock.

This very ingenious and simple improvement is designed for securing doors in a very convenient, safe and permanent manner, dispensing with the bolt now used in addition to the ordinary latch. There has been presented to the public a device for a similar purpose, but found impracticable. This simple apparatus is formed by inserting in the latch a metal pin, which works up and down in the strap, said strap is secured to the door in a similar manner of the ordinary door strap, to confine the latch thereto. The following is a description of the above cut: —A, Latch ; B, catch or pin on latch A ; C, strap with a slot G, for catch B, to work in ; D hasp, which being thrown up over catch B, permanently secures latch A ; E, joint in which the hasp D works ; F, catch to hold latch A ; H, strap with slot.

Extensive arrangements have been made for the manufacture and sale of this Patent Latch, for which a *Premium* was awarded by the American Institute at their late Fair. All orders and communications addressed to Messrs. Engelbrecht & Eddy, No. 132 Nassau st. New York, sole proprietors for the United States, will receive prompt attention. The price for this improvement will not exceed $1 50, per doz.

Munger's Yankee Turbine Wheel.

We have been informed that Mr. Hiram Munger, of Manchester, N. H. has made some very important improvements on his Water Turbine Wheel, which has been pronounced by those who have used it to be most excellent, from its real practical results, the only test of its merits. He can drive one wheel according to the supply of water, from three to one hundred horse power. These kinds of wheels are coming more and more into general use, and we have frequent enquiries respecting their size, power, &c. Those who desire more information about them, will receive the same cheerfully by addressing Mr. Munger, post paid, who has made arrangements to sell rights at a very reasonable price.

We notice in a foreign exchange that a machine has been invented to make spectacles. It is said to perfect them glass and all, but we doubt this.

Instantaneous Alarm.

The Rev. Charles Brooks of Boston, has communicated to the American Academy of Arts and Science three plans—one by which the hours of time may be struck, at the same instant, on every public bell of the city, and in every private dwelling ; another, by which the alarm of fire may be given at the same moment, throughout the city, and the place of the fire indicated at each of the engine-houses simultaneously. A third plan is one by which all the lamps in the streets may be lighted or extinguished together, at any given moment.

We have seen the same plans proposed before, and in respect to the clock alarm, it is not a new invention. We should like to see the latter plan carried out, and if it is a practicable invention why should it not be adopted at once.

BANVARD'S PANORAMA.---Figure 1.

We here present an engraving of the machinery employed by the renowned artist Banvard in operating his wonderful Panorama of the Mississippi. The mechanical devices employed are very simple but answer the purpose in a most admirable manner. The canvass is wound upon one large vertical roller while it is being unrolled from the other.— This is done by level gearing A and E. As there is a great extent of canvass spread at once, which being painted is very heavy, it is very important to hold it up between the rollers and prevent it from what is technically termed *sagging*. To accomplish this object well, there is a cross beam erected in which there are set a double row of pulleys C C C. The manner in which this is done will be better understood, however, by examining fig. 2, which is an end section. A, is a beam running along above B B, in which the pulleys C C, are erected. These two pulleys C C, are fixed in B F, so as to receive the panorama canvass between them—therefore the edge of the canvass is only seen in this view. On

Fig. 2.

the upper edge or it may be called " a selvage," there is sewed a thick cord or small rope D, and as this rope rests on part of both the pulleys—running along the tops of the whole of them in the like manner—the canvass is rolled up along the whole length of the line without any sensible dropping of it at one place more than another. This is a very ingenious way to hold up the canvass and yet allow it to be wound freely on the large rollers.

The distinguished artist is now in the Old World, and in the capital of the British empire he has been treated with that consideration which has so uniformly distinguished the English people in respect to American artists. The Panorama of the Mississippi has had an astonishing effect upon all classes in London The most of the English people think that our Western country is nothing but a wild-man-of-the-woods region, and no doubt but many places on the Mississippi are wild enough, but Banvard's panorama presents many scenes where the poet might indulge his fancy and the lover of the picturesque sigh to behold in reality. We hope that Mr. Banvard's success will be commensurate with the greatness of his Panorama, which is the largest ever exhibited.

Combined Wrench and Screw Driver.

This is a very neat and useful tool, for machinists and especially tentors in factories, who are obliged to carry a wrench always in the pocket. It is simply a wrench such as we have before described in the Scientific American combined with a screw driver, or it may be combined in the same manner with other tools fitted for that purpose. A is the handle, D, is a screw nut with an interior thread worked by the thumb which raises or lowers E, the upper jaw of the wrench, by the nut of the same which extends through the nut. B is the screw driver. It is made with a round head and passes into a circular recess cast in the end of the handle. This recess has a small groove cut in one side of it extending upwards and another crosswise. These grooves are for the purpose of retaining the screw driver in the handle by a spring C, with a nib on the inner end of it which fits into the cross groove, and the spring itself which answers the purpose of a feather in the other groove, thus serving to keep the driver firm and snug in the handle. This tool is manufactured by and secured to J. O. Lewis Worcester, Mass. There is nothing that facilitates work more than a good handy tool and nothing keeps a mechanic in better temper. We therefore think that this tool will soon be universally introduced as its very simplicity proclaims its utility.

INVENTOR'S CLAIMS.

We have concluded to publish no more of the Patent Claims, as we are not able to keep up with the date of the patents granted, without occupying too much of our space. Those of our subscribers, who wish to know the claim of any patent granted during each current year will be furnished with the same if they desire. Those who wish to get claims for patents prior to the current year, will be furnished with the same by a reasonable compensation for our trouble.

Rock Drilling Machine.

It will be seen by our list of Patents that Messrs. Foster and Bailey of this city have been granted a patent for their valuable machine for drilling rocks. This Machine has justly been pronounced the best portable rock driller ever constructed. Its mechanical construction for drilling underground in mines, is the most perfect of any that ever has come under our notice, and this is the opinion of all who have seen it operate. Messrs. Foster & Bailey can receive their Letters Patent by calling at this office.

It is reported that Commodore Parker and Commanders Dupont, Buchanan and Barron, of the Navy, have received furloughs from the Department, for the purpose of proceeding to Europe, to organize the new Navy recently created by the Federal German government.

Figure 2.1   Banvard's Panorama.

Source: Scientific American 8.13 (March 28, 1863), Courtesy of Cornell University Library, Making of America Digital Collection.

above the majority of his competition, earning his show an appearance at Buckingham Palace.

Arriving in London, the river panorama's mechanized system and transitory simulation ushered it in as a theatrical wonder. Charles Dickens sensed its indirect influence after seeing the panorama in London: "New Worlds open out to them [the spectators] beyond their little worlds, and widen their range of reflections, information, sympathy, and interest.[84] Shows over the Christmas season saw crowds that drew fashionable society and the aristocracy. The encoded grandeur and upstart ambition solidified notions of the shrewdness and simplicity of the rebellious country. The alleged legitimacy of the panoramas aura telegraphed racial, ethnic, and frontier impersonations of 'American.' Other marvels captivating Londoners were the wit and charm of seeing what was assumed an actual Yankee, which Banvard dutifully performed. The panorama was scrutinized for its artistic merits, which the London *Examiner* found lacking in 'refinement' and the *Illustrated London News* equated to scene-work."[85] Although, the latter admitted it was one of the finest views of the "United States."

By the spring of 1850 at least eight other American-made panoramas arrived in Liverpool and London.[86] The exportation of Americana flooded the city and provinces. Adding to the market was interest around escaped slave, playwright, and lecturer William Wells Brown's political history, named in the press the *Panorama of American Slavery*. His performance detailed the life of a slave in the United States from plantation to "his death or escape from bondage," yet omitted "disgusting details of American slavery that would be offensive to English taste."[87] Banvard's competitors experimented with different strategies to add new ingredients to the scenic recipe. Theatrical scene painter turned panoramist Englishman John Rowson Smith competed head to head with Banvard. They waged public battle in England accusing the other of poor workmanship and inaccuracies. The simultaneous performances are held responsible for a decline profits from a weary public. Another factor may have contributed to flagging interest.

Smith was a resident in St. Louis, where he was employed as a scene painter as early as 1832.[88] The immigrant story was his forte. He entered the panorama business alongside Banvard, with less fanfare, only to have his first installment destroyed by fire.[89] He acquired a partner, acrobat John Risley. They completed a large-scale panorama advertised as four miles in length to outdo Banvard. This "leviathan" panorama of the Mississippi was installed in the wealthy city of Saratoga. Its six week run earned a reported $20,000; its touring life in the United States lasted under a year. Success came to Risley's and Smith's *Original Gigantic Moving Panorama of the Mississippi River, Extending from the Falls of St. Anthony to the Gulf of Mexico*, abroad. It raises questions whether the Englishman had difficulty gaining support among xenophobic, local American audiences in the face of Banvard's homegrown celebrity. European audiences were largely left to compare the two versions without actual knowledge of the regions depicted. Comparisons focused on the qualities of the shows. Smith's river journey was consistently upheld as dramatically satisfying, artistically fulfilling, and of thrilling interest.[90] American endorsements testified to its accuracy at promoting land leasing. The Bishop of Dubuque, Iowa, wrote for "Emigrants seeking information, it is invaluable, as it gives the qualities price, and appearance of Land in America and the Rolling Prairies."[91] The work was installed in the Grand American Hall of the Leicester Square Rotunda in 1849. It traveled from London to Dublin, and Edinburgh. The panorama also exhibited for six weeks in Christiania over the summer of 1852, giving rise to speculation that the visionary narrative of the "American dream" spurred immigration to the Mississippi Valley by Scandinavians. In the United States, settlement became more viable for immigrants and citizens as federal land policies were implemented to sell land in the public domain at reduced prices. After the 1841 election of "old Tippecanoe" William Henry Harrison to the Presidency, The Log Cabin Bill was passed by Congress granting US citizens (legal immigrants) preemptive rights to purchase and improve land.[92] The magnified scenic economy allowed both domestic and foreign audiences to survey land and occupational options available in the Midwest.

Risley's and Smith's panorama allegedly recreated nearly "four thousand miles of American scenery in three sections, running through nine states of the union."[93] The storyline (published in London the same year; Dutch and German in 1851) partitions the Mississippi Valley into interlinking economies bridging Northern industry, farming, and the Southern agricultural beltway of ports and distribution centers. The imagery broadly represented the diversity of racial "complexions" and the "variableness of scenery," which the accompanying performance implied dwelling in peaceful coexistence. Skippering the departure from the "emporium of commerce," New Orleans, on a steamer, the ship's captain paints a swelling serenade in a harmonious concert of bells as "twenty-five or thirty negro firemen and deck hands stand on the gang-way plank" singing spirituals. The immersive views of land wealth and occupational variety: "from the wheat of the North to the oranges of the South," encased sectarian habitats: between city and country, slave labor and luxurious plantations, and migrating Indians and stabilized frontier homesteads, in a colonial structure. Risley's and Smith's comparative graphics split regional enterprises into three major agricultural industries. A pan down the West bank traced "The Corn Regions" from Falls of St. Anthony to the Mouth of the Ohio; the "Cotton Regions" transitioned to the East bank from the mouth of the Ohio to Natchez; Continuing on the East bank from Natchez to the Gulf of Mexico displayed "The Sugar Regions." The panorama took two and half hours to revolve, with a minutely timed lecture on each scene lasting two to three minutes.

Unlike Banvard's Yankee storyteller, the performance provided real-time correspondence on land acquisition, climate conditions, and federal support for industrial development to acquaint audiences with the Mississippi Valley as the "only part of America fitted for Emigration." [94] The use of abrupt scenic cross cuts also superimposed ethnographic "complexions" of racial diversity for bolder contrast. A section on the "Great West" opens on the extent of white settlement to date. Spectators were cued to the particularities in legal and civic organization and constant change along the river. In fact, extensive tracts retailed the economics of industry, property costs, and potential income of different cities and regions on view. Audiences learned that Illinois farms "formed by the hand of nature" could be purchased for $1.25 an acre and that the region was a "greater El Dorado than the gold mines of California." Smith's treatise scripted a free society built on exclusionary rights of citizenship, for the economy of slave labor and territorial gains from the purchase of Indian lands inscribed the premise of white liberties on land ownership.

The panorama coopted the "story" of the "Mormon City" of Nauvoo, Illinois, possibly to quell fears of regional violence or religious extremism. The steward of The Church of the Latter Day Saints, John Smith, along with his brother Hyrum, were murdered in Nauvoo by a mob of approximately two-hundred men that included State militia. The death of Smith led to the community's exodus from over the Rocky Mountains abandoning the city. The Mormons' long migration from New York to Pennsylvania, Ohio, and Missouri to Nauvoo was a bloody one.[95] They were driven from city to city by aggressive extra-legal militias and rogue gangs, who viewed the community's missionary work among local Indians threatening and their concentrated affluence a political and economic encroachment on self-preservation. The white majority in Missouri used sectarian tensions to label them radical abolitionists. The Mormons fought back. Under the leadership of Smith, who briefly sanctioned a "riot of right," a defensive legion was formed. The "Saints" preempted and counter attacked anti-Mormon vigilantism. The escalating violence proved too viscous. They fled to settle and worship freely in Nauvoo, with members legally serving in the Nauvoo Legion.[96] A Temple was built, but a public campaign by Illinoisans began the cycle of anti-Mormon agitation all over again. The final blow came when in retaliation for the destruction of an opposition newspaper, the *Nauvoo Expositor* (June 1844), exposing the practice of polygamy, Smith was charged with treason and inciting war against Illinois.[97] He and his brother were ambushed on leaving jail. In Risley's and Smith's version of the history, the promised "kingdom" of the Mormons is reflected in the vacated Temple left behind. No mention is made of Smith's murder. Only a vacant space was shown. However, the architectural specs of the Temple are depicted in detail. Smith's account takes time to "explore" the ruins left behind of a reviled community that included "living representations of the 'Forty Thieves.'"[98] The signature on this cautionary tale of banished heretics reaffirmed norms of law, order, and religious orthodoxy.

The Mormons reclaimed the history of Nauvoo in the *Mormon Panorama* (1869).[99] The narrative function adopted by the Mormons had a didactic purpose in memorializing years of exile and persecution before arriving in Salt Lake City. The site of Nauvoo is now "sacred space."[100] The faith-based panorama started out to aid missionary work among Utah Indians in the reservation system. Danish artist Carl Christian Anton Christensen began working on a biblical panorama in the 1850s. He began a second panorama in 1869, possibly commissioned by Brigham Young, to preserve the history of the Church's own trail of tears to Utah. It circulated locally. The completed work of 19 scenes ran on vertical rollers. The *Mormon Panorama* depicts attacks by "gentiles" and exodus across the country in caravans. Religious persecution is illustrated in graphic detail. Events leading to Smith's murder in Nauvoo are portrayed as a lynching. A panel titled, "Death of Joseph Smith," places an angry mob of men wielding sticks outside the jail with Smith pinned against a wall where he had been shot in the chest. The tormentors are painted in blackface with no features, including William Web. He is identified in the accompanying narrative as drawing his knife and attempting to cut off Smith's head when "God supposedly paralyzed him and the crowd dispersed." A shaft of light falling from heaven brought him to his knees.[101] Vilified in racist dualities of aggression and impersonation, the "gentiles" are stripped of Christian supremacy. The origin story of founding the city comes by way of sacrifice and religious conquest. The mission of preserving historical memory for the community asserts minority control to claim freedom of worship.

The sociological refrain of Risley's and Smith's performance mythologized the pragmatic aptitude of the American vista: equality, opportunity, and enterprise. Its landscape rhetoric personified pluralism: "where the prairies roll into regions so far off as to be untrodden by the foot of civilization—where the Andes are reared, and where the Mississippi rolls, where the Rocky Mountains mock the clouds, and Niagara plunges into the bowels of the earth—where the forests spread over territories and the lakes are oceans."[102] The interplay of narrative and visionary coding predicated "natural" affluence in abundant land wealth that reiterated the ethos of America back to cramped industrial European cities. The visionary sensorium of open land, where nothing is fixed, placed the spectator on a ground plane within the immeasurable reach of one's own aspirations. By replicating models of territorial colonization, Risley and Smith pitched free systems of democratic society in terms of a mercantile status quo.

The Western Response

Overshadowed by the wide success of Banvard and Smith, Stockwell, Lewis, and Pomarède also had each other to contend with. Beaten to the goal, the St. Louis artists concentrated on distinguishing their own versions. They separated their work from the first wave by vivifying frontier life along the upper Mississippi. In doing so, they supplement Western genres. With the push to open the Pacific Northwest, the techno-color presence of the "Great West" intercepted real-time mythologies. Disenfranchised populations absorb the darker tonalities of romantic terror and excess. Dramatic impersonations encased the aberrant sensibilities of imaginative freedom as trophies of recent battles. Indian histories are dismembered for souvenir artifacts or appropriated to label conquered territories. The entrepreneurial vigor of machinery, river boats, and factories showcase local commerce and innovation. The sturdy signs of civil progress are crowded with American architectural models along the river, from log cabins to forts. The pristine wilderness recedes into the picturesque, modes of transportation: steamships, flat boats, and commercial craft, commute the workforce of growing metropolises. A military presence increases. Realistic flourishes become more pronounced en route to the Civil War. Disaster scenes become more frequent: destructive fires and horrific steamboat accidents among the most common. The lower Mississippi recedes from visibility. The scenic course is less literal, resulting in regional adaptations rather than a cohesive journey.

The rapid growth of the Midwest illustrated in these shows mounted regional perceptions of an "advancing spirit of civilization," pronounced by the new Whig president Zachery Taylor. His election to the presidency in 1848 was surrounded with "fearful responsibilities," among them balancing Texas's annexation to the United States, the US Mexican War, and the extension of slavery in the newly acquired territories. [103] In general, the metaphorical appeal of exploring the Western margins Miller suggests, may have stirred "a degree of anxiety and awe over obtaining a glimpse at the fringe between two aspects of freedom, the feel of the wild and the material life of the domestic."[104] Western panoramas, in particular, initiate sectional reclamation. Not to be overlooked are other residual factors, both political and psychological, tripping performance narratives of the Western panoramas. At this time, constitutional collapse became a pressing danger under the growing thunder of secessionists. Curtailing land speculation abuse in new state's legislative agenda, such Wisconsin, took on importance. The transappearance of different pioneer histories intercepts an admixture of representational claims occurring. The precarious "nature" of aggressive colonization appears in cross sections of the Western elevation from the anecdotal to the monumental.

First out the gate was Samuel Stockwell, who patterned the panoramic experience after the mythos of "the people" bordering the river that brought the "ever changing, ever new" sensibilities of the "Great West" to scenic life.[105] His anecdotal style staged a pageant of Indian scenes, river craft, and plain-spoken settlers. Lewis's *Great National Painting* upheld the internal Mississippi beltways as the economic pin uniting old country—the East—and new frontiers—the Great West.[106] Pomarède experimented with mechanization and dioramic effects to animate the landscape with sensation scenes that anticipate their appearance in melodramas.[107] All trumpeted "Great Missouri," Wisconsin's Prairie du Chien, and Lake Pepin, a final strategic acquisition of territory in Minnesota.

The field of Western panoramas enjoyed rising prestige from local literati and social establishments. "The best panorama in a panoramic age," glowed a report in the Boston periodical *Literary World* when Stockwell's work appeared in his birth place (1849).[108] Advance articles in the nationally respected St. Louis *Weekly Reveille* followed each stage of Lewis's preparation. With aesthetic authority of American-made media advancing internationally, the Midwest artists competed for artistic merit. Stockwell's panorama toured only four months then disappeared. What is known of it has been duplicated in historical accounts from numerous reviews and printed dialog from the accompanying narrative. Stockwell looked to gain an edge by painting lesser parts of the upper river to set his panorama apart. It is clear that he sketched the vast range of "characters" making up the Midwest, adding to the ever popular prints and stage galleries of representational stereotypes of Indian, frontiersman, and settler. Stress was placed on appealing to the assorted interests of the "Emigrant, the Speculator, the Tourist."[109]

Stockwell unveiled his panorama for the *Weekly Reveille* in October 1848 in a saloon of the Planter's House. He completed it before Lewis and Pomarède, possibly with assistance. The narrative was delivered by hired lecturer J. M. Weston, former stage manager of the St. Charles Theatre where Smith had worked as a scene painter. St. Louis gave Stockwell's panorama a "warm reception" during its two week display.[110] His views of the city included both sides of the river.[111] His second stop was New Orleans. *The Spirit of the Times* assented there is "one opinion of its truthfulness" that it belonged "among the lions."[112] The showing there was viewed at night with the panorama illuminated by gaslight, "producing dramatic effects."[113] From Baltimore to Boston, comments reprinted from the "very high authority" of the *New Orleans Picayune* commended its accuracy and comprehensive scope "unhesitatingly to public patronage." Stockwell's work is most often mentioned in comparison to Banvard's widely circulated version.[114] Backhand assaults on Banvard's bravado were not always kind. Bostonian society validated Stockwell's artistic pedigree as "the first representation in the city "painted by a professional artist," adding "it is emphatically a Mississippian picture for the artist mixed his paint with the water of the river."[115] Stockwell was one of the few to tour the Southeast. Many of the Southern tour stops were cities the former scene painter had worked in: Mobile, Alabama, Macon and Savannah, Georgia, and Charleston, South Carolina.

Measuring 625 yards by 12 ft, the show featured ten states "of the Union" from the Gulf of Mexico to the Falls of St. Anthony in four sections alternating East and West banks. Upper river landmarks were added to the lexicon of regional wonders. The low horizontal rapids of the Falls of St. Anthony symbolized the rugged open range of Midwestern life; its treacherous churning currents marked a stark contrast with the majesty of Niagara's thunder. The Falls of St. Anthony formed the internal gateway to the Pacific Northwest and to opening Minnesota for settlement; the Iowa territory was a critical strategic avenue on the Oregon Trail. Rock Island (Ft. Armstrong), Davenport and Dubuque, Iowa, Nauvoo, and Fort Snelling become common monikers of upper river views. The catalog of local folk and actual cities and towns blended in with the theatrical fabrication of temporary "Indian villages" and encampments along the river banks.[116]

The section of the lower river compressed conventional route markers from New Orleans to the mouth of the Ohio in order to move through the section quickly. The condensation of the region irked one Boston critic's evaluation that the shorthand approach to the lower river detracted from its geographical value.[117] Attendees in New Orleans did not seem to mind. There, spectators' called out the names of prominent buildings before Weston, which threw him off his performance.[118] Stockwell was no longer mapping a geographical course, but abbreviating the genre's makeup to magnify the profile of working communities. Notably, the show lingered over river traffic, modeling assorted steamers, rafts, flatboats, and canoes. Detailed replicas of steamboats caught them in all phases of work: tied to landings, billowing up river, and gliding past cities.

A populist ethic injected political jabs in support of Whig policies promoting nongovernment interference on states' rights. Remaining sections of the narrative suggest the performance reenacted humorous sketches of the artist's journey along the river, which were widely reprinted. One running bit features Stockwell's young Dutch assistant George, who often falls in the river. The peppered dialect of immigrant and settler voices captured local discourse, while serving up comic relief. The device muddles the political maelstrom around expansionism and slavery, and takes stabs at elite Northern industrialists, who purchased large tracts of land in the Northwest. One anecdote appears to have had local bite; it circulated in Missouri news.[119] In trying to dislodge the boat Stockwell sketched from when it hit a snag in the water, both George and the artist fell into the cold water. The frosty dunking leads to the punch line from Stockwell: "if he hadn't been a democrate[sic] and voted for Polk, the snag would have been removed a long time ago" Well, replies George, "I shall vote for General Jackson's next time." Anti-democrat barbs mocking then current President Polk's allegiance to unpopular Jacksonian federalism in St. Louis would get a laugh. The swipe may have been directed at the federal Amy of Engineers responsible for mapping, cleaning out, and deepening navigation routes along the Ohio and Mississippi rivers.[120] In the most famous sketch, artist and assistant stop along the river to sketch a squatter's log cabin. The puzzled owner wants to know if the pair is electioneering. Once the purpose of the visit is explained, the farmer tells the artist: "When you show me to them Inglish fellars, jest tell 'em I'm a Mississippi screamer—I kin hoe more corn in a day than any Yankee machine ever invented." The fiercely folksy jabs of Stockwell's populism struck at the anti-authoritative sentiment of self-regulation pitting the ordinary needs and common sense of grass root political agency against the oratory of statesman proffering political ideals.

With "panorama fever" glutting a booming market, manufacturing methods were adopted to speed up production.[121] After attempting to contract Stockwell and Pomarède, Lewis outsourced sections of the river surveys to different local artists: Charles Rogers, George B. Douglas, and enlisted writer John S. Robb. [122] He accelerated execution by employing a team of local artists in the field and a team of theatrical scene painters in the studio. Lewis sketched the upper river from a floating studio built on a catamaran to facilitate the work. He collaborated with manager Henry Stagg and William Warren, then director of the St. Louis Museum, to orchestrate exhibiting the Northwestern section of the panorama in St. Louis before anyone else.[123] Working in Cincinnati, he convinced John Bates, manager of the National Theatre to invest as business partner in the panorama.[124] He galloped through painting 825 yards of the upper half of the river in a reputed nine months with help from four other respected scenic artists: John L. Leslie, Edwin F. Durang, John R. Johnston, and James B. Laidow.[125] The 500 yard lower section of the river was completed once the initial exhibit was open in St. Louis. The two sections, costing $15,000, were completed within a year, if Lewis's word is accepted. [126] In December 1849, both paintings were shown in Buffalo, New York. The panorama toured over a year domestically with modest success. Receipts for a two week run in Louisville only brought in $429.

Two factors impeded the kind of windfall profits the first wave achieved. A cholera outbreak in the Mississippi Valley reduced the number of venues to exhibit, and an "overstocked" market in the United States ruined box office prospects. Lewis surmised that there were at least "20 panoramas" on view in the United States as he scrambled to finish his work. [127] A report in the St. Louis *Weekly Reveille* groaned that there are too many to enumerate but there are always two or more open at the same time."[128] Lewis also correctly predicted a cholera outbreak risked touring potential. Stockwell's run in New Orleans was cut off when the epidemic spread during the height of success; another in New York resulted in cancelling its appearance there. Lewis confessed these worst case scenarios to his brother George. In addition to panorama fatigue in domestic markets, the attraction of the river panoramas flagged as well in England. Paris, too, had its fill; it was entertaining Banvard's work with Pomarède's to follow. Lewis saw his only chance in Germany, where interest remained strong. He followed Hudson and Cassidy and Risley and Smith to Germany, where his painting was compared as superior.[129] He was the first to show in Holland. Dutch and German audiences, many with family or relatives who immigrated to the Midwest, could see desirable farming, factories, and industrialization occurring in the Northwest. Also visible was assurance of transportation routes and government protection. He managed to open markets in Canada, touring for a year in rudimentary conditions in Halifax, Toronto, Kingston, Ottawa, and Montreal. In four years of performances, he struggled disappointedly to turn a profit. Lewis eventually sold the work in 1857 to a Dutch plantation owner (Hermens), who brought it to the East Indies. He then left the country to study painting in Dusseldorf. Lewis left behind an illustrated book *Das Illustrirte Mississippithal* (published in parts between 1854 and 1858) with 78 colored lithographs from drawings and paintings. This publication remains the most substantial visual evidence of the river panoramas.[130]

The English-born Lewis occupied himself with settlement conditions during his survey of the upper river. His panorama traverses the upper river from St. Louis to Prairie du Chien, Wisconsin.[131] Traveling up river on the steamer the US Senator in June 1848, incidental events witnessed on the journey forged storylines. The six day route headed from St. Louis to the confluence of the Mississippi and Minnesota rivers. Destinations featured Dubuque, Iowa, Prairie du Chien, Wisconsin, Stillwater, Minnesota, and Fort Snelling in St. Paul.[132]

Joseph Earl Arrington observes that Lewis's motivation selected the picturesque, the historical, and current events to capture "the contemporary thriving settlements and future prospects of the region."[133] However, one of Lewis's stated goals for his journey was "seeing Indian life in all its rudeness."[134] His movements overlapped with the last vestiges of removal of Northwest Indian nations from surrounding ancestral lands or recently acquired farm lands negotiated in The Treaties of Prairie du Chien (1827–1831). The Fever River district of Northwestern Illinois and Southwestern Wisconsin not only was coveted farmland but also saw a mining rush from 1822 on. The area shipped 15,000,000 pounds of lead yearly to New Orleans.[135] The dismantling of Indian power on the upper Mississippi, dating back to French and British hostilities, completed one phase linking the Northwest corridor to Northeastern ports. Control over the Wisconsin territory led to statehood in 1846.[136] Lewis rendered the growing federal presence of military camps and newly erected forts "designed to throw a protecting screen between Indians and pioneers."[137]

The last two Indian uprisings in the area of Prairie du Chien were the Winnebago (1827) and the Black Hawk War (1832).[138] Winnebago Chief Red Bird led an attack against farmers who were encroaching on Indian lands in the Fever River area. Red Bird was unable to rally support for a general uprising and the attack was quickly thwarted. The resistance ended with the Winnebago ceding their lands in Prairie du Chien, and being removed to Iowa. On the ground where Red Bird surrendered Fort Crawford was erected and nicknamed Fort Winnebago. The Black Hawk War, involving Sac and Fox Indians return to ceded lands in Illinois, ended in a massacre on the Bad Axe River as remaining bands tried to escape the artillery of federal forces and cross the Mississippi back into Iowa. All three Western panoramists commemorated some allusion to Wabasha prairie and the Bad Axe River. Metaphors of battle and self-preservation attached "native" sites to scenic icons of surrender and defeat. The memorial attributes of noble grandeur or savage ferocity memorialize a militant democracy. Lewis recorded a sequence of scenes relating social and political ceremonies he witnessed in Indian treaty deliberations with each other or federal troops. The scenic compilation recreates military stratagems used in treaty signing protocols that replicate civil codes of oratory and debate in procedural rituals instituted in state and federal government systems.

Lewis's arrival in Minnesota (1849) coincided with the removal of the Winnebago from Iowa to a Minnesota reservation at a tense time.[139] The Winnebago remained unsatisfied with treaties signed at Prairie du Chien. Now, claiming the sale of their lands was given without their consent, and recoiling from being given a track of land situated between Sioux and Chippewa with whom they did not get along, they refused to leave Wabasha (Winona) during a stop at a military camp. The small federal force in place, led by Captain Seth Eastman, waited uneasily when a grand council was called to deliberate. Among the 1,200 representatives were Fox, Chippewa, Menominee, Sauk, and Dakota. Lewis admired the Captain's diplomacy in the situation.[140] Eastman pressed negotiating a treaty to avoid forceful removal. His strategy cut off any means of escape by the Winnebago, when he suspected they would not comply. He deployed troops and wagons to block any means of flight.

Lewis's panorama reenacts many of the events he encountered, including "The Grand Council." It adjoins a different scene of a federal military encampment. The serial narrative evokes a joint spectatorship, observing military proceedings. The council scene (Figure 2.2) shows an assembly of over 1,000 representatives of the local Indian population standing in a circle. In the center a Chief speaks to the assembly. Lewis entwines a theatrical display of a Grand Council and Eastman's

Figure 2.2   Henry Lewis, The Grand Council.
Source: Das Illustrirte Mississippithal, 1855, Minnesota Historical Society.

military strategy in one. A formidable aspect of the pageantry in the scene is the subtle entrapment of the assembled Indians. The Indian council is sandwiched between a towering mountain range behind and the river in the foreground. It is posed to be *overseen* from a distance. The miniature assembly is defenseless on the flat prairie in the middle ground. Onlookers surround the council on three sides. There include military on horseback, Indian scouts, and what appears to be Lewis perched on a rock sketching. These exterior figures frame the large group within the encircling surveillance.

Following the Grand Council scene is Lewis's recreation of the Battle of Bad Axe River. The central event shows the *Warrior*, a military steamship, sailing into the frame in profile with cannon blazing. The ship's opposition is a retreating raft of Indians, seen from above. Tiny figurines are splayed across the helpless vessel, leveled by the overpowering military cannon. The visual montage layering different vantage points on the scene accentuates the pursuit of fugitives from law and the military machinery in place to stop resisters. The production values mesh on-site sketching and studio embellishment, generating immediacy to the suspenseful action. His synthesis adjusts the framing mechanisms of the medium for a more spontaneous sensation effect. The dramatic editing drives immersive action. Rather than the presence of being on the spot and physically turning in space, panning perspectives change within the scenic space, intensifying feelings of being engaged in battle.

Earlier moving panoramas partition racial boundaries and ethnic identity in segregated scenic frames. When Banvard toured Great Britain, he hastily added 15 scenes on the Missouri River and some views along the Ohio River. Many of the new scenes were wilderness tracks. The opening account of the Missouri dramatized a rousing description of the rivers "wild nature" as it thrashes and ripples down into a gentle stream.[141] The fresh mystique of Indian domains and cultures were an attraction for Europeans, long familiar with colonial acquisitions. Recurrent in the early panoramas are villages (home), hunting scenes (hearth), and burial grounds (sacred rituals). Indian "villages"—so labeled in the panoramas—related a nomadic migratory society, "dwelling in tents" and were often contrasted with permanent settlement and architecture.[142] Hunting scenes confirmed natural aggression necessary for survival. The fixation on tombs and burial rituals awaken compassion and spirituality.[143] The Assiniboin culture, long decimated by small pox and eventually removed to a reservation at Fort Peck, shuttle across the river before six enormous earthen domes in Banvard's panorama. The melancholy scenes group isolated, transient encampments within moody desolate ruins of jagged boulders, clay bluffs, and leafless trees, land uninhabitable for settlement or development. The "prehistoric" appearance of "abandoned" civilizations provided comparative evidence of the emerging empire.

Lewis inscribes mechanisms of power and control within his scenes by placing white observers as sentry point. The guiding point of view modeled the viewer among those standing on the deck of "one of the great floating palaces."[144] The interloping device of the *flâneur*, the strolling observer describing types of objects and social characters, appears throughout. Given modern definition by Walter Benjamin, the commenting consciousness of the outsider within the crowd extenuates an emphatic intimacy with dehumanizing consumption.[145] The *flâneur* exists as normative presence for the viewer who adapts the role of companion to the performer's presence in the scene. On the lower section of the river, a cotton plantation in Memphis illustrates slaves picking and hauling bales of cotton. A white slave owner standing tall with hands behind his back watches the work of the bent over slaves. The viewer is often guided into the narrative by the well-dressed presence of the artist himself, absorbed in looking out over the landscape: pointing, contemplating, or sketching. He stands atop his floating studio, named "Minnehaha" after the falls, with his back to the viewer or is seated in camp by the river side looking directly at the spectator. At other times, surrogates gaze off into the distance as representatives of the *flâneur's* reflective "intoxication." Lewis employs an aesthetic conduit that mingles internal and external viewpoints; the manipulation of subject positions within observed circumstances maximizes empathetic byplay as an ocular strategy of empowerment.

The architecture of law and order increasingly dot the landscape. Sentinels protecting the status quo loom along the river in a range of permanent military structures. Rudimentary military installations and forts spread beyond the canvas boundaries or emerge from rock faces. A view of Fort Snelling, depicted from the opposite bank, looms over lush wilderness, a fortress a top a rocky bluff. Down river, the last section of the panorama approaching St. Louis spans over Rock Island where Fort Armstrong, anchored to a ledge, was erected after the Black Hawk War.[146] Instead of a stable bird's eye view shifting from one shore to another, Lewis often merged both sides of the river in one scenic frame. Lewis includes two views of the Fort. One seizes it from the shore of Davenport close up, protruding off the elevated rock face; the other strikes a distance passing it on the river where the stony fortress stands watch over an approaching steamer.

To increase immersive saturation, Lewis manipulated the vanishing line characteristic of multipoint perspective. Two- and three-dimensional space is synthesized in which material objects gain corporeal volume against a scenic setting. Objects closest to the viewer diminish; objects in the middle ground are seen in close up. In a view of a Northwest steamer wooding at night, figures in the foreground loading the boat with fuel are barely visible. A sturdy oak rising out of the scene and the ship docked in profile consume the scene, projecting the accompanying narration of the "appearance and construction" of the wood burning Western steamboat, with its distinctive flat bottom for speed and carriage of freight.[147] Scenic distortions enhance visceral sensations of inhabiting physical space. Pictorial elements layer social hierarchies, political institutions, and economic markers. The heightened radiance on industrial machinery, timberlands, and wilderness reserved Midwest citizenry equal share in nation building.

The significant natural resources of the Midwest cascade in images of wealth, power, and prestige. Lead mining epitomized the rich mineral region of the upper Mississippi. Entrepreneurs snapped federal land leases beginning in 1837 for lead mining operations. The main port was Galena, Illinois, before 1850 when railroads replaced steamboat shipping.[148] Profits from shipping thousands of tons to New Orleans financed stately mansions in Galena. This wealthy city was a favored jewel in the Western panoramas. The impressive metropolis challenging Northeastern prestige crowns the riverbank, which overlooks industrious factories blasting tall plumes of coal smoke in Lewis's version. The importance of St. Louis among Midwest metropolises gave Lewis the opportunity to satisfy the hometown public. The city is lavished with detailing; it comes into view from across a fertile bank sheltering a covered wagon, a reminder of the city's pioneer origins. The eye is lifted from the rustic bank across the gentle river among busy ships and flatboats to the sprawling cityscape dotted with church steeples and Capitol dome.

Lewis's show was noted for its "magic realism." *The Missouri Republican* received letters from the public praising the "glowing ideas" of the landscapes. One excited individual writes of the artist's success in "imposing on the senses of the beholder and inducing him to believe that he is gazing, not on canvas, but on scenes of actual and sensible nature."[149] For those in St. Louis with actual knowledge of the upper region and Missouri River the "magnificent" imagery was lauded as accurately "delineated."[150] An early testimonial recounted in the Louisville *Courier* mentions an elderly gentleman from the area of Rock River, who burst out "stop the boat and let me get out," when he recognized his house, barn, and white mare materializing on the changing scenes.[151] When there was no prior knowledge of the entertainment or geography, the merits of the performance were accepted in the "spirit" of desire to "ramble through living forest, and beside the flowing river."[152] What irked Missouri citizens were proportional inaccuracies in drawing or perceived historical errors in describing cities. One critic from the *Missouri Republican* suggested "many parts of the canvas might be cut, and the scenes would of themselves form interesting subjects."[153] For some, the live illusion conferred to "nature" transformative beliefs. In practice, media production took to processing landscapes off-site. Location drawing, studio invention, and genre specialization more and more turned out a synthetic landscape. Its hybrid enlivened a physical world that no longer existed yet assumed historical presence. A darkening realism, perhaps holding at bay the approaching war, further distorts immersive filters.

Experiments with standard conventions of the theatrical shows by different panoramists altered temporal and physical relationships to linearity. The geographical chronology of the early river panoramas could be dispensed with. Box Brown's subverted the typical linear stream of imagery in his *Mirror of Slavery* by interrupting the illusion to address the audience directly. Western panoramists used stop action and digressive insertions to remold the dramatic fabric. Pomarède used his experimentations with mechanics and transformation scenes as internal aesthetic mechanisms.

Pomarède called his competitors "daubs" (hacks). The Frenchman arrived in St. Louis through New Orleans. He scratched out a living painting theatrical sets, portraits, Indian scenes, and Church frescoes before turning his attention to panoramic entertainment.[154] Intending to "outlive" his rivals, he tinkered with technology, adding special effects of motion animation. He motorized steamboats so that they traveled against currents and emitted steam. He also may have applied lighting effects to dissolve one view into a new one. Well over a year in the making, Pomarède spared no expense.[155] He insured the 625 yard panorama for $6,000.[156] Opening in St. Louis on September 19, 1849, Pomarède's show coincided with a second viewing of Lewis's panorama in the city. Lewis left town after a month. Pomarède attracted crowds until the end of October with benefits for Catholic and Protestant Orphanages. When a Railroad Convention came to the city, his show was extended to accommodate corporate, state, and government representatives. Unfortunately, before he could ship the panorama internationally, it was destroyed by fire in the middle of a successful run at Washington Hall in Newark, New Jersey.

Fixated on featuring the Northern stretch from the Mouth of the Ohio River to the Falls of St. Anthony, Pomarède designed a circuitous route that moved up river with views of the West bank and back down river to St. Louis with views of the East bank. "Seemingly, this panorama was composed of many unrelated scenes, rather than of consecutive views of the river," remarked a surprised viewer.[157] The four sections did not bind a cohesive narrative of the entire river. Instead, four themes corralled thrills and chills. Each part embraced a specialized genre of landscape: Indian "scenery," wilderness, commerce and leisure, and disaster. The first section compiled travel scenes through Minnesota Indian reservations. Indian genre painter Carl F. Wimar may have assisted Pomarède during his expedition North; they traveled together through Minnesota. Scenic landscape composed another piece. Science and technology activated steamboats and mechanical devices. The grand finale featured a "beautiful dissolving view" of the Great Fire in St. Louis.

Stunning sensation sequences in Pomarède's panorama involve fire scenes. The St. Louis fire that occurred on a spring evening in May 1849 joined the list of river disasters treated in the shows. Steamboat fires and explosions were particularly arresting in the river panoramas. The skeletons of wrecks from fires, collisions, and groundings, or depictions of rescue efforts riveted attention on stories of unexpected death, survival, and heroism. Furthermore, monstrous explosions and deadly fires implicated the irrational fears and symbolic effects of new technology, such as steam engines, in contemporary life. One river tragedy, the burning of the Ben Sherrod (1837), was a highlight of Risley's and Smith's show, which included a riveting eyewitness account by one of the few survivors of the recent steamboat disaster.[158] One hundred lives were lost when the ship exploded. The scene dramatizes the self-sacrifice of the ship captain, who tore off planks from the upper deck of the boat to throw to drowning passengers as rescue vessels surround the burning ship. Stockwell featured the burning of the steamer Clarksville (1848). A survivor of the disaster seeing it in New Orleans rose from the audience and testified to its accuracy.[159] Lewis, or an assistant, inserted the sunken fate of The

Brilliant (1851) that was ripped apart by a boiler explosion. Ball and Duncanson included the burning of the Martha Washington (1852) on a cold winter night, as well as the charges of arson and murder brought against its Cincinnati owners.[160]

The Mormon temple in Nauvoo was the scene of at least two fires in the midst of Church members' exodus from the city in 1847. Some of the faithful stayed behind. When news circulated in the county that church members were returning from Utah, anti-Mormon agitators feared the Temple would become a magnet for repopulation. The temple was razed to the ground by a fire widely suspected of being arson. The abandoned city, in 1849, "lay in ruins."[161] The burned out shell of the temple preserved the defeated rival community. Branding the former Mormon occupants an "extremely dangerous sect" sustained removal of "alien" transgression as part of the heroic conceits in Western panoramas.

The St Louis fire was a different kind of tragedy. On that night, the steamer White Cloud docked on the St. Louis riverfront caught fire. The ensuing blaze ravaged the city all night. Three lives perished in the catastrophe. The major toll of the fire came in property damage to residences and commercial buildings. In all 430 buildings, 23 steamers, 9 flatboats, and several barges were destroyed. Lewis lost his floating studio in the blaze.[162] The financial disaster was conservatively tallied at half a million dollars in one report. The story around the fire passed on terrifying detail to the widespread panic, battling the flames, heavy economic loss, and the collective effort to immediately begin rebuilding the city. Pomarède had not completed his panorama at the time of the fire. Stockwell and Lewis hastened to add the fire scene to their touring works. Lewis added a scene with the blaze rising from the skyline that he placed side by side with the city before the fire. Pomarède included the fire as the crescendo of his show. His view took in the chaos of the city in flames and the aftermath of charred ships, blackened walls and tottering chimneys. The ruins of the smoldering city gave pause to survivors in St. Louis. The city's current resurrection was swift. St. Louis rose from the ashes within a year "new and more beautiful."[163] Pomarède imparted biblical significance to the event according to a St. Louis resident. A transformation occurred in the scene from the fury of the blaze to daylight appearing "like a messenger from God" to extinguish the inferno.[164]

Pomarède contrasted the religious overtones of redemption in the city fire with the purgatory of a wild prairie fire. These fire scenes were singled out by the St. Louis Weekly Reveille, wetting the appetite of its readership prior to a September opening.[165] They may be the work of Wimar. Wimar specialized in Indian subjects and wilderness landscapes. He was famous for burning prairie scenes and buffalo stampedes.[166] In the prairie fire as described, an Indian encampment is viewed in the open air. Night descends, when "a small steady light appears in the distance." The prairie suddenly burst into flames. The village of Indians appears trapped on a small space of land near the edge of a precipice from which they cannot escape. Indian men look down a chasm and women holding children run in terror while horses and buffalo stampede.[167] The bold symbolism confers eternal hellfire on the heathen body. Pomarède propounds an orthodox moral liturgy in defining American consciousness; the omnipotent nature of God graces the citizen body with future glory. His rectitude overwrites the saga of domestic colonization. The spiritual drama is wrapped in unexpected enchantments that divert landscape to artifact. His partitioned scenic wonders: Indian display, pristine landscape, science and technology, and community revolve around a divinely ordained destiny.

As part of his show, Pomarède sold Indian items obtained during his travels while preparing the panorama. The trophies of ethnic violence and cultural appropriation formerly framed in illusionary fare materialize in souvenir commodities.[168] Scenic life remounts a disembodied legacy that exhibits ruins and mementos as historic sites. These artifacts multiply across representational frequencies for entertainment, for decorative consumption, for historical literacy, and for mainstream distribution. The reserved parcels of the past are not only objectified as artifacts or landmarks, but demarcate ritualized vessels of self-invention granted citizenship. The medium of landscape once again annihilates the living Indian body in visionary spaces of white progress. The capacity to battle alien elements, to suffer hardship, to improve conditions rejuvenate land narratives, such as discussed in The *Frieze of American History*, but now advancing aspirational legitimacy: to dream, to create, to redevelop, to risk, to embrace new spaces. It is not surprising that the Dickenson panorama shows methods of excavation and skeletal remains within Indian burial tombs. He anticipates the evolutionary authority of scientific evidence, such as Darwin's theory of natural selection (1859), in reconstituting history.

Mediums of History

The prolific river landscapes embody and disembody transcriptions of political, social, and personal discourse. Their pluralism circulates in the accelerating tempos of media presence. The appearances of live historical consciousness admit perpetual change, reissuing landscape narratives out of the economic fluidity of *natural* autonomy. Regionalism both communicates and challenges notions of disparity and diversity. The land's civil imbalances fold in transgression, discord, and disproportion indefinitely. Yet, the medium's conflation with the commercial entertainment industry serves the economy of a larger political project. Multimedia performance attuned public perception to enter the landscapes of critical social, political, and economic issues: slavery, Indian removal, regional strife, secessionism, community, and property. They also dispersed belief systems. Whether radical or conservative, aimed at fantasy or enlightenment the individual ideological perspectives shaping independent narratives submerge the public in dramatized spaces that commune with democratic principles. The widening trajectories of a moving landscape in multimedia performance reinforce the coming attraction of yet unseen histories, each capable of altering mainstream historical awareness for better or worse.

Ascendant commercial diversions supply a panoramic juncture in multimedia applications that stretch into large-scale theatrical attractions of other entertainment platforms, including destination events and site-specific attractions. Partnering with transportation networks and local government were part of William Burr's 1850 marketing campaign for his colossal *Moving Mirror of the Great Lakes, the Niagara, St. Lawrence and Saguenay Rivers*. This large-scale production touted a "seven mile long" interconnecting river voyage exploring the Northern borders of the United States.[169] Seasonal changes were added to the scenic course. Elevated views from buffs and riverbanks magnified the perceptional effect. In design, unruffled amusement and leisure tourism were the goals. The New York run lasted two hundred performances.[170] Promotions used by Burr and his entrepreneurial partner Josiah Perham to sustain interest involved coordinating with the New England railroad to offer half price excursions fares to bring tourists to Boston when the panorama appeared there and selling lottery tickets for prize drawings. After the Civil War, large-scale spectacle productions harnessed commercial entertainment infrastructure to industrial systems. The natural world became further segmented from the motorized procession, altering the "character" of the landscape from agrarian to industrial terrain.

3

Entertainment Scenes: Industrial Strength Brands of Site-Specific Spectacle

Almost a century before Irving Berlin published "God Bless America," novelist and playwright Robert Montgomery Bird began composing songs that he called national hymns. His own "God Bless America!" blesses the land, "the land beloved ... the land that gave us birth!"[1] Published in 1834, Bird's mantra followed the adoption by Congress a few years earlier of Francis Scott Key's "Star-Spangled Banner" as the national anthem, and the penning of "America" by the Baptist Minster Samuel Francis Smith.[2] In the decades following the Civil War, the scenic heritage of the "land" preserved sentiments of God and country, of violence and conquest, of renewal and change in the stage life of sensory media. At the same time, interstate commerce and transition to multinational markets powered large-scale agendas. Spectacle attractions of the industrial era sprinkled massive visions of war, resurrection, and transformation across the entertainment landscape. Nostalgia rebooted retrospective outlooks in a backward gaze that hailed future promise. In 1888, a panorama of *Jerusalem and the Crucifixion* proved an "attractive summer resort" to revive Christian history for thousands of citizens and visitors to midtown Manhattan in New York; meanwhile the *Battle of Gettysburg*, on view downtown, would recall the fury of the Civil War for 150,000 persons over a two-year span.[3] Multimedia panoramas supercharged theatrical tricks of the trade. Out of Chicago, David Henderson's American Extravaganza Company carved a niche for trippy exoticism breathing transformative presence into magic pumpkins, chambers of horrors, and stormy shipwrecks in *Cinderella, Ali Babba and the Forty Thieves*, and *Sinbad*.[4] Among media-centric attractions, scenic spectacles accelerated immersive engineering, hoisting historical presence onto site-specific stages. These durable yet porous theatrical idioms flaunted trademark styles that engulfed spectatorship in modernizing momentum.

One distinctive type of "American" historical spectacle interlocked many moving parts in urban industrial growth. A principal exponent of the genre was theatrical maverick Imre Kiralfy, a producer at the cutting edge of cosmopolitan diversion. Kiralfy propelled site-specific staging to dizzying levels of invention, including specially built outdoor theatres. The Hungarian immigrant pivots around a blockbuster brand of spectacle drama that drew on global entertainment networks, transportation systems, manufacturing assembly, and marketing. Well known for over 40 years in both America and Europe, Kiralfy began in commercial theatres with storybook dance spectacles, moved onto site-specific gargantuan historical spectacles and eventually began designing exposition grounds. As Brandon Gregory argues, he was in the nexus of transitions in spectacle practices.[5] Kiralfy's connections to, and belief in, corporate culture demonstrates how one type of entertainment commodity articulates economic modernization. His work threaded corporate ideology into mythologies of social progress. Because he straddles multiple channels of economic stimulation, his ongoing revitalization of the spectacle industry provides a close up on the distribution of historical concepts filtering into popular perspectives.

Trends in urban culture, for contrast, have a counterpart in the preservation of natural heritage. In juxtaposition to Kiralfy's diversionary historical landscapes, the opening of the Western territories to large-scale industrialization was engineered by corporate interests and federal policies. A more detailed examination of Western development is taken up in chapter 5. For now, a brief look at the elevation of the Great West to national concept makes its debut beginning with Yellowstone National Park. Government consolidation of undeveloped regions of the far West refashioned wilderness culture for public consumption as a national possession. These sites of "natural" heritage and transformative change serve as broad brackets related to large-scale alterations in economic conditions. Two lines of inquiry emerge. Foremost are panoramic environments that actualize "American" brands. The industrial platforms on which scenic spectacles take shape re(occupy) land myths, particularly territorial dynamics projected in changing sites of wilderness and redevelopment. All of which leads to questioning how experiential landscapes reconceptualize narrative histories, while advancing an ideography of cultural differences.

Appearances of city and country—the vanguard and the wilderness—negotiate the operations of corporate environments that traded on panoramic diversity as American "brandscapes." Maurya Wickstrom's characterization of the subjective interactions corporate brands mimetically embody lends particular reverberations to the aforementioned brands of historic "material" in the industrial age.[6] A cornerstone of Wickstrom's thought is how corporeal desire inhabits product identities in which "the consumer comes to embody the resonances of the brand as feelings, sensations, and even memories."[7] In the nineteenth century, a century of nationalist branding, the contra-appearances of distinct regional commodities emit resonant scenic identities, reformulating the expanding horizon of American ingenuity, as well a visionary assertion that crosses into new conceptual territories. Kiralfy's brand of immersive experience establishes a cornerstone to elaborate destination routes in corporate nationalism. Touching on the profile of government deliberations over Yellowstone National Park, hinges the incorporation of network conglomerates strengthening production and distribution systems of scenic wonder and enterprise.

Cross Currents in Nineteenth-Century Spectacle Entertainments

The exuberant ephemera of site-specific spectacles have precedents in traditions of court tournaments, open-air fêtes, and firework displays. Catherine de Medici's sumptuous "magnificences" during her reign with Henry II of France from 1559 to 1589 subtly disseminated political propaganda that helped solidify reassurance in France's stability and distracted the nobility from political infighting.[8] Political diffusion underlines the seductive distractions indebted to the outgrowth of nineteenth-century grand spectacle drama, circus "specs," and public amusements that entertained a growing working and middle class whose appetite for leisure activities created new cultural outlets. Spurred on by a robust economy of consumers, theatrical entrepreneurs sought ways to partner in novelty markets in order to stay competitive and attract large audiences. Cultural historian Jack Kasson notes that urban modernization and mass culture in the United States were produced, in part, by a growing entertainment and amusement industry.[9] As a contemporary theatrical medium, in addition to multimedia techniques, spectacle vocabularies earmarked specific entertainment commodities dispensing "American" styles. The expressions of spectacle staging bridged all levels of theatrical translation, from the pictorialism of Steele Mackaye to the refined naturalism of David Belasco, from installation and multimedia panoramas to Wild West Shows and live action, proto-cinematic extravaganzas like *Ben Hur*.[10] Belasco's impressionistic interplay with special effects, scenic accuracy, and stage composition is notable in the passage of time of his 20-minute dusk to dawn lighting plot in *Madame Butterfly*. Textual components in spectacle practices are welded to theatricality in an immersive stagecraft of visceral exchange.

Late nineteenth-century scenic spectacles showcased technical artifice in production vocabulary, creating complex, multilayered scenic action, and inducing sensual excitement and visual stimulation, as well as a sense of movement and actuality, especially as realistic flourish became more and more pronounced. The appeal of large-scale spectacles spanned civic performances, amusement parks, commercial theatre, and early cinema. Commercial spectacles, in particular, diversified specialized methods of producing an aesthetic formula that tapped into mainstream desires. They leach off community empowerment, educational reforms, fantasy, and nationalist propaganda. Their eclectic mix of high and low culture was accessible to all strata of society. Although consumer choice gained leverage in respect to profit-minded entrepreneurs that agency is complicated by the sensory architecture of production mechanisms.

The scenic narratives of "specs" coalesced in elaborate special effects, pantomime, music, and dance. Subjects ranged from exotic locales to historical reenactments, even "oriental" medleys. A featured dance style was often classical ballet. The ballets fashioned classical technique into fanciful personifications of food, objects, concepts, and inventions. Racist stereotypes and cultural parodies were common. *Niagara Falls* (1884), a production by Frank Pease in an indoor theatre in Buffalo, New York, featured "pas de wampum" during an Indian ballet. Another of his spectacles, *The Queen of Death* (1883), included a "pas de bon bons" during a carnivalesque "Grand Ballet of Confections."[11]

Commercial and civic spectacles bathed the historical imagination across America with a pageantry of nationhood that celebrated patriotic mythologies on local and national scales. Historical spectacles took audiences on adventures through ancient and local histories, conveying spiritually uplifting and culturally instructive entertainment. Scenic "pictures" were colorfully animated with exotic figures and richly textured with mood and atmospheric immediacy. Story-lines followed exaggerated, melodramatic plots centered on war and romance or transported spectators through multimedia panoramas into strange, new foreign landscapes. Themes of colonial expansion struck cords of "civilizing" missions in works such as John Rettig's *Montezuma and the Conquest of Mexico* (1889), produced for the Cincinnati Opera Festival.[12] The Boer War was the subject of an extravagant recreation "in miniature" of the battle between the British and Boer armies in South Africa's Transvaal at Brooklyn, New York's Coney Island in 1905. Brighton Beach Park was transformed into the "Boer War grounds" with a seating capacity of twenty-eight thousand. Actual soldiers and generals who fought in the war appeared in the production, which was also seen on a slightly smaller scale in St. Louis. The New York Company included cast of one thousand. Advertisements boasted that three-hundred men from the Zulu, Kafir, Swazi, Basutos, and Matabele tribes as well as 150 Boer women and children were brought over from South Africa to take part in the show.[13]

Ancient history was another popular theme. Conquest and romance were key ingredients of Edwin T. Ziegler's *Cleopatra VI, Queen of Egypt* (1895). This pyrotechnic production boasted that the "action, scenery, and costumes were designed from cuts [sic] and illustrations in the art room of ancient history" in Cincinnati's Public Library.[14] The decline of the Roman Empire provided numerous treatments in which the forces of good and evil, represented by Christians and pagans, battled one another. Typically, the moral superiority of the Christian spirit prevailed against the corrupt excesses of Rome's ruling classes. Reimaging republican destiny vilified the privileges of the wealthy few, turning civic responsibility over to the working classes. Henry J. Pain's chronicle of the fall of Rome, *The Last Days of Pompeii*, presented at the Louisville Autumn Carnival of 1889, was originally produced for an indoor stage, but was so popular it was transferred outside for the civic celebration.[15] Biblical epics set in Ancient Rome presented immigrant audiences with the struggle to build a Christian nation. Two stupendous productions appeared in American theatres. *Quo Vadis?* arrived on stages in England and America during the 1899–1900 seasons. The dramatization of Henryk Sienkiewicz' novel on the decline of Rome and the persecution of Christians was even staged simultaneously in some cities. *Ben Hur* made its stage debut the same year in New York at the Broadway Theatre. Adapted from a best-selling novel by Lew Wallace on the life of Christ, it depicted the birth of Christianity on a gloriously bloody scale. One of its chief attractions was a live action chariot race. After running a season in New York, it was taken on the road by numerous companies.[16]

Natural phenomena continued to fuel experiments with artificial sensation. The mechanics of water effects surged briefly in theatrical spectacles in the early nineteenth century. In addition to its panoramic predecessors, the formidable sight of Niagara Falls had a long association with sensory experiments in scenic transformation.[17] Multimedia applications continued exploring temporal-mechanization with transitory lighting and scenic transparencies to create a variety of ambient illusions channeling moody impressions.[18]

The "American" landscape was broadly recognized by domestic and foreign audiences in Niagara attractions. When the watery monument crossed the Atlantic, the crashing downpour of the falls were particularly appealing for playing with technical and lighting effects of wave motion, liquidity, and reflective hues.[19] Richard D. Altick describes a rush of Niagara shows stemming from a short-lived vogue for cascading water scenes in London.[20] Niagara's rushing waters on stage garnished the ferocious mountain with three-dimensional effects, effects that overwhelmed audiences with awe and astonishment. A pair of paintings for a diorama display in Belgrade's Pantechnicon in 1832 ushered a perception of this world wonder as "the very life and energy of nature," even though the illusionary properties of the trick fell short.[21] The success of the somatic experience depended on delighting and satisfying spectators' belief in the existence of the illusion. If the technology faltered, the immersive "reality" was ruined. Visitors could be swept away in 20 moving views of the torrential falls in the Langenheim brothers' thrill-filled environment called a Physiorama.[22] German immigrant Gottfried Nikolaus Tracht, who took the American name Godfrey N. Frankenstein, introduced a rousing *Moving Panorama of Niagara Falls* in 1853 that coincided with the opening of a railroad line to Niagara.[23] By the end of the nineteenth century, a "little" Niagara Falls was spilling real water that "tumbled from the flies to the stage."[24] In step with these immersive currents, the Kiralfy brothers infused media technologies of modern spectacle tradition with an industrial strength brand stamped with a reputation for quality and innovation.

The Enterprising Vision of the Kiralfy Brothers

Brothers Imre and Bolossy Kiralfy rocketed from specialty dancers to leading spectacle producers of the late nineteenth century. Born in the Austro-Hungarian Empire city of Pest, Imre was the oldest of seven children born to Jacob Konigsbaum, a clothing manufacturer, and his wife Anna (Rosa) Weisberger. They were a prosperous family of Jewish descent. However, the Konigsbaum family business was ruined during the 1848 Hungarian Revolution. The family suffered temporary poverty and Jacob narrowly escaped imprisonment by the Austrians. The Kiralfy Brothers, as they billed themselves, started their careers touring Europe as folk dancers. Shortly after arriving in the United States, they started choreographing and producing spectacles in which visual narrative and dance predominated, beginning with a stupendous revival of the burlesque *The Black Crook* (1873). The production ran 18 seasons at Niblo's Garden Theatre.[25] The brothers had a bitter breakup in 1887, which neither publicly addressed. Although, Bolossy intimated that his brother was making business deals behind his back.[26] Working independently, Bolossy's particular flair leaned toward fantasy and fable; Imre embraced the ramp up to the progressive era armed with science, technology, and the industrial machinery that bonded corporate growth to independent entertainment enterprises.

In the summer of 1887, Imre brought spectacle entertainment to new levels of installation with a blockbuster outdoor staging of *The Fall of Babylon* at St. George, Staten Island (Figure 3.1). The following summer, he returned to produce *Nero, or The Destruction of Rome* on an even grander scale. The productions integrated advance electronic effects and stage mechanics with eye-popping pizzazz. They employed thousands and cost upwards of half a million dollars. Hundreds of thousands of spectators traveled to St. George from June to August to watch Babylon fall and Rome burn. The widespread appeal of open-air commercial spectacles, such as *Babylon* and *Nero*, translated Judeo-Christian religious narratives into edifying historical reconstructions. These pseudobiblical stories of religious persecution, perseverance, and the spiritual advent of civilized humanity valorized the struggle of "outsiders" seeking the promise of freedom. This form of dramatic dance-spectacle eliminated concentration on the spoken word, replacing speech with a panoramic display of social progress. Its processional pageantry invokes the serialized scenic scope of political narratives seen earlier in the US Capitol panorama,

Figure 3.1   Imre Kiralfy, *The Fall of Babylon*.

Source: Circus Poster Collection, Graphic Arts, Department of Rare Books and Special Collections, Princeton University Library.

but now realized in live media on stage. The conceptual narrative embodied historical events in nonstop action that saturated spectators in spellbinding tales.

The Kiralfys push off and pull in trends in spectacle practices from all directions. Their contemporary, director/producer Steele Mackaye, searched for representational unity in spectacle drama. With a background in visual arts and an interest in science, Mackaye investigated new means to bring a more integrated dramaturgy to nineteenth-century commercial theatre. Mackaye wanted theatrical representation to "realize" an artistic rendering of nature.[27] The purpose, he argued, emphasized "the most inspiring idealism."[28] He began experimenting with stage realism after opening his Madison Square Theatre in 1880.[29] A leading exponent of the pictorial stage in America, Mackaye molded scene, acting, and text into a more circumstantial method of play production. He also employed, as well as invented, media technology toward creating spectacular immersive effects with the use of the cyclorama, electric lighting, and elevator stages. The last years of his life were spent in carrying out an architectural dream of building a ten thousand-seat, fully mechanized, grand spectacle-musical theatre called a Spectatorium for the 1893 Chicago World's Fair.[30] In sharp contrast to Mackaye's auteur approach, the combined company was a type of management partnership of producers and theatre owners formed to consolidate regional distribution. David Henderson, W. J. Gilmore, and Charles H. Yale joined forces to establish the Interstate Theatre Company, which specialized in visual spectacles. With headquarters based in New York and a repertory niche of fantasy, opera, and musicals, their theatres in Philadelphia, Boston, New York, and Chicago maintained a steady stream of caprice.[31]

The Kiralfys entered the United States during vast social movement. Educational standards became a primary concern during post-bellum reconstruction. In 1873, an annual report by the United States Bureau of Education was released by John Eaton Jr, Commission of Education. The 1870 census revealed that 17 percent of adult males and over 23 percent of adult female—nearly one in four—over ten years old were illiterate. The situation, as accounted for by Eaton, proposes "those who have the power" to increase the facilities for the education of the masses."[32] Promoting methods to "normal schools," Eaton recommends curriculum standards to foster "original investigation in science, history, and in political and social economy."[33] Technical knowledge and the humanities were vital he argues to "include the culture which our institutions and modern times unite in demanding" in order to improve political institutions and advance "our vast material prosperity."[34]

In the latter half of the nineteenth century, educational institutes were founded to train young men and women in applied sciences and art. Industrial tycoons often established these schools. They were guided by philanthropic principles devoted to advancing common cultural values and social betterment through policies of open enrollment and instruction in commercial art, architecture, and engineering. Two of those that have endured are Cooper Union in New York and The Drexel Institute in Philadelphia. In major cities where industrialization, European immigration, and Northern migration by African Americans fragmented daily life, the merger of entertainment media and corporate industry spawned institutional systems dedicated to the cultural improvement and social advancement of all classes.[35]

Between 1870 and 1900, the United States asserted itself as world leader in industry, manufacturing, and mining. Economic investment in transportation, raw resources, technology and low-cost energy fueled industrialization. A large, cheap labor force accelerated its growth. According to census data from 1850 to 1930, the foreign-born population of the United States increased from 2.2 million to 14.2 million, reflecting large-scale immigration from Europe during most of this period. [36] Records indicate that almost half of New York City's nearly one million people in 1870 were immigrants.[37] By 1880, 6.6 million of the more than 50 million people in the United States were foreign born. Within this national environment of swelling, ethnic diversity and modernization, the worldly sensibilities of an eclectic mainstream powered an economic engine in the entertainment industry that would, in turn, append global reach to urban enrichment.

Imre's social philosophy gripped science and media technology as methods of visionary empowerment to invoke social exchange and positive feelings for violent upheavals in democratic processes. He forged partnerships with businessmen as well as railroad and ferry directors to secure promotional advertising and access to the destination venue. When he produced *Nero* and *Babylon* the economic redevelopment of Staten Island served the local political economy by broadening regional infrastructure. Day tourism was part of the marketing strategy. The impetus of Mackaye's design for his Spectatorium was to "present the facts of history with graphic force while suggesting, by music and poetic symbolism, the true philosophy of history."[38] Kiralfy understood the power of imagery as an immersive tool of storytelling; his media vocabulary sponged off contact with state-of-the-art technological developments in the US and abroad. With a more pragmatic approach to integrating productive commodity markets into progress narratives, he gentrified the political thrusters of industrial multinationalism. By cultivating emerging networks of sponsorship and combined companies, he developed short and long-term destination venues. His brand of conceptual spectacle married historic confections to economic identities through a processional lens of trains, telecommunications, consumer appliances, and engineering marvels.

Imre and Bolossy, ages 24 and 22, along with two brothers and three sisters sailed into New York harbor in 1869. Their first appearance was in George L. Fox's *Hickory Dickory Dock*.[39] Led by the two elder brothers, the family of dancers performed Hungarian folk dances. While touring European cities, the brothers schooled themselves in the Paris boulevard theatres and variety theatres in London. They also studied the grander confections of the Paris Opera and English pantomimes. With cultural trade in European dance, acrobatics, and spectacle novelties increasing during the era, the itinerant climate of possibility was immediately apparent to Imre.[40] On his arrival in New York City, Imre recalled that "I saw instantly that the great popular want in America was spectacle, spectacle that was more or less familiar to Europeans. Spectacular dramas there were, but they were on a very small scale, and greatly deficient in either color or magnificence."[41]

In partnership, the brothers traveled back and forth to Europe to purchase exclusive rights to popular productions, to contract English, French, Italian, and German dancers, or to import sets and costumes. Italian and French ballet masters were hired to choreograph the ballets. A Kiralfy production always promoted its continental credentials. In fact, the family motto was "All the World's a Stage."[42] The early ballets employed two hundred or more dancers, with the action of the episodes characteristically expressed in mime or tableaux against extravagant, picturesque panoramas. Glamorous, leggy, high kicking "belles" executing precision choreography earned Imre an epitaph as the "pioneer of 'girl' shows of the first rank."[43] By the 1880s, the name Kiralfy was synonymous with quality dance spectacle; it became attached to ebullient, bustling scenes around town and effervescent literature: as "gay as a Kiralfy spectacle," and of the "Kiralfy species" became comparative refrains.[44] The brothers pluck and enterprise garnered a meteoric rise as the most sought after spectacle producers of their generation. They embody a storied myth of meritocracy in the land of opportunity; they also branded it into a spectacle identity.

The Kiralfy Brand

Dance historian Barbara Barker observes that Imre understood American audiences, "especially the steadily growing immigrant audience with its multiplicity of languages, its need for affordable entertainment, and its love of spectacle and visual theatre."[45] He was famous for his ability to generate rhythm and patterns with enormous numbers of people on stage. He combined fantastic tableaux and transformation scenes—familiar to him from English pantomimes— with a keen eye for visual narrative. Behind the dazzling array of motion effects, storylines followed fables of democratic colonization through the virtues of patriotism, religious tolerance, and moral fortitude. Imre participated in the national celebration commemorating the four-hundredth anniversary of Columbus's "founding" of America with a production in 1892 of *Columbus and the Discovery of America* at the Madison Square Garden Theatre. Fifteen thousand spectators attended the production, bringing in receipts amounting to $900,000.[46] The ballets morphed products into scenic parades personifying modern conveniences, such as Edison's Electric Light and the Fulton steamer. The following year it was featured at the Auditorium Theatre at the Chicago World's Colombian Exposition. The international exposition was a focal point of the national anniversary, showcasing American ingenuity and its increasing power.

In the competitive establishment of New York theatre managers and producers, Imre was a "Midas among showman," writes Edward Marks. [47] His shows turned profits for his backers and himself. In the press, he was described as "ingenious and shrewd" in the same sentence.[48] Imre believed himself "a great chef who placed before his customers a superb meal, rather than simply a jumble of rich food."[49] The organization, labor, and coordination of mounting and producing these feasts were itself part of the spectacle. When Imre's production of *America* arrived at the Metropolitan Opera House in 1893, following its premiere at the Chicago World's Fair, *Life* magazine lauded it as an intoxication of color, light, and form in which "Kiralfy out-Kiralfy's himself."[50]

As a youth, Imre studied magic, music, and civil engineering. He relates that by the age of 12, I spent "hours and days studying the railway locomotives," resulting in an attempt to build a motor for a horseless vehicle.[51] The "color of prismatic effects" and "all kinds of spectacle" fascinated him.[52] One enduring impression was a visit to the International Exhibition in the Champ de Mars, Paris, in 1867. Forty years later he wrote, "This was the supreme achievement in the way of pageants and exhibitions. Not a single detail escaped me. I went about daily viewing this great spectacle, in whole and in parts from every point of view."[53] With his brother, Imre began to erect theatrical exhibitions—live animated tracks of swirling colors that consolidated hundreds of chorus girls into dazzling, mechanized loops, spirals, and blocks.

One of the Kiralfys' first explosive successes was their 1883 ballet-spectacle *Excelsior*. It opened in the three-thousand-seat Niblo's Garden Theatre. First created under the direction of the Italian ballet master Luigi Manzotti at La Scala, Milan, it was imported to the Eden Theatre, Paris, before reaching New York. *Excelsior* employed over four-hundred people. It was touted to cost $75,000 and boasted of advancing "the stage at least one hundred years."[54] An allegory of civilization, *Excelsior* tracked the "progress of science, thought, mechanics, freedom, invention, art, and civilization" from the beginning of time to the current age, the age of illumination—electricity.[55] Episodes traveled over time and across countries reflecting a struggle between Light (Madelaine Nani) and Darkness (Ettore Coppini), between the grace of freedom and the tyranny of repression. Civilization (literally) dances forward but progress is laborious and fraught with the threat of failure and danger at every turn. Recent feats of human invention, from the telegraph to the opening of the Suez Canal (in 1869) materialized, illustrating the advance of applied science, transportation, technology, and communication. The rustic countryside and the sand whipped desert gave way to travel by steamship and harmonious trade among nations. The recently completed Mount Cenis tunnel—the first railroad tunnel connecting France and Italy—was depicted from start to finish with a train of flag waving passengers appearing out of it.[56]

Scenic displays were synchronized with grand, act-ending ballets to symbolize the beauty of modernization. Civil achievement was not only the great commonality uniting all races and religions, but championed the ethical choices to change the world. The monumental finale promoted electricity as the next revelatory invention. A transformation sequence heralding the "Triumph of Light over Darkness" culminated in the "Peaceful Union of Nations." The Kiralfy brothers enlisted the help of the Edison Electric Light Company for the final "Ballet of Light." Five hundred glass globes were lowered from the ceiling while the sets sank and a young woman representing humankind's hope—Excelsior—rose on a huge globe. Hundreds of dancers with "electrified costumes" held battery powered wands that illuminated the stage with incandescent light.[57]

Imre's historical spectacles joined an urban wave of Roman entertainments replicating "harmonious and coherent civic symbols."[58] Margaret Malamud observes that contemporary interest in the rise and fall of the ancient Roman Republic conflated hope and fear in the political model of republican identity.[59] The notion of disintegration associated to the imperial period of Roman history evoked the perils of political and religious empires, perhaps a through back to British rule for some. As dramatic fodder, overreaching, wealthy tyrants awakened fresh memories for new immigrants who may have fled religious or political persecution. Rome's fatal legacy also intimated the more ambivalent threats of internal combustion. The hidden fiber in Roman political spectacles often revised the circumstances of aristocratic corruption targeting plebian aspirations. The site-specific spectacles of Imperial Rome, as Richard C. Beacham points out, were not "just for spectacular diversion but for the mass communication of popular sentiment as well."[60] They symbolically mediated desired social outcomes in a display of national characteristics. Kiralfy resituates the political propaganda in the social identification with private struggle and personal achievement. Modifications occurred in the polarizing treatment of subject matter, which tilted toward perils to family, community, and liberty when selfish ambition takes root. Youthful, Romanized heroes come to be snared in a web of contradictory impulses: to honor private loyalties or to collectively stand against a tyrannical moral order. The modeling of ethical dilemmas put forward responsible citizenship as agent of democracy's survival.

Characteristic of Imre's style was the efficiency of his methods. The recognizable formula of his production techniques had much in common with assembly line manufacturing. The mechanized precision of his dance patterns devalues individual labor. Its rotating human geometry glamorized machine-made automation. The technicolor cascade of lines and shapes anticipate the "Taylorized choreography" of kick lines and mass formations, exemplified in Busby Berkeley's films of the 1930s. The effect Mark Franko observes dehumanizes the dancer to a commodity within the production values.[61] Kiralfy humanized a landscape of capital enhancement. He did this by mythologizing commodity markets. The montage of historical personifications embodied a kaleidoscope of animated systems. Heritage expressed democratizing brands in the progressive iconography of benevolent consumption and improvement. Voluminous, impersonal color blocks rotated against moving panoramas of typographical landmarks, while technological inventions emotionalized the magnificence of modern wonders. A reporter for the *Brooklyn Eagle* wryly noted empirical and factual discrepancies in the scenographic scale:

> One scene represents the Brooklyn Bridge. The bridge looks about three feet wide and 600 feet high. Several scores of ships in full sail are moving briskly under it. Palm trees grow on either shore and Indians sit on picturesque rocks around the Brooklyn entrance. At the New York end of the bridge is the Capitol at Washington.[62]

Stepping out Niblo's Garden Theatre in lower Manhattan, perhaps audiences marveled at the bounty of the "new world" occurring outside the auditorium. Towering over the streets stood the latest feat of American engineering, The Brooklyn Bridge, which opened in 1883. The urban city was in motion. *Excelsior* fleshed out the encroaching chaotic and jagged persona of cosmopolitan growth, of national and religious differences, with the dreamy luminosity of infinite possibility.

The hustle and bustle of urban congestion slips away in regional vantage points. At the same time city landmarks dotted the horizon, natural landmarks expressed uninhabited spaces. Environmental attractions aligned archeological sites with tourism. Kentucky's Mammoth Cave, now a National Park, is the longest cave system in the world. Tours of the caves began in 1816. It quickly joined the catalog of national possessions. Anticipating science-fiction lore, the mysterious allure of subterranean archaeological exploration held dramatic fodder for writers and artists. George Brewer's multimedia panorama of Mammoth Cave (1849) appeared alongside other "wonders and natural curiosities of the American continent," among which was Niagara Falls.[63] Brewer's "you are there" virtual tour made the dimly lit, dank caves sparkle and "glow." The guided expedition crafted an extraordinary psychological odyssey of departure and return after an underworld descent into the bowels of the cave floor, a chasm known as the "Bottomless Pit." Peter West notes how in the Mammoth Cave panorama that the visual treatment of the authority of black guides and excavators, who worked at the actual site, is submerged in spectral animations, haunting the cave's interiors or depicted in minstrel codes as entertainers. Much like the Mississippi river panoramas, race anxiety ripples beneath the fabric of the new popular science (fiction) genre. The reaffirmation of control implied a type of "national spectatorship that transcended the fraught model of white subjectivity."[64] The undercurrents also validate domestic "natural" antiquities and dissolve human subjects into labor systems.

John Skirving's assemblage of a 25,000 yard 80-scene moving panorama of the Overland Trail to California (1849–1850) was largely based on field artists' sketches taken during publicized topographical and geographical survey expeditions, the most famous led by John Charles Fremont, whose name headed broadsides. It figuratively traversed "more than half a million square miles" of new territory acquired by the United States following the Oregon Treaty (1846), the annexation of Texas, and the US Mexican War 1846–1848.[65] Its sweeping landscape upheld migration and territorial amendments of the national project to develop the continent. Alan Trachtenberg speaks of the momentum of Westward expansion and industrialism as the "incorporation of America." One aspect of formalizing national heritage to compete internationally served to define the natural rights of citizenship and endow it with monumental spirit. The far Western landscape branded the regional *scene* a separate yet equal site of the "American" panorama. After the Civil War, the scenic spectacle of the Western territories identified "native" wilderness areas that preserved an illusionary framework of natural heritage. It is during this period that the national park system is established.

The Natural Wonders of Yellowstone

Muscling US policies in trade and foreign relations built the undercarriage of socioeconomic exchange and geopolitical alliances. The political narrative of future prosperity under construction was rooted in aggressive legislative policies, domestic lobbying, and diplomatic negotiations to increase domestic mass production, expand transcontinental transportation systems, and insert footholds in Trans-Pacific, Latin American, and European trade. When the constitution of the United States was adapted, the three executive branches of government established were the Department of Foreign Affairs (September 15, 1789; the name was changed to the State Department), the Department of War (August 7, 1789), and the Treasury Department (September 2, 1789). The Treasury Department and its first Secretary Alexander Hamilton administered to the commercial and industrial life of the country. This cabinet post was designated "Secretary of Commerce and Finance at the first constitutional convention."[66]

In the postbellum decades, commercial and trade associations began lobbying for Congressional action to establish a fourth executive branch, a Department of Commerce that would supervise the increasing volume of capital investment in commerce and manufacturing. One such organization The National Board of Trade, an association of Boards of Trade, Chambers of Commerce, and other chartered organizations, declared itself in 1868 in Philadelphia. By 1874, its mission to secure "unity and harmony of action in reference to commercial usage, customs and laws" pressed the national scope of the "financial, commercial, and industrial interests of the country."[67] A comprise was reached in the formation of the Interstate Commerce Commission (1887). However, the influence of commercial lobbying power continued to grow in favor of a separate cabinet position. One argument levied in continued petitions stated that "the United States was a distinctly commercial and industrial nation, that the 1900 census showed the aggregate value of the product of manufacturing establishments of the United States exceeded 13 billion dollars (nearly four times the value of agricultural products)."[68] Yet, it was not until January 15, 1903 that the Fifty-seventh Congress passed a bill creating the Department of Commerce and Labor.[69] When the Taft administration took office in 1909, the Republican Party took credit for over two decades of prosperity and expansion under the leadership of William McKinley and Theodore Roosevelt.[70]

The political narrative framing US history was animated by the geographical mapping of the continent. Prior to creation of The US Geographical Survey by Congress (1879) topographic and geologic expeditions were dispersed throughout the West to gather data on natural resources, Indian populations, and trails, mainly under the Department of War.[71] Wilderness conservation was backed by corporate conglomerates and federal trade policies. The successful military containment of the Great Plains Indians on Western reservations laid open the region for large-scale industrialization. Development of the "natural wealth" of the land was aided by rail transportation, linking Eastern and Western ports. The administrative, corporate view of nature as natural resource contradicted growing public perceptions of the sublime character of the untouched wilderness.[72] In acting to preserve the institutional idea of America as rising historically from the land itself, the conservation of uninhabitable lands was translated into national reserves, fomenting perceptual legacies of cultural tradition on par with Western Europe. The vision of the Grand Canyon diverted attention from decades of war and genocide. The iconic monument justified the goals of military conquest. Much like the regional elevation of the Niagara landscape, the wide-open splendor of the Western landscape evoked the grand ideal to achieve the American dream.

President Grant signed a bill in 1872 establishing Yellowstone as the first National Park. Today, the US Department of the Interior lists over 21 million acres, 25 national parks, 80 national monuments, 45 national historic parks, national battlefields, and other classifications of areas.[73] The United States Geographical Survey of the Territories was formed in 1861 under the Land Office.[74] Civilian explorers led the first expeditions into the Rocky Mountain territories. Legend tells that the idea of establishing a national park was first expressed by Montanan Cornelius Hedges to his companions as they sat around the campfire on the night of September 19, 1870 near what is now called Madison Junction:

The members of the party quite naturally fell to discussing the commercial value of such wonders, and laying plans for dividing personal claims to the land among the personnel of the expedition. It was into this eager conversation that Hedges introduced his revolutionary idea. He suggested that rather than capitalize on their discoveries, the members of the expedition waive personal claims to the area and seek to have it set aside for all time as a reserve for the use and enjoyment of all the people. The instant approval which this idea received must have been gratifying to its author, for it was a superb expression of civic consciousness.[75]

According to a commemorative pamphlet issued by the US Geographical Survey in 1940, the purpose of exploring the far Western frontiers was to "gain a measure of the vast lands and natural resources in the region now occupied by the Rocky Mountain States." Survey teams collected detailed scientific information about terrain, mineral, and timber resources, climate and water supply. When the bill to establish Yellowstone as a national park was presented to Congress, it was evaluated in terms of practical use value. Based on the surveys report, Congress found the area "not to be susceptible of cultivation with any degree of certainty." The winter climate was seen as too severe for "stock-raising." Settlement was problematic due to extreme altitude, "unless there are valuable mines to attract people."[76] The first National Park was created because the region was considered economically worthless for development, but potentially valuable as a tourist attraction. It fell to photographs of the Yellowstone area, as well as a viewing for Congress of Thomas Moran's panoramic paintings *The Chasm of the Colorado* and *The Grand Canyon of the Yellowstone* (Figure 3.2) that is said to have finally convinced Congress to pass the bill in support of establishing Yellowstone National Park.[77] Moran was among the artists and photographers on the expedition into Yellowstone. Congress purchased Moran's wondrous paintings and displayed them in the Capitol Rotunda until 1950.[78]

An unflappable geologist Ferdinand Vandiveer Hayden headed Moran's survey team. Hayden wanted photographic documentation of the expedition to bring back to Washington in order to raise funding for yearly summer expeditions. At the time, the Western school of photography, or what was known as field photography, was gaining commercial popularity.[79] Eadweard Muybridge, one of the pioneers of field, concentrated on human and animal locomotion. Nature landscapes such as Niagara Falls and the Grand Canyon reached mass

Figure 3.2 Thomas Moran (1837–1926), *The Grand Canyon of the Yellowstone*, 1872. Oil on canvas. 84 × 144¼ in. (231.0 × 266.3 cm).

Source: Smithsonian American Art Museum, Washington, DC, Lent by the Department of the Interior Museum, Photo Credit: Smithsonian American Art Museum, Washington, DC/Art Resource, NY. Image reference: ART128918.

circulation. The most famous scenes of the Rocky Mountains were the work of William Henry Jackson. Jackson Canyon near Casper, Wyoming is named after him. Hayden hired Jackson, who ran a small commercial photoshop in Omaha to join his expedition into Yellowstone. With an assistant, Jackson carted up to three-hundred pounds of equipment that included two large cameras with glass plates coated with chemicals ("wet-plate" technique) into the unmapped regions of Yellowstone.[80]

In his panoramic photographs of Colorado, Wyoming, and Utah, Jackson developed his own style. He would climb to one peak in order to gain a higher vantage point another.[81] Typical in panorama painting, the placement of the horizon line establishes a centralized overview. Jackson manipulated the vantage point to activate spatial volume. He moved the viewer above or below the horizon. In doing so, he skewed the viewer's perspective so that foreground objects appear magnified or the irregularities of the natural geography were exaggerated. By destabilizing the horizon line, the distance or proximity of actual phenomena was set in motion. The effect imparts a sentient scale of physical magnitude. Jackson's shifting perspectives sculpt a felt iconography. The static and the dynamic simultaneously reciprocate the grasp of natural statuary and the sense of physical expansion through an inexhaustible expanse. His panoramic photography dissolves empirical appearance, giving way to an intangible aesthetic. The perceptional streams did not just immerse one physically in a felt space, they orchestrated a steady stream of "natural" sensations—an immersive mobility in the scene space.

Jackson's iconic images of Mammoth Hot Springs, the Mountain of the Holy Cross, and Teton Ridge, became some of the most enduring *sights* that entered homes and magazines. Over one season, Jackson snapped nearly four-hundred negatives. His photographic prints of the Hot Springs basins, Old Faithful geyser, Grand Teton ridge, and the Lower Falls were the first to reach beyond the West and roundly credited with publicizing the "value" of the Yellowstone region.[82] His prints reached mass distribution when he partnered in the Detroit Publishing Company or published compilations in mass-market viewbooks.[83] *National Geographic* republished one of his most famous photographs of Jupiter Terrace in 1940 for an article titled "Fabulous Yellowstone."[84] A year earlier John Ford filmed the first of nine Westerns, *Stagecoach* in Monument Valley, an area on the border of Arizona and Utah is now a protected Navajo park. It was named for the monolithic rock formations erupting up from the desert floor.

The lure of site-specific destinations echo antebellum narratives of crossing boundaries into new frontiers. In the gilded age, commercial and institutional agents consolidated vantage points over scenic heritage. The crafting of diversionary pleasures advanced wealth creation as privileges in "civil" society. Speaking of museum practices, Barbara Kirshenblatt-Gimblett distinguishes between "context" and "*in situ*" in display. Where the former organizes interpretive frames; the later involves filling out fragments in a mimetic location.[85] As scenic attractions, site-specific environments suggest a blend of dramatic context and *in situ* installation in heritage production. Spectacle sites converted environmental narratives, filling out sensations of belonging and continuity that downplayed poverty, labor exploitation, and disenfranchisement. The sensible occupation of felt perspectives momentarily could distract or push out of the frame lived conditions. In doing so, the altered intimacy of immersive mobility refres-hed new conditions coming into existence. Symbiotic transactions with illusionary sentiments of mobility stirred evocative, transformative spaces for desire to occupy.

Reflecting back over his life in theatre, Imre felt gratified by the "thought that I may have helped to raise the standard of spectacular entertainment and that I have contributed something to the artistic needs, as well as to the gaiety of the nations."[86] When, in 1887, Imre was enlisted to direct the outdoor summer dramatic offering at St. George, Staten Island, he was inspired to experiment beyond the constraints of indoor architecture. "No theatre would serve to exploit the vast pictures which I began to conceive in my mind," he wrote of this period.[87] The scope of Imre's vision moved beyond interior spaces; the landscape became scenic architecture.

Staten Island Stages *Babylon* and *Nero*

Canadian-born businessman Erastus Wiman (1834–1904) contacted Imre Kiralfy. Wiman was a staunch advocate of commercial union, or unrestricted reciprocity (free trade), between Canada and the United States and served as director of the Western Union telegraph company. A committed family man, he lived on Staten Island, where he was instrumental in developing bridge and rail lines to and around Staten Island in partnership with Robert Garrett, president of the Baltimore and Ohio Railroad. [88] With transportation and ferry service under his control, Wiman opened the Staten Island Amusement Company in the mid 1880s. Day-trippers could ferry over to the island to watch the Metropolitan Baseball Club, attend the circus—laid out on 11 acres or, by evening, see wholesome entertainment.

For his first season at St. George, Imre planned the "Grand Historical Biblical Dramatic Musical Spectacle" *The Fall of Babylon*. Both *Babylon* and the following year's spectacle *Nero, or The Destruction of Rome* originated in Ohio with the Order of Cincinnatus. The Order was named after the legendary Roman general/farmer, and held in postrevolutionary America as a symbol of republican virtue. The civic organization sponsored extravagant outdoor historical pageants and parades. Christian values and colonizing ideals underscored themes of "civilizing" missions. Works produced for the Cincinnati festivals, such as *Montezuma and the Conquest of Mexico* and *The Fall of Babylon*, struck cords of righteous conquest over barbaric, pagan cultures.[89] These civic spectacles were the creation of John Rettig, an artist and scene designer. Imre amplified Rettig's design into an historical landscape inhabited by all.

Babylon was based on the Book of Daniel from the Old Testament. It illustrated events surrounding Daniel's prophecy of the city's destruction "tolerably strictly."[90] Great care was taken to sanction what was seen as accurate and educate the public in lengthy program notes detailing the history of Babylon. The program text highlighted descriptions of the enslavement of the Jews, as well as the divine design of that civilization's destruction. Like a storybook, action scenes blended into visual tableaux and vice versa (Figure 3.1). Three parts in sequence brought viewers to the city, led them inside the city, and let them witness its fall—all within two hours. These sensational vistas allowed spectators to arrive at the exterior of the city along with the grand entrance of Belsahzzar, who was first seen returning from the hunt before the mythical walls of the city. Suddenly, great numbers of Persians appear in red and blue, preparing to attack the city. During the ensuing battle, the soldiers "discharged a copious flight of arrows at the orchestra."[91] In the second section, the walls "disappeared" before spectators, who gained entrance to a magnificent palace, a lake, and the legendary Tower of Babel. Within, there were victory and wedding processions. Scenes of drunken orgies ornamented with dancing girls were juxtaposed with the desecration of religious icons and lamentations of the Jews by the riverbank, while a variety of mesmerizing interludes passed over the stage before the viewing stands. These featured sports and races, dancing, choruses, and even a parade of "Africans with animals." Finally, came the "wild" feast of Belsahzzar. The frenzy escalated to the sudden illumination of the Writing on the Wall. Daniel enters to decipher the Hebrew script, delivering the divine judgment: "Thou hast been weighed in the balance and found wanting." With that the Euphrates is drained, the Persians physically attack the city with catapults, the great walls fall, and the city burns.[92]

The production promised to be the "finest ever seen in this country."[93] It did not disappoint. It opened on June 22 with plenty of advance buzz. The immensity of the undertaking included a running tally of the army of labor and huge costs involved. Kiralfy transported the sets from Cincinnati to Staten Island in five train cars. In addition to managing a cast of over one thousand performers, three-hundred carpenters were involved in building a 450 by 250 foot stage and mounting twenty carloads of scenery.[94] Estimates on lighting equipment alone ranged from $20,000 to $150,000.[95]

This included a centralized system for regulating electric lights. One report noted that the payroll exceeded $27,000 weekly.[96] Technical problems hounded many a Kiralfy production and on opening night, the show was delayed one hour. The much-anticipated fiery blaze consuming the city fizzled. Only a few palaces flamed; the tower did not burn down, and there was merely a "slight change before the walls slid in."[97]

Once corrected, Babylon fell gloriously throughout the rest of the summer. It was *the* event. It had everything: sumptuous colors, scantily clad showgirls, and, to some, moral fiber. It earned praise for its "intelligence" and gained the respect of the social elite, who filled the grandstand nightly.[98] Six nights a week thousands of people shuttled over to the island to attend.[99] Extra ferries were added to accommodate the crowds. Group excursions from surrounding counties became common, including a contingent from the Order of Cincinnatus, who remounted a more Kiralfyesque *Babylon* in Ohio the following summer.

"Great as the success of this experiment was," Imre stated, "I had something still more ambitious in my mind. This was *Nero*."[100] Carrying a cast of two thousand, the format of *Nero* followed the same montage-like momentum, shifting from massive patterns of rhythm and colors to intimate close-ups or action packed battles, Olympic Games, and chariot races. Like *Babylon*, *Nero* brought to life a time and place, "where luxury and crime ran riot."[101] The cautionary tale intensified violence and bloodshed with heroic gladiatorial combats and the ominous slaughter of Christians in the Circus Maximus. It concluded with Nero dying as the city dissolves in flames. Alongside history culled from Tacitus and Seutonis, *Nero* introduced fictional characters and tragic romance in order to enable "all who view this remarkable spectacle to be transported in imagination to Early Rome and *read through the eyesight* a novel of love, adventure, cruelty, slavery, gladiatorial efforts, and tortures of the early Christians."[102] It followed the story of Thirza, a Christian virgin who successfully fends off the Emperor Nero by having her brother kill her rather than become Nero's mistress. Unlike Thirza—the virtuous virgin—Rome falls. All the pagan decadence of the city is swept away in the fiery flames of eternal purgatory as an illuminated cross and one-hundred floating angels, symbolizing the "Dawn of Christianity," ascended over the blazing stage.

Imre wanted to create the feeling of being in a Roman amphitheatre for this production. He devised new means to realize this vision.[103] The proscenium opening of the stage was 465 feet wide.

A chariot track was set up around the stage. In order to expedite communication among crew, section "heads," and performers over such a huge distance he set up a central control from where he could "conduct" the performance. "To do this," he explained, "I caused thirty electric bells, invisible and inaudible to the public, to be placed on the stage at intervals, and so, by a code of signals operated from a gigantic keyboard, I was master of the situation." By pressing one button, he rang numerous bells in order to keep all the singers and dancers in unison, which unison "greatly mystified the audience."[104] However, in practice, the performers could not always hear the bells over the music of the orchestra. In order to shift massive scenery, some of which was two to three stories high, Kiralfy built a circular rail track 800 ft in circumference far upstage to roll sets on stage. The device trucked in a fully loaded "pictures." One such wonder was a riotous scene outside Nero's palace. Five-hundred singers, dancers, and extras positioned on steps and terraces were assembled in the wings then rolled on stage.[105]

Average attendance to *Nero* in July was reported to be fifteen-thousand people a week.[106] This influx of consumers was a bonanza for transportation systems and the economy of New York. For *Nero*, special trains were arranged to bring people from Chicago, St. Louis, Cleveland, and Pittsburgh or from Washington, DC, Baltimore, and Boston. The round-trip fare included hotel and admission to grandstand seating. Two new ferries were constructed to carry thirty-five-thousand people each. The time schedule of the show (8:30–10:00) was geared to allow ample time for the crowds to arrive and end early enough so that people could be home at a comfortable hour. No less significant was P.T. Barnum's interest. Already partnered in the Barnum and Bailey circus, the lavish extremes of "cruelty and excess" suited the titan's conceit of bringing the "pastimes of the Caesars" to the masses.[107] He snatched up both productions, hiring Kiralfy to package *Nero* into a crowd-pleasing circus spec for the London premiere of "The Greatest Show on Earth" in 1889.

Imre demonstrated that he could transpose any production to suit both given architectural or environmental space and audience. The Olympia Exhibition Hall held seating for twelve-thousand people. Imre had a stage installed along one-half of the great hall across from the viewing stands. It was reportedly half a mile long. Over one-thousand performers, danced, paraded, and battled across the arena. Camels joined at least a dozen elephants in the menagerie of animals on view. The sheer "audacity" of the show bedazzled

London crowds.[108] The "titanic" spectacle was again transplanted to the New York Polo Grounds as the feature attraction opening the famed circus's 1890 season.[109] By this time, the machinery of Rome's destruction had acquired the "agreeable habit of falling with persistent regularity to the intense delight of thousands of persons."[110]

That summer, *Babylon* launched Barnum's own outdoor amusement center located in Oakland Gardens, Boston.[111] The resort area was also strategically situated near a transportation hub in order to move thousands daily to and from the amusement park. The production played twice a day for three months. Special viewing stands were built with seating for ten-thousand people. The stage was so long one amused reporter noted that "by the time Daniel made his way across the huge stage to the wall, the writing on it had long disappeared."[112]

Clergy of all denominations attended both *Babylon* and *Nero*. Wiman invited them and their families personally by letter with the offer of free tickets. One pastor found *Babylon* blasphemous, protesting over the "slurring of the handwriting on the wall by a hundred chorus girls" in the pages of *The New York Evangelist*. The climax of the piece, he charged, "is *not God's hand but their legs*."[113] In his invitation to *Nero,* Wiman asserted:

> The closing scenes of the life of Nero have always had a special interest for the Christian world. The final triumph of the cross is a sermon in itself, rising as it does, amid the strains of the "Stabat Mater" above the ruins of the great city whose terrible destruction is so vividly set forth.[114]

Within the Christian community, there appears to have been more charges of vulgarity. Yet both onstage and off, the effort to exert respectability was rigorously upheld. During *Nero*'s run, three-hundred male extras were fired for inappropriate behavior toward female cast members.[115] In response to those "short-sighted persons" who were not won over by such spiritual refreshment, an article appeared in *Life* claiming that Brother Wiman and Brother Kiralfy "deserve the gratitude of the Christian world for the evangelical propaganda they have established on Staten Island in the grand ballet, *Nero*."[116] It is a striking statement, since Kiralfy and his family were of Jewish descent. Although when Kiralfy shortly settled in Britain, he gained social prestige and important patronage for his new projects through joining the Grand Lodge of Freemasons and mingling among the aristocracy, including the Duke of Cambridge.

The stage was a medium of faith for Imre. To understand his worldview, one only has the evidence of his earliest memories as a child growing up in Budapest, where he not only experienced ethnic discrimination, but witnessed from his doorstep the 1849 Austrian invasion and occupation of his homeland. Terror and totalitarianism were repressive forces to unite against. But he also came of age in the abundance of European artistic experiment and scientific advance. The statuesque merger of technology and art, symbolized by the Eiffel Tower (1889), announced the "miracles" of modern life. Imre's outlook consistently personified a forward-looking spirit of optimism, independence, and equality that could overcome intolerance, enslavement, and fear.

Kiralfy fed the historical imagination with the splendors of citizenship. Belonging to the momentum of global infrastructure, he exported immersive memorials of independence, possibility, and individual achievement in an idiom of entertainment brandscape. With *Babylon* and *Nero*, he served his audiences a banquet. Corporate ideology was assimilated into landscaped habitats of machine-made beauty and material worth. As ferries shuttled back and forth in New York harbor to St. George, the recently dedicated Statue of Liberty (1886) watched over the masses assembling on the shore. At that very moment, on stage and off, the crowds could feel the United States taking its place within Western civilization. Imre served his audiences *the popular want*, the exhilaration of feeling a shared history, the immediacy of a land created out of individual labor and sacrifice, the sensation of hope, of a commonality that allowed a polyglot of people to believe that they were part of this new wondrous world, part of its future, part of the myth. On the other side of the continent, the Grand Canyon branded the United States a monumental nation of common possession. The reiterated ideal recalling the quest of historical destiny infused corporate interests in wilderness heritage. Both sides forage to supply destination networks that promise experiential renewal.[117]

Envisioning Global Environments

Imre transported his worldview throughout Western Europe. He easily adapted the political content depending on the country he was working in. Kiralfy was fully involved in exhibition design in London by 1889, exerting an influential connection in transitions from industrial exhibitions to cultural centers. His exhibition work continued to promote a multinational climate of exchange. The impetus he brought to exhibition planning consolidated production concepts honed in spectacle entertainment that served the dominant political economy yet expressed global citizenship. While settled in Great Britain, he gained the social prestige that appears to have eluded him in the United States. He was enlisted as a consultant on the British sections of exhibitions outside the country. His travels took him to exhibitions in Antwerp (1895), Hungary, Dresdon, Nurnberg, Berlin, Genoa, Copenhagen (1896); Brussels, Nashville (1897); Omaha (1898), Paris (1900); and Buffalo (1901).

In London, Kiralfy experimented with the notion of mixed-use cultural complexes with multiple attractions. He acquired the lease at Earl's Court. There, he staged nine multinational theme exhibitions between 1893 and 1903, working with a consortium of exhibitors. Patronage for his private projects came through associations among the aristocracy. The Grand Lodge of England's Freemasons awarded Kiralfy with the honor of Commander of the Order of Leopold in 1905. Initially, Kiralfy's vision fixated on creating an international repertory network of theatres in Paris, London, New York, and Venice. [118] Global commerce dovetailed with international exhibition schemes pushed by organs of business federations, especially the British Empire League to take advantage of industrial exhibitions as a vehicle to prepare the public for national expansion. The British Empire League was a turn-of-the century society operating as board of commerce to secure industrial networks, trade policies, technology, communications systems, military protection, and banking regulations in British-held colonies.[119]

Earl's Court was originally established as a pleasure garden by John Robinson Whitley in 1887. Whitley held ideas of launching cultural destinations derived from Victorian sociology of international social capitalism. The main impetus for Whitley was the marriage of internationalism, education, and trade as a means to socialize the masses.[120] Creating interdependent buyers and consumers of imported and exported goods was believed to lessen international conflict. Earl's Court stemmed from theory but became widespread practice. Kiralfy was able to experiment and test out ideas he encountered visiting and working at numerous international exhibitions throughout Europe and the United States. He established a consortium of exhibitors with selective exhibition themes designed to present a quartet of "Life Pictures" of colonial "empires," such as America, Italy, France, and

Germany, to show the people of England how foreigners lived.[121] Kiralfy was put off by static object classification of exhibition layout. He brainstormed ways to market mass tourism by staging resort destinations theatrically. Hotel owners would have the opportunity of seeing what foreigners do. His marketing strategy saw a chance for hotel owners to gain consumer feedback while advertising their own resorts. He thought a less monotonous style of exhibiting culture would attract railway or steamship companies. One conception he picked up along his travels were fantasy spaces replicating world sites and pleasure resorts.

Fantasy habitats, reproducing medieval castles or legends, were temporary structures wrapped with panoramic painted views and infused with scented oils. The objective was to envelope visitors in exotic environments. Kiralfy gleaned the idea from a visit to the 1896 Budapest Millennium Exhibition where this type of *Pokol* was the rage. A temporary circular structure of wood, canvas, and stucco was a one-third scale reproduction of Buda Castle as it may have looked under Turkish occupation during the Middle Ages. During the day, it was refreshment house; at night, it became a watering hole for Budapest society and the demi-monde. It was said to be a favorite haunt of King Edward VII.[122] "History is no longer a matter of dates and "dry-as-dust" facts," one of Kiralfy's later guide books states. "We see its progress in the wonderful collections of relics and treasures, and we realize its meaning in the results pictured for us. Geography, previously a science of maps and lines becomes an entrancing pastime, a magic carpet taking us to scenes and lands of which we have only dreamt."[123]

Kiralfy introduced season tickets and discount rail/entrance fees at Earl's Court, which opened from May to October from 11:30 am to 11:30 pm. Within the grounds, garden areas were surrounded by 50 ft high scenic backdrops hiding nearby houses. Panoramic backdrops were used and repainted with appropriate landscape vistas for each exhibition.[124] The illuminated grounds held thousands of gas and electric light designed by James Pain and Co.[125] At night the whole area was lit with a reported million fairy lights. The permanent, specially built six-thousand-seat Empress theatre ran two shows daily. Museum exhibits and an amusement park featuring a 300 ft Ferris Wheel encouraged visitors to spend the day. Landscape gardens and lakes were interspersed with exhibition halls and restaurants. Restaurants drew fashionable crowds from London Society. *Venice in London*, a site-specific spectacle first seen at the Olympic, London

(1891/1893), was the first show presented there. It was composed of one-third replicas of many of Venice's tourist attractions, including the Bridge of Sighs, and a variety of industrial exhibits, including a working glass-blowing "factory." [126] In 1895, Kiralfy celebrated British colonial rule in India as part of his "Empire of India" exhibition on the grounds of the garden with a massive production of *India* staged in the Empress Theatre.[127]

In 1898, Kiralfy returned to the United States to stage a *Grand Naval Spectacle* at Madison Square Garden. American military propaganda added to his international repertory of "empire" spectacles. Well aware of linkage to past genres of nautical entertainment and fresh forms of naval shows held in Berlin, Stockholm, Brussels, and London, he conceptualized a "history lesson" on the "American naval victories" in the Spanish-American War.[128] United States intervention into Cuban independence from Spain triggered events that escalated the conflict. In its aftermath, Kiralfy coordinated with Frank W. Sanger, manager of Madison Square Garden, and Lieutenant Commander Chenery of the US Navy and officers of the battleship *Texas* to reconstruct key battle scenes of the US blockade of Cuba and Commodore George Dewey's tactical maneuvers to secure Manila Bay.

Kiralfy's ongoing augmentations to site-specific installation synthesized international practices into his vision of cultural commerce. The British Empire League enlisted him to manage a single national Empire exhibition; instead, the Victorian model gave way to multinational arenas. At the helm, Kiralfy instituted a series of bi-national exhibitions between 1908 and 1914. As Director General, Kiralfy formed a management company, and gentrified a twenty-four acre site into a permanent entertainment destination. The company, "Exhibitions Ltd." raised capital, negotiated expansion of rail lines, and replaced temporary structures with permanent buildings at a leased site on the outskirts of West London, Shepherd's Bush.[129] On May 25, 1908, the first in a series of "allied" expositions formally opened at what came to be known as the Great White City. Promoting a new era of diplomatic accord between France and Great Britain known as *Entente Cordiale*, King Edward VII and President Armand Fallières of France arrived at the fair grounds to the playing of the Marseillaise before leading a procession of two-hundred dignitaries and committee members for their entry into the Court of Honor. The Franco-British exhibition evolved from the economic stance that international commerce could promote international peace. King

Edward VII supported the enterprise to "promote an undertaking which has for its object an increase in commercial prosperity"[130] The site of Shepherd's Bush was leased and designed as a permanent exhibition venue, privately financed and institutionally organized.

The ensuing binational exhibitions marked diplomatic and trade agreements to secure continental alliances in Africa, the Americas, Asia, and the Pacific toward calculated commercial expansion and non-interference with colonial territories. The Franco-British exhibition was followed by the Anglo-Japanese Exhibition in 1910, marking a critical trade agreement. The Latin-British Exhibition of 1912 showcased the trans-Atlantic reach of industrial allies with the important trade economies of Argentina and Brazil representing South America.[131] On the eve of World War I, the 1914 Anglo-American Exhibition wistfully looked back over a century of peace and progress between the two nations, only to close within two months when War broke out.

The 120-acre Great White City included 120 exhibition buildings and 20 pavilions for participating countries and merchants. The principal buildings were constructed from steel and concrete, then ornamented with stucco domes and arabesque arches. Many of the ideas integrated into the design were influenced by Chicago's World's Columbian Exposition's White City, where Kiralfy produced his other blockbuster spectacle *Columbus and the Discovery of America*. By 1911, concessions included tea stalls, cigarette kiosks, and seventeen different restaurants—frequented nightly by London Society.[132] Available to all, imported fine goods from Brazilian coffee to French chocolate and Turkish tobacco. Season tickets were popular; each exhibition spiked tourism to the city by participating countries. At Merryland, a Luna park styled amusement area, the ever-popular Flip-Flap swung riders 200 ft (60 meters) up in the air. An estimated 8.5 million people attended the first exhibition, although attendance dropped by 1914.

The six international exhibitions Kiralfy organized were the culmination of his work where "spectacle and exhibition were fused into one self-choreographing show."[133] Such site-specific perspectives route the entertainment landscape at intersections of a conceptual economy. The destination spectacle burrowed into desires to create anew. Traveling into historical identity returned a transformative embodiment of possibility. Yellowstone National Park encapsulated pioneer legacies, raising the profile of US expansion internationally while laying permanent trails for Western tourism. Imre Kiralfy gave corporate agendas inroads to resituate cultural trade and consumer exchange in site-specific venues that branded progressive mythology. As bookends in the industrial era, scenic life remounted the experiential proportions of circulating viewpoints without physical or temporal restraints. The fragmented idioms of historical "nature" immersed feelings in the conceptual framework of production effects, the tricks of the trade. Government involvement in exhibition practices forges an adjacent domain in site-specific productions. Exhibition events in the US showcase the interactive role of administrative coordinates entering cultural affairs. Institutional entities establish a new context for the changing borders of political economy.

Nationalized exhibitions promote a robust international exchange of industrial exploration. These momentary, seasonal show lands pulsated with the now, of crossing into a new realm of modernization. Over time exhibition "specs" articulate changing scenes of socioeconomic momentum. The descriptive display houses of contemporary inventions, products, and merchandise typical of early nineteenth-century industrial expositions migrated into multifaceted threads of midways, amusement parks, and metropolitan splendors of the international city in concept fairs by the turn of the century. By the first decades of the twentieth century, multinational fairs blanketed the landscape with stupendous cultural complexes.

4

Theme Scenes: Producing Global Strategies on US Exhibition Stages

The United States intensified diplomatic negotiations to secure inroads into competitive multinational trade networks between 1876 and 1916. During this push into global economies government-authorized world's fairs were held in Philadelphia (1876), New Orleans (1884–1885), Chicago (1893), Atlanta (1895), Nashville (1897), South Carolina (1901), Omaha (1901), St. Louis (1904), Portland (1905), Jamestown (1907), Seattle (1909), San Francisco (1915), and San Diego (1916). Of pivotal importance is the Philadelphia Centennial Exposition. On July 3, 1873, President Ulysses S. Grant pressed the US seal on a bill authorizing the appointment of an independent corporate council to manage it. His stamp of approval beckoned the marriage of trade and global expansion. The Philadelphia Centennial was largely planned by moderate Republicans from the Northeast and Midwest. Majority party objectives allied with President Grant's heated policies over protecting (the appearance of) equal rights, currency regulation, and separation of church and state to boost industrial output and strategically acquire noncontiguous territories.[1] Marking the hundred-year anniversary of the democratic revolution, the "great exhibition" proclaimed the industrial revolution underway.

The Philadelphia Centennial initiated a major shift from single building exhibition sites to immersive grounds in which visitors moved through a self-reflecting, dynamic, and ever changing landscape. "How long will it take to see everything thoroughly" was the question asked when the massive international exposition opened. "At least a month," came the reply.[2] Covering 485 acres, the geographical installation of the exhibition reassembled the mythic synergy of wilderness and settlement popularized in earlier panoramic media. In the fair's wake, government-sponsored exhibitions successively swept through the South, Midwest, and West, each designing scenes of current socioeconomic habitation. Chicago's World's Columbian Exposition, stylizing the architectural gloss of the symbolic "White City," is perhaps the most recognized. In equal proportion, the New Orleans Cotton Centennial Exposition, and the San Francisco Panama-Pacific International Exposition correspond to a procession of regional redevelopment—East to West and North to South—asserting sectional difference in large-scale geopolitical destinations. The New Orleans organization was forged out of a minority (party) coalition of state, city, and private interests to elevate interstate business by drawing investment to Southern industries, while deepening trade relations with South America; the San Francisco exhibition was spearheaded by the city's business community to invent a "new West" and relocate the Pacific states as a destined crossroads of the "universe."[3] These cultural landscapes tease out the changing aims of political economy in the *in situ* materialization of new scenes. US exhibition "specs" bounce off a far ranging background of "old world' exhibition spaces. Considering how industry-minded ambitions gain social traction, the production strategies of the Philadelphia Centennial supply one context to contemplate the adaptive vantage points of institutional creativity. The alternate configurations of the New Orleans Centennial and San Francisco Panama-Pacific International Exposition accent other organizational means trafficking large-scale cultural migration.

Robert Rydell's valued work on American world's fairs describes the overarching function of nineteenth-century expositions in consolidating moral standards in a symbolic universe. Rydell develops an interpellation of civilian order perpetuated by elite political and intellectual perspectives. The exertion of hegemonic power, he writes, "is the normal means of state control in a pluralistic society."[4] His concerns unravel racial assumptions structuring ethnographies lining fair culture. Yet, the binding "universal" or totalizing construct attached to nomenclature from exhibition culture obscures the particular geopolitical nuances of these nineteenth- and early twentieth-century assemblages. Versatility and compact messaging make exhibition environments, Alfred Alles argues, effective dispersal systems that stem from variety of marking objectives and range of marketing techniques."[5] Administrative tactics coincide with changing power shares in political economy, which can be seen as a discursive set of practices. Another way to view the regional aims of exhibition cultures is within an active diplomacy of geopolitical circumstances. As producing organizations, administrative ideologies adjudicate a participatory presence in spectacle tradition.

Theme Space and the Economies of US Exhibitions

Initially, government-appointed commissions functioned as independent producing corporations working in concert with majority political objectives. Toward the latter half of the nineteenth century, exhibition management operates more as an ad hoc consortium of producing agents challenging majority interests. In the first decades the twentieth century prior to World War I, exhibition companies absorb profit-making margins into fair culture. In the march from the Atlantic to the Pacific, Northeast manufacturing, Southern mining and iron works, the Midwest farm belt, and Western ports resituate regional independence by reforming a US worldview. "Multiple modernities" open a framework in mainstream modernization, argues Shmuel N. Eisenstadt, toward disassembling Westernization as a singular globalizing practice of industrial progress.[6] In respect to this notion, US management practices further distinguish cultural differences. They respond to fluid, competitive situations, and adapt conventional methodology to redirect economic shares in local, national, and global markets. Andrew Slap recounts in his history of the postbellum Republican reform movement how liberal republicans understood political parties as short-lived organizations advocating change.[7] Institutional forums express a similar ongoing advocacy. In the compositions of fair sites, different management models set renovation in motion.

The rise of a "new American culture" over the nineteenth century in William Leach's determination summoned consumer power as ethical.[8] US exhibition sites lather the scenic values for the American way of life into a spectacular ethos. These tangible yet impermanent environments resituate economic conditions to propel forward momentum. In planning, exhibition producers dramatize a short-term effect that instates long-term objectives. Augmentations to the production values of exposition "spaces" increasingly hyphenate media platforms. Installation design adopted many trends found in zoos, performance, and museums display. Amusement parks, three-dimensional dioramas, moving panoramas, midways, and natural history habitat tableaux carried into theme space—a synthetic spatial construct elaborated by Eric Ames in terms of fabricating natural environments.[9]

Theme space merges real and imaginary elements to engage sensible interaction. In Ames theory, this type of geographical habitat lodges spectatorship in live immersion. Exhibition administrators extend vigorous investment in erecting interactive attractions, inviting the spectator-citizen to wade among automated sensibilities, geographical proximity, and technological animation.

While theme spaces expound new sites to inhabit, the more nebulous thematics converging in large-scale patterns compound a tricky intermedial sensibility molding exhibition geography. Alexander C. T. Geppert's recent study of fin de siècle European expositions points to the intercommunication of exhibition networks as "a transitory yet recurrent meta-media," establishing internal and external traditions.[10] Particularities of local economies, political systems, and administrative goals trying to influence public agency dwell in transformative circumstances. Production themes compose the appearance of a new "scene." Thematically forecasting the "World of Tomorrow," the 1939 New York World Exposition swallowed the despair of the Depression era by cuing up the next wave of technological ascendency, the coming telecommunications revolution.[11] In 1876, the Philadelphia Centennial Exposition management believed the economic accomplishments of its fair were yet to be seen: "the material benefits accruing from the Exhibition are manifold, and will be realized for years to come."[12] Following the Philadelphia Centennial, exhibition producers parallel the widening grip of corporate and private enterprise agitating for governing powers. Trade organizations, chambers of commerce, and "amusement enterprises" asserted greater visibility in administrating exhibitions for specific industries, for publicizing political alliances, to launch competitive initiatives, or to market tourism. Transmigrations of exhibitions over the nineteenth century and into the early twentieth century seed local and external infrastructure that expose the decline of insular national economies and colonial holdings of empire.

Thematic Models of Nationalized Industrial Fairs

Models of trade fairs date back to the bustling market places of the eleventh and twelfth centuries held at well-trafficked intersections. Migrating conventions radiate into and out of these communal spaces of commercial activity. The debut of a formal trade exhibition is credited to one held in a town hall in Nuremberg in 1569.[13] Credit

for an official public exhibition aimed at manipulating national
sentiment occurred in Paris amidst the turmoil of the French
Revolution. In an effort to prop up the failing monarchy, the Marquis
d'Avize was appointed Commissioner to organize an exhibit of royal
manufactures.[14] The sale of Sevres porcelain, Gobelins tapestries,
and Savonnerie carpets attempted to shore up revenue and contain
unemployment. Planning was interrupted when the nobility was
banished from the country by decree of the Directory. However, the
Marquis returned a year later. In 1797, he organized an exhibition at
the Museum D'Orsay of aristocratic finery that wetted popular taste
for "beautiful and rare objects."[15] It was immediately followed by
an official government-sponsored public installation that successfully
celebrated the refinement of French culture with the most magnificent
examples of domestic fine art, manufacturing, and merchandise.

The graphic industrial themes of nationalized exhibitions communicate underlining schemas aiding commercial redevelopment and
gentrification. Early nineteenth-century exhibition grounds needed to
be within seaport and railroad access to transport building materials, labor, foreign exhibitors and exhibits, products, and later visitors.
Initially, European monarchies set aside the use of Royal Parks within
city centers, investing in urban reform. Queen Victoria granted use of
centrally accessible Hyde Park for the London 1851 exhibition. The
Vienna Exposition of 1873 was held at the immense Royal Park, the
Prater. A site-specific transportation system was developed that ran
various train tracks to the grounds from a carriage park on the perim-
eter.[16] The Philadelphia Centennial would use a similar light rail to
carry visitors within the exhausting exhibition grounds. In France,
the use of public land symbolized fraternal sentiments. The Champ de
Mars on the Left Bank of the Seine in central Paris was used numerous
times: 1798, 1867, 1878, 1889, and 1900. Within view of the Eiffel
Tower—a central feature of the 1889 exposition—portions of public
green space were used as the drilling grounds of the Ecole Militare.
Once the site of the beheading of the first mayor of Paris Jean Sylvian
Bailly in 1791 and the gathering place for Bastille Day festivals celebrating the revolution, the historic blood stained grounds of the new
republic ebbed into a central tourist district.[17]

In the United States, land was leased or transferred from municipality to exhibition management. State and corporate investors
of the Philadelphia Centennial capitalized on the use of a section
of the two-thousand acre Fairmount Park to upgrade accessibility
within the city, to expand rail and steamship transportation, and

build new roads.[18] The Pennsylvania Railroad controlled most of the passenger traffic to the exhibition. A new terminal was erected opposite the exhibition site to convey passengers directly to the main entrance. The Philadelphia, Wilmington & Baltimore Railroad had exclusive control of the South and Southwest. A Northeast regional line brought visitors from New York and New Jersey. The Philadelphia and Reading Railroad built a station within the exhibition grounds to accommodate visitors from Central and Western Pennsylvania. The site of the New Orleans Cotton Centennial was located on a former plantation purchased by the city of New Orleans in 1871. With tourism one of the objectives, a commuter electric railway was built to comfortably bring visitors the six miles from the city to the exhibition grounds.[19] One visitor guide sketched downtown points of interest contributing to the "future" of the city with a section devoted to retail advertising.[20] Exhibits on the grounds featured commuter and regional railroad companies, national banks, and insurance companies set up within state zones to market interstate services. Rebuilding the infrastructure of San Francisco for commercial investment went into planning for the Panama-Pacific exhibition. Initial plans to engineer an urban boulevard from Golden Gate Park to the Harbor proved too difficult to realize. An undeveloped stretch of land on the San Francisco Bay was settled on by the directors. Designated a marshy strip of "waste land," the wetland was dredged and filled; seventy-six city blocks with over four hundred existing buildings were demolitioned under agreement that exhibition management insure complete restoration. [21]

The spread of geocentric exhibitions launched in the mid-nineteenth century relocated separate working economies to heterogeneous scenes of productivity. One imposing feature of exhibition space as it shifts locations is how the comingling of art, science, technology, and industry formulate a currency of the good—as comfort, convenience, improvement—and the beautiful—as material splendors and currency. Producing creeds motivated public attraction to discriminate among cultural powers within competing domains of economic growth and geopolitical influence.

The landmark London Exhibition of 1851 was sanctioned by a Royal Commission, chaired by Prince Albert for the purpose of comparative instruction, with the support of the Queen, government, and aristocracy. Funding was raised by subscriptions collected from exhibitors, merchants, bankers, and traders. Members of the Society of Arts, an academic council, were instrumental in its planning and execution. Clearly, the prime symbol of the rising middle class was the architectural marvel of Sir Joseph Paxton's publically approved design of the Crystal Palace.[22] The architecture deposited an urban zone in an agrarian landscape. The single building of prefabricated iron, glass, and wood rose above the treetops of Hyde Park, with the majestic sweep of a grand indoor promenade.

Classification systems supplied critical logic to graphic themes. Descriptive categories synthesized plot points for visitors, reinforcing systemic references to the speed and convenience of industrial processes, scientific technique, and technological innovation. In London, contributors were grouped into six divisions: raw materials, manufactures of textiles and metals, mechanical inventions, and applied arts.[23] Its hierarchical ligature accorded social importance to applied science and manufacturing. The statuesque placement of machinery in large galleries lent sculptural form to the hard geometrics of "working" metal objects. British exhibitors and foreign exhibitors were separated. Visitors were thus guided according to predetermined coordinates that magnified the ranking of what was on view.

The aristocratic wrapping of the "Palace," decorated with colored banners, encased commercial wealth as material productivity. The interior layout of the Crystal Palace also framed a linear display hall, cataloguing the processes and methods by which natural resources became agricultural and manufactured goods. Traffic flowed back and forth along a wide avenue, with a spatial repetition of galleries. The promenade through empire allowed visitors consecutive rows of "windows" or viewpoints to survey, to become familiar with strange new technology, to compare the latest luxury imports, to see and be seen in one place. The spatial framework articulated an empirical geography of colonial cohabitation. The spectator not only had an external vantage point to explore a consolidated domain, but was also an active part of the internal circumstance.

The Victorian model of the empire exhibition summoned the producing energy of a growing middle class. It excited social appetites for the beneficent rationale of international cooperation to support trade expansion during a period of peace. The façade of aristocratic authority held up under wider deliberations with private interests to graft civilian sensibilities on industrial majesty. Its unitary form expressed the legacy of imperial nationalism; its impetus triggered embryonic components of globalization.

Government-supported expositions spawned a similar pattern in linear spatial design and classification system in Dublin (1853) Munich

(1854), and Paris (1855) over the next decade. The first US universal exposition took place in New York in 1853. It was housed within a single two story "Crystal Palace" designed by the firm of (Georg J. B.) Carstensen and (Charles) Gildemeister.[24] New York's Crystal Palace's dazzling statement was a central rotunda with a dome 100 ft high. The circular dome was joined by the Latting Observatory tower, where visitors could enjoy panoramic views of the city. The 315 ft tower was the tallest silhouette on the horizon, forecasting the vertical ascent of the city's architecture. Already momentum for the metropolitan "high rise" was appearing in the form of elegant and multileveled "commercial palaces."[25] Inside the exhibition space, the 360-degree views around the circular rotunda, vertical ascent, and horizontal halls opened panoramic sight lines in contrast to the linear system used in European exhibition structures. Rather than movement through a horizontal spatial realm, democratic space circulated in all directions.

The 1853 New York fair promoted the "Work's and Industries of All Nations." Robert Post treats the event as a manufacturing wonderland of invention and authoritative scientific discovery that "heralded the moment in US history when science and technology modulated from a minor to a major key."[26] Public support for the exposition waned over its first season, marking its legacy as a financial failure. [27] Behind the scenes trade partnerships established precedents that stretch through the postbellum decades. Cooperative efforts between US Trade Commissions and a private consortium of New Yorkers with close ties to Wall Street, Washington, and London made the fair possible. Edward Riddle, the American Commissioner in London, returned from that city's exposition eager to gather interest in a US version. August Belmont, Alexander Hamilton Jr, J. J. Roosevelt, William Cullen Bryant, and Theodore Sedgwick were among the socialites, politicians, legal reformers, literary luminaries, and business executives entering into collaboration to launch the exhibition.[28] They formed an independent corporation, the Crystal Palace Association. Riddle helped to secure a lease on undeveloped rural land four miles north of the city boundary and garnered legislation to proceed.[29] Capital was raised through the efforts of a Board of Directors by the sale of stocks to individuals and companies.[30]

Opposition to a proposed allowance admitting foreign goods tariff free raised a recurrent debate over free market policies being hostile to domestic industry.[31] The red tape was cut by Federal presence acting on behalf of the Association. A waiver of import duties to encourage foreign trade was arranged through Secretary of State Daniel Webster, who also used foreign consulates to promote participation.[32] The polemics of party politics intensified partisan goals over expansionism. Daniel Walker Howe elaborates the moral imperatives guiding divisive notions of conquest in the antebellum period: geopolitical assimilation or domestic appropriation.[33] Jeffersonian Democrats mostly from Southern and Midwest states argued for enforced protectionism of internal territorial expansion as a means of harvesting natural resources. Northeastern Whigs sought principles based on economic improvement that exerted trade relations and missionary influence "through example."[34] In his capacity at the State Department Daniel Webster "put Whig principles of foreign policy into practice by both resolving tensions with Britain and extending US commercial opportunities in the Pacific."[35] The New York exposition served a Whig agenda that created a portal for a colonizing methodology of "economic and cultural imperialism."[36] Newly elected President Franklin Pierce straddled party divisions by holding forth a constitutional stance on states' rights but launched an administrative policy that backed expansion to secure national growth for "commercial preservation and world peace."[37] On opening day July 14, the presence of President Pierce, cabinet members, Governors, bishops, and judges ceremoniously endorsed a private enterprise with the united front of government, church, and state. International involvement came from countries in Western Europe (Germany, Austria, Great Britain, Sweden, and Belgium) that suited trade relations with desirable colonial partners, as well as to draw in immigrant labor. If public support flagged, private interests took over the government lead in waging incentive arguments in the press and in Congress for and against participation in overseas exhibitions. The 1867 Paris International Exposition threw open that door.

The Paris exhibition, strategically dedicated to the "History of Labor," weighted the event with a monolithic symbolism. Imperial control of the Bonaparte dynasty under Emperor Napoleon's Second Empire was limping toward its end. Beset by a budget crisis, economic downturn in trade, foreign policy and military failures, pressure to relax censorship, and an agitating working class, Napoleon III negotiated with nationalists, populists, and liberals in order to balance his hold on power. "Why should not commercial and industrial affairs assume a new development," he argued in an opening session speech to the French Chamber of Deputies."[38] To that end, economic reforms meant to increase agricultural, commercial, and industrial production involved subsidized tariff reductions and diplomatic negotiations to "contract" commerce treaties with England and neighboring countries in order to facilitate "everywhere the means of communication and of transport."[39] The Paris International took place in a climate of anxious foreign and domestic diplomacy against a backdrop of economic and social turmoil. In June 1863, by imperial decree, the dramatic impetus of the Paris International set out to prophesize a new era of harmony and progress, idealized in the geospatial union of an "agglomeration and confederation of great nations."[40]

Frédéric Le Play oversaw the construction of an oval exhibition palace for the fair, resembling the Roman Coliseum. [41] It was as much a monument to shore up the imperial legacy of Napoleon III as it was a structural concept of bringing all countries—one might say all knowledge—into view under one roof. This fractured universe, still clinging to a mythic totality, emitted multiplicity. The main exhibition building was laid out in a grid system.[42] Its wide oval concourse was inset with seven concentric halls, conceived as architectural abstractions of the Northern and Southern hemispheres.[43] The main exhibition space was largely dedicated to French exhibitors, who made up one fifth of the fifteen-thousand participants. Foreign exhibitors were housed in the adjoining halls. The segments of the building divided participating countries like "slices of cake."[44] Segregation by sectional "blocks" articulated geopolitical passageways through ethnographic division. The 10–15 million French attendees, who made up the major portion of spectators, could in effect tour different countries. The layered traffic allowed visitors to browse the main avenue or move in and out of various national displays within a single multidimensional space. In addition to the monograph of communicating "domains," the complex of intersections energized a public habitat of spectatorship as a reflexive theme of colonial occupation. The ring design stood in palatial splendor to the surrounding park grounds of the Champ de Mars. France, Germany, Belgium, and England, the four industrial pillars of Europe, each received a quadrant on the grounds. Spotted with individual pavilions erected by exhibiting nations, inviting refreshment booths, and a hot air balloon ride, the park supplied a "natural" populist atmosphere contingent to the palatial luxuries filling the internal avenues.[45]

Beneath the surface of propaganda, the thematic stratagem set out a competitive showcase of "industrial wealth."[46] The theme of the Paris exhibition stressed the country's lineage and contributions to civilization. Citizenship from the Imperial Commission's point of view was illustrated in an expansive account on the history of labor, for which material deriving from the Stone Age up to the nineteenth century was made available. Emphasis on social productivity wedded cultural supremacy to modernity. The hydraulic elevator was one of the primary technical inventions on display. Unlike London's industrial exhibition, which did not list prices, consumer goods and artisan products were marketed. A comprehensive classification system was introduced that divided civil industries into ten umbrella categories that governed catalog layouts. Fine and commercial art held top designation, followed by household furnishing and appliances, clothing, and applied arts. In an attempt to ease apprehensions and reestablish domestic confidence in the Second Empire regime, the "active care" of working class interests publicized how industry and cultural sensitivity improves affordable housing, quality of life, and education. The "universal" creed of the vehicle ministered to the French imperial agenda. A primary motive politically was a final grasp at consoling flailing social and political relationships alongside retention of old world aspirations. Napoleon III called the "momentary brilliancy" of the exhibition an occasion that cast off the past. [47] The Second Empire soon followed.

Merle Curti relates that opposition to US participation at the Paris exposition in political circles was broken down by arguments over the social and economic good it would accomplish. The desire to "publicize the nation's resources, industries, and social and economic institutions," was one motive. Elevating the status of Northeastern commercial industries in Europe was another.[48] Secretary of State William Henry Seward presented a report recommending participation on economic grounds to President Andrew Johnson.[49] Expansionist preferences set in motion Congressional support. Members of New York's Chamber of Commerce (1866) were urged by Executive Committee Chair Elliot C. Cowdin to join in.[50] Cowdin had attended exhibitions in Paris (1855) and London (1862). The influential importer of fine French silks and accessories spoke passionately at length, arguing the benefits of acquiring technology, machinery, and skilled labor to boost domestic production not only from "large capitalists of Europe but also from those of smaller means." US participation in Paris secured the viability of American manufacturing as an alternative source of production in world markets. When the Franco-Prussian war broke out in 1870, US arms manufacturers and other branches of trade, having exhibited in Paris, increased exports.[51]

Cowdin raised a call for action during his speech to his business associates to secure global territories: "A continent is ours midway between Europe and Asia in a position to serve and control both. Crowned with the victories of war, and, holding such a position, shall we fear any conflict?"[52] His confident prediction of the country's commercial supremacy infiltrates the worldview of US diplomacy that braces exhibition scenes. The official theme of the Panama-Pacific International Exposition celebrated the opening of the Panama Canal as a "union of the world seas" (under US shipping control). The historic moment securing US pathways to new commercial settlements and geopolitical alliances dominated publicity. The "world character" of the United States jettisoned forth into every hemisphere, unchained by continental landmass, annihilating distance while binding Europe, the Americas, and Asia into "one brotherhood" fulfilling "world-commerce, world-friendship, and world-peace."[53] Before that, the Philadelphia exposition unfurled a bird's eye view (Figure 4.1) of the mounting quest.

Figure 4.1 Bird's Eye View of Philadelphia and Centennial Grounds, 1875.

Source: Print. John Bachman, Popular Graphic Arts, Library of Congress, Prints and Photographs Division.

The Great Exhibition

The idea of a commemorative exhibition had been raised by a professor from Wabash College, Indiana, John L. Campbell in the wake of the Civil War.[54] General Charles B. Norton, an appointed commissioner to the Paris world's fair, was among the first to enlist political and civilian leadership in Philadelphia to endorse an international exhibition. Momentum for accessing international markets started to build in the Northeast. The Franklin Institute of Philadelphia, an academy of applied science and mechanical arts, drafted a proposal to the municipality of the city for the use of Fairmount Park. Once the city agreed, a Council was formed led by Campbell, Norton, John Bigelow, and M. Richards Mucklé. With backing of the state legislature, a bill was brought before Congress by Pennsylvania Congressman Daniel J. Morrell, another early advocate of the exhibition. The Chairmen of the House Committee on Manufactures, Morrell made his fortune and reputation from iron manufacturing. He was later elected to serve on the Executive Committee of the Centennial Commission.

Congress passed an Act on March 3, 1871 legally incorporating the US Centennial Commission to independently author the commemoration of a one-hundred year celebration under the auspices of the government of the United States. The bill stipulated that the Commission consist of "not more than one delegate" from each state and from each territory of the United States. With passage of the act of incorporation, Congress retained financial oversight in order to guard against failure in an undertaking concerning "national dignity and prestige."[55] A point of friction over passage of the bill involved whether or not government funds would be appropriated toward the projected ten million dollar cost. Section 7 of the bill was amended to assure that the US Government "shall not be liable for any expenses."[56] Most of the startup revenue was raised from corporate and private subscriptions in Pennsylvania, including $500,000 from railroad companies with offices in Philadelphia, and a one million appropriations bill brought before the State Legislature.[57]

The appointed President of the Commission was General Joseph R. Hawley. Hawley had a distinguished resume among Republicans: Civil War veteran in the Federal Army, former Connecticut Governor, respected journalist and editor of the *Hartford Evening Press*, as well a staunch member of the antislavery "Free Soil" party before the war. He was a leading member of the (progressive) "regular," as opposed to (reactionary) liberal Republican Party, that first nominated Grant to candidacy of the party's bid in the 1868 election.[58] Hawley managed a "congress" of committees, directors, bureaus, and departments under the banner of the Centennial Commission, whose officers represented important commercial networks of the country, from manufacturing to shipping.[59] The Commission replicated a government institution, which it also served. It acted as a centralized voice of the governing entity. The degree of "representation" was exclusively white, socially prominent, and politically connected. The model established a governing structure with three main branches: Commissioners, Executive, and Board of Finance. Constituent committees and subcommittees were bound in a legislative system of checks and balances by a separation of powers. The organ of a centralized administration coordinated the moving parts of each division to accord with the Centennial theme. Its unseen authority granted this particular partisan entity oversight on budget, contract negotiations, and translating corporate, municipal, and political objectives into a consensual realization of cultural revenue. The practical operations of the core internal committees were carried out by the Director General Alfred T. Goshorn. The Cincinnati manufacturer, owner of white lead factories, was elected by the Executive Committee. All subcommittees, bureaus, and departments reported to him.[60]

Although the concentration of power was held by the executive boards at the Centennial, they executed government mandates. Routine procedural processes moved slowly through administrative chambers. Internally, committees had to find middle ground within private deliberations. Decisions were transmitted in regular reports to Congress and faced continuous press coverage. An initial logjam was the architectural plans, which took eight months to resolve.[61] Public scrutiny dogged decisions. The appointments of Commissioners and the financial organization of the Centennial took two years to settle. A second bill was passed by Congress on June 1, 1872 authorizing the election of a Board of Finance to raise the estimated ten million dollars from state and city subscriptions. Public stock at $10 shares were offered to raise a third of the estimate.[62] Seventy-one year old John Welsh, of the Philadelphia shipping firm J. &W. Welsh, was unanimously elected to chair the Board. The composition of the elected Board, "curiously" consisting of local Philadelphia bankers, politicians, and businessmen, fueled cries of political manipulation and demands for resignations.[63] The Commission defended the election by reporting that the availability of local residents assured a quorum of members would always be present at meetings.[64] The lack of representation on the Board from major "trade" and finance" centers: Chicago, St. Louis, Cincinnati, New Orleans, and San Francisco generated distrust and skepticism toward the exhibition that affected subscription projections. Each of these cities held government-authorized fairs between 1893 and 1915 that magnified historical linkage to national status.[65] St. Louis held the 1904 Louisiana Purchase International Exposition in commemoration of the one-hundred year anniversary of the land acquisition by the US through which the Missouri territory became the portal to Westward expansion. Hosting the first Olympic Games in the US, the fair reasserted the city's pioneering profile as a gateway of the national enterprise.[66]

While state and city support behind the project moved cautiously, the public campaign of resurfacing a united national landscape began with the official transfer of 450 acres of Fairmount Park by the city of Philadelphia to the Centennial Commission. On July 4, 1873 amid great pomp, municipal land was turned over to a corporate division of private individuals.[67] President Grant did not appear at the ceremony due to the death of his father a week earlier. His administration's second term was under duress from political corruption scandals and a stalled economy. The symbolic occasion set the stage for the President to broadcast the platform of national expansion trumpeted by his "old guard" radical Republicans. He released a proclamation, delivered by Secretary Robeson, describing the approach of a bold bright future by the "interchange of national sentiment" that might bring "greater advantage to science and industry," and "strengthen the bonds of peace and friendship."[68] The forward-looking vision reached out to national and international audiences. Copies were given to diplomatic representatives of all participating nations. The reach of mass print media came into play as an agent of public diplomacy. Hawley directed his remarks on that day to the national press assembled. He called on the "agency" of the news media to communicate the unprecedented scale of the Centennial to "every family in the land" on a daily basis. It was, he said, their patriotic duty as "heralds and Generals" of the national cause to make the enterprise a "glorious success."[69] In setting the thematic notes to the "great exhibition" countdown, public relations spin trumpeted peaceful expansion to foster belief in US influence internationally.

Prior to the land transfer ceremony, the first of an annual Merchants Banquet gathered at Delmonico's in New York. J. Pierpoint Morgan, Joseph Drexel, and Louis Tiffany were among the prominent assembly joining ranks among bankers, manufacturers, and industrialists. The President of the Centennial Commission Hawley appeared at the prestigious party as invited guest.[70] A legion of distinguished judges and dignitaries were also present, including the Consul General of Russia, a member of the Japanese Treasury, and Dr. Lunderman, Director of the United States Mint, who updated the room on a new coinage act to encourage monetary "conformity" throughout the world that used gold as an exchange rate for international commerce. Among rounds of toasts, attendees projected legislative forecasts and statistical graphs that set out internal and international agendas for a "majestic and far-reaching future." The gathering was of the opinion that Chambers of Commerce made "the best conservators of commercial principles and the most efficient organ through which merchants may exert their proper influence upon commercial legislation"[71] Two common refrains held sway. The first tied national security to the expansion and influence of "democratic" political economies internationally: commercial diplomacy "discourages war, destroys national prejudice, and brings within the reach of all products of every climate." Promoting trade relations as a political strategy endowed business with the power of arbitration to create conditions for peace. The second agenda anchored the material growth of internal commerce on interdependencies that binds democracy, rendering "possible a continental and perpetual Republic."[72]

The Treasury Department acted on behalf of the Philadelphia Centennial Commission to induce foreign participation by placing customs officials in charge of supervising foreign exhibitor shipments. Import duties and examination of the contents on exhibition shipments entering all US ports were waived, unless merchandise was sold.[73] In President Grant's 1873 report to Congress, the United States located itself as the only Western power in the Northern hemisphere. The nation held "cordial and friendly" relations with France, Germany, Russia, Italy, and "the minor European powers [Sweden, Norway, Denmark, Austria-Hungary]"; with Brazil and most of South American republics [Peru, Argentina, Venezuela and Chili]; and with Japan." In 1867, a treaty with Russia "acquired possession" of Alaska territory, then known as "Russian America." Desired for its harbors, the treaty opened the whaling industry to the North Pacific, enabling trade flow with China and Japan.[74] The United States was determined to wedge itself into the opening of diplomatic relations between an unsteady China, under the Qing dynasty, and the Western powers, of which Great Britain took the lead.[75]

Within China, there was strong opposition against opening new ports to foreign trade from merchant factions.[76] Secretary Seward negotiated a new treaty in 1868 that augmented an existing agreement, and which pitched escalating tension over Chinese immigration in California and Oregon when the federal government interceded in state legislation deemed discriminatory.[77] China's trade value was in imports, including raw cotton, woolen goods, and furs, for which nearly a quarter of a million dollars was spent annually according to US statistics.[78] Coal, minerals and sulfur in Northern China were also hungrily viewed.[79] China, along with all other trade partners participated in the Centennial, each exhibiting in an independently designed pavilion.

US diplomacy approached foreign territories as cooperative partners. The girth of market economies interlinking international expositions hawked development and export of natural resources. The Chilean government held an exposition in 1875 to accent its vast "wealth" of mineral resources: gold, silver, and copper, to "induce" South and North American investment as well as attract immigration of skilled labor to the country.[80] The United States seized the opening to increase trade with Mexico when Great Britain, France, and Canada withdrew diplomatic relations with the country in 1868. Most coveted were Mexico's silver deposits and produce.[81] Industrial economies were treated as diplomatic trade partners while land-based economies fell under the nomenclature of diplomatic settlements. As diplomacy transitioned to multinational power alliances, the outlets for colonial territories to enter modern political economies provided increasing public visibility and self-defining power.[82] The US approach to trade alliances strategized legislative tariffs to engage free trade that ingratiated American business methods into developing economies. By 1909, the Taft Administration rationalized that the territorial "dependencies" of Puerto Rico and the Philippines would profit by improved trade with the US as business conditions improved, and that the influence of democratic "traditions of "civil liberty" and "increasing popular control" would take root.[83] The popular theory defended the spread of commercial democracy as instrumental to national security. When two nations are commercially and financially interdependent" advised the *Wall Street Journal*, "they can ill afford to plunge into war at slight provocation." [84]

Diplomacy was a two way street. Treaty and trade agreements with "independent nations" had reciprocal advantages or disadvantages for both signers. Exhibition appearances externalized diplomatic accord derived from strengthening geopolitical allies. Internal dynamics were more delicate. Sustaining Japan's interest in renewing US trade agreements since its first pact in 1854 was a critical foreign policy priority to control the Pacific-rim and chip away at European influence and markets internally. Japan's participation at the Centennial was the first of many international exhibitions. Modernization in Meiji Japan transitioned quickly from agricultural to industrial economy. Exhibition events served diplomatic propaganda for colonial and military expansion by corporate factions in charge of the army and navy. In 1902, Japan formed a defense alliance with Great Britain to increase trade. This East-West alliance was broadcast in an Anglo-Japanese Exhibition in 1910 at the state-of-the-art fairgrounds of Shepherd's Bush, London. Mentioned earlier, the series of "allied" expositions held there—designed by Imre Kiralfy—beginning with the 1908 Franco-British Exposition underscored competitive diplomatic relations. Opposition within Japan's Imperial Diet viewed the agreement with Great Britain dangerous to relations with the United States and Pacific trade.[85] Corporate interests wanted to strengthen ties with United States. Foreign Minister Komura prevailed in the government belief perceiving the United States a threat to Pacific domination. During the Anglo-Japanese exhibition, Japan declined to renew long standing trade agreements with the US. Growing rapprochement between the two countries may have influenced Congressional authorization to look West in its selection of San Francisco over New Orleans's hard lobbying to host the Panama-Pacific International Exposition. The bill granting San Francisco the right to hold the fair was passed on February 5, 1911. President Taft arrived in top hat and tails, photographers in tow, to ceremoniously break the ground nine months later.[86]

The timing of the Philadelphia, New Orleans, and San Francisco exhibitions arose as a means toward interlocking municipal and regional economies to catapult national resurgence. Such market stimulus supplies an interesting subtext to the strategic planning. The Philadelphia Centennial was held during an economic downward spiral for domestic industries precipitated by the panic of 1873.[87] In its aftermath a commentary by Eugene V. Smalley in the mainstream news journal *The Century* surveyed its impact as a "turning point" that broke the "spell of lethargy," holding economic investment in stasis."[88] The windfall from the exhibition did not come from profits.

Revenue from ticket sales and concessions barely reached half of the eight million dollar cost. The fair did reactivate the domestic economy in both consumer spending and corporate expansion. The Centennial Board of Directors' assessment of the exhibition's economic influence reported:

> Undoubtedly, the setting in motion of millions of people, each with money to spend, has had an effect in breaking the lethargy that has stifled enterprise in the business world, and in causing the hopeful beginnings of a revival of trade which we have been witnessing this fall. Many improvements in manufactures and the introduction of new branches of industry will soon follow the result of the study by investors, skilled mechanics, and men of enterprise of the products of the globe. They have discovered that many articles which we have been buying from other countries can be profitably made here, and that many which we already make can be improved in quality or in the element of taste, or produced at lower cost, so as to command new markets, and the result will be a still wider development of our national industries.[89]

The attitude that private economic interests lead to general wealth and well being echoes classical Republican theory beginning with Adam Smith's treatment of political economies in *An Inquiry into the Nature and Cause of the Wealth of Nations* (1776).[90] The exhibition set a standard for the presentational achievements of a free market economy. The national publicity sounding the success of the Philadelphia World's Fair gave exhibition venues cultural status with wide public relations value. Deployment of exhibition events following the Centennial expressed selective agendas.[91] The idea for a Cotton Centennial Exposition arose in a letter to the *New York Herald* by political economist Edward Atkinson, advocating New York City as host. It was quickly coopted by leaders of the Cotton industry.[92] President F. C. Morehead raised the idea at an October 1882 Cotton Planters' Association's Convention in Little Point, Indiana, according to *The American Architect and Building News*.[93] After the much-publicized New Orleans Centennial, Cincinnati's Mechanics Institute and Chamber of Commerce organized an Industrial Exposition to promote local trades and urban development in 1888.[94] When Democrat Grover Cleveland took the presidential reigns in 1885, he called for a return to constitutional adherence and a "spirit of amity, mutual deference, and coexistence."[95] The medium of the New Orleans exhibition attempted to balance sectional disputes with a forum of productive cohabitation.[96] Increasing labor unrest, wealth disparity, and corporate abuse of interstate antitrust laws shifted economic debate away from notions of civic virtue toward social responsibility.

Congressional politics butted heads over corporate morals in terms of self-regulation or the need for federal legislation. Labor and social theories agitated for reform. Henry George's *Progress and Poverty: An Inquiry into the Cause of Industrial Depression and of Increase of Want with Increase of Wealth ... the Remedy*, published in 1879, argued an influential labor theory of "democratic economics." [97] He asserted environmental alienation as a rationale for social inequities, pointing to land value as the systemic detachment of wealth creation from labor use to corporate ownership.[98] The Republican Party maintained progressive economic platforms rooted in reforming competitive market policies that afforded the private sector and business greater opportunities. Long simmering controversy over regulatory measures involving railroad monopolies, interstate commerce, import tariffs, or national incorporation laws for large corporations eventually breached Republican ranks during the Presidency of William Henry Taft. President Taft's reactive stance on tariff reduction and deregulation pitted conservative (free trade) factions against liberal (protectionist) reformers aligned with Theodore Roosevelt.[99] Party divisions opened the door to Democrats, who took up the progressive movement under the mantle of enforcing federal trade legislation. They regained majority footing with the election of Woodrow Wilson. The route to the Panama-Pacific fair defused party politics in venture capitalism.

If the Philadelphia Centennial Exposition, and later fairs, inspired "continued vitality," what ingredients contributed to that?[100] One aspect to consider is how the micro-geographical stages of exhibition designs are pliable formats. Exhibition landscapes dovetail with the migratory, trangressive *nature* of the "American" spectacle itself, given definition by Guy Debord in the notion of autonomous mobility or fetishistic nature.[101] In doing so, industry provocation teases out spatial "territory" to gain advantage of alternative (alien) and competing revenue sources conducive to economic growth. The *in situ* spectacle does not mask the economic habitat, but elevates geospatial crossings in the scenic occupation of unlimited wealth creation, property, social diffusion, and material productivity. Changing cultural infrastructure pressures the ways producing organizations deliberate a visionary interface with citizenship.[102]

New World Perspectives

The designation "New World's Fair" given the Philadelphia Centennial by the *New York Tribune* informed readers of their transformative identity.[103] In contrast to the defense mechanisms of "Old World" hegemony, the advancing edge of American culture fueled itself on offensive strategies of economic belonging for growth and diversification. Unbridled commercial competition encouraged alternative perspectives and aggressive exploitation. Alan Trachtenberg observes during late nineteenth-century consolidation "corporations formed themselves as superior fighting units."[104] Economic behavior motivated business and labor, who differed over productivity as unequal market share or equal share in wealth creation. Exhibition management settled on a middle ground, celebrating productive change as historic cultural values that redistributed wealth, diversified output, and amalgamated power. Mona Domosh isolates the economic transactions of American exhibition arenas in the confluence of corporate capitalism.[105] The battle for territorial assimilation was always part of the American design. The violent course of border transgressions over the antebellum era charted constant threat to national survival over colonizing territorial amendments. The call to a geospatial destiny now approached a solidified phase of maturation.

The official title of the Philadelphia Centennial Exhibition was the "International Exhibition of Arts, Manufactures, and Products of the Soil and Mine." Newspaper leads carried it under the welcoming banner of the "Great Exhibition." The missionary theme of the event asked postbellum citizens to pledge allegiance to one nation. The fragile coexistence felt in post-Civil War trauma muddled collective consciousness.[106] The tri-color flag raised over the exhibition grounds at Fairmount Park tied the success or failure of the event to the multitudes bound to the perpetuity of "this Union." Public events around the Centennial shifted attention to patriotism and state independence in order to bury lingering acrimony. At the first official public ceremony in Philadelphia, the presence of Judge A. R. Butler of Virginia valorized a conciliating confederate presence. His keynote pledged his state's commitment to move forward. "Whatever differences there were in the past," he said, there is "no other point for their [citizens] patriotism but the flag of their country."[107] Six months before the May opening, flags of all shapes and sizes decorated the city. On the street, the tri-colors adorned young and old. "Little girls tied up their hair in tri-colored ribbons," while older women wore neckties. "Gentlemen carried miniature flags on their lapels, and boys ran the streets decorated with flags and badges of red, white, and blue."[108] The oath to the flag, penned by J. Bellemy, and officially adopted in 1892, formalized this latest chapter of an amended constituency.

The communion of a United States, rather than a union of states, testified to the survival of the American institution. A British commentator dryly observed that the Declaration of Independence, signed in Philadelphia one hundred years earlier, was "rather the resolve to create a new Government than the actual birth of a nation."[109] The celebration of peace-time prosperity, "in which the people of the whole country should participate," supplied the effervescent message of the exhibition; purposefully, the girders of participation supported an offensive economic agenda dramatizing a new worldview: "by an exhibition of the natural resources of the country and their development, and of its progress in those arts which benefit mankind, in comparison with those older nations."[110] The iconography of this economic wave was not a monolithic palace but the narrative body of the landscape.

Its design was conceived by a youthful twenty-seven year old engineer and chief gardener of Fairmount Park from Bavaria, Hermann J. Schwarzmann. On his selection, the Architect-in-Chief was immediately dispatched to the 1873 Vienna Exhibition to study its installations, grounds, and the city's famous zoo. Departing from the self-contained central building of European predecessors, Schwarzmann spread separate pavilions and six exhibition buildings over a 285-acre portion of Fairmount Park. This triangular area was adjacent to the Northern side of the city. Locally it was known as West Park, lying west of the Schuylkill River below Belmont Street and George's Hill. A natural elevated plateau of approximately 120 ft crowned views of the river. Below the peak ran deep, wooded ravines.[111] The "roominess of the national domain," urged the *Independent* to readers, invites all people to "see the conquests over Nature which were achieved by us in a single century of our country's life."[112]

Bird's eye views cast recessive perspectives that intimated the storied "character" of natural progress and regional intercommunication. Panning vantage points offered wide or partial views over the grounds from peaks or valleys, across artificial lakes, and through lush forest. Distributed across the landscape, over 250 exhibition pavilions were constructed and arranged by subject, country, state, and theme. For six months between 8 and 10 million visitors wondered the sprawling fairgrounds. "Do not come with the idea that you are going to see an enlarged State fair that can be 'done' in a single day. Nothing less than a week of steady application will suffice for a rapid survey of the great show," warned the *New York Tribune* in its detailed overview of the exhibition. [113] The "American" century moved beyond perspective grasp. The grounds did not hold forth a scene, but endless scenes. Freely circulating around the seemingly unscripted course of natural diversity, different cultural landscapes appeared or disappeared from view. The geo-embodiment of the United States, with its forms of mass production, system of states, regional industry, but especially its appearance in the "world," dissolved fixed sight lines. Visitors inhabited cityscape and country simultaneously.

Mining, metallurgy, manufacturing, technology, and industrial equipment claimed center stage. The two most important and largest buildings on Belmont Avenue formed an imposing avenue with parade grounds between them. These were Machinery Hall, where the Corliss steam engine roared powering all machines in the building, and a one story Main Hall for industrial products, education, and science. From the grand promenade named Administrative Avenue, other Departments: Art, Agriculture, and Horticulture, in separate buildings were positioned North and South of the main complex.[114] Each of the main buildings teemed with machinery, equipment, textiles, minerals, and produce from every hemisphere. Numerous inventions were premiered among the thirty-thousand plus exhibitors with American technology outdistancing all other nations.[115] The first sewing machines and typewriter, along with Alexander Graham Bell's telephone were on view. Just north of the Main Hall, perched on a plateau was Memorial Hall (destined to become the Philadelphia Museum of Art) stuffed equally with all categories of fine and commercial art: painting, sculpture, photography, engravings, lithographs, graphic design, and ceramics. International painting and sculpture was closely compared to examples from American academies in news reports.[116] Northeast of the main buildings, food exhibits grouped around Agriculture Hall. In the Northwest quadrant, states' pavilions lined State Avenue forming a chain of architectural styles. Assorted eccentricities reflected the showy attributes of state identities. Mississippi built a log cabin. New York erected an opulent, ornamented two-story building. Colorado, entering statehood the same year, joined with Kansas to erect a Gothic framed building with a floor plan in the form of a Greek cross. Private individuals from nonparticipating states invested in the pageant as well. A gentleman from Tennessee pitched a canvas tent to exhibit iron ore.

Cooperative trade agreements granted foreign partnerships mutual inroads to influence consumer spending. Pavilions built by trade nations and private companies exhibited commodity specialties from glass blowing and ceramics to Japanese cabinetry and Viennese leather goods. The borderless "free" market nations showcased sovereign status in commodity goods that appealed to consumer tastes and spiritual beliefs. China's "most striking" Pavilion bore the inscription "Ta-Shing-Lo" reported to announce visitors were entering the "Chinese Empire."[117] The architecture elaborated an ornamented façade with carved dragons curling up the pillars. A "brilliant" interior pagoda and "odd-looking" cases filled with lacquer ware and silks sealed the culture in spectral, decorative allure.[118] Specialty products shown by foreign nations domesticated ascendant styles and luxuries, carpeting mainstream fashions in the empowerment of international relations. One could stop for refreshments in an Algerian café or listen to a variety of musical styles in the rotunda of the main hall, see Turkish baths, a Mexican temple, stroll past a Hunter's camp tucked away on the grounds, visit the New England kitchen, or a Canadian log cabin. The dramaturgy of this event in the words of one chronicler laid before the world a complete "panorama of American progress during the last century."[119]

The dream of a better future materialized in Philadelphia; it was a competitive race. Skilled labor along with technological innovations paved avenues into the social economy. Independent entrepreneurs also carved out new markets. Small business edged into the cultural foreground. Joseph Campbell exhibited his canned preserve company based in Camden New Jersey, better known as Campbell's Soup, at the fair.[120] James W. Tufts and Charles Lippincott installed a 30 ft soda fountain in their own building. The $20,000 investment, dispensing flavored water, earned them an estimated $52,000. Sales of their drug store soda fountain blossomed nationally.[121] In addition to thousands of exhibitors from all participating countries displaying everything from horse rakes to children's toys, private businesses flooded the grounds with service industries. The great American restaurant and the German restaurant became favorites. Retail businesses held a separate area from major industries. One could browse burial caskets, swings, and roofing or wander the Brewer's building among the "special exhibits.[122] On the parameter of the site, the large hotels that opened near the main entrance of the exhibition grounds came up with the idea of an "Operti Garden" serenading visitors in a music garden with 50 piece orchestras. Springing up daily on the fringes of the fair, were theatrical entertainments, independent art galleries, and out-door shows.[123] All of which would migrate into official fair culture before the end of the decade. Radial and peripheral visibility dispersed elastic cultural scenes that set mainline creative enterprise in motion.

White women claimed a measure of self-representation with their own industrial exhibit devoted to "women's work." Their inclusion was capital driven. It came as an afterthought when the Centennial Board of Finance had difficulty raising money.[124] The institutional acceptance granted them partial recognition after decades of protest and legislative lobbying. At an annual meeting of the American Woman Suffrage Association in October 1873, reflections offered on the "progress" of the movement over a twenty-five year period named associations in each of the twenty states of the union, greater employment opportunities, and how in many of the state legislatures "friends have been found."[125] The Executive Women's Committee, was presided over by Philadelphia social elite Edna Gillespie, great grand-daughter of Benjamin Franklin and daughter of William J. Duane, who served as Secretary of the Treasury under Andrew Jackson. Highly active in traditional fund-raising for religious and charitable causes during the Civil War, Gillespie also lobbied for the creation of the Philadelphia Museum of Art.[126] With patrician zeal, in just over four months the committee raised over $93,000 dollars, and an additional $45,000 to independently build a separate pavilion, when exhibition space offered proved inadequate for the overwhelming response.[127] In addition to selling stock in districts of Philadelphia, they established a national committee with chairwomen in thirty-seven states and territories. The New Orleans organization adopted such a plan to set up auxiliary committees across the country to promote the Cotton Centennial and build financial support.[128]

The women's committee was initially praised as a stepping-stone in women's rights. The announcement of a significant women's presence was seen as one that would help "build the pedestal on which the American woman is destined, through her work, to stand."[129] However, exhibits confined women's industry to domestic ingenuity, fashion, painting, and social duties: charity work and education. A six horsepower steam engine developed by Emma Allison drove the looms and spinning frames in the pavilion. Contemporary commentators admiringly highlighted the elegance and precision of the exhibited embroideries and textiles collected from around the world.[130] Yet, the social snobbery of the Executive Committee earned a reputation for being "exceedingly disagreeable and disobliging" to visitors.[131] A bust of Iolantha modeled in butter by a woman from the Southwest, popularly called "The Butter Woman," highlighted the conservative hodgepodge of pressed flowers, wax fruit arrangements, wood carvings, and paintings of mothers and children.[132] One acknowledgment of political agitation for women's rights was a deliberate plan to hold a "Women's Day" at the fair on November 7, 1876 in order to join with Suffragettes, who gathered in Philadelphia to protest the vote on Election Day. On another note, visibility brought female labor to national attention but did so as an outgrowth of women's usefulness to the larger aims of industrialized labor. Little attempt was made to shine a light on civil rights, conditions for working women, or advocating employment opportunities.[133]

The presence of a Women's Executive Committee joined the administrative establishment in succeeding fairs. Centennial Commissioners denied African Americans participation either in the formal organization or by a share of construction contracts issued. The Centennial suppressed reference to the institution of slavery, and any suggestion of inequality or civil discord. As ceremonies for the exhibition unfolded, an item of news from Washington reported the US Department of the Interior began the forced removal of the last Winnebago from Wisconsin to a reservation in Iowa.[134] The United States took control of the final parcel of land for Northwest development. The long bloody battle to colonize the continent lay entombed at the Centennial. The afterlife of Native American cultures at this fair were written in past tense, as an embalmed archive of artifacts collected for ethnographic narratives of "savage life and conditions in all grades and places."[135]

Reconstruction altered the status quo. In the South, the "Negro question" erupted in fresh waves of terror and violence against African Americans by a surging Ku Klux Khan. Liberal Republicans and Southern Democrats sought reactionary legislative policies to suppress human rights and suffrage granted in the Fourteenth and Fifteenth Amendment to restore white supremacy. In counterpoint to the Centennial Exposition in which African American self-representation was excluded and Southern states were largely absent, the 1884–1885 "colossal" World's Cotton Centennial Exposition in New Orleans saw Southern Democrats siding with reformers to promote the invention of a "New South" inclusive to the national enterprise. A coalition of organizers joined forces to plan and construct the venue within two years. F. C. Morehead from the Planters' Association partnered with associate Edmund Richardson, a cotton planter involved in mass manufacturing. They were joined by Edward Austin Burke, editor-in-chief of the *News Orleans Times-Democrat* and Treasurer of Louisiana, who became Director General of the fair.

Commemorating the one-hundredth anniversary of the first shipment of cotton from the United States to Europe in 1784, Kevin Fox Gotham relates the replacement of the slave-based economy of the antebellum period with wage-labor and factory production signaled the transformation of the agrarian economy to an industrial one.[136] The year 1884 was selected because it marked the availability of cotton for manufacturing was ready for practical demonstration.[137] One of the primary aims of the New Orleans exposition was to corner trade relations with Latin American republics "South of the Rio Grande."[138] A promotional salvo for the New Orleans Centennial in the *New Orleans Times-Democrat* promised the "worldview" of internationalism: "All the nations, civilized, semi-civilized, and barbarous, have poured the wealth of all their possessions into the monster lap of the Exposition."[139] A principle design of the exhibition arose from the conviction that if the port of New Orleans could become the gateway to a larger share of cotton and agricultural trade with Latin American countries along the Gulf of Mexico and the Caribbean, Northern industries would invest in openings for commercial activity in the Southern hemisphere. According to Mauricio Tenorio-Trillo's account of Mexico's involvement in world's fairs, establishing trade relations in Latin America came with assurances from the US of a commercial "protectorate" from European intervention in the region. The elite Porfirian government of Mexico seized on exhibition trends in the wake of the French-Mexico war as a means of political preservation and economic consolidation.[140] The Philadelphia Centennial was Mexico's first appearance in a US exhibition. At the New Orleans Centennial, the federal government launched a major offensive to polish an image as a commercial trade partner of unexploited resources to draw investment and skilled labor.[141] The "full representation" of tropical produce from Mexico, Guam, Guatemala, Honduras, Venezuela, Brazil, and Jamaica with "machine the machinery for their preparation" excited potential investors.[142] European presence was subdued. Private exhibitors from Europe outweighed official government presence aside from Western European industrial allies and US trade partner Japan.

A conciliatory effort was made to demonstrate racial integration and social harmony existed in the South. The first African American Commission, chaired by Blanche K. Bruce, was appointed to independently manage a "Colored Department" of exhibits. Director General Burke ignored the Committee's input and restricted African American opportunities at the fair to work "in the fields and shops."[143] Economic emancipation was only marginally recognized. Executive management directed the separation of the "colored" exhibits from "white" exhibits. Rather than join the majority of industrial exhibitors in the Main Hall, setting the display in the Government Building masked the community's current role in rebuilding the Southern economy. A prominent motto placed on a historical chart in the department's exhibition space recognized the economic forces steering representational themes: "we must unite; we must acquire wealth; we must educate, or we will perish."[144] The issues for black management in fair culture splintered over the means to achieve social autonomy: whether to compromise with white centralized authority or resist the reactionary constraints. In rebuttal to continued exclusion from full representation in exhibition administration, civil rights leaders Frederick Douglass, Ida B. Wells, Irving Garland Penn and Ferdinand L. Barnett published a pamphlet coinciding with the opening of the World's Columbian Exposition, *The Reason Why the Colored American is Not in the World's Columbian Exhibition*. It enumerated ongoing contributions while holding up the ideological grip of sustained racial violence and distortion in contradictions of liberty and progress for black America.[145]

The site of the New Orleans Cotton Centennial covered 62 acres of Upper City Park (now Audubon Park), Southwest from the center of the city.[146] Organizers modified the epic landscaping used for the Philadelphia fair for a multinational perspective. The main building, housing "private exhibits" was plagued by construction problems and unfinished opening day.[147] Many of Philadelphia's construction contracts remained in state. Contracts at New Orleans were distributed nationally in order to include "active commercial rivalry."[148] Iron framework salvaged from Philadelphia's dismantled buildings was used.[149] The roof of the main building was built in Cincinnati. Nine million feet of lumber was delivered from Mississippi. Four thousand kegs of nails were shipped from Wheeling, West Virginia.[150] The main building grew to cover half the grounds, with over one million square feet of space and skylight roofing.[151] The largest exhibition structure to date was seen by architects as an oversized "barn." Criticism levied at management scoffed over contracting an "unknown Swedish immigrant" from Mississippi, rather than an established Southern firm.[152] Southern planters claimed it as the "most remarkable edifice" ever built.[153] Cotton mills, iron works, as well as forestry and mining process for developing mineral resources featured working models. Above the central music hall ran second floor galleries. Views of the bustling Mississippi River beyond, the gardens and exhibits, sectioned equally side by side for "varied effect," stitched together a real-time "panorama of the world's industry."[154]

Samuel Mullen, Chief of Installation, partitioned the display floor into fourteen-foot aisles with four-foot square cubicles for exhibitors. The floor plan arose as solution to giving prominence to any one exhibitor over another. Lengthy aisles crowded with merchandise reflected the new South's "representational" integration. It also reinforced a separate but equal clamor for power.[155] Vendors battled for visibility in the chaotic Main Hall. Advertising found conspicuous modes of drawing attention to exhibitor stalls.[156] Many companies branded products with three-dimensional mascots. Edward L. Wilson's photographs of the exhibition include many examples, one of which was The American Salt Mines, which produced rock salt. Its exhibit hailed customers with a life size statue made of salt, called Lot's Wife.[157]

The New Orleans Centennial played up Southern unity to challenge the economic stronghold of the North. Every state and territory participated; Northern industries flocked to exhibit. The motorized labor-intensive processes of iron works and cotton manufacturing inserted agriculture and forestry into the national economy by increasing the efficiency and quotas of industrial output. Separated from the Main Hall were buildings for farming machinery, saw mills, brick making, and livestock. The multiethnic deposit of "all the wealth of the world" collided in a "bewildering" arena that flopped financially but buttressed tourism to the city.[158]

By the twentieth century, the San Francisco Panama-Pacific International Exposition wrapped multinational trade agreements in multipurpose cultural complexes. Over 18 million visitors made San Francisco's exhibition in the words of Burten Benedict, the "last collective outburst" of optimism before the outbreak of World War I.[159] Rather than an end, the fair marks a turning point. Its state-of-the-art composition ushers in the roiling terrain of corporate globalism. Celebrating the opening of the Panama Canal, the San Francisco World's Fair was the first to commemorate a simultaneous event.

The occasion solidified US control over transcontinental shipping channels, once Panama signed an administration agreement with the United States.[160] The agreement met with protests from Great Britain, rattling decades of "friendly" relations.[161] It unnerved US European allies France, Italy, and Germany. The outbreak of World War I further shook up official participation by Great Britain and Germany, but did not hinder private involvement. A sanitary, upbeat atmosphere hid the rough parts of the city. A separate police force patrolling the grounds was aided by a "moral protection" guard in charge of travelers' safety to and from the city in order to keep criminal activity, drunkenness, and women's virtue in check.[162] The city on the bay proudly stepped up its frontier reputation to light the beacon as a cosmopolitan world city, only nine years after the 1906 catastrophic earthquake and fire.

R. B. Hale suggested the idea of holding a world's fair to mark the opening of the Panama Canal to fellow business associates of the San Francisco Merchant's Association in a 1904 editorial.[163] The idea took almost ten years to realize. The city of San Francisco competed with Boston, Baltimore, Washington, San Diego, and New Orleans in a lengthy political "contest" to win Congressional support for the "honor and profit" of hosting the fair.[164] Lobbies from California and Louisiana plied members of the House Committee on Industrial Arts and Expositions with gifts of oranges and sazarac cocktails.[165] The 50 million dollar price tag was funded by private and corporate investment from businesses, shipping, utility, and railroad companies.[166] Local millionaires William H. Crocker, president of the Crocker National Bank of San Francisco, and Frank L. Brown, later named Director of the Exposition, formed a Panama-Pacific Exposition Company on March 22, 1910 and began raising shares of stock.[167] Over four million dollars were raised in less than two hours when the sale of subscriptions opened at the Merchant's Exchange. Stockholders held a majority share in the company. The sum of 20 million dollars was raised by the state of California through private and district tax levies.[168] Sponsorships by the Union Pacific and Sante Fe railroads supplied $250,000. They not only competed in fare reductions to attract East coast visitors but also set up rival exhibits in the popular Palace of Transportation.[169] Even the public became a financial statistic. Projected sources of the gate receipts from anticipated attendance figured into the budget calculations.[170] The estimate approximated daily averages of paid admissions equal to near 20 percent of the city population, assumed at half a million inhabitants. Attendance shattered all projections; it brought in over 13 million dollars, lifting the exhibition company into the black with a rare profit of two million dollars.[171] The Panama-Pacific Exposition Company was dissolved and its assets liquidated in August 1920, having completed a mission lasting ten years.

Great effort was taken to promote the appearance of a bipartisan administration. The titular head of management was President Charles C. Moore. The owner of a prominent engineering firm, Moore's election was "agreeable" to factions on the Board of Directors concerned about graft. He reassured his partners appointments would be based on merit alone.[172] A committee of three hundred "representative" citizens of San Francisco chose the thirty members on the Executive Board, apparently major investors in the exhibition company as well.[173] Four executive divisions along with the President, and the Director-in-Chief Dr. Frederick J. V. Skiff coordinated as producing management. In addition to the Division of Exhibits (Capt. Asher Carter Baker, Director), Division of Works (Harris D. H. Connick Director), and Division of Concessions and Admissions (Frank Burt, Director) was a publicity department bluntly named Division of Exploitation (George Hough Perry, Director). The marketing department published press releases, informational brochures for foreign exhibitors and visitors, stickers, and maps to target audiences. Corporate sponsors had consultants appointed to administrative positions. W. D. A. Ryan, General Electric Company's Illuminating Engineer was commissioned to design exposition lighting systems.[174] It fell to the architectural commission to brand the "world character" spectator-citizens would inhabit.

The theme of the exhibition grounds was "pictorial."[175] The site spanned a 635-acre stretch of land along the bay, now known as the Mariana District. Chief Architect George W. Kelham explained that the design meant to unify painting, sculpture, engineering, and architecture.[176] Its execution involved collaboration among specialized experts, working with separate divisional committees. The blueprint organized eight main buildings into a "block plan." The compact worldscape divided a central group of buildings into three courts or intercommunicating districts, each designed by a different architect. Broad avenues, named Progress or Palms or Administration, directed traffic flow. The surrounding Palace Courtyard was conceived by architect W. B. Favilles as a "walled city" of antique origin. Its pseudo intercultural architecture blended Mediterranean influences with Moorish domes and Pacific inspired pastel tones of blue, pink, green, yellow, and ochre. The coloring and diagrammatic scheme determined by the architectural committee was intentionally panoramic. Extending the complex was the bay to the North, the surrounding hills of the city to the South, and the mountains in the distance. Navigational ease and scenic variety obscured the methodical block system. Planning took into account multi-perspective views from elevated lookout points around the city. Special attention was paid to creating impressionistic effects from above the grounds as well as from inside the complex. The domed roofs of exhibition buildings were painted to absorb and refract changes in natural light.

San Francisco's "man-made" landscaping staged the world city in technicolor grandeur. The production values of exhibits, the grounds, and the amusements pulsed with an electrifying beauty of internal diversity. Its wonderland glow departs from the conceptual wedding cake layers of authoritatively named "white cities." The white city came from uniformly painting the facades of their architectural pastiche. The preeminent model of this urban idealism was the World's Columbian Exposition, which gave inspiration to the city beautiful movement. [177] Chicago architects Daniel H. Burnham and George W. Root's oversaw the selection and coordination of five national firms and five Chicago firms as part of architectural design.[178] Its final unifying conceit, supervised by Burnham when Root unexpectedly passed away, overlaid monumental neoclassical building styles and sonorous plaster detailing onto the modern engineering feats of US architecture rising in the Midwestern metropolis.[179] Landscape architect John McLaren (long time superintendent of Golden Gate Park) and the New York firm McKim, Mead, and White involved in the Chicago's fair continued to reinvent the immersive fabric of the fair in San Francisco. At that exhibition, the architectural hybrid of "Oriental" facades and precolonial South American inspired pastoral colorings came to be known as the "City of Domes." Instead of surfacing buildings with plaster and paint that degraded quickly, Paul E. Dennerville created a recipe for mass-producing stucco in imitation of ancient Roman travertine marble.[180] The Philadelphia and New Orleans exhibitions brought attention to architectural engineering, construction materials, and manufacturers.[181] The Chicago world's fair stirred the stylish metropolitan whimsy of the beaux-arts movement. [182] San Francisco pushed forth a synthetic globalism that vented a cinematic charisma.

One of the crowning features of the "jewel city" was an electric light system composed of state-of-the-art projectors and floodlights that refracted off crystals strung on every tower, roof, and façade. It

Figure 4.2   Night Illumination of the Panama-Pacific International Exposition, San Francisco, 1915.

Source: Poster, Edward H. Mitchell, Yale Collection of Western Americana, Beinecke Rare Book and Manuscript Library, Yale University.

lit the night sky with constellations of glimmering jewels. Searchlights wove across the grounds in changing colors from the Tower of Jewels (Figure 4.2).[183] The effusive landscape architecture conveyed a fragmentary geography of spontaneous occupation. Mingling practical and imaginary, motion and stasis, marginal and central, proportion and exaggeration, mechanical and organic, released freewheeling abandon. In the words of Louis Christian Mullgradt, member of the Architectural Commission, "international expositions are independent kingdoms in their corporate relations with other countries." [184] The existence of these "phantom kingdoms" is "established without conquest" and "vanish like the setting sun in their own radiance.[185] The transient shell of flickering experiences internalized tactile emotions, memories, fantasies, skepticism, or desires occurring on the spot, leaving narrative control open to self-inscription.

A montage of sites put in motion a prismatic spectacle, a fabrication of a golden city within a struggling San Francisco, a digressive gateway to sophistication and tranquility, a travelog that internally cross-cut interactive habitats. Visitors pursued their own course of action, determining privileged sites and attractions. The wide streets directed strollers to centralized locations, scenic vistas on the bay, garden sanctuaries, concerts, concessions, a competitive sports venue, or the amusement park, called the Joy Zone. Over two hundred concessions in the Zone, as it was known, packed a one-mile long "bizarre" with the latest "amusement ideas." Within, a series of ethnic villages confined nonwhite communities to "minority" neighborhoods.[186] The counter site of street life, as opposed to the wide avenues of main street, in the Zone challenges the orthodox sheen of "fair" order. Rosemarie K. Bank notes the incompatible collisions emitted in and external to the status quo often overflow into unexpected disorder.[187] The mixed-use space let visitors crop their own vantage points near or far, close up or from a distance, from above or below. The convulsing dynamics of the grounds may have marketed a retail traffic of choice but spectatorship entertained its own design.

In the official history of the exposition, Frank Morton Todd conferred that the unknown outcome—that unwritten blank space—had to inspire a marketplace of ideas: "The job is only half done when you show what men are manufacturing. You must go ahead and show what they are thinking."[188] Exhibit planning, headed by Asher Carter Baker, oriented historical viewpoints on contemporaneous stages of progress. Industrial exhibits sustained the next big things. The Corliss steam engine, the "prime mover " at the Philadelphia Centennial, was replaced with a Diesel engine in the Palace of Machinery. A twenty-thousand horsepower hydroelectric generator pointed to new energy sources on the horizon. Contrasts of then and now, keyed visitors to inhabit historical themes. The highly popular Palace of Transportation emphasized the ease, comfort, and convenience of personal travel. Automobiles, electric trains, and powerful steam locomotives modeled the art of engineering. The first Central Pacific locomotive, part of the transcontinental route from Utah to California, was placed beside the latest high speed train, the Mallet Articulated engine. The Ford Motor Car Company maintained a factory exhibit that assembled a continuous rolling line of Ford cars, which were driven away every ten minutes. Instructional films came into vogue giving the observer a bird's eye view over the choreography of skilled labor working in precision with production processes. Films carried viewers into industrial scenery demonstrating farming, logging camps, mining, fisheries, mills, and factories. The ambience of benevolent corporate industries massaged vocational jobs into attractive behavioral systems.

The Social Habitats of Commerce

Educational standards billowed into all aspects of exhibition practices under the auspices of scientific criteria that continued long practiced government policies of cultural assimilation, segregation, or erasure. Scenic displays of Louisiana swamps and Massachusetts fisheries at the New Orleans exhibition created instructional storybooks combining panoramas and habitat display.[189] Increasingly, amusements filtered educational content into intimate attractions, further domesticating the vocabularies of commerce. Social legacies, histories, and achievements came alive everywhere at the

Panama-Pacific fair. Behavioral standards were introduced by the Binet-Simon test, named after French psychologist Alfred Binet. Lewis Terman presented his "Stanford Revision and Extension of the Binet Scale" to the national educational assembly convening at the fair.[190] The move toward assessment was based on mathematically measuring intellectual aptitude, which by result predetermined students' economic potential as well. The appellation of a scientific scale of IQ testing shifted educational outlook to individual achievement. The singular issue scrutinized by conference attendees was mass socialization in public education. They were not alone. The logo of the fair was an illustration of two intersecting globes that lashed "commerce" and "education" to the slogan "The Panama Canal Divides the Continents to Unite the World."

Home, work, and leisure were major themes of social interconnectivity sponsored by institutions, corporations, and the entertainment industry. Investments in "amusement enterprises" according to one report amounted to a million dollar industry.[191] The range of entertainment commerce removed the static shelves of object lessons. General Electric Company masterminded the radical and practical uses of electrical engineering to motorize rides, pump water, as well as illuminate the grounds and exhibition spaces. GE's "guarantee of excellence" brought electricity to life. Its "Home Electrical" walk through a model house was one of the most popular habitats next to the Machinery Building, where the company constructed a wholesale exhibition space for industry investors.[192] In addition to sales offices throughout in the US, the company had representatives "in all countries."[193] In the Palace of Liberal Arts, The American Telephone and Telegraph Company told the "Story of a Great Achievement." There, access to daily transcontinental phone calls dialed individuals into "universal" connections.[194] The Southern Pacific Railroad section in the Transportation Pavilion at the Panama-Pacific fair drew visitors inside its structure through a tree-lined entry leading to a central ticket office, and male and female waiting rooms. Adjacent to the ticket office was the Sunset Theatre, modeled after a trendy New York City "little theatre" where potential customers could watch movies and hear lectures given every hour on routes and industries along the rail lines.[195] The fun house doubled as model house or the reverse. Earlier moving river panoramas continued their traveling life as scenic rides. Cars, trains, and ships took passengers on scenic railways, toboggans, and spiral railways. The famous Panama Canal ride in the Zone was conceived by midway showman Fred McClellan.[196] Riding along a moving belt, visitors traveled through a scenic waterway of the Canal Zone while a telephonic recording narrated different points of interest on its internal engineering and operations. Commentator Ben Macomber asserted its temporal and spatial contraction is "better than a trip through the canal" and more "instructive."[197] Speed, immediacy, and the play action of interactive adventures encoded the behavioral energies of automation, results, and risk taking, all agents of productive performance systems.

Benedict Anderson's well known theory of "imagined community" intercepts the ascent of nationalism as a sensible construct of cultural references.[198] The cultural landscapes of US exhibitions revoke permanence for change. Their differences locate but also dislocate nationhood by reconstitution. What lay ahead temporarily underwrites what lay behind. A cardinal feature of the spectacle is the evasive logic of its vociferous sensibilities. Where there is not entirety, no end or beginning only limitless extensions. Unscripted movement through the "world's" stages recovers somatic rhythms that valuate immersion not as an illusion but as a migrating economy of performed actuality that momentarily grafts perspectives to a phase of current occupation.

Social commerce is one such scenic medium that percolates behavioral interactivity in exhibition cultures. The spectacle encounter yields a purposed matrix of administrative ideography. It absorbs instructional trends from numerous institutional forums, among which are museum authorities. In museum culture, the disciplinary project of the institution curates history. As custodians of heritage diffusion, museum preservation efforts enlist educational media as part of its cultural mission. Scene spaces seep into many forms of educational content to humanize heritage exhibits. In particular, habitat dioramas, drawn from painted panoramas and three-dimensional staged models became popular in display design to show wilderness conservation and historical preservation in the twentieth century.

5

Instructional Scenes: Heritage Preservation, Commerce, and Museum Dioramas

In October 2009, the "controlled crash" of a NASA probe producing a crater 60 miles wide and 2 miles deep bore into the surface of the moon to mine for evidence of water that would make future settlement possible.[1] Recovered data from the groundbreaking lunar mission played into the debate over where the National Aeronautics Space Administration's human spaceflight program should aim next, whether to return to the moon or head elsewhere in the near solar system. At the time, the Obama Administration was actively revamping NASA to join a growing commercial space industry. An independent panel appointed by President Barack Obama weighed in on the lunar expedition. MIT professor and panel member Ed Crawley was quoted as saying, NASA should explore the inner solar system "to interest the American public in new destinations."[2] In anticipation of lucrative government contracts, the Boeing Company announced that it was entering the space tourism business.[3] The ensuing space race has seen the successful launch of the private SpaceX Dragon: the first "reusable" commercial cargo craft successfully reached the International Space Station in May 2012.[4] Two months later NASA's third Mars Rover, equipped with a panoramic camera, safely landed. Named Curiosity; the rover joined eight-year-old companions Spirit and Opportunity to survey soil and moisture. The popular notion of intergalactic exploration may conjure William Shatner's voice of *Star Trek*'s dogged Captain Kirk announcing, space ... the final frontier. But then, the current crowd of space expeditions follows a long lineage of US Army Corps of Engineers topographical surveys dating back to 1785 before territorial containment, colonization, and integration into the economic landscape.[5]

Among the phases of nation building from colony to Superpower the visionary stage often evokes destination in terms of spatial quest. John O'Sullivan's crusading theorem of manifest destiny sounded at a turning point in continental control. Territorial acquisition advanced a scenic landscape occupied with the restless anxiety of change. Amid the sweeping disappearance of Western forests and public lands in the late nineteenth century, historian Frederick Jackson Turner proposed the receding Great West "the true point of view" of history.[6] His influential frontier theses, published in 1920, interpreted the defining trait of American ideology as a transient space. In an early address, "The Significance of the Frontier in American History" (1893), Turner speaks of the frontier as motion; "it is not merely advance along a single line, but motion toward a continually advancing frontier line; a fluid area in which nature has been conquered and one in which it prevails."[7] The frontier poses an edge along the visible and the invisible. In this wrested void occurs the visionary space of social democracy. Destination in this adaptive motion is a marginal threshold of freedom, or as Hubert Damisch observes a scene out of which projects ideals, hope, opportunity, promise, onto which is grafted numerous desires, dreams, fantasies, horrors.[8] The creation of the frontier, the origin point into the unknown, sustains the immersive dimensions of social democracy in perpetual movement. The passage of geographical mythology into historiography preserved the invention of the frontier as natural strife of enduring freedom, a striving toward destiny.[9] Yet, what Turner signifies as frontier, laying at the "hither edge of free land," reissues the contours of democratic renewal as spatial transgression.[10] Since boundaries are arbitrary, they can be broken, contested, resisted, constructed, or erased. If instability is a condition of democratic agency, sensory media increasingly becomes a competitive tool of social discourse.

That enigmatic ligature lurks in the vanishing lines of the nineteenth century. With the closing of public land sales on the Western frontier by the 1880s, swift industrial encroachment brought attention to land conservation and historic preservation. Amassing US heritage held a reflective grip over reconstituting spectator models of social history in the turn to the modern era. A period threatened with social and economic collapse is bracketed by two World Expositions trumpeting national heritage in past and future tense. Looking back at pioneering prowess, the refractive Chicago 1933–1934 "Century of Progress" came at the height of the Depression when 1.5 million people were unemployed, while the 1939–1940 dazzling New York

"World of Tomorrow" lifted off into the technological future. The retrospective slant to the so-called century of progress gained immutable scenic presence in US government, state, and historical institutions as the country spilled violently into the twentieth century.

Between the World Wars, vantage points over heritage filter into public consciousness through the "moving" economies of museum institutions.[11] Tony Bennett details how these public complexes served a key function in mediating public knowledge of social organization and naturalizing citizenship to "position people on this side of power, both as its subject and beneficiary."[12] A tangent to issues of public influence in modern era museums blossoms out of disciplinary agencies imprint on historical discourse. US naturalization law—regulating open borders to citizenship—was modified in 1906 to introduce uniform court procedures, which were placed under the control of the Bureau of Immigration and Naturalization of the Department of Commerce and Labor.[13] One stipulation maintained Indians living with a tribe were ineligible for citizenship, cutting off economic access through sustained denial of representational rights. The law's reform was one among a series of centralized attempts toward managing labor and political dissent through economic colonization and coordination of immigration policies, industrial management, educational standards, and government programs rearing national debate beyond the war years.[14] During a period of policy consolidation, wilderness conservation and heritage exhibits ventured a curatorial role in memorializing an indigenous "American" point of view. It poses a scenic circuitry through which "taming" counter narratives raises a buried part of American landscapes. These fault lines continue to yield an ambiguous creative relationship to "the true point of view of history."

Instructional Scenic Models: Museum Dioramas

Museum practices keep pace with other forms of spectacle absorbing immersive trends. The installation of scenic exhibits in museums branch out into instructional methodology. One method that gained popularity was diorama displays. Permanent museum exhibits of state, civil, and scientific histories postured an immobile existence in hand-crafted habitat environments and three-dimensional dioramas. Miniature and large-scale forms of dioramas dramatized the specimens of history in "natural" circumstances. In place of actual objects or artifacts, stationary scenes encased a physical recreation of animal or human activity. Painted panorama techniques helped stylize environmental terrain. Early staging methods adopted techniques used in theatrical dioramas devised by scene painter and inventor Louis Jacques Mandé Daguerre. Daguerre and associate Charles-Marie Bouton introduced the theatrical diorama in 1822. These scene illusions combined two-dimensional painted scrims to achieve impressionistic dissolving views with three-dimensional elements placed in front of the screens or moving panoramas to create immersive effects.[15] Multimedia accessories eventually budded alongside trending visual technology such as photographs and motion pictures. Keeping up with "appearances," the stationary manufacture of diorama display anticipates the intimate screen of broadcast television.

Although stationary dioramas resemble static "theatres," their production values share numerous characteristics with other spectacle mediums: the immersive effects of installation environments, interaction with multidimensional scenic episodes, aesthetic standardization, and the discreet framing of dramatic narratives. On a broad scale, the recapitulations of nineteenth-century continental topographies: regionalism, architecture, transportation, technology, industry, and domestic life, resonate in disciplinary pluralism. Conceptual systems developing in institutional collections often interconnected historical or civic education to scenic habitats. Narrative content held flexible functions: to empathize with a species' cultural diversity, to situate community in relationship to country, or remold artifactual beauty to perpetual renewal. Two sets of dioramas examined later demonstrate the varied use of scenic narratives. They reside in state and government museums. One series, created for the Colorado State Museum (History Colorado Center) in Denver, conserves state history. It was produced by a team of artists, architects, and historians between 1934 and 1941, funded in part by the Works Projects Administration (WPA). Labor relations and tourism factored into the economic recovery of the city during the Depression. Another important collection of dioramas is displayed in the US Department of the Interior Museum. Opened in 1939, the installations depict the work of civil industry carried out by its different bureaus. This outreach institution of the Federal Agency focused, in part, on civic education and tourism.

First, it is important to elaborate how diorama assembly emerges as a distinct form of educational media. The rendering of diorama collections presented disciplinary contexts ways to storyboard instructional content for cumulative effect. Elements combined visual setting, taxidermy subjects, and set pieces. "Colorado Huntress" Martha Maxwell used her skills to create a "complex diorama" for the Women's Pavilion at the Philadelphia Centennial Exposition.[16] Preserving animals for decorative mounting was behind infant methods of taxidermy. Posed behind a wrought iron fence, her Rocky Mountain and Great Plains deer, wolves, eagles, bison, bear, as well as a leaping cougar were arranged with smaller animals and mounted birds. The American Museum of Natural History introduced bird habitats for public display in 1887. Otis T. Warren from the Smithsonian Institution, curator of ethnology at the new US National Museum in Washington DC, and colleagues modeled educational exhibits of live human groups staged in habitat exhibits at the World's Columbian Exposition.[17] By the post-World War I period, diorama manufacture increased exponentially as a systematic style of educational media in curatorial strategies. Fabrication procedures differed depending on the resources and mission of the organization.

Three particular patterns that crop up in scenic spectacles throughout the nineteenth century resurface: genres of wilderness, settlement, and industry. When examined side by side these alternating story lines conjugate syndicated iterations of economic heritage. They reset in historiography, and in particular through social modeling. Humanities discourse is parcel to the development and range of educational media. Mounting human-interest stories for instructional purposes conscript interpretive interdependencies in conventional applications of productive knowledge. Historical dioramas, specifically, preserve an arbitrated mythology of American-made civil liberty. As custodians of artifactual terrain, institutional canons enact the creative transmission of social histories. Simultaneously stable and unstable, heritage dioramas reenact recorded interplay with narrative repositories. This exchange occurs through a scenic medium that confers to historic spectatorship, a sensible site, a placeholder. It presents a confounding autonomy that entertains the realm of pseudospectacle. Provoked in Rebecca Schneider's theatrical undoing of live reenactment, the lack of boundaries, as she states "between faux and real might not necessarily be failures or threats to the project of accessing, remembering, crossing the paths of the past."[18] Remnants of historical flux also negotiate somatic sensibilities. Perceptional engagement transects the ways pseudospectacles activate tangible spaces. Less uniformly regimented than propaganda; more complex than advertising slogans, the pseudosphere includes facets of redundancy, persuasion, exaggeration, justification, actuality, and errant claims. It is a believed status. Scenic dioramas creatively distribute convictions that manage, drive, contest, conflate, distract, or omit alternate viewpoints. On these artful stages, disciplinary perspectives preserve stages of scenic heritage. These vantage points dovetail with other historical trails.

Historical Preservation and the Conservation Movement

Cultural historicism aimed at preserving *natural history* concurred with activism toward land conservation attracting political and public attention from the 1870s onward. Lee Clark Mitchell examines an underlying ambivalence in nineteenth-century civil society over uprooting nature and decimating indigenous populations that begins to occupy cultural perceptions in the 1820s.[19] Western artist George Catlin first articulated the idea of national park during an 1834 visit to the Great Plains, where he painted the Lakota, Pawnee, and Mandan among others in their own territories on the eve of removal to reservations.[20] His image of a "specimen of America," containing human and beast in the wild, resembled "something approaching a living history museum," notes John C. Freemuth.[21] An assumption in Catlin's projection of historical preservation captures Indians and animals in natural habitats as anthropological subjects or zoological species of an open scene. It holds up a disturbing inversion of real-time fragmentation and eradication that would be erased and restructured for scenic adventure in Wild West Shows.[22]

A decade after Catlin's travels, nature artist John James Audubon, an avid hunter, recognized the decline in buffalo herds, which only escalated.[23] Over a ten-year period, hunters flocking to the Western Plains decimated buffalo populations in order to ship hides to Eastern tanneries. Once the gridirons of railroad routes were in operation, they were killed for pure sport by rail travelers, who shot at herds near the tracks.[24] W. T. Hornaday writing in the *Chautauquan Magazine* lamented the "extermination of American animals" by travelers and local residents "for every conceivable purpose," noting wild bison were practically extinct.[25] The preservation of two-hundred bison in Yellowstone National Park amounted to "a zoological garden" in the words of Hornaday.[26] The idea of scenic reserves gathered urban cache with zoo parks and wild animal spectacles. Animal dealer and showman Carl Hagenbeck devised "living habitats," for his approach to ethnographic performance in the 1870s.[27] With the launch of his *Tierpark* in Stellingen, Germany in 1907, he integrated animal display into wilderness reenactment and wildlife theatre. His "zoological garden" enchanted the cosmopolitan spectator with trained animal shows and exploratory paths for viewing animal habitats through different theme spaces. He replaced barred cages with trenches to permit "free" exchange. Intimacy with wild animals removed the barriers between stage and audience. Visitors explored unencumbered sites to tour a menagerie of exotic beasts, or watch a lion tamer risk life and limb in the arena. Nature spectacles traded on capturing the fearsome stronghold between human and nature by fabricating wilderness for "thrilling excitement."[28]

By the end of the nineteenth century, anxiety over industrial consumption of the land overflowed into public empathy for environmental protection. The visible crisis of the issue concerned national policies. The establishment of Yosemite National Park (1890) took over two decades to accomplish. A failed attempt to reserve California's Yosemite Valley and Mariposa Big Tree Grove from private development was led by landscape architect John Olmsted in 1865. Olmsted argued the reserve of a wild park a duty of democracy. He foresaw in the indigenous botany a "museum of natural science."[29] Following Olmsted, naturalist and amateur geologist John Muir waged a public campaign. His undaunted efforts on behalf saving Yosemite popularized the virtues of natural heritage in his widely read essays.[30] In his history of the conservation movement, Stephen Fox names him "press agent for the mountains."[31] In 1888, Muir teamed up with Robert Underwood Johnson, then editor of the high-end *Century* magazine. With Underwood's support, Muir's articles for the magazine deposited the preservation cause in the homes of the social elite. A leading figure of the conservation movement for over 40 years, he advocated attentive future planning of protected lands. His ardent mission championed environmental education the gateway for sustaining public awareness of legislative policies.

Wilderness preservation placed responsibility on active citizenship. It enlarged public empathy for conservation, challenging the industrial economy of progressive civil order, what Muir called the belief "that the world was made especially for the uses of men."[32] Naturalists, hunters, and outdoor enthusiasts took the lead in organized protection of endangered wildlife, forest, rivers, and wilderness.[33] Theodore Roosevelt and future president of the National

Parks Association George Bird Grinnell gathered hunting friends to form the elite Boone and Crockett Club (1888) to consider preventive measures of staving off the declining population of big game. During his Presidency, Theodore Roosevelt's domestic policy increased land conservation and legislative measures to protect wild game.[34] The San Francisco based Sierra Club (1892) fought for Yosemite forests. The Eastern Appalachian Mountain Club (1876) was joined by numerous others in the West.[35] State Audubon Societies dedicated to protecting bird populations merged into a National Association in 1905. Fox observes, "the conservation movement began as a hobby but became a profession," yielding to the complexities of legislation and centralized bureaucracy.[36]

Complicating demand for pure wilderness preservation were commercial aspirations. Public legislation seized on the antique mystic of the frontier, while pursing economic motives to lay transcontinental infrastructure. Assessment of territories natural resources documented regions for the potential cultivation of forestry, mining and agriculture, and to establish centralized domestic land management. From the 1820s onward, topographical surveys of the Western territories transmitted to Congress extensive field findings detailing the potential for settlement that included evaluations of water, wood, soil, and stone for agriculture, fuel, and housing.[37] Among ongoing surveys reported to congress by the Secretary of War is an 1832 letter from surveyor Isaac McCoy reporting from the field recommendations for Indian removal two-hundred miles West of Missouri and territory of Arkansas.[38] Government practice of land assimilation methodically identified the economic conditions for development and harvesting natural resources. Field surveys moved in segmented yet purposeful ways that were compiled into comprehensive narratives. One such exploratory "tour" commissioned the Reverend Jedidiah Morse for a hefty sum of $500 to study the religions, institutions, politics, educational systems, leaders, and daily circumstances of Indian tribes in the country. Ethnographic reports of Indian cultures within the "immediate neighborhoods" of advancing territorial interest were used to "promote the object of government in civilizing the Indians."[39] Antebellum field research structured the political goals of continental expansion.

Mounting pressure on Congress from trans-Mississippi Western States succeeded in the creation of a new executive branch, the Department of Home and the Interior in 1849.[40] The Department of the Interior (DOI) administered domestic policies. Before the creation of federal surveys following the Civil War, civilian exploration parties coordinated with Pacific Railroad surveyors, mainly under direction of the War Department. Early expeditions were dispatched in various directions over the mountain regions of the Far West. The reports were compiled in thirteen lavishly illustrated volumes called the *Pacific Railroad Reports* (1855–1860).[41] This "encyclopedia of the West" detailed descriptions of Western geology, botany, animals, birds, fish, ethnographic reports of Indian tribes, and comprehensive geographical maps. Field surveys laid the ground for the legal sale of land grants and "reservation" of Native American tribes within defined boundaries.

The US Geographical Survey of the Territories was formed in 1861 and placed in the charge the Land Office under the offices of the Secretary of the Interior in 1869.[42] One mandate under the control of the Commissioner of the General Land Office in the DOI, involved "sectioning the public lands, preparatory to opening them for settlement or entry"; the other was "to complete a map of the country" in topographical and geographical detail of unexplored regions.[43] This work was undertaken with Army escorts to protect expedition teams from Indian resistance. Fieldwork by four extensive federal surveys was conducted between 1867 and 1879.[44] Commonly called the "Great Surveys," scientists, artists, and government agents charted and secured the territories across the trans-Mississippi West for over a ten-year period.[45]

The first of the Great Surveys was led by geologist Clarence King to map an area of 86,290 square miles from the Sierra Nevada to the Eastern slope of the Rocky Mountains (1867–1872).[46] Professor Wesley Powell led an expedition of the Colorado River and tributaries, covering approximately 67,000 square miles (1871–1878). George Wheeler, First Lieutenant in the US Army Corp of Engineers, scouted more than 359,000 square miles over parts of Nevada and Arizona along the One Hundredth Meridian (1871–1874). Geologist Ferdinand V. Hayden headed surveys through 10,000 square miles of territories that would comprise much of the Yellowstone region: Colorado, Wyoming, Utah, New Mexico, and Idaho (1873–1878).[47] Mentioned earlier, his name became fused with the Yellowstone legacy. Backing the Hayden expedition was Jay Cooke. A primary interest holder of the Northern Pacific Railroad, Cooke used the survey to excite investment for the Western line of the railroad being built from Chicago to the West coast. He publicized the expedition to arouse public support for tourism; he envisioned a tourism industry, claiming the area "America's Switzerland."[48] The exotic terrain of the Northwest was reached by passenger train through Montana in 1883. Cooke enlisted publicity from Montana native National Langford, who lectured on behalf of the Northern Pacific Railroad in Eastern cities and published articles on "The Wonders of Yellowstone" in *Scribner's Magazine*.[49] The American Switzerland transitioned into an educational series. Under the State Department of Public Instruction, an illustrated narrative tour of "Colorado and the Grand Cañon" was featured in a series of public lectures by Board of Education member Professor Albert S. Bickmore at the American Museum of Natural History.[50]

Where data on the mineral, water, and soil resources of unexplored interiors of the Northwest was studied for the "cultivation" of settlement, industry, and agriculture, imagery returning from the region roused astonishment over the magnitude of its natural wonders. Documentation included visual records of the terrain illustrated by artists and field photographers. Timothy H. O'Sullivan, former apprentice to Civil War photographer Matthew Brady, joined the Wheeler expedition. He stereographic views panning up the walls of the Grand Canyon were taken while on a month long boat trip down the Colorado River.[51] *Scribner* engraver Thomas Moran, artist Henry W. Elliot, along with official field photographer of the US Geological and Geographical Survey William Henry Jackson joined the Hayden expedition. Jackson's publication of the *Beauties of the Rockies* canvassing the Rocky Mountains, Colorado, and Utah and New Mexico with panoramic scenes of city of Denver distributed wilderness attractions, much as nineteenth-century Mississippi river moving panoramas charted Midwest regionalism.[52] William Welling ties the rise in public interest in panoramic photographs of popular sites from the 1870s to increasing transportation access for tourism.[53] Landscape photographers paid less attention to aesthetic value than capturing souvenir scenes with which "tourists could more readily identify."[54]

Land preservation rallied public affection for the collective treasures of wilderness symbols: the Grand Canyon or the Rocky Mountains, and inspirational scenery of "spectacular sites."[55] The luster of cultural prestige in the world played a role in Congressional support for Yellowstone. The Committee on Public Land endorsed legislation of the 55-mile by 65-mile tract of uninhabitable land recognizing its economic value as a cultural resort that would interest travelers and scientific communities. "The geysers of Iceland, which have been objects of interest for the scientific men and travelers of the entire world," the committee reported, "sink into insignificance in comparison with the Hot Springs of the Yellowstone and Fire Hole Basins."[56] Evidence of a preexistent "native" heritage supplied the US with an ancient identity. Discoveries of Indian ruins in the Southwest unearthed the archaeology of a prehistory. They also drew looters, and vandalism became an alarming problem. [57] Congress acted to preserve heritage locations by passing the Antiquities Act in 1906. It designated historic sites, landmarks, and structures "national monuments" by presidential proclamation, ensuring their federal protection.[58] The outgrowth of federally mandated conservation emerged in a system of National Parks and Monuments under the charge of the DOI.

The opening of the West to field research drew attention to the vitality of new scientific subjects: zoology, ethnology, archaeology, paleontology, and botany. From the field, geologists, anthropologists, and archaeologists intercepted indigenous contexts as evidence of native pluralism. However, the autonomy of natural diversity advanced in nineteenth-century faith in scientific proofs contradicted the exclusionary parameters of ethnocentric cultural norms.[59] Anthropologists recorded cultural differences among Indians that challenged representative assumptions of racial homogeneity and tribal stereotypes, but the urgency to record languages, philosophies, and institutions of regional tribes was qualified as means for distinguishing strategies to further legislate civil assimilation within the reservation system.[60] Intellectual investment in the preservation of Indian cultures encouraged white reassessment of stereotypical representations of romanticized Indian identities as noble or savage. Cultural autonomy fed contexts toward reconstructing a native heritage in which Indian civilizations were absorbed in geological, paleontological, and archaeological evidence of "American" history. In Southwest Colorado, discoveries at Mesa Verde of the ruins of an ancestral Puebloan civilization were claimed as the "first Americans." Anthropologists assembled classifications such as "Cliff Dwellers, named" for their settlements on rock ledges and narrow, elongated shape of the skull, or "Basket Makers, a moniker" for cave settlers whose skulls were found buried under baskets.[61] Discoveries of ice age human remains in New Mexico and Nevada, named the Folsom Culture, ignited competition by research institutions to claim excavations sites. The American Museum of Natural History in New York had camps in New Mexico and Utah. The discovery of a Paelo-Indian culture revised theories over "the conceptions concerning the antiquity of man in America"[62] The study of human ethnography, artifacts, geology, and specimens involved research institutions that helped amend disciplinary narratives of evidential material for both practical application and as intellectual property. Adaptive reasoning informed ideas of Charles Sanders Pierce. In an article published in *Popular Science Monthly* (June 1878), Pierce argued an evolutionary theory of natural contexts that departed from an established treatment of uniformity.[63] The mathematician and influential founder of American pragmatism developed his theories of interpretive logic and semiotics, while employed mapping coastlines for thirty-two years by the US Coast and Geodetic Survey in the Department of Commerce and Labor.[64] Scientific investigation of uncharted regions had a practical side: to assess minerals and natural resources for economic value. It also provided cultural worth "for the use and wants of all classes."[65] The semiology of the Great West roused a hyperhistorical consciousness.

Soil, water, climate, and mineral data informed the "great industrial interests of the country" of potential investment.[66] In the late 1870s, the pursuit of field research in American Indian studies founded the Smithsonian's Bureau of Ethnology and the privately organized Archaeological Institute of America. Powell's expeditions were placed under the direction of the Smithsonian Institution. He later became Director of the Department of Ethnology there. He was accompanied by amateurs, naturalists, and scientists, including Professor A. H. Thompson overseeing the execution of geographic maps.[67] Each survey team used assorted methods and instruments for mapping. Because there was no general system in place to create and reproduce a comprehensive map, the National Academy of Sciences was enlisted to recommend standards.[68] Secretary of the Smithsonian Institution Joseph Henry lobbied on behalf of the Powell expedition for Congressional appropriations. Justifications for funding painted a synoptic vantage point of commercial and educational benefits. Henry argued the Colorado and its branches presented a "highly interesting" scientific point of view, including an "economical application of a portion of it to agricultural purposes" of irrigation.[69] Smithsonian holdings from geological expeditions formed public exhibits of the National Museum. In 1879, after Henry's death, the National Museum, by an act of Congress, was granted funding to erect a separate building. Its function had both a domestic agenda and the elevation of cultural stature internationally. The National Museum exhibited "resources of the country" in a collection of natural and artistic specimens, with the intention to:

> Present at a glance the materials essential to a condition of high civilization which exists in the different States of the Union; to show the various processes of manufacture which have been adopted by us, as well as those used in other countries; in short to form a great educational establishment by means of which out inhabitants as well as foreign visitors may be informed as to the means which exist in the United States for the enjoyment of life and for future improvement.[70]

Civic institutions interlaced material, artistic, and intellectual property in historical preservation. Adapting existing scenic mediums was one way to transmit cultural signage.

Between 1862 and 1871, US Congress made land grants of more than 174 million acres of public land in the Western interior for construction of four transcontinental railroads. Jackson became a member of the World's Transportation Commission (1894–1896), traveling through Asia, North Africa, Australia, and Oceana recording modes of transportation from rickshaws to bicycles. By commission for railroad companies, he documented the construction of transportation networks and locomotive travel in the 1890s. His work for the New York Central and Baltimore & Ohio companies were exhibited at the World's Columbian Exposition. Beside the hidden boundaries of territories and wilderness sites, industrial narratives recorded transformations of rapid modernization occurring in the West. Jackson was there too, photographing the building of the Pacific Railroad through Colorado's Rio Grande into Utah. His panoramic "windows" amplify tracks, machines, mining towns, mountains, rivers, and valleys in blended motion. Recalling the vocabulary of earlier visual media, human figures, when they appear, are landscape elements.[71] The steam locomotives of the Denver and Rio Grande passenger trains fill the frame in profile; their glistening bodies projecting sleek portraits of power and luxury. Colorado's dusty mining camps and smoky smelting towns relay working coexistence with the soft-edged surrounding mountains. Adventure tales sprout out of locomotives charging in tandem at the viewer or seize on a snaking passenger train in Ruby Canyon beside the Colorado River (Figure 5.1). Jackson inscribed a sensual harmony on the industrial landscape. His photographic scenes dramatized perception of machinery as an emotional, humanized content of natural geography.

Figure 5.1 William Henry Jackson, Ruby Castles, Canon of the Grand, Utah, 1900.

Source: Photograph. Detroit Publishing Company, Photograph Collection, Library of Congress, Prints and Photographs Division.

The moving gaze of Jackson's panoramic communion mingles wildner-ness in a transportation landscape.[72]

Dioramic Developments in Educational Media

Habitat displays repurposed instructional content with ideographic narratives. Their formal use in natural history museums paralleled the sensory invasion of immersive media in visual culture, theatrical entertainments, and exhibition environments. Early curatorial models of natural history exhibits documented white hierarchical narratives of civilization canvassing mineral, vertebrae, mammal, and ethnography. Late eighteenth-century and early nineteenth-century popular museums of natural sciences began creating armature for artificial *in situ* settings with taxidermy specimens, botanical models, and painted environments. Natural history groupings of birds and large animals used by portrait painter Charles Willson Peale in Philadelphia (1786), at Bullock's Museum (1815) and by E. T. Booth, who specialized in ornithological groups, began displaying illustrative specimens within an evolutionary taxonomy of preexisting order. Peale's ongoing collection of artifacts and specimens rooted nationalism in its providential assembly of visual and material exhibits: portraits of Revolutionary heroes, domestic artifacts, and specimens, which included expeditionary material from the Lewis and Clark surveys and wax figures of Native Americans.[73] His great-grandson Albert Peale was a mineralogist on the Hayden Survey team.[74] Peale's Americanized evolutionary theme of natural heritage answered the sting of European intellectual prejudices, particularly the theory of American degeneracy forwarded by French naturalist Buffon (George Louis Leclerc), who determined a weaker diversity and size of animals in the New World than from continental Europe.[75] Peale set forth material proof of American stature and historical prestige. The centerpiece of his unofficial national museum featured the mythical "American" Wooly Mammoth, an 11 ft by 17 ft giant mastodon skeleton, excavated in Newburg, New York, and mounted in 1801. His attention to recomposing "natural" life in scenic form used display art as an instructional tool. With an unorthodox artistic flourish, he added design elements to physical specimens:

> It is not customary in Europe, it is said, to paint skies and landscapes in their cases of birds and other animals, and it may have a neat and clean appearance to line them only with white paper, but on the other hand it is not only pleasing to see a sketch of landscape, but by showing the nest, hollow, cave or a particular view of the country from which they came, some instances of the habits may be given.[76]

By localizing the specimen's habitat, naturalized scenic identity made iconographic veracity accessible.

Svetlana Alpers denotes the crafted visibility of exhibition format informing cultural sight the "museum effect." Granted, curated points of view instill methodical ways of seeing or not seeing.[77] Early habitat fabrication is rooted in the production of static installation art that sways personal interpretation with semiotic concepts. To shift the notion, the media effect marshals immersive exchange in the sight lines of cultural perceptions.

Pedagogical approaches to historical content objectified scientific discovery. Ancient "American" archaeological sites and unknown ethnographies integrated North America into a contiguous global narration. Harvard's Museum of Comparative Zoology and the Peabody Museum, the Smithsonian Institution, and the American Museum of Natural History coincided with the completion of US geological surveys.[78] With the close of the Western frontier, research institutions dispatched scientific expeditions to the Great West. A team of paleontologists from the American Museum of Natural History excavated the complete skeleton of "prehistoric" million year old horse in Northeastern Colorado. The discovery of the Upper Miocene Period skeleton captured conclusive evidence that the ancestors of the horse were a "native of America" before appearing in Asian or Africa.[79] The discovery was considered of such importance a private donor funded further study and costs of mounting for display in order that "the complete story of the remarkable development of the horse can be told in a series of practical illustrations."[80] Prehistoric giant fossils of sabre-toothed cats, "American rhinoceros," mastodons, and dinosaurs refreshed landscape in a national antiquity that equaled Old World civilizations.[81]

The media effect deepens complications in regard to normalizing "characters" of race, society, geography, and history. Ethnographic exhibits muddled the margins of rational order. Live media extensions of natural history habitats lent performative sensation to ethnographic exhibits of humans and living villages. Transported human attractions displayed for profit in commercial halls and staged at expositions exploited scientific anomalies, normative epistemologies, and exploratory excursions, the exotica of travel, irrational distortions, and subjective disorder. Human curiosities famously staged by P. T. Barnum in his American Museum in New York (1842) marketed popular science myth and fantasy.[82] The media frenzy Barnum engineered to humbug the public with the Fejee mermaid or the bearded ladies traded on "natural wonders" that had to be seen to be believed.[83] The provenance of World Expositions became a public avenue for the educative authority of scientific institutions and ethnographic installations of stationary, miniature habitat groups placed in front of environmental backdrops. Simultaneously, imported ethnic villages and living habitats lined midways and alternative amusement zones. The blurry boundaries of educational content, ideographic consumption, and entertainment novelty skewed perceptual stability of deciphering recreation and reality. Barbara Kirshenblatt-Gimblett approaches live ethnographic display as a "panoptic mode" of increasingly ubiquitous effects.[84] "Live displays," Kirshenblatt-Gimblett writes, "whether recreations of daily activities or staged as formal performances, also create the illusion that the activities you watch, are being done rather than represented, a practice that creates the effect of authenticity, or realness."[85] Critical intervention may divest the panoptic of its subject power. The oblique illusions of habitat dioramas invite visitation to speculate on intangible presences.

In transitions from research institutions to public museums over the latter half of the nineteenth century, exhibit practices underwent reorganization. Curatorial ideologies experimented with narrative gesture. Display showcases aggregated exhaustive disciplinary narratives into intelligible, tactile conceptual stories that exemplified general principles. Artistically designed case studies vivified proximity to sites of scientific expeditions and engagement in rational evaluation: observation, inference, and deduction. Natural history models were among the first instruments used to attract the critical imagination of the public. Bennett elaborates the transformations in curatorial function that separated intellectual research and instructional pedagogy. Edward Grey of the British Museum's Zoological Department proposed "study-series" distinct from established comprehensive "exhibition-series" in 1858.[86] Educational methodology was adapted at the London Museum of Natural History in 1884 during the tenure of Sir William Henry Flower.[87] The American Museum of Natural History in New York (1868) mainstreamed preservation of a native heritage. Among exhibits were bird displays overseen by Morris K. Jessup, Director of the AMNH. An initial exhibit featured regional birds, such as American robins nesting on the bough of a flowering apple tree. Portraying the species domestically associated animal life with human attributes of home and family.[88] The first diorama of North American Birds was installed in 1887 in order to "nurture a reverence for nature by creating illusions of its beauty and grandeur."[89]

The art of nature recreation transposed wildlife to dramatic still life. Ornithologist Frank M. Chapman became the first curator of birds involved in crafting "habitat groups" for the Hall of North American Birds, which took 25 years to compete.[90] He established curatorial standards, sending expeditions to geographical sites with a team of specialists that included artists and taxidermists. Yet, taxidermy methods were not very sophisticated. Skins were mounted on crude armatures or specimens were stuffed with straw only to decay. Early displays were often misshapen or unrealistic. Comprised of glass cases, exhibits contained taxidermy specimens and botanical models with a painted background of the birds' environment. Manicured scenes attempted to portray wildlife as a realistic encounter. Although barely "distinguishable from a snapshot of the same subject in real life," one reporter noted that the actual drama of survival in the wild is "hidden beneath scientific reports."[91] Groupings staged a tranquil coexistence occurring among natures' aggressors, scavengers, and docile species. Stylizing "nature at glance" harkened back to the scrolling illusions of stationary panoramas. Tactile models of nature habitats joined already familiar reconstructions of popular scenic sites within the larger exhibition chronology of natural selection.

Wildlife dioramas proposed a common view of existence; the taming of the natural world aimed instructional coordinates at holistic concepts. The aesthetic identity of habitats shaped wildlife sentiments. The recreation of wildlife settings engaged human interest in story form. Their appearance in the waning nineteenth century mimics conservation efforts following the close of the Western frontier. According to Stephen Christopher Quinn, the habitat dioramas in the American Museum of Natural History "evolved in response to the public's growing awareness of wildlife and wilderness." Chapman's system of exhibiting preservation narratives replicated scenic reserves. His conservation efforts on behalf of endangered birds underlie his curatorial plan for the Hall of North American Birds. The ornithologists' union partnered with the Audubon society to protect bird populations. William Dutcher addressed a convention of ornithologists at the museum in 1897.[92] In addition to the destruction of nests, one of the most serious threats to bird populations was the millenary demand for feathers ornamenting women's hats. The fashion for the plumage of snowy herons and egrets at the time nearly brought these Southern dwellers to extinction. Chapman's display design modeled bird sanctuaries to raise empathy for wildlife protection. His Pelican Island group of 1902 is credited with assisting in establishing this nesting site in Vero Beach, Florida, the first federal bird reserve a year later.[93]

Industrial fabrication altered the methodology of mounting diorama exhibits. Self-taught taxidermist Carl Ethan Akeley joined the museum's staff in 1909 under president Henry Fairfield Osborn. Akeley reformed processes of taxidermy and diorama production.[94] He replaced stuffed specimens with the construction of manikins made from clay molds out of wood, wire, and skeletal parts. Plaster molds were then made from the clay model. The prepared animal skin was attached to the manikin. Full-scale habitat dioramas were constructed in workshops by large teams of scientists, taxidermist, fabricators, and artists. Competition, egos, and differences riddled collaborators.[95] The installations consisted of integrating three components: a curved panorama painting, manikins, and three-dimensional elements. Technical production required a fixed perspective for the panorama, providing a level vantage point for frontal viewing. Construction design manipulated mounted elements: plants, rocks, and other geographical set pieces, to fuse with a curved horizon line. One of the largest dioramas in the museum is the Bison and Pronghorn (1842) in the Hall of North American Mammals.[96] Cumulus clouds enter the frame from the left, while a group of four bison in the middle ground move right. In the distance, another herd painted on the panorama deepens the recessive span of spatial expanse. The herds curving shapes emulate the rolling prairie terrain. A pronghorn stands to the left of bison, staring directly at the interloper/visitor, while the largest of the bison, head tilted toward the foreground, is set off against an azure sky. The bison used were "taken" from a wildlife reservation in Western Montana. Background artist and designer James Perry Wilson studied the Wyoming plains for the panorama. His motto "art to conceal art" (*ars celare artem*) introduced the primacy of aesthetic values.[97] Albert E. Butler prepared foreground elements. Drawing out a felt encounter of being in the field, the composition holds a stable point of view for the visitor to infiltrate the scene. The rarified stage life grants visitors' a contemplative, on the spot immersion, whether absorbed in roaming within the scenic world or admiring it from a distance. The sensible exchange expands spectatorship into an artifactual presence that has no antecedent place. Its deliberative collaboration actively navigates the live and the synthetic. The spectator becomes a transformative agent to locating sensate presence.

Collaborative methodology of research and fabrication dislodges authorship from individual purpose to disciplinary mission. Diorama models express aesthetic standards in exhibition layout beyond scientific rationale. Osborn believed in bringing "a vision of the world to those who otherwise can never see it."[98] As a presentational system, the habitat diorama overwrote human exploitation of wildlife areas and ecosystems with an aesthetic subject hood organized out of embedded principles of appropriation for scholastic empowerment. Reconstituted references to perceived life engrossed viewership to not only appreciate a substitute for the natural world but also accept its absence and endow the illusion with existence. The manipulation of literate signs suited an adaptive range of instructional schemes.

Federal promotion of the Americanization of foreign-born populations announced by Theodore Roosevelt's Administration sounded the roll out of liberal reforms with the Americanization movement that peaked in the 1920s.[99] In 1915, the Bureau of Naturalization issued a letter advising that English language acquisition for immigrants was a first priority for American citizenship training.[100] Workplace control, denuding labor activism and regional migration guided approaches to philosophies and objectives. Liberal reformers, government and state agencies, educators, and corporate industries concentrated on educational reforms that implemented programs in civic education. In a study of methods and the function of different Americanization programs, Howard Hill from the School of Education at the University of Chicago formulated three criteria emphasized in defining a good citizen: intelligence, cooperation, and self-sacrifice.[101] Modifying attitudes and behavior to actively support workplace standards of efficiency and loyalty or to intensify patriotic attachment to dominant beliefs enunciated the benefits of self-compliance to achieve the American dream. Michael R. Olneck inverts complex arguments around Americanization that diverge over concerns of assimilation and ethnic conformity.[102] He finds educational mechanisms of control and order in a "symbolic reconfiguration of civic culture" that delegitimized collective ethnic identity by validating individual autonomy as a personal stake in the ethos of mass modernization.[103] Affirmative literacy invested citizenship with acquisition of an entitled identity within permanent infrastructure of social and material progress.[104] Deliberations over representative social change energized centrist narratives in New Deal cultural politics. [105]

Dioramamania

By the 1930s, wide-spread use of animated, mechanical, and stationary dioramas intersect with the social commerce of historical literacy. Diorama artists were classified with display painters in a new group established by the United Scenic Artists of America to ensure fair employment practice.[106] Educational media splintered into different syntax of cultural rhetoric. Museums of fine art, science, industry, history, and combinations of fields removed the "high hat" of cultural elitism.[107] A revitalized curatorial discourse entered museum practices making them "powerful educational forces." Metropolitan Museum of Art Secretary Henry W. Kent divided the modern museum function into three parts. In addition to the traditional role of acquisition and clean layout, the new purpose looked for ways to immerse visitors in the social application of history: "trying to get people to see what the exhibits mean" in contemporary life.[108] A classical aesthetic criterion of proportional beauty is no longer enough to cultivate common moral character, suggested R. L. Duffus. The sociological value of history exhibits served an interpretative function to empower public control over the "ugly" "jerry built, "nervewracking" machinery of modern conditions.[109] Diorama technology automated educative properties designed to attract and mold the imagination of the public. "How easy it is to learn by admiring!" asserted critic Waldemar Kaempffert, who argued dioramas bring "facts" to life, convinced that multimedia exhibit practices were leading the way for mass education in social sciences. [110] The vitality of the museums in the new era he claims, "dramatize knowledge by a skillful staging of exhibits, and the next step is the linking of art and natural science to man's social rise."[111] Dioramamania conversed with the parlance of humanities driven narratives.

Technical museums installed dioramas to contextualize industrial manufacturing as the social arm of applied science. The museum of Science and Industry opened an exhibition of food industries in 1931. Dioramas and miniature models taught methods of food transportation, preservation, and urban distribution"[112] Organized as the story of agriculture covering the global evolution of food industry over five-thousand years, the exhibit's messaging underscored how science aids farmers, and how the agricultural industry contributes to the health and welfare of society. In Chicago, the Field Museum of Natural History told "the story of man," with the opening of the Hall of the Stone Age of the Old World. Eight dioramas dramatized geo-global habitats: housing, tools, and food sources, of prehistoric races beginning with the Paleolithic period and ending with late Neolithic era. Life size figures of Neanderthal man and Cro-Magnon man breathed corporeal existence into comparative anthropology. The manikins were sculpted by Frederick B. Laschke, who accompanied assistant curator and anthropologist Henry Field to European archaeological sites. The evolutionary synthesis of "primitive" social organization associated ethnographies of difference to the domesticated productivity of white Indo-European cultures.[113]

The versatility of dioramas went beyond collaborations among artists, scientists, and researchers targeting specialized fields of knowledge. Corporate sponsorship of dioramas implanted consumer confidence in special exhibits producing attractive "man-made" wonders on the horizon. A block long, multimedia diorama of New York City constructed for the Consolidated Edison Company for the New York 1939 World's Fair required 100,000 hours of work to build it. Designed by Walter Dorwin Teague, the architectural model replicated more than four-thousand buildings, and employed time-lapse illumination to show, in 12 minutes, a day in the life of the charismatic cosmopolitan city. Each show accommodated eight-hundred spectators. From Times Square to Coney Island, the diorama sprang to action with motion, light, and sound effects synchronized with a spoken word lecturer. Miniature elevators rose and fell, a six-car subway sped beneath city streets, ocean liners arrived at piers, and transparencies rotated scenes of work and play, including a hospital operating room.[114] The underlining conceit imparted the radical new ways gas, electric, and steam revitalized urban living. Not to be outdone, General Motors sponsored Futurama, which became the most popular attraction at the fair.

Paul Mason Fotsch investigates General Motors' exhibits in connection to the Depression.[115] Lurking beneath problems of urban traffic congestion and highway planning were corporate designs on interstate growth. Futurama he argues, "like the fair as a whole, emphasized hope for the future at a time when daily life contained fear and uncertainty."[116] Designed by scenic artist Norman Bel Geddes, the diorama imagined a free flowing superhighway moving people and goods. Visitors felt the rush of the beltway by sitting on a rotating platform above a panoramic stage that held a fixed model of the "magic motorway" of tomorrow.[117] The open roads of suburban destinations free from urban congestion distributed the sensible aims of corporate objectives. The Insterstate Highway Act eventually passed in 1956. Futurama tickled synoptic patterns to construct a personal vision directed at lifestyle infrastructure. In popularizing the depiction of a future superhighway, the technology of change promoted the growth of interstate economies benefiting community, city, and state. Commerical dioramas optimized consumer choices by placing visionary desires in front of them; they made corporate identification with economic investment a stabilizing agent of uncertainty.

Another premise designed into commercial dioramas compassionately rendered labor relations. Consolidated Edison appealed to working class insecurities with a "forceful" labor advertisement at the fair.[118] The exhibit portrayed a brand mascot named Bill Jones, an "average Edison employee." Currently earning a standard of living one-third higher than in 1929, Mr. Jones enjoyed a pension, insurance, sick pay, medical service, and paid vacations. Employment in the electric light, power, and gas industry did not decline as much during the Depression due to the growth in use of electric energy according to a report by the National Bureau of Economic Research.[119] The lure of prospective job security that would improve standards of living offset the energy industry from the instabilities of labor-intensive industries struggling under Depression era stresses of declining revenue.

Social education disseminated Americanization by authenticating differences as interdependent plots of national heritage. Museum exhibits expanded educational outreach in coordination with public schools as virtual texts. Elementary school children in New York were taught the city's "story of communications" by means of "portable history sets." One series created by the Museum of the City of New York constructed transportable dioramas in metal cases (18 × 12 × 10 inches). These were loaned to schools in order to enhance lessons in the various ways human exchange occurs over time: the story ranged from ships signals and the telegraph to telephones and the future of telecommunications—another growth industry.[120] "To read in a history book," explained Museum President Courtlandt Nicoll, "no matter how eloquent, about an event naturally cannot be expected to make the same impression on a child's mind as to see the event, together with the background of the times in which it occurred."[121] In Washington, DC, the trend was nationally recognized with an exhibition at the National Museum devoted to new educational media for social science instruction drawn from museums' "extension work and visual aids."[122] The spotlight fell on an array of diorama models, showing "some of the possibilities of bringing history and other subjects to life."[123] Presented by the WPA and the DOI, the exhibition foregrounded WPA "American-made" activities around the country related to the integration of educational projects occurring in urban centers and rural schools.[124] In 1937, WPA white-collar professionals, artists, sculptors, and craftspeople boosted recovery efforts in 50 museums.[125] They worked as archivers, guides, lecturers, and diorama or display fabricators. WPA artists executed a series of dioramas for the Mamaroneck children's museum in Westchester County, New York. The Westchester project was supervised by historian William G. Fulcher, Chair of the Social Science Department of the Mamaroneck High School. WPA project coordinator Louis Bromberg directed the model making. Instructional methodology in WPA diorama projects standardized narrative techniques for historical reenactment. Four generic types are common: topographical, architectural, equipment, and human. The genres could then be serialized for dramatic groupings.[126] The first completed set followed an origin allegory—reminiscent of early nineteenth-century painted panoramas—through the life of the first colonist John Richbell. He is depicted landing at Mamaroneck and being warmly welcomed by Indian Chiefs Wappaquewam and Mahatan. Other story groups reproduced local landmarks, showed transportation milestones, depicted natural resources, such as water sources for irrigation and energy production, or reenacted significant events.

Federal work relief and public work projects administered throughout the country invested in modernizing regional infrastructure and reforming "American" culture. Colorado, along with 16 other Western states received a windfall of New Deal legislation and program funding.[127] The State Historical Society museum in Denver was among the beneficiaries. Its diorama collection resituated the independent enterprise of state heritage among the wonders in Western tourism.

The Heritage Trail of the Old New West

During his thirty years as historian for the Colorado Historical Society LeRoy R. Hafen recalls "the WPA years of the 1930s were the most fruitful in the history of the state historical society."[128] Hafen brought attention to the society's historical and field research with funding from New Deal programs. Hampered by financial downfall in state support, Hafen proposed a project for the State Museum through the Colorado offices of the WPA. The exhibit grew incrementally. It repatriated frontier mythology into a contemporaneous site of intercultural heritage. Plains Indians life, white settlement, mining, agriculture, and hydroelectric power encapsulate landmark scenes. The dioramas are set in wood frames; some are entirely sealed behind glass, others are free standing with no glass top. They were conceived as serial groups. One of the first series was the Western "story of transportation." Compositions modeled different means of travel over time, from Indian sleds and fur trapper carts to steam locomotives.[129] Business firsts feature dioramas of Pass Brown Bank and a local barbershop run by African American Barney Ford. Writing in the *Rocky Mountain News*, Lee Casey told readers in 1936, "there is nothing on exhibition in New York City or the celebrated Washington historical collections to exceed the results of the deft fingers and keen artistic taste of these Western artists."[130] With the director of the society's museum Edgar C. McMechen, Hafen supervised the research and construction of 78 dioramas between 1934 and 1941 with federal aid.[131] Relief funds enabled the "authenticity" of Western artists, architects, and researchers to recreate Western identity in the "American" fold. The Federal Writers' Project (FPA) relied on the local representational communities in the same way, inventing what Susan Schulten tags the "Old New Western History."[132]

The Colorado State Museum (Colorado History Center) began as a one-room attraction in Denver at the Glenarm Hotel over 130 years ago. The State Historical and Natural History Museum branched into specialized institutions in the early twentieth century: The Colorado State Museum and the Denver Museum of Nature and Science.[133] Its institutional development is tied to the growth of Colorado—it entered statehood in 1876—from US incorporation as a Western territory in 1860. The largest diorama in the collection, a 12 ft sq. plaster model of Denver's first white settlement along the South Platte River in 1860 is spotted with 350 tiny structures.[134] According to Tom Noel, education volunteer of the museum in the 1960s, the diorama always captivated fourth graders with its reconstructed streets of the "baby town."[135] The federal purchase of Indian land in Colorado was completed by 1880.[136] Many Plains Indians ceded their land prior to the Reservation period (1871–1887). The organization of a research society was instated by the State Congress in 1879 with a vision of recording the as "yet unwritten history" of white Colorado settlement.[137] Of more urgency was protecting proprietary rights over excavations as the influx of relic hunters and outside scientific institutions sponsoring field research removed artifacts and specimens.

The site of Mesa Verde was discovered accidently by local ranchers Richard Wetherill and Charles Mason in 1888. The Wetherill brothers became legendary for selling pottery and artifacts. They also guided explorers and archaeologists into the ruins, who infamously removed artifacts to Eastern and European institutions.[138] A cotillion of women from the state society and the Colorado Federation of Women's Clubs forged the Cliff Dwelling Association to claim proprietary rights. Since an area of the ruins was located on the Ute Mountain Ute reservation, the women, headed by Mrs. Gilbert McClurg and Mrs. George T. Summer, spent years negotiating a treaty to lease the land for excavation. Their ministries frequently bestowed gifts on the highly suspicious, elderly Chief Ignacio. On hearing the plans to "show" the site, the sage veteran is reported to have said: "You want to make a show of the cliff houses as they made a show at the festival at Denver last fall. White man always wants to make a show of everything."[139] A thirty-year treaty was signed in 1901 for $300 annually, which was immediately authorized by the DOI. The preservation campaign to take permanent control of the site as a park continued in Congressional lobbying efforts that contributed to the passage of the Antiquities Act.[140] Because of its significance as a national commodity, Mesa Verde became the first public reserve designated an archaeological national park. Its marketable values as a tourist attraction, generating jobs and income from hotels, trails, and roads, overtook preservation efforts based on intellectual or educational criteria. [141]

The fabrication of the Colorado dioramas applied research as a means of practical consideration. Texas born artist Juan Menchaca joined the project in 1936 and was involved in creating 40 of the dioramas. His first assignment was on the art project team, painting portraits of different important "characters" in state history from old photographs and "very sketchy research."[142] People moved around the different projects. He soon shifted to diorama models, becoming a supervisor. At times, 25 people were working on a series. Among his associates were A. A. Dubbs, Virgil Willis, Jules Ambruch, Harvey Garrill, Carlos Valencia, and Frank Gaton. Researchers gathered historical accounts of the subjects, from which the model makers arrived at an interpretive vision. A conceptual frame was developed for each series. Models in a series comprised nature views, habitat groups, and human activities. The framework supplied a dramatic spine, as well as a degree of continuity among different aesthetic sensibilities of model makers in charge of compositions. In one pioneer set, conceived as trapper groups, a beaver at work becomes the entry lure for the trapper. Another scene depicts mountain men in a canoe arriving or preparing to depart a trading post. Because the dioramas were assembled by different teams at different times, one personalized aspect is that they vary in size and shape. Fabrication consisted of a painted environment, plaster figures—casts were made to speed up production—and hand-made set pieces. Over time process techniques developed to speed up assembly of three-dimensional elements. To simulate different seasonal effects trees were made with sawdust; wire was used for the limbs of cast figures. In the back and forth between researchers and model makers refining details shaped a collaborative creative process as the dioramas were fabricated.

Scenes of Plains Indian life assimilate cultural authority in the "primitive" wilderness of indigenous autonomy. The reproduction of Mesa Verde brings scientific ethnographies to life. Dark haired, naked, rose-colored figures materialize in daily activities upon the cliffs. A diorama of a Pawnee buffalo hunt across the prairie was derived from George Catlin's naturalistic drawings of Comanche hunts almost one hundred years earlier. A contemporary disclaimer on display labels diverts attention to a preserved art object rather than the authority of its narrative treatment: "the scenes depicted in these dioramas are accurate in detail, but the artists chose their subject matter primarily for dramatic effect rather than as a systematic representation of tribal or frontier life." Cheyenne and Arapaho occupied practically all of Colorado East of the Rocky Mountains prior to the treaty of Fort Laramie in 1851. A diorama titled "Arapaho Indians Preparing Buffalo Meat" details methods of skinning, tanning, and preserving buffalo. Yet, the Arapaho and Cheyenne suffered one of the worst massacres in history—the Sand Creek Massacre.[143] During negotiations to lease lands in 1864, Colonel John Chivington led an unprovoked attack slaughtering two-hundred or more women, children, and men. Eye witness accounts relate pregnant women were disemboweled and mutilated for war trophies.[144] An artifactual stasis rears itself in present tense. Pioneering narratives justified atrocities of "winning" the West. The static, aesthetic monuments of Indian "habitats," amended to lifestyle reenactment, bump social histories against political narratives such as The *Frieze of American History* in the Capitol Rotunda.

Old new tales of a natural prehistory excavated material proof of an autonomous past, surmounting policies of ethnic cleansing in memorial social lore. Military scenes include a bustling Fort Bent. The fort was a stop along the upper Santa Fe Trail and used as a staging ground during the first American Intervention on Mexico (1846–1848).[145] Signs of Mexican presence are rare. In one diorama, it is reduced to a Spanish mule harnessed to a mill grind. Branded corporate mythology is cemented in regional icons. Illustrating water uses, prehistoric irrigation is juxtaposed with the new Boulder hydroelectric power station. The architectural model of the public utility company stands sentry without human presence. A transportation group reanimates Jackson's panoramic photography with three-dimensional replicas of The Denver & Rio Grand Railroad Company, founded by

General William Jackson Palmer in 1872. A model of the Narrow Gauge Denver & Rio Grande train, linking Colorado to the Pacific Coast, glides past in profile as it moves across the tracks. Working life in the dioramas elides the strong-arm tactics of union busting in neutralized tones. Labor flows in cooperative harmony with technology and machinery that crowd the series of mining, agribusiness, and manufacturing dioramas. The Denver & Rio Grand became an affiliate of the prominent mine, smelter, and mill operators, the Colorado Fuel and Iron Company (CFIC). CFIC coal miners and operators in Ludlow were massacred by militia in a strike breaking episodes that garnered national attention.[146] Corporate industries centralized power as major land-administering agencies in the West. In addition to considerations of passenger access, land and colonization departments promoted farming, mining, and ranching so they could also profit as shipping companies.

A statuary state sovereignty pervades historiographic distortion. State identity spackles habitat groups into regional commodities. Constructing exhibits for general appeal needed to balance a wide swath of visitation from in-state residents or out of state travelers. The theatrically tweaked realism of the dioramas revives the frontier as wonderland. Rugged terrain, hard work, individuality, and unadorned lifestyle revised the violent, rough and tumble Western mystic. What glue remains in the fashion of historical memory preserves the ethno exotic spirit of the region, the pioneering pluck of white cultivation, and the heroic, self-reliant character erecting an industrious economy that contributes to the greater welfare. The permanent preservation of "scenic reserves" on one side locates the interpretation of power relations granted by editorial control. On another side, the dioramas static perspectives uphold iconic tropes of historical interpretation that narrative migration revisits.

Civic Perspectives at the US Department of Interior

The logo of the US DOI is a buffalo with a sun rising above a mountain range. The monumental icon well suits the DOI, which is ironically called "the Mother of All Departments." Established in 1849, the DOI was empowered as an executive agency to administer domestic management of Federal lands, becoming a field agency in charge of Indian relations and land surveys. Its offspring included the Department of Commerce and Labor, as well as the Smithsonian Institution. Today, it consists of six agencies: the National Park Service, the Bureau of Indian Affairs, the Bureau of Land Management, the Bureau of Reclamation, the US Fish and Wildlife Service, and the US Geological Survey. New Deal liberal reforms augmented the public presence of the department as a broadcast channel of conservation policies, the work of the National Park Service, and changes to federal Indian policy that began restoration of the right to self-determination (1975).[147] One guiding mission is to educate the public about resource use and preservation.

The DOI museum was the brainchild of Secretary Harold Ickes. With $10,000 from the Public Works Administration (PWA) of which Ickes was director, the museum was built on the first floor of the Interior Department building in Washington, DC. Under Ickes prickly thirteen-year stewardship of the DOI, the public persona of the agency played offense defensively.[148] Ickes began public relations campaigns to market the National Parks and Monuments for domestic and international tourism. In February 1936, he established the US Tourism Bureau. He then mapped an ambitious five-point plan to interest business and government agencies in sponsoring an international advertising campaign to promote travel to the United States. On the surface, the proposal sought to "increase international good will and understanding."[149] In practice, the program had targeted marketing goals: publicity of US scenic and climatic attractions in foreign countries; travel and recreational exhibits at world's fairs representing the attractions of all states, regions, and territories; supervision of a permanent US recreational and travel exhibit with literature and travelog motion picture.[150] As part of the plan, participation from individual states was encouraged to sponsor the creation of permanent exhibits displaying scenic, health, and recreational attractions of the various states and territories. Contributions were deemed advantageous to "disseminate information."[151] The Interior Museum answered what Ickes' saw as a "long-standing, if not minor, identity problem."[152] His vision formulated narrative intervention in cultural politics.

Ickes' contrarian reach during his tenure as Secretary increased park lands while pursuing new legislative control for hydroelectric power and the leasing of public lands for oil, gas, forestry, and mining. National policies regulating environmental commerce amended the ethic of preservation. They intensified a tug of war with conservationists in favor of environmental protection.[153] "True conservation" Ickes argued is the "priceless heritage of natural resources which made our past possible, supports us the present, and upon which our future rests."[154] Museum exhibitions realized a way to orient the public to civil projects and educate them on the varied domestic activities of the agencies. Federal funding distributed two hundred white collar and skilled "technicians" to create heritage exhibits within National Park Museums to advertise the park system. The WPA aided this agenda. The Western Museums laboratory in Emeryville, California, received an infusion of federal aid to employ two-hundred technicians, artists, and fabricators involved in reproducing "natural wonders" and historic lore in different types of media: diorama, cross-section models, relief models, photographs, slides, and sketches, for onsite park museums.[155] Heritage preservation traversed the sociological mission of the National Parks Association (1919) to bring awareness and appreciation for science and history, while shifting gears into destination tourism to refuel state and city economies.

Enthusiasm was high when the DOI museum opened in 1939.[156] Ninety-four-year-old William Henry Jackson trekked to Washington from his studio in New York for the first private viewing. He painted for the museum four expedition scenes, one for each of the Great Surveys tying the 90-year-old institution to its roots. A reported 3,000–4,000 people, largely schoolchildren visited monthly. According to museum curator J. Paul Hudson, a year later the visitor count rose to 130,000.[157] However, stagnation set in after WWII.

Exhibition layout divided a cavernous ground floor space with walls to create separate galleries and alcoves for each bureau's exhibits. The dioramas were conceived as fixed installations within the architectural structure. Curators codified a rigorous methodology around the design and planning of diorama exhibits. Much of the methodology was developed by museum superintendent Ned Burns and chief curator Louis Schellbach. Burns accumulated a staff of 21.[158] Artist Ralph Lewis and assistant fabricators Donald Johnson and Albert McClure collaborated closely. As Chief of the museum division of the National Park Service, Burns had extensive knowledge of diorama fabrication. He published a field manual detailing all types of exhibition layout that ranged from design modules to educational function.[159] Preparations began in 1935. By the end of year, Burns moved his workshop from Morristown, New Jersey, to Washington, DC.

Eleven large-scale dioramas were created between 1937 and 1940.[160] The story of conservation concentrated on land development and the use of natural resources, helping to humanize the work of each bureau. Each agencies storyline is compiled through juxtaposing artifacts, instruments, photographs, maps, watercolor illustrations, drawings, models, and dioramas. The aggregate stitches together a panoramic view over a division's working life; the educational purpose was to "interpret for the public in comprehensive and attractive form" a conceptual identity. A chapter in colonial history depicted the Louisiana Purchase, with George Washington welcoming Lafayette on the steps of the Ford House in Morristown. Jackson worked with artists on costumes to tell the story of the founding myth of Yellowstone—when Hayden's scouting party sat around a campfire dreaming up the idea of a national wilderness park. A scene of an Indian Hogan continued paternalist attitudes of nineteenth-century wilderness stereotypes. [161] Offensive exhibits have since been removed from exhibition space. In the revisionary life of the DOI, its museum, Indian Craft shop, and installation

Figure 5.2 "Coal Mine Explosion Diorama," Ralph Lewis featured in the photograph.

Source: Historic Photograph Collection, Digital Image, Courtesy of the US Department of the Interior Museum..

of commissioned murals by artists of different Indian nations now showcase self-representations of Native American culture.[162]

The Bureau of Land Management exhibit relates land grants and regulated use of public lands to homesteading, crop irrigation, and oil production; the US Geological Survey section represents typographical models and a river measurement station. The defunct Bureau of Mines (Figure 5.2) includes the recreation of rescue efforts during the 1929 Kinloch coal mine explosion in West Virginia; the Bureau of Land Reclamation features Hoover Dam. Multimedia dioramas rely on motors to sync lighting effects. A scene of the Alaska-Juneau Gold Mine Company shows the port view of transporting minerals to Juneau around the clock. Lighting effects transverse a scene cycling through night and day.

The placement and design of dioramas were part of museum planning. They were constructed to be set into the walls; they glow from alcoves with the allure of miniature theatres. Cases are placed at eye level five feet from the floor to provide a dominant vantage point. Perspective depth is achieved with filtered light directed against the curved wall of the panorama. Figures are made from hard wax, molded on wire framework and enforced with fiber. Materials for set pieces are made from wood, metal, and plastics. Architectural elements are constructed out of paper maché or composition board. Diorama exhibits follow prescribed content areas:

> Close-up of the climax of an important and dramatic event or showing plants in operation.
> Close-up of details of violent action (fire, earthquake, wreck, battle scene).
> Panoramic view of violent action.
> Close-up of subdued or limited activity (everyday village street, garden, period interior, forest, or ecological setting).
> Panoramic view of above, small scale.
> Manufacturing plant in operation—employing animating devices.
> Panoramic view of whole city or countryside with no activity in extremely small scale.[163]

The various dramatizations evoke standard educational genres. The river survey scene is a heightened close-up of a surveyor suspended over the water in an open basket while taking a measurement in the rushing currents. A small structure on the riverbank shows the measurement station. The human focus amplifies the risky actions of field agents working to ensure the safety and health of the country's water sources. A close-up view detailing the Kinloch coal mine explosion depicts disaster response. The perspective draws the visitor into the recovery scene as a team rescues workers, who were trapped underground when the mine exploded. The intricately costumed figures, features, and gestures of rescue workers, police, and bystanders are highly expressive. Rescue workers have white backpacks strapped on, replicating the McCasa breathing regulators used. The life saving regulators tell the story that protecting mine workers was behind the formation of the Bureau of Mines, and its work with developing safety equipment.

Environmental destruction in the West motivated conservation legislation. Unregulated mining processes, oil and gas drilling, deforestation, and agribusiness polluted water, endangered wildlife, and drained wetlands.[164] Several dioramas amplify government empathy with proper land management or restoration. In one setting, a DOI agent stands amid a lush farmstead intently checking an irrigation pump. Seen from above is a smaller scale topographical view of Hoover Dam, illustrating flood control, navigation, and power development. The torrential cascade of water spilling down Nevada's Black Canyon supplants the mighty falls of Niagara with human engineering harnessing nature for new energy sources. Not visible is the consortium of contractors or banks financing New Deal energy projects.[165] Another tight view shows an architectural model of Kettleman Hills Oil Field in operation. Regulated use of natural resources magnifies how public land leases create common profit, as well as employment. The California petroleum producer was hailed as the largest domestic producer of oil in the country at the time. An accompanying display label points out leased lands for oil and gas production accounted for annual revenue of $3,000,000. The steel structure swells out in all directions beyond the diorama's frame. Two human figures in the scene are scaled down to emphasis the monumentality of the working plant.

New Deal reforms left behind pioneer history. In 1887, the Dawes Act secured the Western break up of tribal lands, which were allotted to non-Indians through land grants. A panoramic activity diorama recreates a tent camp springing up around an Oklahoma land office; it landmarks closing the frontier for Western settlement. A topographical scene of a DOI agent speaking with a sheep rancher illustrates The Taylor Grazing Act (1934), conserving grazing ranges through cooperative conservation. Small, uncased capsule views of scenic landscape were used to visualize year round vacation use of the National Parks. A skiing diorama shows figures flying down Yosemite Mountain.

The educational storyline in the DOI dioramas is oblique. Burns stated the overarching goal is to tell "a larger story which embraces the whole nation—the story of America."[166] The museum initially stood as a monument to the revolutionizing politics of liberalism. The episodic circulation of heightened dramatic encounters renders for the visitor a pan-American effect of public servants preserving the bountiful resources of natural heritage. Positive role models demonstrate compassionate care of food and energy production, job creation, ensuring safety from floods and work hazards.[167] Since the museum functioned within the larger interpretative programs of the DOI, it served as a training ground for the system national parks. The explicit methodological approach to installing educational media articulates artifactual existence. By design, exhibits devised complex diagrammatic intersections in order to spawn a radial "diffusion of knowledge."[168] Burns's curatorial philosophy dispensed with recreating models of linear, evolutionary relationships. The function and methods of interpretation are arrayed within the immersive narratives of institutional aspiration.

Crossing into Spectacle Autonomy

Disciplinary genres of scenic spectacles tread widely in institutional settings, while remaining conversant with new immersive styles of entertainment. Possessing broad functions of interpretive power, educational media powered social spectatorship. Dioramas formalize an interactive instrument of productive reason. The collaborative art of diorama manufacture ratified a medium that tunnels into psychological and imaginative internment. Its static model of physical order in paint and wax and wire dissolves anchorage to physical phenomena. The preset expression of stage life instills the transitory tensions of felt reception. Interaction with a creatively structured existence grants spectatorship responsive control to evaluate difference, multiplicity, and systemic viewpoints. Immersion in artifactual presence confers an empathetic position to the attraction of spectacle sensibilities. Fixed perspectives determine accessible vantage points of locative mobility; narrative conceits encourage cooperative powers of exchange to reconstitute, contest, assent or redress scenic models. The pseudospectacle is autonomous. Its discursive currency is self-perpetuating, all embracing, and multidimensional. Scenic visibility temporarily occupies a staged space that frames a new scene. What is buried surfaces; what is absent comes into existence; what is present is replaced. The blank slate appears again.

The transgressive voids creating "American" heritage suggest the preserved illusions of history recuperate an interpretive order in landscape resonators of phantom memory: the vast enterprise of working life, regional identities, and monumental rights to free agency. The remains of an "American-made" past are recovered in productive concert edging toward sight lines of future occupation. Spatial flux yields a yet unsettled frontier. Modern era heritage underwent geospatial renovation. Landlocked battles wielded narrative sparring over vacillating perspectives, over differences. Scenic landscapes reimagined fixed sight lines on the instabilities of history. The protracted historiography of the Western frontier disturbed then and now in contradictory environmentalism: having secured the boundaries of a "wild" continent, the vanquished past modulated in retroactive wonders and enterprise.

We arrive at a circuitry in the passages among the actual, the illusionary, and ideals. The forward trajectory of this visionary principle floats through protracted negotiations of spatial boundaries, we the people. Scenic discourse redeemed systematic regeneration of cultural identity, economic potency, and national myths by colonizing novelty as inclusive to the natural order. Recessive trajectories slip and slide, yielding or surfacing while remaining in motion. The fabric of sensory media courses out in all directions across spectacle landscapes through progressive stages, through reactionary stages, through grass roots populism and radical protest, dipping into economic depressions and out, over the fight for civil rights, marginalizing communities or demonizing alien identities. What remains of tradition may reside in the conscious territory of citizenship that illusion is the nature of the quest.

Epilogue: Visionary Spaces

US scenic history, a history that pierces topographical memory, preserves its own vacillation. Scenic spectacles occupy the transient course of national design, reviving the blank spaces of a moving quest. If movement is a dialogic of political economy, it not only interchanges disintegration as an unbridled, visionary territory but also returns a social discourse interwoven in the ricochet of awe and terror—presently resounding in a post-9/11 landmarked consciousness. Niagara Falls boldly stated this unrelenting potential in the Northeast. Economic disparities and disenfranchisement rode along the Mississippi River, and the Western summits occluded the destructive passages laying claim to nation. Landscape's admixture of actual, illusion, ideal rummages through scenic life with immersive vitality: to rewind a few, cultural landscapes rouse new sensations, new destinations, or new vantage points; political landscapes reinstate, retract, reform, protest, and decompose. Diana Taylor's inflection of the archive is worth pausing over in respect to historic scene spaces. Taylor retrieves cultural expressions from the acts of performance; the unwritten repertoire of embodied practices braces, too, the vocabularies of scenic memory in motion and stasis that elude language.[1] The repertoire in Taylor's words "requires presence: people participate in the production and reproduction of knowledge by 'being there,' being part of the transmission."[2] Trying to access what the repertoire does entangles social praxis as well in spectacle activity. Spectacle mediums of transmission further confound scenic mediation. Even when scenic heritage is reproduced, sensory technology actively relocate the immersive exchange of (dis)embodiment. In this manner, spectacle practices continue to alter how sensory perceptions occupy new spaces. I began this study with present landscapes in mind, which I have yet to address. In a few final scenes, I jump forward to rejoin sensory media's complicated pathways in contemporary spectacles.

From installation panoramas to multimedia performance, "specs" on stage and into site-specific productions, architectural design and public spaces, theme parks, tourist resorts, malls, and into twenty-first-century virtual sites, what now is referred to as the media of spectacle, continue to exude immersive regeneration. Angela Ndalianis's treatment of neo-Baroque aesthetics across contemporary entertainments wraps spectacle efficacy around the "architecture of the senses."[3] Intriguingly, the commonplace technosensorium of spatiality also reenacts landscape narratives that directly and indirectly funnel antecedents in the embodied phenomenology of nineteenth-century scenes of wonder and enterprise. Illusion technologies of nineteenth-century entertainment conventions pushed out perceptual boundaries. Christopher Kent questions scholarly constraint around the ocular construct of "realism." He offers the challenge that nineteenth-century interception of vision technology "created new definitions of visual realism which, contrary to the apodictic truth claims of the camera obscura's image, depended on deception and even falsehood."[4]

Convincingly, perceptional deception no longer accounts for the effect of "natural" illusion. The interface of social space and sensory mediums: static, live, and virtual, occupy a multifarious terrain of spectacle presence. Both the Colorado History Museum and the US Department of the Interior Museum closed to renovate their exhibit spaces. The renamed History Colorado Center has since moved to a new facility, reopening in 2011. Following trends in immersive design, HCC also linked its governance of 12 other museums and historic sites statewide in the lucrative heritage tourism industry.[5] The Interior Museum is still in process of its update at this time. Earlier, I mentioned a recent exhibition at the Smithsonian Institute's National Museum of American History in Washington, DC. *America on the Move* charts the economies of the transportation landscape in making US history. Its state-of-the-art techniques employ sensory methodologies in the form of audio labels, overheard theatrical dialogs, interactive multimedia technology, and life-size dioramas. Visitors are moving parts of the panoramic display floor, meandering around the trains, cars, subways, cargo containers, and maps that diagram the exhibits. Display themes reference a winding path through immigration, technology, leisure, labor, and industry. Interdependent systems of commercial trade scaffold the educational historiographies of nineteenth-century supply routes. Consumer models of transportation, such as a 1950s Portland Oregon Buick dealership, transition to global industries with an aerospace exhibit lining the exit route. The transtemporal avenues of traffic animate a corporate history interlocking country, community, and family, all building a "progressive" American way of life. The exhibition magnetizes the lived landscape rather than a miniature habitat, one in which the spectator creates and consumes its segmented scenic stories. Strangely, the inviting dioramic windows do not stray far from the traveling shows of white constructed Mississippi River panoramas, the working models of exhibition displays, or the empathetic machinery of Jackson's panoramic photographs of the Denver and Rio Grande passenger trains.

Institutional-corporate partnership reproduces a machine-driven tour. The exhibition's installation artworks were actual objects; its habitat environments artfully staged by museum teams. Socioeconomic integration paves conduits: work, home, leisure, back and forth among the physical object hood of interactive scene spaces. Spectatorship activates the panoramic presence. A life-size child mannequin stands in a suburban driveway beside the family station wagon. Audio of vacationers at a country cabin unpack in the wilderness. The visitor's sensible invigoration can skip or deliberate with the exhibitions educational sight lines. Passing by the diorama of suburban migration, one can pause in reflection at the child in the driveway—as I did, recalling a dormant childhood memory—or eavesdrop on the vacationers surrounded by rustic wilderness. Transportation exhibits featured in fair culture resurface as well. A 1903 Winton, the first car to be driven across the United States, and a set of roadsters heading down the highway in a Route 66 diorama generically recover the nostalgic lore of road trips. A Chicago Transit Authority train landmarks urban development. The mass transit car lets travelers enter and sit down to observe other passengers conversing at the head of the car on a video loop. Weaving among artifacts of commerce and leisure infrastructure, the typology of daily life fragments in polycentric ways. The show's immersive mentality tripped openings and partitions to cross through and against its boundaries; its elliptical monuments and memories ensnared my own artifactual existence.

In recent decades, large-scale production values of a spectacle "nature" are saturated in scenic patterns and media-centric predecessors of nineteenth-century entertainments. I offer a few more threads that maneuver over implications of how the precedents and prototypes of panoramic installations and multimedia performance lurk in contemporary practices. My starting point is static and moving installation environments treating landscape as history. The opening ceremonies of the 2008 Summer Olympics in Beijing, China, and Robert Lepage's theatrical odyssey *Lipsynch*, which I attended in 2009 at the Brooklyn Academy of Music in New York, supply examples of mythmaking and myth-busting historical spectacles.

Visual artist Kara Walker directly references nineteenth-century visual narratives and panoramic traditions in her installations to question race assumptions in American mythologies. Her use of black silhouettes floating in white spaces negates the structural perspective of the horizon line used to construct the *natural order* of panoramic space. Recurrent references to colonialism and slavery in her work are enacted in vignettes that couple shame and desire, presence and absence. The disturbance of panoramic illusion in her work forces one to reckon within the scale and scope of white cultural entrapment. "Most pieces have to do with exchanges of power, attempts to steal power away from others," says Walker.[6] Cutting into white representational supremacy, she draws on imagery from narrative sources from the antebellum South, testimonial slave narratives, historical novels, and minstrel shows. She slices into fact as fiction to uncover the living myths of racial and gender discrimination. The monuments of heroic normative values, such as home, family, country, are swallowed in acts of sex, violence, love, exclusion, and humiliation. If we consider the orientation of space derived from the manipulation of perspective (from the Renaissance), Walker's silhouettes cast shadows on conventional thinking about race representation in the context of relocating the terrain of racism in its monolithic destruction.[7] Her panoramic installations vacate the illusionary qualities of spectacle to confront the viewer with the empty spaces provoking disenfranchisement. In projecting the historical performance of cultural genocide, Walker's silhouettes carry forward haunted global localities of ongoing traumas.

Another side of panoramic perspective is (Danish-Icelandic) Olafur Eliasson's color installations and site-specific environments. He internalizes the horizon line by removing perspective anchorage between viewer and object. The experiential nature of space becomes a public spectacle. Eliasson's circular rooms typically have no order to the sense of space, no imagery, and no descriptive link to experience, except the external motion of light and space. In an installation called *Beauty*, the spectator stands in an empty "white" room, a rainbow emerges from a curtain of mist and vanishes. In *Take Your Time*, a huge slanted oval mirror suspended across the gallery ceiling leaves visitors to wait and watch and discovers things happening or not.[8] His precocious denial of reference and mediation encourages the spectator to enter processes of revelation by sharing in instances of illumination and variation. Eliasson's work in contrast to Walker's revalidates panoramic entertainments by recovering the scenic expressiveness of immersive landscapes, such as Frederic Church's *Niagara*. Holland Cotter termed Eliasson's social activism "a politics of enchantment."[9] Site-specific environments such as the *New York City Waterfalls*, where he deployed four sculptural ergonomic waterfalls on the East River leans back to landscape art of the nineteenth century that assimilated the sublime modalities of romanticism. Eliasson revises the natural power of landscape art past and present in panoramic civic events. His ongoing work, which he documents in the 2009 film *Space is Process*, attempts to reengage spatial depth and volume in the surrounding social communion of the event.

Large-scale theatrical spectacles recover hallmarks of mass movement, temporal mechanization, and multimedia effects. In particular, cross-cultural transmission of site-specific spectacle events occasions their own transappearances. Global spectacles are reproductive accelerants. They are often generated in real-time, yet produced to cross over from live format to world media streams for multipurpose appeal. With world viewership segmented and fractured into multiple screens, real time, and virtual environments, spectacle excursions float among media savvy audiences, who reframe the mechanisms of a scene into many. By design, panoramic vantage points are seen in whole and in part. Physical production values take into account that a portion of the audience is live at the event, global audiences are in different time zones, and networks of online spectators are viewing isolated scenes of unfolding live action. Different time-captures, narratives, and panning frames of the live performance are edited by media outlets into various broadcast editions. The monolithic branding of cross-cultural spectacles takes on other existences across local, national, and global interaction.

Australian director David Atkins signaled the technological wave of immersive geoglobal landscapes scoring special event spectacles with the orchestrations of the opening and closing ceremonies of the 2000 Sydney Summer Olympic Games. The twenty-first century mode of these diversionary Kiralfyesque offspring is mediated by political and cultural propaganda yet often dismantled by global media and social networks.[10] When David Atkins again returned to direct and produce the Vancouver 2010 Winter Olympic ceremonies with a team of Canadian designers, the narrative theme "Landscape of Dreams" packaged travel through Canadian history with the enhancements of 100 projectors, LED screens, and 3D holographic imagery. The performance was not without its own technical mishaps with the failure of a hydraulic beam of the Olympic cauldron that did not rise on cue. Many of the razzle-dazzle effects of the performance were steered to "brand" the host's cultural landscape in an episodic narrative of historic mythology.

Two months after a horrific earthquake in Sichuan province, the much-anticipated 2008 Beijing Olympics opened. The lead up to the Games occurred in a politically charged climate.[11] International criticism saturated media coverage when Tibetan independence protesters raised a "Free Tibet" banner near the National Stadium in March and were speedily deported. China spent forty-three billion dollars building roads, stadiums, parks, and subway lines in trying to transform Beijing into an Olympic city. The lucky number eight was aligned with the event. At 8pm on the eighth day of the eighth month of the eighth year of the twenty-first century, the opening ceremony began. "The historic moment we have long awaited is arriving," President Hu Jintao said at preceremony luncheon with visiting heads of state: "The world has never needed mutual understanding, mutual toleration, and mutual cooperation as much as it does today."[12] Two years in the making, the proceedings were designed to project a new face to the world, while trying to overwrite a troubled human rights record. Composer Tan Dun, speaking for the record, summed up the pride swelling around the country. "This is a great honor for my culture," he said, "This is a lot more than about China. If we think this is only China's moment, it's a big mistake. It's the moment of the world."[13] The stunning opening ceremony, directed by China's most famous film director, Zhang Yimou, cost a reported hundred million dollars. Zhang, whose early films were banned by government censors found himself criticized for entering political favor.[14] He is a controversial example of China's shifting economic agenda. Chinese artists adapting to changes in the political economy over the past decade are busy shaping China's global landscape. Wu Tianming, a well-known producer and director, related, "Now, the government wants directors to promote the country's economic development."[15]

Rising pride in China's empowering stature in global economies was injected into the production. Its theme was "One World, One Dream." The elaborate performance included fifteen thousand performers and a three-part production, compressing Chinese culture, history, and the economy of modern China into a four-hour pageant of resplendent goodwill with the rest of the world. State media giant, China Central Television (CCTV) drew an estimated 80 percent of Chinese households in its coverage.[16] The global television audience was estimated to surpass four billion viewers (in the United States, the opening ceremonies were not carried live). The processional style of dance, music, special effects, as well as the mechanized precision of thousands of performers included the ornamental choreography of dancers on a giant calligraphy scroll. Illustrative patterns depicted traditional forms of Chinese music, dance, and visual art. The live audience experienced the panoramic environment of the stadium setting and participated in the scenic episodes. Cameras substituted alternate angles on the mass movement in panning perspectives around the stadium for US television audiences. However, delayed action also used retooled footage that was broadcast live. Mark Magnier of the *L.A. Times* noted a final explosion of fireworks was recreated by the visual effects team, who "worried about the difficulty of cameras capturing 29 sequential explosions." Except for one "big bang," everything was reproduced in an animation studio, and "inserted the 55-second clip into the live TV coverage."[17] The studio-generated rhythms coordinated a carefully regimented makeover. China is investing heavily to compete globally, carving a share in entertainment and art industries.[18] However, the glazed effects choreographed to showcase a new world cultural landscape excavated persistent wounds.

Despite the outward confidence of the national spectacle, the monumental moment uncovered tears in the mesmerizing color fields of the live performance. In the wake of glowing praise for the opening ceremonies—and a nod to future promise—revelations began to surface of behind the scenes manipulation. Embarrassing stories started to surface about dubbed voices and digitally animated fireworks streamed as live to television viewers. The overnight celebrity of the "smiling angel," nine-year-old Lin Miako, turned to national shame and humiliation when her lip-synched "Ode to the Motherland" was discovered. Alongside the image of her in a pretty red dress the scandal broke.[19] Under the pressure of intense internal outrage and international scrutiny, Chinese officials admitted deceiving the public.[20] The switch was made because a senior party member attending a dress rehearsal found the actual singer unattractive. The substitution of a picture-perfect schoolgirl was ordered. Once the illusion ruptured, public criticism flew across social media with many online condemning the hypocrisy of falsifying "national honor." The Beijing Olympics opening ceremony indicates how swiftly political narratives are unhinged, and how the crafted geopolitical space of market reform divests spectacle "integration" of a stabilizing vantage point. The scenic appliqué cannot hold its stitching; the technospatial landscape defies narrative consolidation, even when acting to advance marketplace ideals.

A counterweight to the engines of economic globalism and effusion in special event spectacle is experimental multimedia performance. The ever-evolving interdisciplinary language of Robert Lepage is one example among contemporary directors and companies. For the past 20 years, Lepage's work with Ex Machina has explored the borderlands of multimedia aesthetics. At times, the overlay of visual narrative and multimedia tricks in his work has overwhelmed the dramatic or operatic content. In one of his recent collaborations *Lipsynch*, multimedia dramaturgy and dramatic substance liquefy a protean storytelling sensibility. A synthetic presence pulsates in the 8.5-hour epic that stretches in multiple directions moving from wartime Vienna to present-day London, Nicaragua, and Quebec City. Travel landscapes interweave the communal and the contemporary.[21] The mythic tropes used to unify and reference sociopolitical discourse are carefully erased. The theatrical odyssey launches a quest to locate identity that fragments geographical place and spatial sense to reach into the body of emotions. The action arises out of a baby's cry. The sound of the primal cry signals both the mystery of the child's mother in whose dead arms the child wails and the beginning of the journey on a transcontinental flight.

Lepage relates through the art collective website epidemic, "up until now our work at Ex Machina had focused mainly on telling stories using image, movement, space, and music. Voice was rather an afterthought. This time around we have decided to make it our focal point and see where the exploration of oral communication in all its forms would take us."[22] Sensory communication unbinds the logic of order and control. It creates a fabric of the different ways human beings communicate—from the isolated cry of the orphaned baby to opera singing and computerized synthesizing. The performance portrays all human vocal emanations; its creation was a collaboration with Spanish, German, British, and Quebecois performers, who built the piece with everything from clinical research to personal reminiscence.[23]

The branching storylines open into the illusions, hallucinations, dreams, pain, or desires of nine lives, which open onto other lives. To find one's voice, to recapture family, to record memory, to lose one's voice, the composite trek opens portals through the reified voice of opera, to synthesized dubbing, and voiceovers. Lepage breaches the architecture of myths: home, family, country, in sentient perspectives. The spectator is thrown in the murkiness of differentiating urgent human dilemmas: mental illness, disease, sex trafficking, and death from among sound tracks of looping noise. Sherry Simon notes that "Lepage's work nourishes our understanding of translation today as a reality and as an ideal that has more to do with discontinuity, friction, and multiplicity than it has to do with commonality, precisely because culture no longer offers itself as a unifying force."[24]

Lipsynch infiltrates the perplexing trajectories of voids, where narrative fails and the lived situation strains to communicate. Contact is fleeting; the human body and the technological body sync presence in a search of unknown identity. Immersion in empathy trespasses physical mediation in the spatial wiring disconnecting time, place, and body. This disjointed sensorium severs panoramic presence, of landscape, of scene, and of embodiment beyond any physical factum. The phantom tissues of its origin quest afflict breakage with illusion as mere effect; the scenic dimensions detach and replace sight lines from the fabric of the live, shattering locative placement. Departure vocalizes the near and far, appearing and disappearing in a synchronic landscape exchanging real time and virtual time. This type of immersive synthesis suggests the approach of a borderland. Such turning and returning to the yet unwritten space recoils on the historical repertoire.

The shape-shifting span of spectacle behavior launched this study, which I come back to. Landscape and spectacle share a mutual induction into the American project as immersive mediums: one transmitting environmental mediation, the other sensory mediation. In the nineteenth century, the swirling expressions of sensory media were novel. Scene space communed with active expressions of wonder and enterprise. Commercial and institutional industries of scenic spectacles surging forth from the nineteenth century divulge evasive sentient distension. Commercial "specs" branded entertainment infrastructure and media technologies into social legacies. Institutional philosophies poached entertainment practices and massaged disciplinary heritages for educational consumption. Current transitions advance the depletion of these spectacle vocabularies; their destabilizing rejuvenation leaves the archival sites to tradition while adding new scenes to the repertoire.

The novelty that expires, revises, and dismembers itself revisits the fissures in which economic and political interests negotiate instabilities—movement in stasis, vying to define what one from many. In the motion of amending and remaining American vernaculars change and recover the search for who we are. New sites reframe environmental forces, such as "alien" terrors, gun violence, economic depression, civil rights, and natural disasters. New scenes disclose the battlegrounds and memorials that reoccupy landscape with divisive views. Ground Zero, New York City, Somerset Country, Pennsylvania, Washington, DC, and Boston, Massachusetts, landmark ruins of post-911 cityscapes accumulating an altered stasis. Natural wonders of destructive and productive energies are joined by post-Katrina New Orleans, Superstorm Sandy's damage to the tri-state region of New York, New Jersey, and Connecticut, and tornado ravaged Oklahoma. Spectacles of wonder and enterprise deploy to capture scenes of trauma and triumph that are distributed, replayed, recomposed in the sensible modalities of changing vantage points that reclaim differences; scenic sites perpetuate the internal schisms that mask, segregate, and interrogate the transient discourse of belonging or not belonging, pressing the margins of democracy beyond sight lines. Reproductive momentum crosses into the blank space in which rebuilding moves forward; the present scene embalms memory in the immersive tremors of pain, loss, and suffering that pass through the fearsome disappearance.

Spectacle culture complies with the boundaries that isolate radical sentiments; it also resists inclusionary bounds. Whether retreating from or confronting the ongoing maelstrom of economic uncertainty, war, and human rights scenic life occupies landscape views. As visionary space, scenic spectacle's fluency with immersive praxis embraces its own transgressions. The next frontier might well be called the sensory revolution.

Notes

Introduction

1. Throughout this book, I use the United States when referring to the post-Civil War national climate and America when discussing the antebellum period or nationalist projections.
2. Walt Whitman, *Leaves of Grass* (1855; reprint. New York: Dover, 2007), 4.
3. A select overview includes, Richard D. Altick, *The Shows of London* (Cambridge, MA: Belknap Press, 1978); Ralph Hyde, *Panoramania! The Art and Entertainment of the "All-Embracing" View* (London: Trefoil, 1988); Bernard Comment, *The Panorama* (London: Reaktion, 1999); Denise Blake Oleksijczuk, *The First Panoramas: Visions of British Imperialism* (Minneapolis: University of Minnesota Press, 2011); Ivan Karp and Steven Levine, *Exhibiting Cultures: The Poetics and Politics of Museum Display* (Washington: Smithsonian Institution Press, 1991); Tony Bennett, *The Birth of the Museum: History, Theory, Politics* (London: Routledge, 1995); Barbara Kirshenblatt-Gimblett, *Destination Culture: Tourism, Museums, and Culture* ((Berkeley: University of California Press, 1998); Sadiah Qureshi, *People's on Parade: Exhibitions, Empire, and Anthropology in Nineteenth Century Britain* (Chicago: University of Chicago Press, 2011); Eric Ames, *Carl Hagenbeck's Empire of Entertainments* (Seattle: University of Washington Press, 2008); John E. Findling and Kimberly D. Pelle, eds, *Encyclopedia of World's Fairs and Expositions* (Jefferson, North Carolina, and London: McFarland & Company, 2008); Edward Alexander and Mary Alexander, *Museums in Motion: An Introduction to the History and Functions of Museums*, Second edition (Lanham, MD: AltaMira Press, 2008); Alexander C. T. Geppert, *Fleeting Cities: Imperial Expositions in Fin-de-Siècle Europe* (London: Palgrave Macmillan, 2010).
4. Among studies of panoramas, site-specific performance considered in reenactments or "living histories," exhibitions, and museums are John Francis McDermott, *The Lost Panoramas of the Mississippi* (Chicago: University of Chicago Press, 1958); John Bell, "The Sioux War Panorama and American Mythic History." *Theatre Journal* 48:3 (October 1996): 279–299; Robert W. Rydell, *All the World's a Fair: Visions of Empire at*

American International Expositions (Chicago: University of Chicago Press, 1984) and *World of Fairs: The Century of Progress Exhibitions* (Chicago: University of Chicago Press, 1993); Linda P. Gross and Theresa R. Snyder. *Philadelphia's 1876 Centennial Exhibition* (Arcadia Publishing, 2005); David Glassberg, *American Historical Pageantry: The Uses of Tradition in the Early Twentieth Century* (Chapel Hill: University of North Carolina Press, 1990); Rosemarie K. Bank, *Antebellum Stagings: Theatre Culture in the United States, 1825–1860* (New York: Cambridge University Press, 1997); Mike Pearson and Michael Shanks, *Theatre/Archaeology: Disciplinary Dialogues* (New York: Routledge, 2001); Daphne A. Brooks, *Bodies in Dissent: Spectacular Performances of Race and Freedom, 1850–1910* (Durham: Duke University Press, 2006); Scott Magelssen, *Living History Museums: Undoing History through Performance* (Lanham, MD: Scarecrow Press, 2007); Rebecca Schneider, *Performing Remains: Art and War in Times of Theatrical Reenactment* (London: Routledge, 2011).

5. Historical accounts of immersive and virtual spaces lean toward further understanding media lineages in cinema, gaming, and special effects. Landscape theory addresses the interpretive frames of perception to understand the discourse of social formation. *The Panorama Phenomenon: Mesdag Panorama 1881–1981*, eds. Evelyn J. Fruitema and Paul A. Zoetmulder (The Hague: Foundation for the Preservation of the Centenarian Mesdag Panorama, 1981); Jay Appleton. *The Symbolism of Habitat: An Interpretation of Landscape in Art* (Seattle: University of Washington Press, 1990); Angela Miller, *The Empire of the Eye: Landscape Representation and American Cultural Politics, 1825–1875* (Ithaca, NY: Cornell University Press, 1993); Stephan Oettermann, *The Panorama: History of a Mass Medium*, trans. Deborah Lucas Schneider (New York: Zone Books, 1997); Malcolm Andrews, *Landscape and Western Art* (Oxford: Oxford University Press, 1999); Jonathan Crary, "Géricault, the Panorama, and Sites of Reality in the Early Nineteenth Century," *Grey Room 9* (Autumn, 2002): 5–25; Oliver Grau, *Virtual Art: From Illusion to Immersion* (Cambridge, MA: MIT Press, 2003); Angela Ndalianis, *Neo-Baroque Aesthetics and Contemporary Entertainment* (Cambridge, MA: MIT Press, 2004); Alison Griffiths, *Shivers Down Your Spine: Cinema, Museums, and the Immersive View* (New York: Columbia University Press, 2008); Anne Friedberg, *The Virtual Window: From Alberti to Microsoft* (Cambridge, MA: MIT Press, 2008); Rachael Ziady DeLuxe and James Elkins, eds, *Landscape Theory* (New York: Routledge, 2008).

6. Brooks, *Bodies in Dissent*, 68.

7. Kirshenblatt-Gimblett, *Destination Culture*, 8–9.

8. Drew Gilpin Faust, *The Republic of Suffering: Death and the American Civil War* (New York: Vintage, 2008), 3-31.

9. Tavia Nyong'o, *The Amalgamation Waltz: Race, Performance, and the Ruses of Memory* (Minneapolis: University of Minnesota Press, 2009), 5.

10. Douglass C. North, *Understanding the Process of Economic Change* (Princeton: Princeton University Press, 2005), 13–22,108–112.

11. Ibid., 107.

12. Kenneth Clark, *Landscape into Art* (New York: Harper & Row, 1976), 56. Clark considers Breughel's naturalism a fantasy technique that bridges Northern style with Italian mannerism.

13. "Panorama of Versailles," *Zion's Herald*, August 8, 1827, 2.

14. "Panorama, *The Time Piece and Literary Companion*, November 29, 1797, 3; see also Comment, *The Panorama*, 23, Figure 7, 23–24.

15. Grau, *Virtual Art*, 57, 58.

16. Alison Griffiths, *Shivers Down Your Spine*, 3.

17. Oettermann, *The Panorama: History of a Mass Medium*, 5–6.

18. Grau, *Virtual Art*, 13.

19. In aesthetic philosophy, Western tradition of cognitive (rational) philosophical thought and perception form the two parts of the higher and lower faculties. The classical division of mind and body divorces the physical sense from knowledge of the world (consciousness). The transfer of aesthetics into an autonomous philosophy of beauty or art begins in the eighteenth century. With the study of aesthetic experience as a separate realm of understanding, the body once again becomes a source of inquiry. The initial step is taken by Alexander Baumgarten, who unfurls a theory of perceptional cognition that translates the precepts of rational philosophy into the attributes that contribute to poetic perfection—the aesthetic. In his *Reflections on Poetry* (1735), Baumgarten cuts a path from perception to beauty, and restores aesthetic experience to the body. Baumgarten's distinction that aesthetic experience is distinct from moral value departs from eighteenth-century theories of sensibility, particularly moral philosophy in England, which reached into the public sphere through the writings of Anthony Ashley Cooper, Third Earl of Shaftesbury and Francis Hutcheson at the beginning of the century. Immanuel Kant develops the discussion of aesthetic experience further. He moves from the perception of the *thing* to the effects on the individual. In the *Critique of Pure Reason* (1781), Kant proposes that knowledge of the world (consciousness) is indiscernible as external phenomena. Consciousness is an intuitive process by which sense impressions are measured and judged. Thus, perception is a faculty of the subjective instrument, a self-perpetuating reference. This philosophical idealism lies behind aesthetic judgments, giving rise to the troublesome issues of aesthetic standards and normative values. Alexander Baumgarten, *Reflections on Poetry*, trans. Karl Aschenbrenner and William B. Holther (Berkeley: University of California Press, 1954), Immanuel Kant, *The Critique of Judgment*, trans. James Creed Meredith (Oxford: Clarendon, 1952), §1, 1:41–42. See Terry Eagleton, *The Ideology of the Aesthetic* (Oxford: Blackwell, 1990), 31–89; Gunter Gebauer and Christoph Wulf, *Mimesis: Culture, Art, Society*, trans. Don Reneau (Berkeley: University of California Press, 1992), 27–75, 151–232; George Dickie, *The Century of Taste* (Oxford: Oxford University Press, 1996).

20. Guy Debord, *Comments on the Society of the Spectacle* (London: Verso, 1998), 8–11.

21. Douglas Kellner and Steven Best, "Debord, Cybersituations, and the Interactive Spectacle," *SubStance* 28.3 (1999): 129–156.

22. Douglas Kellner, *Media Spectacle* (London: Routledge, 2012), 2.

23. Aristotle, *Poetics* (Loeb Classical Library, Cambridge: Harvard University Press, 1995), 13–18, 53–55; Oxford Greek-English Lexicon, Ninth ed., s.v. ὄψις.

24. Among treatments of cultural politics in spectacle performance history are Roy Strong, *Splendor at Court: Renaissance Spectacle and the Theatre of Power* (Boston: Houghton Mifflin, 1973); Glassberg, *American Historical Pageantry*; Richard C. Beacham, *Spectacle Entertainments of Early Imperial Rome* (New Haven: Yale University Press, 1999); Jody Enders, *The Medieval Theater of Cruelty: Rhetoric, Memory, Violence* (Ithaca: University of Cornell Press, 1999); Lynn Avery Hunt, *Politics, Culture, Class in the French Revolution* (Berkeley: University of California Press, 2004).

25. Transappearance is articulated by Paul Virilio as an optical technology of temporal acceleration or simultaneity whereby long distance transmission drives real-time perspectives. Virilio, *Open Sky*, trans. Julie Rose (London: Verso, 2008), 36.

26. Maurya Wickstrom, *Performing Consumers: Global Capital and Its Theatrical Seductions* (New York: Routledge, 2006).

27. Shmuel N. Eisenstadt, ed., *Multiple Modernities* (New Brunswick: Transaction Publishers, 2002).

28. Rebecca Schneider, *Performing Remains: Art and War in Times of Historical Reenactment* (London: Routledge, 2011), 24.

29. Additional sponsors included AAA, State Farm Companies Foundation, The History Channel, United States Congress, US Department of Transportation, Exxon Mobil, American Public Transportation Association, American Road & Transportation Builders Association, Association of American Railroads, National Asphalt Pavement Association, and the UPS Foundation. The exhibit has since been placed online. See <http://americanhistory.si.edu/onthemove/exhibition/>.

1 Immersive Scenes: Visual Media, Painted Panoramas, and Landscape Narratives

1. The scenes move clockwise, beginning from the West door. They are as follows: "America and History"; "Landing of Columbus"; "Cortez and Montezuma at Mexican Temple"; "Pizarro Going to Peru"; "Burial of de Soto"; "Captain Smith and Pocahontas"; "Landing of the Pilgrims"; "William Penn and the Indians"; "Colonization of New England"; "Oglethorpe and the Indians"; "Battle of Lexington"; "Declaration of Independence"; "Surrender of Cornwallis"; "Death of Tecumseh"; "American Army Entering the City of Mexico"; "Discovery of Gold in California"; "Peace at the End of the Civil War"; "Naval Gun Crew in the Spanish-American War"; "The Birth of Aviation." The history, execution, and images of the entire panorama, as well as individual scenes can be

viewed online. "Frieze of American History," The Architect of the Capitol. <http://www.aoc.gov/cc/art/rotunda/frieze/index.cfm>.

2. The dome was built in 1863.

3. The panorama was completed in 1951. See Barbara A. Wolanin's, *Constantino Brumidi: Artist of the Capitol* (Washington: US GPO, 1998), 149; Myrtle Cheney Murdock, *Constantino Brumidi: Michelangelo of the United States Capitol* (Washington, DC: Monumental Press, 1950).

4. New York Senator Martin Van Buren stood against admission of Missouri as a slave state. He spent his presidency fending off national collapse when the banking panic of 1837 hit a few months into his term. In his inaugural address, Van Buren framed the American "experiment," in terms of preserving white national prosperity. Labeled the "little magician," he reversed position to support the existing domestic institution of slavery. (Van Buren again switched positions in the 1848 Presidential campaign as a third party candidate of the anti-slavery Free Soil Party.) He pledged unflinchingly to oppose "every attempt on the part of Congress to abolish slavery in the District of Columbia against the wishes of the slaveholding States, and also with a determination equally decided to resist the slightest interference with it in the States where it exists." Martin Van Buren, "Inaugural Address" March 4, 1837, 6, 13, Library of Congress; Walter A. McDougal, *Throes of Democracy: The American Civil War Era* (New York: Harper Collins, 2008), 91–92.

5. The reference to panoramania appeared in the *Illustrated London News* in 1850. Cited in Ralph Hyde, *Panoramania! The Art and Entertainment of the "All-Embracing" View* (London: Trefoil Publications, 1988), 11.

6. Rosemarie K. Bank, *Antebellum Stagings: Theatre Culture in America, 1825–1860* (Cambridge: Cambridge University Press, 1997), 4.

7. Michael O'Brien, *Intellectual Life and the American South, 1810–1860* (Chapel Hill: University of North Carolina Press, 2010), 213.

8. Ibid.

9. "Andrew Jackson," Inaugural Address, March 4, 1833, American Presidency Project. <http//www.presidency.ucsb.edu>.

10. Daniel Walker Howe, *What Hath God Wrought: The Transformation of America, 1815–1848* (New York: Oxford University Press, 2007), 489.

11. Branches of landscape theory include aesthetics, anthropology, environmental studies, and literary studies. Dramatic literature is represented in Elinor Fuchs's and Una Chauduri's edition of *Land/scape/theater* (Ann Arbor: University of Michigan Press, 2002). For current art historical discussions in the field see Rachael Ziady De Luxe and James Elkins, eds, *Landscape Theory* (New York: Routledge, 2008). Malcolm Andrews also provides a useful overview of the various applications of theoretical framework in *Landscape and Western Art* (Oxford: Oxford University Press, 2000), 1–22. Influential treatments on the aesthetic politics are Jay Appleton, *The Experience of Landscape*, Second ed. (London: Wiley, 1996) and W. J. T. Mitchell, ed. *Landscape and Power* (Chicago: University of Chicago Press, 1994).

12. Denis E. Cosgrove, *Social Formation and Symbolic Landscape* (Madison: University of Wisconsin Press, 1999).

13. Mitchell, *Landscape and Power*, 14

14. Stephan Oettermann, *The Panorama: History of a Mass Medium*, trans. Deborah Lucas Schneider (New York: Zone, 1997), 31.

15. Hyde, *Panoramania!*, 15.

16. Ibid. Bernard Comment dates the use of term from 1792. Bernard Comment, *The Panorama*, trans. Anne-Marie Glasheen (London: Reaktion Books, 1999), 7.

17. Oettermann, *The Panorama: History of a Mass Medium*, 25–32.

18. Hyde, *Panoramania!*, 17.

19. "The Panorama," *Parley's Magazine*, January 1, 1838, 95.

20. See "A Collection of Descriptions of Views Exhibited at the Panorama, Strand" and "Leicester Square Panorama," 1802–1831, Manuscripts, British Library. Denise Blake Oleksjiczuk examines reception strategies of colonial display in *The First Panoramas: Visions of British Imperialism* (Minneapolis: University of Minnesota Press, 2011).

21. Hyde, *Panoramania!*, 38.

22. Burford cites his use of Ingraham's guide. Compare Joseph Wentworth Ingraham, *A Manuel for the Use of Visitors to the Falls of Niagara* (Buffalo: Charles Faxon, 1834), 23 and Robert Burford, *Description of a View of the Falls of Niagara* (Boston: Perkins and Marvin, 1837), 12, British Library.

23. Hyde, *Panoramania!*, 15, 45.

24. Ibid., 17.

25. Ibid., 15.

26. "Panorama of Versailles," *Zion's Herald*, August 8, 1827, 2.

27. Oliver Grau, *Virtual Art: From Illusion to Immersion* (Cambridge, MA: MIT Press, 2003), 57, 58.

28. Hyde, *Panoramania!*, 36; Comment, *The Panorama*, 25; Evelyn J. Fruitema and Paul A. Zoetmulder, ed., *The Panorama Phenomena: Mesdag Panorama 1881–1981* (The Hague: Exhibition Catalogue, 1981), 35–39.

29. On European academies reception see Comment, *The Panorama*, 23.

30. Examples include Pompeii, *Villa dei Misteri*; *Chambre du Cerf* in the Papal Palace at Avignon; Baldassare Peruzzi's *Sala delle Prospettive;* Andrea Pozzo's Nave of Sant'Ignazio in Rome. Grau, *Virtual Art*, 25–52.

31. Ibid., 13, 57.

32. Edmund Burke, *A Philosophical Inquiry into the Origins of Our Idea of the Sublime and Beautiful* (Oxford: Oxford University Press, 1990), 29.

33. "Catherwood's Panoramas, *The Albion, A Journal of News, Politics, and Literature,* May 30, 1840, 379.

34. Ibid.

35. The remarks are part of an extended discussion on theoretical formulations of "Natural Beauty." Theodor Adorno, *Aesthetic Theory*, trans. Robert Hullot-Kentor (Minneapolis: University of Minnesota Press, 1997), 64, 61–78.

36. For assembly methods and specialist roles in the industry, see Oettermann, *The Panorama: History of a Mass Medium*, 55.

37. For accounts of the history of the camera obscura in relationship to the complexities of technique and types of discursive perspectives, see Jonathan Crary, *Techniques of the Observer: On Vision and Modernity in the 19th Century* (Cambridge: MIT Press, 1990): 25–66; also *Suspensions of Perspective: Attention, Spectacle, and Modern Culture* (Cambridge: Cambridge University Press, 1997); Anne Friedberg, *The Virtual Window: From Alberti to Microsoft* (Cambridge: MIT Press, 2006): 60–75.

38. Crary, *Techniques of the Observer*, 39.

39. Ibid., 34.

40. Richard D. Altick, *The Shows of London* (Cambridge: Harvard University Press, 1978), 187.

41. Panoramas came into theatrical vogue in the 1830s. The Paris Opera adopted the new medium. Scenic Designer Pierre-Luc Ciceri and Opera Manager Henri Duponchel elaborated the increasing delight in visual spectacle. Fitted with gas lighting and a water system for waterfalls and realistic fountains, the Opera's sumptuous staging blended transcendent imagery with transitory special effect impressions. Their innovative settings for Giacomo Meyerbeer's *Robert le diable* (1831) launched a period of grand opera. Ciceri combined new technology with soaring romantic scenic décor; his use of panoramic perspective, topical color, picturesque historical settings, and atmospheric effects suspended the viewer in the illusionary vantage point of being part of the changing scene. See Karen Pendle and Stephen Wilkins, "Paradise Found: The Salle le Peletier and French Grand Opera," in *Opera in Context, Essays on the Historical Staging from the Late Renaissance to the Time of Puccini*, ed. Mark A. Radice (Portland, Oregon: Amadeus Press, 1998), 171–208. For specific graphic techniques used by Honorie Daumier, see Judith Wechsler, "Movement and Time," in *Daumier Drawings* (New York: Harry N. Abrams, 1993): 41–47.

42. Robert Barker, *View of the City of Edinburgh*, Maps, British Library.

43. "Panorama of Mexico," *Atkinson's Saturday Evening Post*, June 15, 1833, 1.

44. Michel Foucault's reckoning with internalized structures of visual power found modern comparison in Jeremy Bentham's unrealized eighteenth-century prison blueprint of the Panopticon. *Discipline and Punish: The Birth of the Prison,* trans. Alan Sheridan (New York: Vintage, 1979), 195–228. Allan Wallach notes the coincidence of panoptic power, and panoramic mass media marks a new epoch in the history of visual domination. "Between Subject and Object," in *Landscape Theory*, 318.

45. The panorama was exhibited in a tavern on Chatham Street. Richard Moody, *Drama from the American Theatre, 1762–1909* (New York: World Publishing, 1966), 176.

46. William Dunlap, *History of the Rise and Progress of the Arts of Design in the United States,* ed. Alexander Wyckoff, Vol. 2, 1834, revised (New York: Benjamin Blom, 1965), 77.

47. The sum signaled a box office success. It is equivalent to over $1,000 today. "Panorama of Athens," *Christian Register*, October 10, 1821, 39; September 28, 1821, 27.

48. Richard McLanathan, *The American Tradition in the Arts* (New York: Harcourt, Brace & World, 1968), 305.

49. *Weekly Museum*, February 4, 1797, 3.

50. There are approximately 20 surviving panoramas worldwide.

51. See "New Panorama," *Weekly Museum*, February 4, 1797; February 11; April 8.

52. Grau, *Virtual Art*, 65–72; Comment, *The Panorama*, 18. For techniques and industrial aspects of panoramas, see *The Panorama Phenomenon*, 17–34.

53. American artists typically studied in England and Italy. Vanderlyn studied in Paris, the first American painter to do so. Patron Aaron Burr sent Vanderlyn to Philadelphia to study painting with portraitist Stuart Gilbert. Gilbert trained with American Benjamin West, who was appointed by King Georges III to the post of historical painter to the court, and founded the Royal Academy of Arts in London. McLanathan, *The American Tradition in the Arts*, 72–74.

54. Fulton opened his rotunda with James Barlow in 1799. The famed engineer studied painting with Benjamin West. Ibid., 13–14. See also Hyde, *Panoramania!*, 58–59.

55. The panorama was created from sketches of the palace and gardens of Versailles between 1814 and 1815.

56. Quoted in Kevin J. Avery and Peter L. Fedora, *John Vanderlyn's Panoramic View of the Palace and Garden of Versailles* (New York: Metropolitan Museum of Art, 1988), 23.

57. Funders each paid $8,000 in exchange for free admission. Ibid., 19.

58. For background on the Park Theatre as well as the developing theatre districts in New York City, see Mary C. Henderson, *The City and the Theatre: New York Playhouses from Bowling Green to Times Square* (Clifton, NJ: James T. White, 1973), 38–88.

59. Although portions of the top and bottom of painting are lost, the restored painting is on view in the American Wing of the Metropolitan Museum of Art in New York.

60. Bank, *Antebellum Stagings*, 1–26.

61. The Senate House Association of Kingston gave the Metropolitan Museum of Art in New York the painting in 1952.

62. See for instance, "Panorama of Versailles," *Boston Centinel*, April 18, 1827, 110. The review goes into substantial detail.

63. The idea of establishing an American "museum" of art was a mission—self-serving perhaps—that Vanderlyn promoted until the end of his life. In 1851, a year before his death, he proposed the creation of an "Academy or Gallery of Fine Art" to the federal government. The petition was ignored. See Avery and Fedora, *View of Versailles*, 30–31, 33–34.

64. See Jonathan Crary, "Géricault, the Panorama, and Sites of Reality in the Early Nineteenth Century," *Grey Room 9* (Autumn, 2002): 5–25.

65. Precipitated by Congressional action to the end the sale of public lands on credit, the Panic of 1819 is considered the first deep slide in the economy. Howe, *What Hath God Wrought*, 142–147.

66. Among the numerous studies opening up thinking toward a multidimensional topography of American theatrical culture are Maxine

Schwartz Seller, ed., *Ethnic Theatre in the United States* (Westport, CT: Greenwood Press, 1983); Bank, *Antebellum Stagings*; Bruce McConachie, *Melodramatic Formations: American Theatre and Society, 1820–1870* (Iowa City: University of Iowa Press, 1992)); Lisa Merrill, *When Romeo was a Woman: Charlotte Cushman and Her Circle of Female Spectators* (Ann Arbor: University of Michigan Press, 2000); Henry Elam and David Krasner, eds., *African American Performance and Theatre History: A Critical Reader* (New York: Oxford University Press, 2001); Joel Berkowitz, *Shakespeare on the American Yiddish Stage* (Iowa City: University of Iowa Press, 2002); Brooks McNamara, *The New York Concert Saloon: the Devil's Own Nights* (Cambridge: Cambridge University Press, 2002); John W. Frick, *Theatre, Culture, and Temperance Reform in Nineteenth-Century America* (Cambridge: Cambridge University Press, 2003); James V. Hatch and Errol G. Shine, *A History of African American Theatre* (Cambridge: Cambridge University Press, 2003); Renée M. Sentiller, *Performing Menken: Adah Isaacs Menken and the Birth of Celebrity* (Cambridge: Cambridge University Press, 2003); Daphne A. Brooks, *Bodies in Dissent: Spectacular Performances of Race and Freedom, 1850–1910* (Durham: Duke University Press, 2006); Tavia Nyong'o, *The Amalgamation Waltz: Performance, and the Ruses of Memory* (Minneapolis: University of Minnesota Press, 2009).

67. The first president of the American Academy John Trumbull was chosen over Vanderlyn to execute four monumental paintings of the Revolutionary War for the Capitol Rotunda. In 1817, Vanderlyn received a commission from the House of Representatives for a portrait of Washington. His last major commission was *The Landing of Columbus* for the US Capitol Rotunda. When he exhibited a classical nude now considered his masterpiece, *Ariadne Asleep on the Island of Naxos* (1807), several members, including Trumbull, viewed the painting as indecent and forced him to leave. The acrimony continued throughout his career. In 1826, he turned down Academy membership. It appears that some members, such as Trumbull and Samuel Morse, looked down on his panorama project, while other members sought to use the Rotunda in order to exhibit their own works. Avery and Fedora, *View of Versailles*, 18, 27, 31, 33.

68. The American Academy of Fine Art was originally established as the New York Academy of Arts in 1802. The first president of the National Academy of Design was Samuel F. B. Morse. From "New York: Patronage and Collecting," *Grove Art Online*, 2007. <http:/www.groveart.com>.

69. Dell Upton, *Architecture in the United States* (Oxford: Oxford University Press, 1998), 72.

70. See Homer T. Rosenberger, "Thomas Ustick and the Completion of the United States Capitol, *Records of the Columbia Historical Society* 50 (1948/1950): 273–322.

71. See Kent Ahrens, "Nineteenth-Century History Painting and the United States Capitol," *Records of the Columbia Historical Society* 50 (1980): 191–194.

72. "Paintings for the Rotundo," 23rd Congress, Second Session, House of Representatives, December 15, 1834, Register of Debates, 791, Library of Congress.

73. Ibid.
74. Ibid.
75. Ahrens, "Nineteenth-Century History Painting and the United States Capitol," 195. A two-day debate ensued over a proposal by James Hamilton to commission Washington Alliston to paint the Battle of New Orleans, which was led by fellow Southerner General Andrew Jackson. Hamilton argued the Navy was not represented among the military subjects. Representatives of the Northern states resistance to the proposal suggest a blocking tactic against raising General Jackson's public profile. The resolution did not pass along sectional lines. "Historical Paintings," 20th Congress, First Session, House of Representatives, January 8, 1828, 930–954, Register of Debates, Library of Congress.
76. The Anglo-French wars launched Robert Barker's *The Battle of Waterloo* (1815) into a commercial bonanza, bringing in a profit of $10,000 pounds.
77. Robert Ker Porter's celebrated battle scenes aided the propaganda campaign in England. Paul Philippoteaux collaborated with his father Felix, who achieved fame with *The Siege of Paris* (1873) during the Franco-Prussian war. Former army officer Charles Langlois also gained notoriety for his panorama paintings of battles from the Napoleonic wars. Among other battle panorama specialists were Theophile Poilpot, Charles Castellani, Edouard Detaille, and Alphonse de Neuville.
78. John Bell, "The Sioux War Panorama and American Mythic History," *Theatre Journal* 48.3 (October 1996): 283; see also Bertha l. Heilbron, "Documentary Panorama," *Minnesota History* 30.1 (March 1949): 14–23.
79. William Wehner, *The Battles of Chattanooga* (Chicago: W. J. Jefferson, 1886).
80. Drew Gilpin Faust, *This Republic of Suffering: Death and the American Civil War* (New York: Vintage, 2008), 34.
81. "Gettysburg Again on View," *The New York Times*, December 24, 1887, 3.
82. From the catalog of the Boston Cyclorama Company. *Cyclorama of Gettysburg of the Battle of Gettysburg by Paul Philippoteaux* (Boston: M. J. Kiley, 1886).
83. The work was valued at $360,00 when purchased. It earned a revenue of $550,000, according to one report. "Art and Artists," *The New York Times*, November 7, 1896, A5; "City and Suburban News," *The New York Times*, April 3, 1888, 2.
84. Josephine Gillenwater Tighe, "Brumidi, the Michael Angelo of the Capitol," *The Washington Herald*, September 4, 1910, 3:1.
85. Kent Ahrens observes the remodeling of neoclassical style with domestic subjects among the artwork in the US Capitol. Ahrens, "Nineteenth-Century History Painting and the United States Capitol," 202.
86. The Western construct of world domination has precedents in the Hellenistic period. One of the most elaborate tours followed the occasion of Charles V's coronation in Bologna in 1520. Roy Strong, *Splendor at*

Court: *Renaissance Spectacle and the Theater of Power* (Boston: Houghton Mifflin, 1973), 80, 84–98.

87. *Documentary History of the Construction and Development of the United States Capitol Building and Grounds* (Washington, DC: Government Printing Office, 1904), 994.

88. Russell F. Weigley, "Captain Meigs and the Artists of the Capitol: Federal Patronage of Art in the 1850s," *Records of the Columbia Historical Society* 69/70 (1969/1970): 295.

89. The revolution lasted from 1849–1851. Wolanin, *Constantino Brumidi*, 15–23.

90. Weigley, "Captain Meigs and the Artists of the Capitol," 291.

91. Quoted from a letter by Meigs to Thomas Crawford and Hiram Powers in Ibid., 290–291.

92. Whether the change was made due to the expense or inability to execute it is not clear. The adjustment was reported to Congress on March 5, 1860. *Documentary History of the Construction and Development of the United States Capitol*, 1015.

93. Ibid.

94. Nathans traces counter narratives in the visibility of black vernaculars that agitated abolition debate to the postrevolutionary war Federalist Period. Heather S. Nathans, *Slavery and Sentiment on the American Stage, 1787–1861: Lifting the Veil of Black* (Cambridge: Cambridge University Press, 2009), 38

95. For a biography on Tecumseh, see John Sugden, *Tecumseh: A Life* (New York: Holt, 1997).

96. Ray Allen Billington, *Westward Expansion: A History of the American Frontier*, Third ed. (New York: Macmillan, 1967), 291.

97. The change may have been Meigs idea, but it occurred most likely after the civil war. The fresco design was submitted to congress in 1866. Brumidi began lying in the painting after the Western frontier was officially closed. Wolanin, *Constantino Brumidi*, 149–151.

98. Immanuel Kant, *The Critique of Judgment*, trans. James Creed Meredith (Oxford: Clarendon, 1952), §29, 2:115–133.

99. Burke, *A Philosophical Inquiry*, 36, 53.

100. He eventually received a raise to $10.00 a day. He was paid a flat commission of $40,000 for his fresco of Washington. Murdock, *Constantino Brumidi: Michelangelo of the United States Capitol*, 6.

101. "May Finish Frieze of 'Michael Angelo of the Capitol," *The Sun*, March 22, 1914, 6.

102. Charles Ayer Whipple also unsuccessfully tried to propose a World War I design. It was considered inconsistent with the existing painting. Allen Cox followed Whipple. An appropriation of $20,000 was made to finish the work. Jay Walz, "Unfreezing a Frieze: A Capitol Eyesore May Presently Be Beautified," *The New York Times*, November 5, 1950, 197.

103. Charles Sellers, *The Market Revolution: Jacksonian America, 1815–1846* (New York: Oxford University Press, 1991), 4.

104. President James Madison managed to convince Congressional leaders to stabilize the postwar economy with federal monetary policies. One of first objectives was reinstituting the first National Bank. Ibid., 70–102.

105. Ibid., 488.

106. In addition to Sellers *The Market Revolution*, a useful examination of the economic politics is Melvyn Stokes and Stephen Conway, eds, *The Market Revolution in America: Social, Political, and Religious Expressions 1820–1880* (Charlottesville: University Press of Virginia, 1996).

107. On the technical and commercial aspects of the panorama business, see Oettermann, *The Panorama: History of a Mass Medium*, 49–97; Grau, *Virtual Art*, 50, 59.

108. Catherwood teamed up with John Lloyd Stephens on an expedition to Central America. Their illustrated book *Incidents of Travel in Central America, Chiapas, and Yucatan* (1841) spreads imagery of South American cultures. See Fabio Bourbon, *The Lost Cities of the Mayas: the Life, Art and Discoveries of Frederick Catherwood* (Shrewsbury: Swan Hill, 1999).

109. The famed pleasure garden and spectacle house Niblo's held the corner of Prince and Broadway. If there was a relationship between the theatre and the Rotunda, it is not mentioned in reviews. Henderson, *The City and the Theatre*, 73–74.

110. "Catherwood's Panoramas," *The Albion*, May 30, 1840.

111. Eli Smith, "Panorama of Jerusalem," *New York Observer and Chronicle*, May 9, 1840, 74.

112. "Burford's Panorama of Jerusalem," *Museum of Foreign Literature, Science, and Art*, August 1835, 200. The panorama was on view in London in 1835. It appeared in New York by 1837 with his panorama of Niagara. It was shown in Boston from 1838 until 1840.

113. Grau, *Virtual Art*, 115–116.

114. "The Panorama," *Parley's Magazine*, January 1, 1838.

115. For an in-depth history of the whaling industry in the United States, see Lance E. Davis, et al., *In Pursuit of Leviathan: Technology, Institutions, Productivity, and Products in American Whaling, 1816–1906* (Chicago: University of Chicago Press, 1997).

116. Kevin J. Avery, "'Whaling Voyage Round the World': Russell and Purrington's Moving Panorama and Herman Melville's 'Mighty Book,'" *American Art Journal* 22.1 (Spring 1990), 50; McLanathan, *The American Tradition in the Arts*, 303–304.

117. Avery, "'Whaling Voyage Around the World,'" 69.

118. "Whaling Panorama," *Boston Atlas*, January 23, 1849, 2; quoted in Ibid., 52.

119. "The Fine Arts," *New York Mirror, or a Weekly Gazette of Literature and the Fine Arts*, August 23, 1834, 63.

120. Roland Barthes, "The Photographic Message," in *Image, Music, Text*, trans. Stephen Heath (New York: Hill and Wang, 1977), 25.

121. Ibid.

122. J. B. Jackson, *Discovering the Vernacular Landscape* (New Haven: Yale University Press, 1984).

123. McGreevy lays out four themes shaping different interpretations over time: pilgrimage, death, nature, and the future. His focus is primarily on literary texts. Patrick McGreevy, *Imaging Niagara: The Meaning and Making of Niagara Falls* (Amherst: University of Massachusetts Press, 1994), 3.

124. Wendy Jean Katz, *Regionalism and Reform: Art and Class Formation in Antebellum Cincinnati* (Ohio: Ohio State University, 2002), 118.

125. See David C. Huntington, "Frederic Church's Niagara: Nature and the Nation's Type," *Texas Studies in Literature and Language* 25.1 (Spring 1983): 100–138.

126. Ellwood Perry, *The Image of the Indian and Black Man in American Art, 1590–1900* (New York: George Braziller, 1974), 53–56; see also McLanathan, *The American Tradition in the Arts*, 235–236.

127. For a study of Trumbull's artworks, see Helen Cooper, *The Hand and the Spirit of the Panther* (New Haven: Yale University Press, 1982).

128. The Iroquis Confederacy was courted by British colonial forces. The Niagara Frontier was the scene of British seizure in 1759, and the Pontiac War of 1763 when the Seneca reclaimed British posts Christopher Densmore, *Red Jacket: Iroquois Diplomat and Orator* (New York: Syracuse University Press, 1999):11–20; A. C. Parke, *Red Jacket, Last of the Seneca* (New York: McGraw Hill, 1952).

129. Granville Ganter, "Red Jacket and the Decolonization of Republican Virtue," *Indian Quarterly* 31.4 (Fall 2007): 559–581. On the courtship by British and American councils he said, "At the treaties held for the purchase of ours lands, the white men, with sweet voices and smiling faces, told us they loved us, and that they would not cheat us, but that the king's children on the other side of the lake would cheat us. When we go on the other side of the lake, the king's children tell us *your* people will cheat us. These things puzzle out heads, and we believe that the Indians must take care of themselves, and not trust either in your people, or in the king's children." Granville Ganter, ed., *The Collected Speeches of Sagoyewatha, or Red Jacket* (Syracuse: Syracuse University Press, 2006), 161–165.

130. George Washington Parke Custis's *The Indian Prophesy* appeared in 1827. It headed the antebellum trend. For a compilation, see Don B. Wilmeth, "Tentative Checklist of Indian Plays," *The Journal of American Drama and Theatre* (Fall 1989): 34–54. Rosemarie K. Bank examines three "cultural intersections" in the antebellum period: the 1828 "leave-taking" visit to New York by Seneca Red Jacket; a performing duo from the Onondage, and a "prisoner of war tour by the Sauk Black Hawk in 1833 that was mandated by Jackson after the Black Hawk War. Rosemarie K. Bank, "Staging the 'Native': Making History in American Theatre Culture, 1828–1838," *Theatre Journal* 45.4 (December 1993): 462–464.

131. Ganter, "Red Jacket and the Decolonization of Republican Virtue," 559–581.

132. Ganter, *The Collected Speeches of Sagoyewatha*, 61–67.

133. Red Jacket, Sagoyewatha, "We are Determined Not to Sell Our Lands," *Great Speeches by Native Americans*, ed. Bob Blaisdell (New York: Dover, 2000), 47.

134. Ingraham, *A Manual for the Use of Visitors to Niagara Falls*, 63–64.
135. "Niagara Frontier," 14th Congress, Second Session, House of Representatives, 1817, American State Papers, 1: 507, Library of Congress.
136. "Niagara Frontier," 15th Congress, First Session, House of Representatives, 1918, American State Papers, 1: 441, Library of Congress.
137. "Niagara Sufferers," 18th Congress, Second Session, House of Representatives, December 27–28, 1824, Register of Debates, 66, Library of Congress.
138. Ibid.
139. Ibid., 67.
140. Wolfgang Shivelbusch, *The Railway Journey: The Industrialization of Time and Space in the 19th Century* (Berkeley: University of California Press, 1986), 91.
141. "Niagara," *The Albion, A Journal of News, Politics and Literature*, October 7, 1826, 137.
142. Richard Moody, *Edwin Forrest: First Star of the American Stage* (New York: Alfred A. Knopf, 1960), 75.
143. Ibid.
144. Frank H. Severance, *Old Trails on the Niagara Frontier* (Buffalo, 1899), 164.
145. US census records report 9,668. <http://www.census.gov/population/www/documentation/twps0027/tab06.txt>.
146. Walter Benjamin, "Daguerre, or the Panorama," in *The Arcades Project*, trans. Howard Eiland and Kevin McLaughlin (Cambridge, MA: Harvard University Press, 2002), 5.
147. These included the Eagle and Lockport in Lockport; Oneida House in Utica, the American in Auburn; Geneva in Geneva; the Eagle in Rochester; and the locally named Frontier. Ingraham, *Manual for the Use of Visitors to the Falls of Niagara*, 20.
148. The other panoramas Catherwood exhibited where Views of Lima and Thebes. Oettermann, *The Panorama: History of a Mass Medium*, 372.
149. R. Burford. "Description of a View of the Falls of Niagara, now exhibiting at the Panorama, Leicester Square" (London: T. Brettell, 1833).
150. For a history, see Celeste-Marie Bernier, *African American Visual Arts: From Slavery to the Present* (Edinburg: University of Edinburgh Press, 2008).
151. After the Civil War, proslavery sentiment turned the climate of free Ohio dangerous for the black community. It was a tornado that destroyed the gallery in 1860. Joseph D. Ketner II, *The Emergence of the African American Artist: Robert S. Duncanson, 1821–1872* (Columbia, Missouri: University of Missouri Press, 1992), 102.
152. Ibid., 103.
153. Katz, *Regionalism and Reform: Art and Class Formation in Antebellum Cincinnati*, 118–119.
154. James Presley Ball, *Splendid Mammoth Pictorial Tour of the United States: Comprising Views of the African Slave Trade of Northern and Southern*

Cities; of Cotton and Sugar Plantations; of the Mississippi, Ohio and Susquehanna Rivers, Niagara Falls, etc,, Program (Cincinnati, Achilles Pugh, 1855) 18.

155. Ball calls the panorama "our" painting in the introduction to the printed description. Several artists working in the gallery's studio may have contributed to it.

156. For additional studies of James P. Ball and Henry Box Brown, see Deborah Willis, *J .P. Ball: Daguerrean and Studio Photographer* (New York: Garland, 1994); C. Peter Ripley, ed., *The Black Abolitionists, I: The British Isles, 1830–1865* (Chapel Hill: University of North Carolina Press, 1985), 174–75; Brooks, "The Escape Artist" in *Bodies in Dissent*, 66–130 and John Ernest, "Outside the Box: Henry Box Brown and Politics of Antislavery Agency," *Arizona Quarterly* 63.4 (Winter 2007): 1–24.

157. Frederick Douglass was editor of the *North Star*.

158. "Ball's Mammoth Pictorial Tour of the United States," May 25, 1855; June 1, 1855.

159. Severance, *Old Trails on the Niagara Frontier*, 232.

160. Ball, *Splendid Mammoth Pictorial Tour of the United States*, 53–56.

161. Severance, *Old Trails on the Niagara Frontier*, 271.

162. The letter was signed G. W. S., *The Liberator*, November 16, 1855.

163. "The Magazine," *New York Daily Times*, July 30, 1853, 1.

164. See McGreevy, *Imagining Niagara*, 41–69.

165. Natalie McKnight, "Dickens, Niagara Falls and the Watery Sublime," *Dickens Quarterly* 26.2 (June 2009): 69.

166. Thomas Cole, quoted in Barbara Novak, *Nature and Culture: American Landscape Painting, 1825–1875* (New York: Oxford University Press, 1980), 5.

167. Ralph Waldo Emerson, *Nature*, 1836, reprint (Boston: Beacon Press, 1985), 5; or Alfred R. Ferguson, ed., *Nature*, in *The Collected Works of Ralph Waldo Emerson*, Vol. 1 (Cambridge: Belknap Press, 1971), 7.

168. Ralph Waldo Emerson, *Nature*, 1836, 5; *Collected Works*, 1: 7.

169. Thomas Cole, "Essay on American Scenery," in *The Collected Essays and Prose Sketches,* ed. Marshall Tymn (St. Paul: Minnesota: John Colet Press, 1980), 16. The essay appeared in the *American Monthly Review*, 1836.

170. John O'Sullivan, "The Great Nation of Futurity," *The United States Democratic Review*, 6.23 (1839).

171. Harvey K. Flad, "The Parlor in the Wilderness: Domesticating an Iconic American Landscape," *Geographical Review* 99.3 (July 2009): 358.

172. E. W. Sherwood, "Frederic E. Church: Studio Gathers Thirty Years Ago," *The New York Times*, April 21, 1900, BR4. For a biography of the Painter, see Franklin Kelly, *Frederic Edwin Church* (New Haven: Yale University Press, 2005).

173. "Frederic Edwin Church," in *Corcoran Gallery of Art, American Paintings to 1945*, ed. Sarah Cash (Washington, DC: Corcoran Gallery of Art, 2011), 109, 112–115.

174. "Church's Niagara," *New York Daily Times*, May 21, 1857, 4.

175. *Charleston Daily Courier*, January 3, 1859, 4.
176. "Picture of Niagara in Europe-Art in America," *The New York Times*, August 22, 1857, 8.
177. Albert Boime, *The Magisterial Gaze: Manifest Destiny and American Landscape Painting, 1830–1865* (Washington, DC: Smithsonian Institution Press, 1991), 1–5.
178. Jackson, "Inaugural Address," 1833.
179. Tavia Nyong'o counters hybrid narratives of integration across a subversive terrain to interrogate the genealogy of amalgamation myth. *Amalgamation Waltz*, 33.
180. Hubert Damisch, *The Origin of Perspective*, trans. John Goodman (Cambridge, MA: MIT Press, 1995).

2   Moving Scenes: Multimedia Performance along the Mississippi River

1. William Dunlap, *A History of the American Theatre from Its Origins to 1832* (Chicago: University of Illinois Press, 2005), 363. Painter Benjamin West influenced Dunlap.
2. *The Albion, A Journal of News, Politics and Literature* 7:25 (November 29, 1828), 199.
3. Dunlap, *A History of the American Theatre*, xix. The measurement of 25,000 ft does not seem accurate. It would require vertical rollers capable of loading five miles of canvas. I have not been able to verify the figure indicated by Tice L. Miller in his introduction to Dunlap's *History*.
4. "A Trip to Niagara," *The New York Mirror, or a Weekly Gazette of Literature and the Fine Arts*, December 20, 1828b, 191. See same, November 22, 1828a, 157; see also Richard D. Altick, *The Shows of London* (Cambridge: Harvard University Press, 1978), 204.
5. "A Trip to Niagara," *The New York Mirror*, 1828a.
6. Both opened in November 1828. "Arch Street Theatre," *Saturday Evening Post*, November 15, 1828, 3.
7. Dewey Fey, "Panoramic Paintings," *Home Journal*, November 13, 1847, 3.
8. John Bell, "The Sioux War Panorama and American Mythic History," *Theatre Journal* 48.3 (October 1996): 283.
9. John Francis McDermott, *The Lost Panoramas of the Mississippi* (Chicago: University of Chicago Press, 1958), 13.
10. Ibid.
11. The Dickinson panorama surfaced in 1941. See accounts by Bertha L. Heilbron, "A Mississippi Panorama," *Minnesota History* 23.4 (December 1942): 349–354 and Lisa Lyons, "Panorama of the Monumental Grandeur of the Mississippi Valley," *Design Quarterly* 101/102 (1976): 32–34.
12. Daphne A. Brooks, *Bodies in Dissent: Spectacular Performances of Race and Freedom, 1850–1910* (Durham: Duke University Press, 2006), 68.

13. Llewellyn Hubbard Hedgbeth, "Extant American Panoramas: Moving Entertainments of the Nineteenth Century." Dissertation. New York University 1977. Ann Arbor: UMI, 1977, 51–99.

14. Angela L. Miller, "The Panorama, the Cinema, and the Emergence of the Spectacular," *Wide Angle* 18.2 (1996), 46.

15. McDermott, *The Lost Panoramas of the Mississippi*, 1–17; Bertha L. Heilbron, "Making a Motion Picture in 1848: Henry Lewis on the Upper Mississippi," *Minnesota History* 17.2 (June 1936): 131–156; Miller, "The Panorama, the Cinema, and the Emergence of the Spectacular," 41.

16. Brooks, *Bodies in Dissent*, 81.

17. Gwendolyn Waltz, "Filmed Scenery on the Live Stage" *Theatre Journal* 58. 4 (2006): 547–573.

18. Angela Ndalianis examines a wide range of connections from the Baroque period in cinematic and installation art in *Neo-Baroque Aesthetics and Contemporary Entertainment* (Cambridge: MIT Press, 2004).

19. Alison Griffiths, *Shivers Down Your Spine: Cinema, Museums, and the Immersive View* (New York: Columbia University Press, 2008), 37–78.

20. Ibid., 4–5.

21. Paul Virilio, *Open Sky*, trans. Julie Rose (London: Verso, 2008), 36–37.

22. Ibid., 36.

23. Quoted in Ray Allen Billington, *Westward Expansion: A History of the American Frontier*, Third ed. (London: Macmillan, 1967), 295.

24. Ibid., 294.

25. Ibid., 290.

26. The mythological and historical treatment of maritime subjects becomes pronounced during the romantic period, notably in Gericualt's shipwreck *Raft of the Medusa* (1820), Turner's seafaring landscapes, and the seascapes of Casper David Friedrich. Nautical spectaculars and melodrama in the early nineteenth century circulated out of trends in England. See Michael Booth *English Melodrama* (London: Herbert Jenkins, 1965); Jeffrey N. Cox "The Ideological Tack of Nautical Melodrama," in *Melodrama: The Cultural Emergence of a Genre*, eds. Michael Hays and Anastasia Nikolopoulou (New York: St. Martin's Press, 1996): 167–189. Jonathan Crary, "Géricault, the Panorama, and Sites of Reality in the Early Nineteenth Century," *Grey Room* 9 (Autumn, 2002): 5–25.

27. James K. Paulding, "The Mississippi," *Graham's Magazine*, April 1843, 215.

28. Walter McDougall, *Throes of Democracy: The American Civil War Era, 1829–1877* (New York: Harper Collins, 2008), 96–101.

29. Bell, "The Sioux War Panorama and American Mythic History," 283.

30. George Catlin, "Letter from the Mouth of the Yellowstone River, 1832," in *Illustrations of the Manners, Customs, and Conditions of the North American Indians*, 1841 (New York: Penguin Classics, 2004), 14–16.

31. Ellwood Perry, *The Image of the Indian and Black Man in American Art: 1590–1900* (New York: George Braziller, 1974), 84.

32. Thomas C. Buchanan, *Black Life on the Mississippi: Slaves, Free Blacks, and the Western Steamboat World* (Chapel Hill: University of North Carolina Press, 2004), 43.

33. James H. Dormon, "The Audiences: Composition and Character," in *Theatre in the Antebellum South, 1815–1861* (Chapel Hill: University of North Carolina Press, 1967), 232, 231–251.

34. The owner-directors from the 1830s to 1840s included Albert Koch, W. S. McPherson, and Mr. Weedon. McDermott, *The Lost Panoramas of the Mississippi*, 8–13.

35. Curtis Dahl argues that moving panoramas had an influence on the content and style of Twain's fiction. Curtis Dahl, "Mark Twain and the Moving Panoramas," *American Quarterly* 13.1 (Spring 1961): 20–32.

36. Irit Rogoff, *Terra Firma: Geography's Visual Culture* (London: Routledge, 2000), 21.

37. For a thorough history of the military surveys, see William H. Goetzmann, *Army Exploration in the American West* (New Haven: Yale University Press, 1959).

38. One contemporary comparison from consecutive viewings in New Orleans in 1849 estimated the size of four different panoramas ranged from 440 yards to 1,325 yards. The largest at 12 ft by 1,325 yards was by Lewis. The size of the upper Mississippi section was approximated at 825 yards, that of the lower Mississippi at 500 yards. The smallest was by Banvard believed to extend to 440 yards, before he added scenes. Stockwell and Pomarède were compared to both be about 625 yards. "Lewis Panorama of the Mississippi River," *Western Journal of Agriculture, Manufacturers, Mechanics, Arts* 3.1 (October 1849), 70.

39. It was in circulation by July1848. McDermott, *The Lost Panoramas of the Mississippi River*, 168.

40. "Things Theatrical," *Spirit of the Times*, June 10, 1848, 204; "Panorama of the Mississippi," *Christian Watchman*, December 25, 1846, 207.

41. "Hudson's Panorama," *Christian Secretary*, July 28, 1848, 2.

42. Quoted in Stephan Oettermann, *The Panorama: History of a Mass Medium*, trans. Deborah Lucas Schneider (New York: Zone, 1997), 326.

43. James Presley Ball, *Splendid Mammoth Pictorial Tour of the United States: Comprising Views of the African Slave Trade of Northern and Southern Cities; of Cotton and Sugar Plantations; of the Mississippi, Ohio and Susquehanna Rivers, Niagara Falls, etc* (Cincinnati: Achilles Pugh, 1855), 36.

44. Banvard notoriously reproduced panoramas of Venice and Jerusalem, cities he never visited. McDermott, *The Lost Panoramas of the Mississippi*, 12.

45. April 1841.

46. Lewis, Stockwell and Pomarède settled in St. Louis by 1836. Lewis later claimed, "There was no one in St. Louis, where I first took up art as a profession to give lessons." McDermott, *The Lost Panoramas of the Mississippi*, 81. Heilbron, "Making a Motion Picture in 1848," 132; Joseph Earl Arrington, "Henry Lewis' Moving Panorama of the Mississippi River" *Louisiana History: The Journal of the Louisiana Historical Association* 6.3 (Summer 1965): 240.

47. He eventually lost it as a theatre manager in New York. See John Hanners, "'Vicissitude and Woe:' the Theatrical Misadventures of John Banvard," *Theatre Survey* 23.2 (November 1952): 177–187.

48. John Hanners, "The Adventures of an Artist: John Banvard (1815–1891) and His Mississippi Panorama," Dissertation, Michigan State University, 1979 (reprint, UMI, 2001), 58.

49. The exact measurements of the panorama are unclear. Estimates range from 300 to 500 ft. The number of scenes varied from 29 to 52. "Lewis Panorama of the Mississippi River," *Western Journal*. Comment, *The Panorama*, 63, 64. John Banvard, *Description of Banvard's Panorama of the Mississippi River Painted on Three Miles of Canvas Exhibiting a View of the Country 1,200 Miles in Length Extending from the Mouth of the Missouri River to the City of New Orleans; Being by far the Largest Picture Ever Executed by Man* (Boston: John Putnam, 1847).

50. Banvard reportedly earned revenues of $200,000 in America. Banvard, *Description of Banvard's Mississippi*, 21; Hanners, "The Adventures of an Artist," 65.

51. The exhibit was held at 652 Broadway in 1863. Called both "entertaining and instructive," it included his panorama of the Mississippi and new works on the Missouri and Ohio Rivers. *Scientific American* 8.13 (March 28, 1863), 195. See also Heilbron, "Making a Motion Picture in 1848," 136.

52. "Panorama of the Mississippi," *Christian Watchman*, 207; "Banvard's Great Painting," *Trumpet and Universalist Magazine*, January 9, 1847, 119; Hanners, "The Adventures of an Artist," 63.

53. "A Painting Three Miles Long," *Littell's Living Age*, September 25, 1847, 259.

54. "A Painting Three Miles Long," *Dwights American Magazine*, October 16, 1847, 668.

55. Banvard, *Description of Banvard's Panorama*, 7.

56. Ibid.

57. Orators agitating the end of the legal slave trade are active as early as 1808. Brooks, *Bodies in Dissent*, 80.

58. Ibid., 5.

59. Sergio Costola, "William Wells Brown's Panoramic Views," *Journal of American Drama and Theatre* 24.2 (Spring 2012):13–31.

60. Austin's essay came in response to an assertion made by Cynthia Griffin Wolff that Box Brown's work is unique for the period. Allan D. Austin, "More Black Panoramas: An Addendum," *The Massachusetts Review* 37.4 (Winter 1996): 636–639; Cynthia Griffin Wolff, "Passing beyond the Middle Passage: Henry Box Brown's Translations of Slavery," *The Massachusetts Review* 37.1 (Spring 1996): 23–44.

61. "Panorama of Slavery," *Liberator*, August 5, 1853, 122; Mary Q. Burnet, "Barton S. Hays," in *Art and Artists of Indiana* (New York: The Century, 1921).

62. Sergio Costola, "William Wells Brown's Panoramic Views," 23.

63. Brooks, *Bodies in Dissent*, 85–86.

64. The critic found the panoramas depiction of slavery unfair and inauthentic. Brown sued the editor of the small newspaper and won. For an analysis of the panoramas reception, see Ibid, 95–101.

65. "Panorama of Slavery," *The Independent*, June 20, 1850, 104; "From Our Special Correspondent," *Spirit of the Times*, May 11, 1850, 133.

66. See Marvin Edward McAllister, *"White People Do Not Know How to Behave at Entertainments Designed for Ladies and Gentleman of Colour":* *A History of New York's African and American Theatre* (Chapel Hill: University of North Carolina Press, 2003), 150–163.

67. Ball, *Splendid Mammoth Pictorial Tour of the United States*, 18–21, 26–35, 37–40, 45–47..

68. Oettermann, *The Panorama: History of a Mass Medium*, 67.

69. John Ernest scrutinizes the performance aspects of Brown's negotiation with antislavery narratives. See "Outside the Box: Henry Box Brown and the Politics of Antislavery Agency," *Arizona Quarterly* 63.4 (Winter 2007): 1–24.

70. Robert C. Toll, *Blacking Up: The Minstrel Show in Nineteenth-Century America* (New York: Oxford University Press, 1974), 13.

71. English comedian Charles Matthews inspired the renovation of the comic type. See Francis Hodge, *The Yankee Theatre: The Image of America on Stage* (Austin: University of Texas Press, 1964), 91, 155–239.

72. Richard Maxwell Brown relates the insidious reach of American vigilantism. In "the absence of effective law and order in a frontier region," extra-legal bands within communities filled the void. Brown distinguishes the different models that emerged. Richard Maxwell Brown, *Strain of Violence: Historical Studies of American Violence and Vigilantism* (New York: Oxford University Press, 1975), 96, 94–133.

73. "John Banvard's Great Panorama: Life on the Mississippi," *Littell's Living Age*, 511.

74. Murrell from Tennessee was a notorious thief. He spent nine years in prison for slave stealing, dying in 1844 at the age of 38. A pamphlet written by Virgil A. Stewart that appeared in 1835 spread the lore. "A History of the Detection, Conviction, Life and Designs of John A. Murrell, The Great Western Land Pirate; Together With his System of Villainy and Plan of Exciting a Negro Rebellion, and a Catalogue of the Names of Four Hundred and Forty Five of His Mystic Clan Fellows and Followers and Their Efforts for the Destruction of Mr. Virgil A. Stewart, The Young Man Who Detected Him, to Which Is Added Biographical Sketch of Mr. Virgil A. Stewart."

75. Christopher Morris, "An Event in Community Organization: The Mississippi Slave Insurrection Scare of 1835," *Journal of Social History* 22.1 (Autumn 1988): 93–111.

76. Edwin A Miles, "The Mississippi Slave Insurrection Scare of 1835," *The Journal of Negro History* 42.1 (January 1957), 55.

77. "A Painting Three Miles Long," *Littell's LivingAge*, 259.

78. "A Painting Three Miles Long," *Dwight's American Magazine*; "John Banvard, the American Artist," *The Eclectic Magazine of Foreign Literature* 12:4 (December 1847), 546; "John Banvard's Great Picture: Life on the Mississippi," *Littell's Living Age*, 511; "Banvard's Panorama," *Scientific American* 4.13 (December 16, 1848), 100.

79. "Banvard's Mammoth Panorama," *Liberator*, January 15, 1847, 17.

80. Longfellow diary, December 1846, quoted in McDermott, *The Lost Panoramas of the Mississippi*, 39–40.

81. "Panorama of the Mississippi," *Christian Watchman*, 207.

82. Banvard, *Description of Banvard's Panorama*, 48.

83. Ibid., 5; Hanners, "The Adventures of an Artist," 65.

84. Charles Dickens, "Some Account of an Extraordinary Traveller," *Household Words*, April 20, 1850, quoted in Hanners, "The Adventures of an Artist," 77.

85. December 9, 1848, quoted in McDermott, *The Lost Panoramas of the Mississippi*, 43.

86. "From Our Special Correspondent," *Spirit of the Times*, 133. Both Banvard and Smith duplicated their own work for simultaneous showings in London and provinces. Oettermann, *The Panorama: History of a Mass Medium*, 331.

87. It was shown in Newcastle first. "General Intelligence," *Christian Register*, November 2, 1850, 175.

88. Smith's father John Rubens Smith, a painter and art teacher, trained his son. He promoted public art classes to make "science available to anyone." To rouse interest and generate revenue toward opening a school, he published a series of lectures he offered on principles of perspective, a practical how to approach on the "geometry" of classical technique. J. R. Smith, *Synopsis of J. R. Smith's Perspective Lectures, or Copy of the Note Book by Which He Gives Perspective Illustrations* (Boston: J. H. Eastburn, 1826), 15.

89. In 1844, according to Heilbron, "Making a Motion Picture in 1848," 133.

90. See Oettermann, *The Panorama: History of a Mass Medium*, 331.

91. Risley and Smith also advertised testimonial from the Vice President of the United States in favor of their "great panorama." *Prof. Risley's and Mr. J.R. Smith's Original Gigantic Moving Panorama of the Mississippi River, Extending from the Falls of St. Anthony to the Gulf of Mexico* (London: John K. Chapman, 1849), British Library.

92. Squatters who settled and developed land wanted federal protection and rights to ownership. For years, they competed with speculators and capitalists who were buying up large plots of land. Political disputes spurred on legislative initiatives, such as the Homestead Act and the Free Soil movement offering free leases for settlers and legal citizens who improved the land. Southern politicians opposed free land proposals fearful it would lead to legislation barring slavery in the rich tracts of land opening in the Northwest. Republicans supported cheaper land sales and Homestead legislation. Many allied with Northeastern and Western politicians to ensure higher tariffs to protect nascent textile and iron industries. The Homestead Act passed in 1863. See Robert V. Hine and John Mack Faragher, *Frontiers: A Short History of the American West* (New Haven: Yale University Press, 2007), 133–146.

93. I draw on several versions of printed descriptions that accompanied exhibitions. Quoted excerpts are from the 1849 exhibition in the Grand

American Hall. *Prof. Risley's and Mr. J. R. Smith's Original Gigantic Moving Panorama of the Mississippi River.*

94. Ibid., 16.
95. For an account of the massacre, see Ronald W. Walker, et al., *Massacre at Mountain Meadows: An American Tragedy* (Oxford: Oxford University Press, 2008).
96. For an in-depth explanation of the charters and constitution of Illinois's legal procedure, see Hamilton Gardner, et al., "The Nauvoo Legion, 1840–1845: A Unique Military Organization," *Journal of the Illinois State Historical Society* 54.2 (Summer 1961): 181–197; John Lee Allaman, "Policing in Mormon Nauvoo," *Illinois Historical Journal* 89.2 (Summer 1996): 85–98.
97. Walker et al., *Massacre at Mountain Meadow*, 86.
98. Quoted in McDermott, *Lost Panoramas of the Mississippi*, 59–60; see also, *Prof. Risley's and Mr. J. R. Smith's Original Gigantic Moving Panorama of the Mississippi River*, 10–11; for a description of different renditions of the Nauvoo temple, see Joseph Earl Arrington, "Panorama Paintings of the Mormon Temple in Nauvoo," *BYU Studies* (1982): 1–13.
99. Hedgbeth, "Extant American Panoramas: Moving Entertainments of the Nineteenth Century," 51–99.
100. For the performance of Mormon origin tales and cultural enactments of sacred space, see Lindsay Adamson Livingston, "'This is the Place:' Performance and the Production of Space in Mormon Cultural Memory," in *Enacting History*, eds Scott Magelssen and Rhona Justice-Malloy (Tuscaloosa: University of Alabama Press, 2011), 22–40.
101. Hedgbeth, "Extent American Panoramas: Moving Entertainments of the Nineteenth Century," 75, 87–92.
102. *Prof. Risley's and Mr. J. R. Smith's Original Gigantic Moving Panorama of the Mississippi River*, 2.
103. Zachery Taylor, "Inaugural address," March 5, 1849, Library of Congress.
104. Miller, "The Panorama, the Cinema, and the Emergence of the Spectacular," 41.
105. "Stockwell's Panorama," *Spirit of the Times*, June 19, 1849, 184.
106. English-born Lewis claimed he was a naturalized citizen. It is now apparent he was not, which adds to skepticism around public statements concerning the manufacture of the panorama. See John Graham Cook, "Artist Henry Lewis: The Case of the Falsified Résumé," *Minnesota History* 57.5 (Spring 2001): 238–243.
107. The popularity of the "sensation scene" became a staple feature in melodrama performance by the 1840s. See Lynn. M. Voskuil, "Feeling Public: Sensation Theater, Commodity Culture, and the Victorian Public Sphere" *Victorian Studies* 44.2 (Winter 2002): 245–274; Nicholas Day, "Blood on the Tracks: Sensation Drama, the Railway, and the Dark Face of Modernity," *Victorian Studies* 42.1 (October 1998): 47–76; Daniel Gerould, ed., *American Melodrama* (New York: PAJ, 1983), 10–22.
108. "Correspondence," *Literary World*, October 20, 1849, 335.

109. Joseph Earl Arrington, "The Story of Stockwell's Panorama," *Minnesota History* 33.7 (Autumn 1953), 290.

110. Ibid., 287.

111. "Father of the Waters," *The Youth's Companion,* December 14, 1849, 132.

112. "Stockwell's Panorama," *Spirit of the Times,* January 7, 1849, 588.

113. *Picayune,* December 7, 1848. Quoted in Arrington, "The Story of Stockwell's Panorama," 288.

114. Augusta, Georgia's *Main Farmer* made it a point to mention his work was "three times longer" than Banvard's *Main Farmer,* October 26, 1848, 2. When appearing in Pittsburgh, Ohio, it was reported the panorama covered areas "unexplored by Banvard." "General Intelligence," *Christian Advocate and Journal,* August 16, 1849, 131.

115. "Correspondence," *Literary World.*

116. See the description in Arrington, "The Story of Stockwell's Panorama," 286.

117. Ibid., 287.

118. McDermott, *The Lost Panoramas of the Mississippi,* 76.

119. Reprints of the dialog all use the title "Taking the Mississippi." *Weekly Reveille,* November 4, 1848, 3; *Spirit of the Times,* October 7, 1848, 386; *The Huntress,* December 16, 1848, 1.

120. Federal legislation in 1824 and 1826 authorized river surveys and engineering projects.

121. William J. Peterson, *Mississippi River Panorama: The Henry Lewis Great National Work* (Iowa City: Clio Press, 1979), 24; Heilbron, "Making a Motion Picture in 1848," 137–138; Joseph Earl Arrington, "Henry Lewis' Moving Panorama of the Mississippi River," *Louisiana History, The Journal of the Louisiana Historical Association* 6.3 (Summer 1965): 239–272.

122. McDermott, *The Lost Panoramas of the Mississippi,* 86–89; Arrington, "Henry Lewis' Moving Panorama of the Mississippi River," 241–244.

123. Heilbron, "Making a Motion Picture in 1848," 140.

124. Peterson, *Mississippi River Panorama: The Henry Lewis Great National Work,* 23.

125. Heilbron, "Making a Motion Picture in 1848," 141–142; Arrington, "Henry Lewis' Moving Panorama of the Mississippi River," 248–249.

126. "Lewis' Panorama of the Mississippi River," *Western Journal of Agriculture, Manufacturers, Mechanics, Arts,* October 1849, 70.

127. Lewis expressed his concern in a letter to his brother George. Peterson, *Mississippi River Panorama: The Henry Lewis Great National Work,* 24.

128. The ballooning market occurred between 1840 and 1850. The article goes on to say that the majority is not making a profit. Popular destination themes, such as the *Shores of the Mediterranean, Voyage to California* and *Ireland and her Shores,* suggest producers wanted to appeal to immigrants and tourism alike. Curiously, among the listing no abolition panoramas are mentioned. From McDermott, *The Lost Panoramas of the Mississippi,* 68.

129. The panorama was shown in Hamburg and Berlin. Oettermann, *The Panorama: History of a Mass Medium,* 335.

130. Portions of text and illustrations from *Das Illustrirte Mississippithal* can be found in Peterson, *Mississippi River Panorama: The Henry Lewis Great National Work*. See also Bertha L. Heilbron, "Lewis' 'Mississippithal' in English," *Minnesota History* 32.4 (December 1951): 202–213.

131. Although Smith had painted the upper river from the Falls of St. Anthony, his panorama was not exhibited in Midwest cities, according to McDermott. *The Lost Panoramas of the Mississippi*, 85.

132. Peterson, *Mississippi River Panorama: The Henry Lewis Great National Work*, 44–71.

133. Arrington "Henry Lewis' Moving Panorama of the Mississippi River," 244.

134. McDermott, *The Lost Panoramas of the Mississippi*, 97.

135. Billington, *Westward Expansion: A History of the American Frontier*, 297.

136. McDougall, *Throes of Democracy: The American Civil War Era*, 301–305.

137. Billington, *Westward Expansion: A History of the American Frontier*, 290–291.

138. See Roger L. Nicols, *Black Hawk and the Warrior's Path* (Illinois: Harlan Davidson, 1992).

139. Bertha Heilbron, "Making a Motion Picture in 1848," 138; "The Father of the Waters," *The Youth's Companion*, 132.

140. Peterson, *Mississippi River Panorama: The Henry Lewis Great National Work*, 62–63.

141. McDermott, *The Lost Panoramas of the Mississippi*, 32–33.

142. Lewis's text of an "Indian cemetery" of the Dakota in Minnesota serves as one example of how such scenes transposed white domestic assumptions onto scenic representations yet appealed to a broader empathetic sentiment over death and burial. Hudson's panorama reflects a similar trope. Lewis's text indicates "this cemetery was ancient; and, although these savages had then, as they now have, no fixed abiding places,—pursuing a nomadic life, and dwelling in tents but a few months of each year, and yet every spring … to this sacred spot they gathered, bearing their dead." Peterson, *Mississippi River Panorama: The Henry Lewis Great National Work*, 52.

143. The spread of disease and urban crowding altered burial customs. Location took on urgency in antebellum period. See Elisabeth Walton Potter and Beth M. Boland, *Guidelines for Evaluating and Registering Cemeteries and Burial Places*, National Register Bulletin 41 (Washington, DC: Department of the Interior, 1992), 4–5.

144. Arrington, "Henry Lewis' Moving Panorama of the Mississippi River," 235.

145. Walter Benjamin's well-known theoretical writings on commodity culture include a foundational description of the *flâneur*'s role in nineteenth-century culture based on Charles Baudelaire's *Les Fleurs du Mal*. His thinking was heavily influenced by Georg Simmel's sociological theories of urban public space. Walter Benjamin, *Charles Baudelaire: a Lyric Poet in the Era of High Capitalism* (New York: Verso, 1997); "The Metropolis and Mental Life," *The Arcades Project*, 448; Georg Simmel, *The Metropolis and Mental life*, trans. Kurt Wolff (New York: Free Press, 1950), 409–424.

146. Arrington, "Henry Lewis' Moving Panorama of the Mississippi River," 239–272.

147. McDermott, *The Lost Panoramas of the Mississippi*, 138.

148. For a wide-ranging river history covering geology to economics see Calvin R. Fremling, *Immortal River: The Upper Mississippi in Ancient and Modern Times* (Madison: University of Wisconsin Press, 2005), 176–177.

149. McDermott, *The Lost Panoramas of the Mississippi*, 137.

150. Ibid., 136.

151. Ibid., 140.

152. "Lewis' Panorama of the Mississippi," *Western Journal*, 70.

153. Peterson, *Mississippi River Panorama: The Henry Lewis Great National Work*, 31.

154. He decorated the St. Louis, Cathedral and the Church of the Holy Trinity in Cincinnati, Ohio. "Church Painting," *The Catholic Telegraph*, February 18, 1836, 92.

155. Pomarède painted the panorama in his St. Louis studio with help from his business partner Charles Courtenay. McDermott, *The Lost Panoramas of the Mississippi*, 148.

156. "New Jersey Items," *New York Daily Tribune*, November 20, 1850, 7.

157. Heilbron, "Making a Motion Picture in 1848," 137.

158. *Prof. Risley's and Mr. J. R. Smith's Original Gigantic Moving Panorama of the Mississippi River*, 30–32.

159. Arrington, "The Story of Stockwell's Panorama," 288.

160. In this section, Ball conveys that the owners were also embroiled in bank forgeries at the time. Ball, *Splendid Mammoth Pictorial Tour of the United States*, no.27 and no.28: 48.

161. Lewis reported to his audiences a population of 20,000 in 1844. Peterson, *Mississippi River Panorama: The Henry Lewis Great National Work*, 85–86.

162. Arrington, "Henry Lewis' Moving Panorama of the Mississippi," 245.

163. Peterson, *Mississippi River Panorama: The Henry Lewis Great National Work*, 93, 92–94.

164. Oettermann, *The Panorama: History of a Mass Medium*, 136.

165. Another highlight was the city of Dubuque, Iowa.

166. Duncanson also painted a Prairie Fire (1862). Joseph D. Ketner II believes Wimar's well-known works may have been one influence. Both artists were in St. Louis. See Ketner II, *The Emergence of the African American Artist: Robert S. Duncanson, 1821–1872* (Columbia, Missouri: University of Missouri Press, 1992), 113.

167. Quoted in McDermott, *The Lost Panoramas of the Mississippi*, 154.

168. For instance, Harvey Young examines how in acts of American lynching the commodification of body parts as fetish objects taken as souvenirs embody the past. Harvey Young, "The Black Body as Souvenir in American Lynching" *Theatre Journal* 57.4 (December 2005): 639–657.

169. Oettermann, *The Panorama: History of a Mass Medium*, 340–343.

170. An estimated 200,000 people attended the event in New York. Ibid., 341.

3   Entertainment Scenes: Industrial Strength Brands of Site-Specific Spectacle

1. Robert Montgomery Bird, "God Bless America," Philadelphia, 1834, Library of Congress.
2. The "Star Spangled Banner" was written in 1814. It became the national anthem in 1831.
3. The midtown rotunda was on Madison Avenue at Fifty-ninth street, formerly known as the Merrimac and Monitor Panorama. The downtown rotunda was on Nineteenth-street and Fourth Avenue. The company behind mounting the Gettysburg exhibition included C. L. Willoughby, O. Wheeler, Paul Philippoteaux, J. M. Hill, T. Bartow, L. Brandus, and H. De Casira. "Pleased with their Success," *The New York Times*, February 14, 1889, 9; "Theatrical Gossip," *The New York Times*, July 9, 1888, 8.
4. Henderson managed the Chicago Opera House. His productions toured the East and West. "Tricks of the Stage," *Current Literature* 16.4 (October 1894), 362; "Chicago's Summer Spectacle," *The New York Times*, June 3, 1892, 1; "Matters in Chicago," *The New York Times*, January 21, 1894, 10; "Theatrical Gossip," *The New York Times*, September 8, 1894, 8.
5. Brendan Edward Gregory, "The Spectacle Plays and Exhibitions of Imre Kiralfy, 1887–1914," Dissertation, 1988, University of Manchester, 4.
6. Maurya Wickstrom, *Performing Consumers: Global Capital and Its Theatrical Seductions* (New York: Routledge, 2006).
7. Ibid., 2.
8. Catherine de Medici's "magnificences" or court festivals were staged at Chenonceaux and at Fontainbleau. Frieda Leoni, *Catherin de Medici* (London: Phoenix, 2005); Roy Strong, *Splendor at Court: Renaissance Spectacle and the Theatre of Power* (Boston: Houghton Mifflin, 1973); 121–168.
9. Jack F. Kasson, *Amusing the Million: Coney Island at the Turn of the Century* (New York: Hill and Wang, 1978), 109.
10. Barnard Hewitt, *Theatre U.S.A. 1665–1957* (New York: McGraw Hill, 1959), 273; Nicholas A. Vardac, *Stage to Screen: Theatrical Origins of Early Film. From David Garrick to D. W. Griffith* (Cambridge, MA: Harvard University Press, 1949), 76–80, 89–151. For cinematic studies of early film technique, see David Robinson, *From Peep Show to Palace: The Birth of American Film* (New York: Columbia University Press, 1996), 136, 155; Ben Brewster and Lea Jacobs, *Theatre to Cinema: Stage Pictorialism and the Early Feature Film* (Oxford: Oxford University Press, 1997), 3–17.
11. David Glassberg, *American Historical Pageantry: The Uses of Tradition in the Early Twentieth Century* (Chapel Hill: University of North Carolina Press, 1990), 27.
12. Ibid., 27.
13. "Boer War Spectacle, Coney Island's Newest Show," *The New York Times*, May 21, 1905, 5.
14. *Cleopatra VI, Queen of Egypt*, Cincinnati, Ohio 1895, Program, American Memory Collection, Library of Congress.

15. Glassberg, *American Historical Pageantry*, 27.
16. *Quo Vadis?* was first filmed in 1913. *Ben Hur* was produced as a short film in 1907. Both were made into feature films by 1925. Compiled from Hewitt, *Theatre USA*, 273; Vardac, *Stage to Screen*, 76–80.
17. Richard D. Altick, *The Shows of London* (Cambridge: Harvard University Press, 1978), 187.
18. Ibid., 184–210.
19. Ibid., 190; Richard Moody discusses the explosion of panoramic entertainments in America, in his introduction to William Dunlap's *A Trip to Niagara; or Travellers in America*, in *Drama from the American Theatre, 1762–1909* (New York: World Publishing, 1966), 175–197.
20. These spectaculars took place at Covent Garden in 1829. Altick, *The Shows of London*, 190.
21. Ibid.
22. The brothers were Frederick and William. Stephan Oettermann, *The Panorama: History of a Mass Medium*, trans. Deborah Lucas Schneider (New York: Zone, 1997), 340.
23. Joseph Earl Arrington, "Godfrey N. Frankenstein's Moving Panorama of Niagara Falls," *New York History* 49 (April 1968): 169–199.
24. "Tricks of the Stage."
25. Lincoln Kirstein, *Dance: A Short History of Classical Theatrical Dancing* (New York: Dance Horizons, 1969), 348.
26. The dissolution of their partnership at the end of the theatrical season was publicly announced in March 1887. Imre reportedly entered into partnership with Edward G. Gilmore of Niblo's Garden Theatre. "Theatrical Gossip," *The New York Times*, March 10, 1887, 5. For Bolossy's account of the breakup and his career, see "Bolossy Tells His Side," *The New York Times*, August 22, 1888, 3; Bolossy Kiralfy, *Creator of Great Musical Spectacles: An Autobiography*, ed. Barbara M. Barker (Ann Arbor, Michigan: UMI Research Press, 1988).
27. I refer to Martin Meisel's concept of "realization," which he distinguishes as a central pattern in nineteenth-century dramaturgical developments. He defines its broad application in terms of the manifestation of words, or pictures on stage toward the "literal recreation and translation into a more real … visual, physically present medium." See Martin Meisel, *Realizations, Narrative, Pictorial, and Theatrical Arts in Nineteenth-Century England* (Princeton: Princeton University Press, 1983), 30.
28. Percy Mackaye, *Epoch: The Life of Steele Mackaye, Genius of the Theatre, In Relation to His Times and Contemporaries*, Vol. 2 (New York: Boni and Liverlight, 1927), 337.
29. See Vardac, *From Stage to Screen*. For an account of the influence of the Madison Square Theatre on nineteenth-century production styles, see J. A. Sokalski, "The Madison Square Theatre: Stage Practice and Technology in Transition," *Theatre Survey* 21 (2001): 105–131. For Mackaye's involvement in trends toward realistic acting in melodrama, see Frank Rahill, *The World of Melodrama* (University Park, PA: Pennsylvania State University Press, 1967), 207–213. See also Hewitt, *Theatre USA*; Glenn Hughes, *A History of American Theatre, 1750–1950* (New York: Samuel French, 1951).

30. Mackaye's financial backers pulled out just before completion of the theatre due to delays, rising costs, and debt. In Mackaye, *Epoch*, 2: 337–341; 345–348; 369–408. See also Hughes, *History of American Theatre*, 236–237.

31. "Another Theatrical Combine," *The New York Times*, September 9, 1897, 7.

32. The figures were collated from the census records. The total school population of 34 states reporting directly to the Bureau was just under 13 million. In the seven territories, enrollment dips to 88,000, but the figure is based on incomplete records. "United States Bureau of Education," *The New York Times*, August 21, 1873, 2.

33. Ibid. Eaton emphasizes the need is especially keen in college curriculum.

34. Ibid.

35. In 1859, Peter Cooper opened the Cooper Institute (later the Cooper Union for the Advancement of Science and Art). One of the first board members of the institute was William Cullen Bryant, editor of the *New York Evening Post*. Anthony J. Drexel founded the Drexel Institute of Art, Science, and Industry in 1891. See "The Copper Union," *Harper's Weekly*, March 30, 1861, 200.

36. According to the decennial census, the first census in which data were collected on the nativity of the population, the foreign-born population rose from 9.7 percent in 1850 and fluctuated in the 13–15 percent range from 1860 to 1920 before dropping to 11.6 percent in 1930. The highest percentages of foreign born were 14.4 percent in 1870, 14.8 percent in 1890, and 14.7 percent in 1910. From Campbell J. Gibson and Emily Lennon, "Historical Census Statistics on the Foreign-born Population of the United States: 1850–1990," Population Division Working Paper No. 29 (February 1999), US Census Bureau, Population Division. <http://www.census.gov>.

37. Ibid. 44.5 percent of the city's 942,292 inhabitants were foreign born.

38. Mackaye, *Epoch*, 2: 337.

39. The family of dancers included brothers Arnold and Ronald and sisters Haniola, Katie, and Emilie.

40. International communication boosted popular markets for performative skills such as the acrobatic comedy of the Hanlon Brothers. See Mark Cosdon, *The Hanlon Brothers: From Daredevil Acrobatics to Spectacle Pantomime, 1833–1931* (Carbondale: Southern Illinois University Press, 2009).

41. Imre Kiralfy, "My Reminiscences," *The Strand* 37.222 (June 1909): 646.

42. Imre Kiralfy, Clippings, Billy Rose Theatre Collection, New York Public Library for the Performing Arts.

43. "Imre Kiralfy's Work," *Dallas Morning News*, June 15, 1919, 2; "Masks and Faces," *The National Police Gazette*, March 2, 1889, 2.

44. "Buffalo Bill's Good-bye," *The New York Times*, April 1, 1887, 8; "Books and Authors," *Christian Union*, June 25, 1892, 1259.

45. Barbara Barker, "Imre Kiralfy's Patriotic Spectacles: *Columbus and the Discovery of America* (1892–1893) and *America* (1893)," *Dance Chronicle* 17.2 (1994): 152.

46. For a detailed account of the production, see Ibid.; also Glassberg, *American Historical Pageantry*, 27.

47. Edward B. Marks, *They All Had Glamour: From the Swedish Nightingale to the Naked Lady* (New York: J. Messner, 1944), 22.

48. "Mr. Gilmore's Plans," *The New York Times*, April 10, 1887, 9.

49. Barker, "Imre Kiralfy's Patriotic Spectacles," 152.

50. *Life*, December 21, 1893, 399.

51. Kiralfy, "My Reminiscences," 646.

52. Ibid.

53. Ibid.

54. *Excelsior*, Program, Niblo's Garden Theatre, August 21, 1883, Billy Rose Theatre Collection, New York Public Library for the Performing Arts.

55. Ibid.

56. Mount Cenis was operational by 1871.

57. Reputedly, Thomas Edison himself oversaw the installations for the production. From Bolossy Kiralfy, *Bolossy Kiralfy, Creator of Great Musical Spectacles*, 117. See also Kirstein, *Dance: A Short History of Classical Theatrical Dancing*, 348.

58. Margaret Malamud, "The Imperial Metropolis: Ancient Rome and Turn-of-the-Century New York, *Arion* 7.3 (Winter 2000): 66.

59. Ibid., 64–65.

60. Richard C. Beacham, *Spectacle Entertainments of Early Imperial Rome* (New Haven: Yale University Press, 1999), 203.

61. Mark Franko, *The Work of Dance: Labor, Movement, and Identity in the 1930s* (Middletown: Wesleyan University Press, 2002), 31.

62. *Brooklyn Eagle*, August 19, 1883, 2.

63. "Mammoth Cave of Kentucky," *Friends' Weekly Intelligencer*, September 1, 1849, 181.

64. Peter West, "Trying the Dark, Mammoth Cave and the Racial Imagination," *Southern Spaces*, February 9, 2010, 4. <http://www.southernspaces.org>.

65. The panorama was the studio creation of a team of painters. Skirving was assisted by Joseph Kyle. J. Lee. Jacob Dallas painted figures and animals. Much of the material for the four sections of the work was acquired from different field artists' renderings of various government expeditions. The most famous survey team was led by John Charles Fremont, whose series of expeditions through the Northwest made national news; the Pacific region drew on expedition voyages of naval commander Charles Wilkes. "Sufferings of Col. Fremont and Party among the Rocky Mountains," *Friends' Weekly Intelligencer* 6.8 (May 19, 1849), 57. Joseph Earl Arrington, "Skirving's Moving Panorama: Colonel Fremont's Western Expeditions," *Oregon Historical Quarterly* 65:2 (June 1964): 134.

66. *The Department of Commerce* (Washington: Government Printing Office, 1915), 2.

67. *Proceedings of the First Meeting of the National Board of Trade Held in Philadelphia, June 1868* (Boston: J. H. Eastburn, 1868), v. The organization included Boards of Trade from the cities of Albany, Baltimore, Boston, Buffalo, Charleston, Chicago, Cleveland, Denver, Detroit, Louisville,

Newark, Oswego, Philadelphia, Pittsburgh, Portland, Providence, St. Louis, Toledo, Troy, and Wilmington, Delaware; Chambers of Commerce were represented by Cincinnati, Milwaukie, New Orleans, New York, Richmond, and St. Paul; agricultural groups came from the Boston Corn Exchange, Dubuque Produce Exchange, and the New York Produce Exchange; the Peoria Merchants' Exchange and the St. Louis Merchants' Exchange also joined.

68. The agricultural industry had actively lobbied Congress to elevate their bureau to the rank of Department. "The Tariff Debate in the House," *The New York Times*, May 29, 1892, 1.

69. The Departments of Commerce and Labor were separated shortly after the bill passed. The mandate of the Department of Commerce remains the advancement of economic growth and job creation. *The Department of Commerce* (Washington: Government Printing Office, 1915), 10–13; see also "What is the Department of Commerce,"< http://www.commerce.gov>.

70. William Howard Taft outlined campaign issues in an article for the Independent, "The Republican Party's Appeal," *The Collected Works of William Howard Taft*, Vol. 3, ed. David H. Burton (Athens: University of Ohio Press, 2004), 36–37.

71. The details of these expeditions are taken up in chapter 5.

72. Alan Trachtenberg, *The Incorporation of America: Culture and Society in the Gilded Age* (New York: Hill and Wang, 1982), 10–37.

73. See National Park Service. < http://nps.gov>.

74. The surveys were placed under the offices of the Secretary of the Interior in 1869. Ten years later, the US Geographical Survey was established.

75. A brief history of the national park service, edited by James F. Kieley, in booklet form was published in 1940. A digital edition is available from The US Department of the Interior, <http://www.nps.gov/history/history/online_books/kieley/index.htm>.

76. *Ferdinand Vandiveer Hayden and the Founding of Yellowstone National Park* (Washington, DC: US Government Printing Office, 1941), 20.

77. Thirty-seven of Jackson's photographs were printed by the Interior Department. *Photographs from the Geological Survey of the Territories for the Years 1869–1873* (Washington, DC: Government Printing Office, 1873a). *Photographs of the Yellowstone National Parks, and Views in Montana and Wyoming* (Washington, DC: Government Printing Office, 1873b). A mass-market narrative of the expedition featuring attractions, such as Hot Springs and Castle Geyser, was quickly published by Hayden with 15 watercolor sketches by Moran in *Yellowstone National Park, and the Mountain Regions of Portions of Idaho, Nevada, Colorado and Utah* (Boston: L. Prang, 1876).

78. Congress transferred the paintings to the Interior Department where they remained until 1968 when the museum lent them to the Smithsonian's American Art Museum Renwick Gallery where they are on exhibit today.

79. William Welling, *Photography in America: The Formative Years, 1839–1900* (New York: Thomas Y. Cromwell, 1978), 211.

80. One camera was an 8×10, the other a stereoscope. He contrived a portable dark room with a wooden box to use on the expeditions. William Henry Jackson, *Time Exposure: The Autobiography of William Henry Jackson* (Arizona: The Patrice Press, 1994), 178.

81. Jim Hughes, *The Birth of a Century: Early Color Photographs of America* (London: Taurus Parke Books, 1994), 154.

82. *Ferdinand Vandiveer Hayden and the Founding of the Yellowstone National Park*, 17–28.

83. Hughes, *The Birth of a Century*, 9.

84. Jackson, *Time Exposure*, 209.

85. Barbara Kirshenblatt-Gimblett, *Destination Culture: Tourism, Museums and Heritage* (Berkeley: University of California Press, 1998), 18–25.

86. Kiralfy, "My Reminiscences," 649.

87. Ibid., 646.

88. They constructed a railway bridge to New Jersey. "Wiman Erastus," *Dictionary of Canadian Biography Online*, Library and Archives Canada. <http://www.collectionscanada.ca>.

89. Glassberg, *American Historical Pageantry*, 27. The order produced numerous large-scale spectacles for the city of Cincinnati. See *The Fall of Babylon*, Programs, Billy Rose Theatre Collection, New York Public Library for the Performing Arts; "The Cincinnati Festival," *The New York Times*, September 7, 1883, 5; "The Ballet Girls Struck," *The New York Times*, June 18, 1890, 1.

90. "Fall of Babylon," *The New York Times*, June 17, 1887, 2. The ballet director for both productions was Ettore Coppini.

91. "Babylon's Fall," *The New York Times*, June 26, 1887, 5.

92. Compiled from program notes. *The Fall of Babylon*, Program, 1889, Programs, Billy Rose Theatre Collection, New York Public Library for the Performing Arts. The production opened on June 25.

93. "Staten Island Attractions," *The New York Times*, April 24, 1887, 7.

94. "Watching Babylon Fall," *The New York Times*, June 19, 1887, 9; "Ancient Babylon's Fall," *The New York Times*, June 12, 1887, 9.

95. See, for instance, "Making Great Preparations," *The New York Times*, June 23, 1887.

96. "Watching Babylon Fall."

97. "Babylon's Fall."

98. "A Wonderful Spectacle," *The New York Times*, July 17, 1887, 9.

99. Attendance figures over the summer range from ten- to fifty-thousand people, but it is not clear whether these are weekly or monthly averages.

100. Kiralfy, "My Reminiscences," 647. The brothers bickered publicly over their roles in *Nero*, even after their breakup. Bolossy credited John Rettig of Cincinnati with the creation of *Nero*, minus the ballet, and insisted that the staging and ballet was his. The Order of Cincinnatus later sued Imre over copyright infringement. "Bolossy Tells his Side," 3; "Imre Kiralfy Sued," *The New York Times*, September 25, 1888, 2.

101. *Nero, or the Destruction of Rome*, Program, 1890, Programs, Billy Rose Theatre Collection, New York Public Library for the Performing Arts.

102. Ibid.

103. Advance press provided detailed accounts of the massive preparations. See, for instance, "Summer at St. George," *The New York Times*, April 25, 1888, 5; "Rome Upon Rails," *The New York Times*, June 8, 1888, 9; "Kiralfy's Big Spectacle," *The New York Times*, June 24, 1888, 3.

104. Kiralfy, "My Reminiscences," 648.

105. Ibid.

106. "England Wants Nero," *The New York Times*, July 1, 1888, 16.

107. Margaret Malamud, "Roman Entertainments for the Masses in Turn-of-the-Century New York," *The Classical World* 95.1 (Autumn 2001): 51.

108. The production ran three months. "Nero," *London Evening News and Post*, November 12, 1889. Review quoted in A. H. Saxon, *P.T. Barnum: The Legend and the Man* (New York: Columbia University Press, 1989), 320.

109. The spectacle was billed as "A Titanic, Imperial, Historical Spectacle of Colossal Dramatic Realism, Gladiatorial Combats and Olympian Displays. Indisputably, Immeasurably, Over-whelming the Most Majestic, Entrancing, and Surpassingly Splendid and Realistic Spectacle of Any Age." The production reportedly grossed over one million dollars. From Fred D. Pfening, Jr. "Spec-ology of the Circus, Part I," *Bandwagon* 47:6 (November–December 2003), 4–20. See also Saxon, *P.T. Barnum*, 323.

110. "The Fall of Rome," *The New York Times*, April 9, 1890, 8.

111. For a description of performances, see James S. Moy, "Imre Kiralfy's 1890 Boston Production of *The Fall of Babylon*," *Theatre History Studies* 1 (1981): 20–28.

112. Quoted in Saxon, *P.T. Barnum*, 323.

113. "The Fall of Babylon," *New York Evangelist*, July 21, 1887, 5.

114. *Life*, September 20, 1888, 158.

115. "No Nonsense Tolerated at Nero," *The New York Times*, August 22, 1888, 8.

116. Ibid.

117. Ken Burns reiterates these ideals throughout his recent documentary *The National Parks: America's Best Idea*, in which panoramic views are used to great effect. PBS Home Video, 2009.

118. Gregory, "The Spectacle Plays and Exhibitions of Imre Kiralfy," 287.

119. Kiralfy had associations with members of the British Empire League, including the President Lord Derby and Lord Strathcona, one of its founders. Ultra conservative Lord Derby, formerly Edward George Villiers Stanley, served as British Minister of War from 1916–1918 during World War I. The British Empire League advocated establishing cheaper and more direct steam postal and telegraphic communication; devising a more perfect cooperation of the military and naval forces of the empire, with a special view to the due protection of the trade routes; assimilating, as far as possible, the laws relating to copyright, patents, legitimacy, and bankruptcy throughout the empire. John M. McKenzie, *Orientalism: History, Theory and the Arts* (Manchester and New York: Manchester University Press, 1995), 151.

120. John Robinson Whitley was from Yorkshire, and worked for his father's engineering firm. He invented an embossed wall covering called Lincrusta that become very fashionable in Victorian society. Widely traveled and fluent in several languages, his visits to the 1876 and 1878 Paris Exhibition

international exhibitions convinced him of the social efficacy of cultural complexes. See Gregory, "The Spectacle Plays and Exhibitions of Imre Kiralfy," 287.

121. Ibid., 287.
122. Ibid., 452.
123. Quoted in Gregory, "The Spectacle Plays and Exhibitions of Imre Kiralfy," 443.
124. Ibid., 10–11.
125. Ibid., 300.
126. Ibid., 145
127. See McKenzie, *Orientalism: History, Theory and the Arts*, 196–197.
128. *Imre Kiralfy's Grand Naval Spectacle*, Program, 1898, Museum of London.
129. Alexander C. T. Geppert examines the Franco-British exhibition in relationship to mass media and globalism, *Fleeting Cities: Imperial Expositions in Fin-de-Siècle Europe* (London: Palgrave Macmillan, 2010), 101–133.
130. "The Anglo-Japanese Exhibition of 1910," *Outlook* 93.1 (1893–1924); September 4, 1909, 11.
131. See Alvaro Fernandez-Bravo, "Ambivalent Argentina: Nationalism, Exoticism, and Latin Americanism at the 1889 Paris Universal Exposition," *Nepanlta: Views from South* 2.1 (2001): 115–139.
132. Gregory, "The Spectacle Plays and Exhibitions of Imre Kiralfy," 385.
133. Ibid., 13.

4   Theme Scenes: Producing Global Strategies on US Exhibition Stages

1. President Grant supported a return to the gold and silver standard to stabilize the economy when the national debt ballooned to 2.8 million dollars after the Civil War. The Republican platform pledged enforcement of the Fourteenth and Fifteenth Amendment. However, the Republicans passed a "universal amnesty" act in 1872 sought by Liberals and Democrats that gave back former Confederate leaders voting rights and the right to hold state or federal office. Between 1867 and 1904, territorial treaties were entered with Alaska (1867); Guam (1899); Hawaii (1898); the Philippine Islands (1899); American Samoa (1900); and the Panama Canal Zone (1904). Through protected trade agreements, the United States proceeded to establish civil governments. Jean Edward Smith, *Grant* (Simon & Schuster, 2001), 479, 481, 550; Andrew L. Slap, *The Doom of Reconstruction: The Liberal Republicans in the Civil War Era* (New York: Fordham University Press, 2008), 126–163. *Statistical Abstract of the United States, 1915*, Department of Commerce, (Washington, DC: Government Printing Office, 1916), 10.
2. "The New World's Fair," *New York Tribune*, May 10, 1876, 1.
3. An open-air intersection called the "Court of the Universe" opened on east and west passageways to main exhibition buildings by a set of Arches of Nations. John D. Barry, *The City of Domes: a Walk with an Architect about the Courts and Palaces of the Panama-Pacific International Exposition*,

with a Discussion of its Arch (San Francisco: John J. Newbegin, 1915), 44–50; Ben Macomber, *The Jewel City: Its Planning and Achievement; Its Architecture, Sculpture, Symbolism, and Music; Its Gardens, Palaces, and Exhibits* (San Francisco: John H. Williams, 1915), 15–20.

4. Robert Rydell, *All the World's a Fair: Visions of Empire at American International Expositions, 1876–1916* (Chicago: University of Chicago Press, 1984), 2.

5. Alfred Alles, *Exhibitions: Universal Marketing Tools* (New York: John Wiley & Sons, 1973), 16.

6. Shmuel N. Eisenstadt, *Comparative Civilizations and Multiple Modernities* (Leidon and Boston: Brill, 2003); see also *Paradoxes of Democracy, Fragility, Continuity, and Change* (Baltimore: Johns Hopkins University Press, 1999) and Frederic Jameson, *A Singular Modernity: Essay on the Ontology of the Present* (London: Verso, 2002).

7. The liberal Republican vision of political parties argued political efficacy as principle of democracy. One of the leaders of the movement, Henry Adams, defended the right of citizens to create political parties for the purpose of reform. Slap, *The Doom of Reconstruction*, 37, 25–50.

8. William Leach, *Land of Desire: Merchants, Power, and the Rise of a New American Culture* (New York: Pantheon, 1993), xiii.

9. Ames makes the distinction that theme space in contrast to fantasy space or virtual space reinvents attachment to a physical environment. He defines theme space as the "physical displacement of the spectacle to the spectator" in which all is good and beautiful. Eric Ames, *Carl Hagenbeck's Empire of Entertainments* (Seattle: University of Washington Press, 2008), 5, 7.

10. Alexander C. T. Geppert, *Fleeting Cities: Imperial Expositions in Fin-de-Siècle Europe* (London: Palgrave Macmillan, 2010), 5.

11. It was five years in the making. Useful curatorial material on the fair include, Frank Monaghan, *Official Guide Book of the New York World's Fair 1939* (New York: Exhibition Publications,1939); Helen Harrison, *Dawn of a New Day* (New York: New York University Press, 1980); a photographic record by Richard Wurts, *The New York World's Fair 1939/1940* (New York: Dover, 1977).

12. *The Illustrated History of the Centennial Exhibition, 1876*, reprint (Philadelphia: National Publishing, 1975), 293.

13. Alles, *Exhibitions: Universal Marketing Tools*, 12.

14. "Centennial Exposition Memoranda," *Potter's American Monthly* 6.53 (May 1876): 375.

15. *Illustrated History of the Centennial Exhibition*, 55.

16. Erik Matte, *World's Fairs* (Princeton: Princeton Architectural Press, 1998), 31.

17. See David Andress, *Massacre at the Champ De Mars: Popular Dissent and Political Culture in the French Revolution* (Suffolk: Boydell Press, 2000) and Lynn Avery Hunt, *Politics, Culture, Class in the French Revolution* (Berkeley: University of California Press, 2004).

18. "Fairmount Park," *The New York Times*, June 14, 1872, 4; "A New Route to Philadelphia," *The Independent*, May 4, 1876, 20.

19. "The New Orleans Centennial Exposition," No. II, *Friends' Weekly Intelligencer*, June 17, 1885, 778.

20. *The Official Catalogue of the World's Industrial and Cotton Centennial Exposition: Held under the Joint Auspices: the United States of America, the National Cotton Planter's Association, and the City of New Orleans, During the Period from the 16th of December to the 131st of May 1885* (New Orleans: J. S. Rivers, 1886).

21. Louis Christian Mullgradt, *The Architecture and Landscape Gardening of the Exposition: A Pictorial Survey of the Most Beautiful of the Architectural Compositions of the Panama-Pacific International Exposition*, Second ed. (San Francisco: Paul Elder and Co., 1915), 4.

22. Sir Henry Cole, the assistant keeper of Public Records, raised the idea after visiting a national exhibition in Paris in 1848. The selection of Paxton's design came at the end of a lengthy review process by a separate Buildings Commission charged with soliciting plans for the exhibition building. Paxton's sketch resembling a country estate conservatory greenhouse—he was formerly gardener to the Duke of Devinshire—arrived ten months before opening day. Its swift approval by the Executive Committee came after it met with public enthusiasm. See C. H. Gibbs-Smith, *The Great Exhibition of 1851* (London: Victoria and Albert Museum, 1981), 11-12.

23. Useful catalogs and guidebooks of the exhibition include, *Official Descriptive and Illustrated Catalogue of the Great Exhibition of the Works of Industry of All Nations*, 4 Vols (London: Spicer Brothers, 1851); *The Art Journal Illustrated Catalogue: The Industry of All Nations 1851* (London: George Virtue, 1851); William Gaspey, *Tallis's Illustrated London: In Commemoration of the Great Exhibition of 1851. Forming a Complete Guide to the British Metropolis and its Environ*, 5 Vols (London: John Tallis, 1851).

24. Carstensen's account remains the most substantial, *New York Crystal Palace* (New York: Rikker, Thorne & Co. 1854).

25. The trend begins in the 1850s with retail store Lord and Taylor. It was not until the 1870s that this new architectural movement took off. Winston Weisman frames his history of these luxurious retail outlets as "the architectural symbol of the merchant prince." Weisman, "Commercial Palaces of New York: 1845–1875," *The Art Bulletin*, 36.4 (December 1954): 286, 285–302.

26. Robert C. Post, "Reflections of American Science and Technology at the New York Crystal Palace Exhibition of 1953," *Journal of American Studies* 17.3 (December 1983): 338.

27. Ticket sales reached over $300, 000 for the first five-month season. Total expenditures more than tripled that amount. P. T. Barnum attempted to jump start flagging attendance the following season during his brief tenure as president when Sedgwick resigned as director. He attempted to lure repeat business with amusement arcades and musical entertainment but was unable to salvage the venue as a permanent installation. It closed in November 1854 at the end of its second season.

28. In Post's account of the history, once the New York community became involved, they wrested control from Riddle. Post, "Reflections of American Science and Technology," 337.

29. The location was Reservoir Square (now Bryant Park) situated between 40th and 42nd street, off sixth avenue. Ed Witkowski, *The Lost History of the 1853 New York Crystal Palace* (New York: Vox Pop, 2008), 108.

30. To obtain a five-year lease for $1.00 per year, certain conditions were agreed on that benefited local trade and carried a civic mission: the use of iron and glass were prescribed for construction; admission was set at an affordable 50 cents; New York City school children were admitted free; and one day's receipts were held as benefit to a New York and Brooklyn Fireman's Fund.

31. Merle Curti elaborates on the arguments. Protectionism for domestic industries was a repeated point of contention. "America at the World Fairs: 1851–1893," *The American Historical Review* 55.4 (July 1950): 834–837.

32. Post, "Reflections of American Science and Technology," 338.

33. Daniel Walker Howe, *What God Hath Wrought: The Transformation of America, 1815–1848* (Oxford: Oxford University Press, 2007). 701–708.

34. Ibid., 706.

35. Ibid.

36. Through expanding trade and Christian missions as opposed to forceful colonial territorial expansion.

37. Peter A. Wallner, *Franklin Pierce, New Hampshire's Favorite Son* (Concord: Plaidswede 2004), 253. Pierce laid out domestic and foreign policy in his first inaugural address a few months before the exhibition: "It is not to be disguised that our attitude as a nation and our position on the globe render the acquisition of certain possessions not within our jurisdiction eminently important for our protection, if not in the future essential for the preservation of the rights of commerce and the peace of the world." "First Inaugural Address," 4 March 1853; Irving J. Sloan, ed., *Franklin Pierce, 1804–1869: Chronology, Documents, Bibliographical Aids* (New York: Oceana Publications, 1968), 19.

38. Speech of Napoleon III; "Opening the Chambers, The Domestic and Foreign Policy of the Empire," *The New York Times*, February 20, 1860; "Emperor's Speech," *Harper's Weekly*, March 2, 1861.

39. Ibid. He pledged 90 million francs of annual receipts toward economic reforms, promising to balance the budget without resorting to new taxes.

40. Napoleon championed European unity as his "great idea" that would lead to lasting peace and prosperity. John Stevens Cabott Abbott, *The History of Napoleon III, Emperor of the French* (Boston: B. B. Russell, 1869), 669, 671; Napoleon III, "Opening Day Speech," July 1, 1867.

41. Three architects designed the palace, the park, and the art exhibition: respectively they were Jean Baptiste Krantz, Adolphe Alfant, and Charles de Chennevières.

42. Faith K. Pizor, "Preparations for the Centennial Exhibition of 1876," *The Pennsylvania Magazine of History and Biography* 94.2 (April 1970): 214.

43. The concept of semicircular insets had been developed by George Maw and Edward Payne for the 1862 London World Exposition, but never realized. Matte, *World's Fairs*, 20.

44. Ibid.
45. *Illustrated Catalogue of the Universal Exhibition*, 1867; a useful visitor account is Eugene Rimmel's *Recollections of the Paris Exposition of 1867* (London: Chapman and Hall, 1868).
46. Elliot C. Cowdin, "The Paris Universal Exhibition of 1867," Chamber of Commerce of New York, January 12, 1866 (New York: Baker & Godwin, 1866).
47. In the aftermath of the 1867 Paris Universal Exposition, Napoleon III basted in its success as an event that cast behind "a past of prejudices and of errors."Abbott, *The History of Napoleon III*, 670.
48. The United States presence at the Paris world's fair had many organizational shortcomings and was roundly criticized. See Curti, "America at the World's Fairs," 833, 842–848.
49. Ibid., 834–837.
50. Cowdin was a "zealous" figure in promoting New York commerce and exercised considerable influence in political circles. An "ardent" Republican, in 1876 he was elected district representative to the New York Assembly. His first legislative act was an attempt to pass a controversial amendment in state law to eliminate taxing bank stock. "Elliot C. Cowdin Dead," *The New York Times,* April 13, 1880.
51. Steinway and Sons pianos experienced a jump in exports when leading French and German manufacturers were curtailed by shipping embargoes. "Effect of the War in Europe on American Exports," *The New York Times*, December 23, 1870, 5. More in-depth analysis at the time on the economic effects of the war are seen in David Wells, "Industrial and Financial Effects of the War," *Lippincott's Magazine of Literature, Science, and Education* 7 (January 1871a): 81–92 and "Contraband of War," *The American Law Review* 5.2 (January 1871b): 247–261.
52. Cowdin, "The Paris Universal Exhibition of 1867."
53. *Panama-Pacific International Exposition: Popular Information* (San Francisco: Panama-Pacific International Exposition Publications, 1913), 1–2.
54. Campbell proposed the idea in a lecture given at the Smithsonian Institution. Scientists from the Smithsonian designed the classification used to organize exhibitions according to racial hierarchy. Rydell, *All the World's a Fair*, 17, 20–29.
55. "The Centennial," *The New York Times*, February 22, 1872, 1.
56. The sections of the bill and Presidential proclamation are reprinted in *The Illustrated History of the Centennial*, 65.
57. Private subscriptions were estimated at $1,600,000; corporate contributions were $575,000. The report was a comprehensive document compiled by "heads" of the Commission mandated by the act of 1871 to provide the opening and closing dates; a schedule of ceremonies; plans for building; the plan for classification; receipt of articles. Forty-five thousand copies were printed for government branches as well as the State Department, the House of Representative, the Senate, and the Commission. 42nd Congress, Third session, February 22, 1873, The Congressional Globe, 1605, 1610, Library of Congress.

58. Hawley presided over the 1868 republican convention in Chicago that nominated Grant and running mate Colfax. He led the delegation to Washington to formerly propose the nomination of Grant to the Republican Party. Smith, *Grant*, 456.

59. Vice Presidents included Orestes Cleveland (New Jersey), John D. Creigh (San Francisco), Robert Lowry (Iowa), Thomas H. Coldwell (Tennessee), John McNeil (Missouri), and William Gurney (South Carolina). John L. Campbell (Indiana), among early lobbyists for a centennial, served as Secretary and was quickly appointed to chair the Committee on Foreign Affairs. The Commission met nine times from March 1872 to January 1879, when it adjourned. Its agenda was accomplished by the Executive Committee, composed of 13 members appointed by President Grant. Divisions included a Bureau of Administration, the Executive Committee, the Board of Finance, a Women's Centennial Committee, a United States Government Board and Departments, the Smithsonian Institution, a Building Committee, Telegraph, Fire, and Award Directors, a Concession Committee, a Bureau of Admission, and 31 different Foreign Commissions, each with a contingent of representatives.

60. *The Illustrated History of the Centennial Exhibition*, 243.

61. Costs, completion schedules, and controversy plagued the Architectural Committee. For an in-depth study, see Faith K. Pizor, "Preparations for the Centennial Exhibition of 1876," *The Pennsylvania Magazine of History and Biography* 94.2 (April 1970): 213–232. See also, "Architectural Exhibition at the Centennial," *Architect and Building News*, June 24, 1876, 202; "Centennial Anniversary Building Plan," *The New York Times*, October 25, 1873, 1.

62. Stock subscriptions amounted to just over two million dollars in Walsh's report of December 1875, 82. The state of Pennsylvania and city of Philadelphia appropriated upwards of three million dollars. A required report of the Centennial Commission to the 42nd Congress by Mr. Scott on February 22, 1873 reassured the senate that an estimated four million dollars raised to date would "insure the success of the exposition, and would justify an appeal to the other portions of the country to subscribe liberally." "Forty-Second Congress," *The New York Times*, February 23, 1873, 6.

63. Seventeen of the twenty-five member Board were from Philadelphia. Other members came from New York, Virginia, Alabama, Rhode Island, Massachusetts, Iowa, New Jersey, and Wisconsin. "Centennial Anniversary," *The New York Times*, April 23, 1873, 1; "Funds for the Centennial" *The New York Times*, August 28, 1873, 4.

64. The State was in heavy debt to the extent that Governor Geary advised repeal of enrollment tax on "private acts chartering industrial institutions, and all taxes on capital stock earnings." "Pennsylvania," *The New York Times*, June 9, 1873.

65. Chicago's celebration marked the four-hundredth Anniversary of Columbus's Discovery of America.

66. Anthropological themes at the fair reissued colonial attitudes. Most notorious was a Philippine living village installed to promote US occupation.

Rydell includes a pointed study of the exhibit in *All the World's a Fair*, 155–183. Contextual perspectives on imperialism and anthropology at the fair is the focus of the recent collection; Susan Brownell, ed., *The 1904 Anthropology Days and Olympic Games: Sport, Race, and American Imperialism* (Lincoln: University of Nebraska Press, 2008).

67. During the third session of the 42nd Congress, the progress of subscriptions was reported to amount to four million dollars. It was taken as a positive sign ensuing the success and useful to gaining the support of other parts of the country. "Forty-Second Congress," 6.

68. The proclamation was widely reprinted. "The National Centennial," *The New York Times*, July 5, 1873, 5; "Government and the Centennial," *The New York Times*, August 2, 1873, 4.

69. "The National Centennial," 5.

70. Hawley was also in Washington lobbying for the restitution of a Japanese Indemnity fund, estimated to be over $800,000. "Washington," *The New York Times*, January 28, 1873, 1.

71. "Merchant's Banquet," *The New York Times*, May 2, 1873, 5.

72. Ibid.

73. Exhibitors arrived through ports in Boston, New York, Philadelphia, Baltimore, Portland, Maine, New Orleans, and San Francisco."The Centennial Exposition," *The New York Times*, December 5, 1873, 3.

74. "Large Territorial Acquisition," *The New York Times*, March 31, 1867, 4.

75. "North China Trade," *Merchants' Magazine and Commercial Review* 57.2 (August 1, 1867), 127. Diplomatic relations with China were carefully monitored when tensions mounted between Japan and China over the island Fomosa. Senate. 43rd Congress, First Session, December 7, 1873, Congressional Record, 13, Library of Congress.

76. "China," *The New York Times*, June 6, 1868, 4.

77. The first treaty was signed in 1858. "New Chinese Treaty with the United States," *The Albion, A Journal of News, Politics and Literature*, August 1, 1868, 366. L. T. Townsend in the *Zion's Herald* argued the fervor against the Chinese was un-American. "The Chinese Problem," *Zion's Herald*, April 20, 1876, 1; Charles W. Wendte, "The Chinese Problem," *The Unitarian Review and Religious Magazine* 5.5 (May 1876), 510.

78. "China," in *International Exhibition 1876: Main Building* (United States Centennial Commission: Centennial Catalogue Company, 1876), 257.

79. "North China Trade," *Merchants' Magazine and Commercial Review*. China resisted the United States efforts to colonize its economy. According to Secretary of State Hamilton Fish in his annual report on trade relations, the United States imports into China over a 10-year period ending in 1873 showed recent decline. "Commercial Relations," *The New York Times*, August 23, 1875, 2.

80. "The Chilean Exposition, "*The New York Tribune*, April 15, 1876, 12. There appear to have been a series of expositions in Santiago. The first opened September 18, 1869. I have come across no documentation of these fairs to date, including in the comprehensive 2008 *Encyclopedia of World's Fairs and Expositions*.

81. "Mexico," *The New York Times,* 18 April 1868, 2. The United States sent an ambassador to Mexico to extend an invitation to participate at the Centennial Exhibition. "Mexico," *The New York Times*, September 8, 1873; "The Crescent City's World's Fair," *New York Tribune*, December 16, 1884, 4.

82. See Loren Kruger, "'White Cities, 'Diamond Zulus,' and the 'African Contribution to Human Advancement' African Modernities and the World's Fairs," *TDR* 51.3 (Fall 2007): 19–45.

83. William Howard Taft, "Inaugural Address," March 4, 1909.

84. The United States relations with Japan held steady until this time. "The Significance of the Visit of Japanese Business Men," *The Wall Street Journal*, October 9, 1909, 6.

85. Corporate factions in charge of the army and navy saw the exhibition as good propaganda. They were from the Satsuma and Chosu clans of the Imperial Diet, who sought foreign and military expansion following the War with Russia (1904–1905). Carol Gluck, *Japan's Modern Myths: Ideology in the Late Meiji Period* (Princeton: Princeton University Press, 1985), 176.

86. October 14, 1911. The path to securing treaties and building the Panama Canal moved through three administrations beginning with Theodore Roosevelt. The closing ceremonies were presided over by Woodrow Wilson with another opportune press shot. The bipartisan accomplishment was highlighted in souvenir books. See *The Blue Book: A Comprehensive Official Souvenir View Book of the Panama-Pacific International Exposition at San Francisco, 1915* (San Francisco: Robert A, Reid, 1915), 7.

87. Frank Leslie, *Illustrated Historical Register of the Centennial Exposition, 1876* (New York: Paddington Press, 1974), 10.

88. Eugene V. Smalley, "The New Orleans Exhibition," *The Century Illustrated Magazine* 30.2 (June 1885b): 199.

89. *Illustrated History of the Centennial*, 293.

90. The book was reissued five times over the nineteenth century. In particular, Book IV defines two forms of political economy, understood as feudal and industrial. The former is based on agriculture, the latter on capital. Smith defines political economy "as a branch of the science of a statesman or legislator." Adam Smith, *An Inquiry into the Nature and Causes of the Wealth of Nations*, ed. Edwin Cannan, 1904, Library of Economics and Liberty. <http://www.econlib.org/library/Smith/smWN12.html>.

91. Forerunners to the New Orleans exhibition were a cotton exhibition in Atlanta 1881, followed by a larger one in Louisville 1883, which did not attract the lower Mississippi Valley. An annual multitribal gathering at Muskogee, Creek Nation, called The International Indian Fair was held for 20 years beginning in 1874. The fairs expressed tribal autonomy and governance within Indian Territories. Smalley, "The New Orleans Exposition," 30.1, 4; for the international expositions held in the South between 1885 and 1907, see Rydell, *All the World's a Fair*, 72–104. Andrew Denson,

"Muskogee's Indian Fairs: Tribal Autonomy and the Indian Image in the Late Nineteenth Century," *The Western Quarterly* 34.3 (Autumn 2003): 325–345.

92. Edward Aktinson, *New York Herald*, August 1880.
93. "The Cotton Centennial Exhibition at New Orleans," *The American Architect and Building News*, April 11, 1885, 171.
94. "Machinery Put in Motion," *The New York Times,* July 5, 1988.
95. Highlighted by Grover Cleveland in his inaugural address, March 4, 1885, Papers of Grover Cleveland, Manuscript Division, Library of Congress.
96. Samuel C. Shepard measures the success and failures of the exhibition "A Glimmer of Hope: The World's Industrial and Cotton Centennial Exposition, New Orleans, 1884–1885," *Louisiana History* 26 (1985): 275–290.
97. Steven L. Piott, "Henry George: Democratic Economics," in *American Reformers, 1870–1920: Progressives in Word and Deed* (Lanham, MD: Rowman & Littlefield, 2006), 25–41.
98. Ibid., 34–36, 39–40.
99. One trigger was a free trade agreement with Canada that liberal Republicans railed against. Lewis Gould examines the ideological divides during Taft's Presidency, *The William Henry Taft Presidency* (Kansas: University Press of Kansas, 2009), 93–120, 139–153.
100. Smalley, "The New Orleans Exposition," 30.1, 3.
101. Debord's concept identifies the fetish in terms of a second nature, a perceptual realm driven by internal forces of economic advance. In his view of late twentieth-century capitalism, spectacle alienates contact with physical nature. Guy Debord, *The Society of the Spectacle,* trans. Donald Nicholson-Smith (New York: Zone Books, 1995), 11–24.
102. Debord, "Self-portrait of Power," in *The Society of the Spectacle,* 19.
103. "The New World's Fair," 1.
104. Alan Trachtenberg, *The Incorporation of America: Culture and Society in the Gilded Age* (New York: Hill and Wang), 100.
105. Mona Domosh, "Selling Civilization: Toward a Cultural Analysis of America's Economic Empire in the Late Nineteenth and Early Twentieth Centuries," *Transactions of the Institute of British Geographers* 29.4 (December 2004): 453–467.
106. "The carnage of the civil war," observes Drew Gilpin Faust, "held representative pull on the bereaved families North and South. Wives, parents, children, and siblings struggled with new identities—widows, orphans, the childless—that now defined their beliefs. And they carried their losses into acts of memory that both fed on and nurtured the widely shared grief into the next century." Drew Gilpin Faust, *This Republic of Suffering: Death and the American Civil War* (New York: Vintage, 2008) 170.
107. "The National Centennial," 5.
108. "The Great Exhibition," *Gody's Arm-Chair,* June 1876a.
109. "English Comments on the Centennial," *Christian Union,* June 7, 1876, 480.

110. Leslie, *Illustrated Historical Register of the Centennial Exposition, 1876*, 11.

111. In 1876, the park was 2,749 acres, extending on both banks of the Schuylkill River.

112. "The Great Exhibition," *The Independent*, May 18, 1876b, 14.

113. "The New World's Fair."

114. *International Exhibition 1876: Main Building*, 7–8.

115. In Machinery Hall, US exhibitors outnumbered foreign participants by 80 percent.

116. "Art at Philadelphia," *The New York Times*, May 17, 1876, 4; "Art at the Exhibition," *Appleton's Journal of Literature, Science and Art*, June 3, 1876, 724.

117. "New World's Fair," *New York Tribune*, 1876, 1.

118. Ibid.

119. Leslie, *Illustrated Historical Register of the Centennial Exposition, 1876*, 10.

120. Andrew Smith, *The National Cookery Book: Compiled from Original Receipt for the Women's Centennial Committees of the International Exhibition of 1876*, ed. Deborah Jean Warner, Reprint (Bedford, MA: Applewood Books, 1976). xxii; *International Exhibition, 1876: Main Building*, Part III, 131.

121. *International Exhibition, 1876: Main Building*, Ibid.

122. "Buildings and Special Exhibits," *Official Catalogue*.

123. "The Centennial Fair," *New York Tribune*, May 17, 1876, 1.

124. The Board of Finance determined to appoint an Executive Women's Committee to "work" in a traditional fund-raising capacity in order to enlarge support for the exhibition. The selection of the committee came with incentives to contribute a women's exhibit and representation in exhibition management.

125. The meeting was held at Cooper Union in New York City. At one point, one-hundred parasol-makers, having a business meeting in another part of the building, entered the assembly to request organized help with an employer. "Woman Suffrage," *The New York Times*, October 14, 1873, 5.

126. She had managed Philadelphia's 1864 Sanitary Fair, raising more than one million dollars to help wounded soldiers during the Civil War. Elizabeth Duane Gillespie, *A Book of Remembrance*, Second ed. (Philadelphia: B. Lippincott, 1901), 114–119; 371–374.

127. Twelve states raised money. $15,000 came from Philadelphia, $10,000 from Ohio, $5,000 from Boston, and $15,000 from New York. In an open letter to the public published in the *The New York Times*, an appeal was made for a final $15,000 to furnish and decorate the interior. "Women's Centennial Union," *The New York Times*, February 23, 1876, 5; Gillespie, *A Book of Remembrance*, 327.

128. Morehead himself visited Cincinnati and Baltimore to check on state committees. He traveled to "every parish of Louisiana to collect materials and prepare exhibits." He also lobbied abroad. Mauricio Tenorio-Trillo, *Mexico*

at the World's Fairs: Crafting a Modern Nation (Berkeley: University of California Press, 1996), 50.

129. "The Women's Auxiliary Centennial Commission, *The New York Tribune*, August 8, 1873, 8.

130. "The Great Centennial Exhibition," *Arthur's Home Magazine*, August 1876, 450.

131. "The Great Exhibition," *The New York Times*, June 4, 1876c, 1.

132. Gillespie, *A Book of Remembrance*, 321.

133. "The Women's Centennial Paper"; "The Great Centennial Exhibition," *Arthur's Home Magazine*.

134. "Washington," *The New York Times*, July 4, 1876, 1.

135. The Indian Bureau of the US Department of the Interior enlisted the Smithsonian Institution to organize and expedite the exhibits. Otis T. Mason, a professor from Columbia University, directed these installations. Mason quoted in Rydell, *All the World's a Fair*, 24.

136. Kevin Fox Gotham, "'Of Incomprehensible Magnitude and Bewildering Variety': The 1884 World's Industrial and Cotton Centennial Exposition," in *Authentic New Orleans: Tourism, Culture, and Race in the Big Easy* (New York: New York University Press, 2007), 49.

137. "The Cotton Centennial Exhibition at New Orleans," *American Architectural and Building News*, April 11, 1885, 271.

138. Trade with Latin America, particularly in Brazil and Argentina continued to increase. "America Buying Freely of Dry Goods and Textiles," *Wall Street Journal*, April 26, 1909, 3.

139. Quoted in Gotham, *Authentic New Orleans*, 45.

140. Tenorio-Trillo details the politics of Mexico's investment in international exhibitions. He illuminates how an idealized image of industrial Mexican culture was conceived at the US fairs. *Mexico at the World's Fairs*, 38–43.

141. Ibid., 19, 40.

142. "Farmer's Department," *New York Evangelist*, November 20, 1884, 7. The "international" scope of the exhibition was questioned. Only the major European industrial countries exhibited: Great Britain, France, Belgium, and Russia. Japan was present, as was China. Herbert S. Fairall, *The World's Industrial and Cotton Centennial Exposition, New Orleans, 1884–85* (Iowa City: Republican Publishing Co., 1885).

143. The complexities of race and racial constructs at the New Orleans exhibition are examined in Rydell, *All the World's a Fair*, 82, 72–104 and Gotham, *Authentic New Orleans*, 60–64.

144. Smalley, "The New Orleans Exhibition," 30.2, 193.

145. Frederick Douglass, et al., *The Reason Why the Colored American is Not in the World's Columbian Exhibition*, ed. Robert Rydell (Urbana: University of Illinois Press, 1999).

146. Philadelphia's fairground covered 48 acres.

147. "The New Orleans Centennial Exposition."

148. "New Orleans Exposition Building," *Southern Planter* 45:8 (August 1884), 404.

149. *American Architect and Building News*, 171.

150. Ibid.

151. The building was 1,656, 300 sq ft. It was 1,378 feet long by 905 feet wide, covering 33 acres. "New Orleans Exhibition Building," *Southern Planter* 45.9 (August 1884), 404.

152. The architect was Gustave M. Torgerson. *American Architectual and Building News*, 271.

153. "New Orleans Exhibition Building," 404.

154. *American Architectural and Building News*, 271; Ibid.

155. Disenfranchised populations were legally excluded from the full rights of citizenship and forced to compete for civil and human rights through long protracted legal and political deliberations, and public campaigns. I am thinking specifically of government policies enacting Indian removal, immigration policies, notably the 1850 Chinese Exclusion Act, legalized segregation in 1896 (Plessy v. Ferguson), and Women's suffrage.

156. Smalley, "The New Orleans Exposition," 30.1, 12.

157. Edward L. Wilson, "Lot's Wife," Main Building, title 567, Centennial Photographic Company 1884. Library of Congress.

158. Quoted from *The New Orleans-Times Democrat*, January 19, 1885 in Gotham, *Authentic New Orleans*, 45, 47. Anticipating over four million visitors, the exhibition attracted a little over one million and incurred a debt of $470,000.

159. "San Francisco 1915: Panama-Pacific International Exposition," *Historical Dictionary of World's Fairs and Expositions, 1851–1988*, ed. John E. Findling (Westport, CT: Greenwood Press, 1990), 225. The fair was open for ten months, from February 20 to December 4.

160. The United States was also in process of completing canals in Cape Cod, Texas, and Louisiana for domestic and international shipping. "Getting Ready to Celebrate the Completion of the Panama Canal," *Current Opinion* 4:4 (October 1913): 229.

161. The United States and Great Britain accord followed the signing of the Treaty of Washington in 1871. Smith, *Grant*, 509–515.

162. Frank Morton Todd, *The Story of the Exposition: Being the Official History of the International Celebration Held in San Francisco in 1915 to Commemorate the Discovery of the Pacific Ocean and the Construction of the Panama Canal* (New York: Knickerbocker Press, 1921), 121–124; Appendix, part iv, 124.

163. First initiated by the Mechanics Institute in 1857, San Francisco held Industrial fairs for decades. Amelia Neville, "World's Fairs of the Past," *Overland Monthly and Out West Magazine* 58.2 (August 1911): 19–21.

164. The decision took nearly a year. California counties endorsed San Francisco over San Diego when the two cities faced off. "Three Cities Want the Panama Fair," *The New York Times*, May 8, 1910, C4; "The Pacific Slope," *New York Tribune*, March 27, 1910.

165. "New Orleans or San Francisco," *The New York Times*, July 26, 1911, 10.

166. The total cost estimate was supplied by the state controller.

167. Barry names W. B. Brown, which is possibly a misprint. Frank L. Brown is listed as well as pictured in the Board of Directors along with Crocker. Each contributed $25,000, which was set as a maximum share. Barry, *City of Domes*, 2; John M. Ingram, Biographical Dictionary of American Business Leaders, Vol. 2 (Westport, CT: Greenwood Press, 1983), 214; "Board of Directors Panama-Pacific International Exposition," in *Charles C. Moore Albums of Panama-Pacific International Exposition Views*, Vol. 1, (Berkeley: The Bancroft Library, University of California).

168. The state tax added five million dollars; district tax contributed three million. The citizens of San Francisco voted a bond issue for another five million. "Panama-Pacific International Exposition, San Francisco 1915," *Brooklyn Eagle Almanac* 30 (1915): 370.

169. *Dictionary of World's Fairs and Expositions*, 230.

170. Revenue projections were used successfully at the 1893 Chicago exhibition and ones that followed. Director Milton H. Esberg researched previous fairs and established the coefficient of 18–20 times the population of the host city. Norman Bolotin and Christine Laing, *The World's Columbia Exposition: The Chicago World's Fair of 1893*, (Urbana: University of Chicago Press, 2002), 4; Todd, *The Story of the Exposition*, 154.

171. The figure was $13,127,103. Detailed financial records were kept of public expenditures on a daily basis. Todd compiles a majority of these. See Todd, *The Story of the Exposition*, 154–163.

172. Moore was guest of honor at a Convention of Engineers that took place during the exhibition in September. It was the first time assorted specialized engineering societies meet together. *Transactions of the Engineering Congress*, September 20–25, 1915 (San Francisco: Neal Publishing Company, 1916), 72–73.

173. *Condensed Facts Concerning the Panama-Pacific Exposition, San Francisco 1915* (San Francisco: Panama-Pacific International Exposition, 1914).

174. "General Electric at the Panama-Pacific Exposition," Pamphlet (General Electric Company, 1915), 3.

175. The concept combined the exterior treatment of the buildings, architecture, sculpture, and paintings. Barry, *City of Domes*, 17.

176. Ernest Coxhead, architect of the city presented initial plans to Congress. He later amplified the schema of a mass grouping of buildings around courts, using the bay boundary. Macomber, *The Jewel City*, 14, 15.

177. Timothy J. Gilfoyle examines the contradictory interpretative range surrounding the World's Columbian Exposition. "White Cities, Linguistic Turns, and Disneylands: The New Paradigms of Urban History," *Reviews of American History* 26.1 (1998): 175–204.

178. The national firms chosen reflected major cities in the Northeast and Midwest: New York, Boston, and Kansas City, respectively, Richard Morris Hunt, McKim, Mead and White, George Post, and Peabody and Stearns, Van Brunt and Howe. Chicago firms were Adler and Sullivan,

Henry Ives Cobb, S. S. Berman, Burling and Whitehouse, Jenney and Mundie. *Encyclopedia of World's Fairs*, 117–118.

179. Allen Trachtenberg examines the pictorial dimensions of design architecture in his study of the fair. In particular, he draws out the discontinuity between the painterly facades of the period's architecture in relationship to the construction engineering design that produced new functional interior spaces. *The Incorporation of America*, 119.

180. Macomber, *The Jewel City*, 40–41; also Barry, *City of Domes*, 10.

181. For instance, four different companies earned contracts to erect the Main Exhibition building. William Sellers and Co. of Moor Iron Works manufactured wrought and cast iron frames; A & P. Roberts of Pencoyd Rolling Mill's furnished wrought iron; Morris, Tasker & Co. of Pascal Iron works furnished cast iron; Watson manufacturing Co. erected the iron work. *International Exhibition, 1876: Main Building*, 23.

182. Sculptor Augustus Saint-Gaudens, an energetic force of neoclassical naturalism or the "American Renaissance" was brought in to the Chicago Exhibition as adviser. See Duffy, Henry J., and John H. Dryfhout, *Augustus Saint-Gaudens: American Sculptor of the Gilded Age*, (Washington, DC: Trust for Museum Exhibitions, 2003).

183. Macomber, *The Jewel City*, 74.

184. Mullgardt was a member of the Architectural Commission in charge of conceptualizing and overseeing the design of the 1915 Panama-Pacific International Exposition held in San Francisco. *The Architecture and Landscape Gardening of the Exposition*, v.

185. Ibid.

186. Macomber, *The Jewel City,* 193.

187. Rosemarie K. Bank, "Representing History: Performing the Columbian Exposition," *Theatre Journal* 54.4 (December 2002): 589–606.

188. General Electric Company defined the exposition as a "monumental tribute to the progress and efficiency of the Electrical Industry." "General Electric Company at the Panama-Pacific Expostion," 10. Todd, *The Story of Exposition*, ix, 335.

189. Gotham, *Authentic New Orleans*, 52.

190. In the US Terman's revisions came to known as the Stanford-Binet test. It was among various models of domestic and international educational curriculums presented during the convention of the National Education Association. Todd, *The Story of Exposition*, 102.

191. Imre Kiralfy was invited to produce a large-scale spectacle, but the plans were dropped when England entered the war. "Kiralfy Show for Panama Exposition," *The New York Times*, October 13, 1912, 6.

192. "General Electric Company at the Panama-Pacific Exposition,"1–10.

193. Sales offices were opened in the cities of London, Sydney, Melbourne, Rio de Janeiro, Buenos Aires, Mexico City, Cape Town, and Johannesburg. Ibid.

194. "The Story of a Great Achievement-Telephone Communication from Coast to Coast," Pamphlet (American Telephone and Telegraph Co, 1915).

195. "Southern Pacific Building-Panama-Pacific International Exposition, San Francisco," 1915.
196. Rydell, *All the World's a Fair,* 147, 227.
197. Macomber, *The Jewel City,* 193.
198. Anderson defines the political community "imagined both as inherently limited and sovereign." His theory views modernization as a horizontal extension of progress, stemming from enlightened principles. *Imagined Communities: Reflections on the Origin and Spread of Nationalism* (London: Verso, 1991), 5. For another orientation to cultural sensibilities as system of performed relations, see Arjun Appadurai, *Modernity at Large: Cultural Dimensions of Globalization* (Minneapolis: University of Minnesota Press, 1996).

5   Instructional Scenes: Heritage Preservation, Commerce, and Museum Dioramas

1. The $79 million dollar mission was named Lcross (Lunar Crater Observation and Sensing Satellite) after the 2.2-ton rocket. NASA, "LCROSS Impact Indicates Water on Moon." <http://www.nasa.gov>. Kenneth Chang, "Two Bull's-Eyes in Test of Water on the Moon," *The New York Times,* October 10, 2009c, A12; Kenneth Chang, "Satellite Found Water on Moon, Researchers Say," *The New York Times,* November 14, 2009b, A1; Kenneth Chang, "Signs of Plentiful Water are Found Below Moon's Stony Face," *The New York Times,* May 27, 2011. A13.
2. Crawley was co-chairperson of a committee that reviewed NASA's progress in technology development for future human space flight missions. He joined a nine-member panel appointed by the Obama Administration to look at NASA's efforts to return to the moon by 2020. The Defense Advanced Research Projects Agency (Darpa) in coordination with NASA has formed the 100-Year Starship Study to seed the study of human space travel. Seth Borenstein, "Panel: NASA Should Skip Moon, Fly Elsewhere," *U.S. News & World Report,* October 22, 2009. Kenneth Chang, "Private Rocket's First Flight Is a Success," *The New York Times,* June 5, 2009a, A11. Dennis Overbye, "Offering Funds, U. S. Agency Dreams of Sending Humans to Stars," *The New York Times,* August 18, 2011, A1.
3. Vice president of Boeing's Space Exploration division Brewster Shaw stated, "one of the goals is to become the Boeing commercial aircraft of human space commerce." The company is partnering with Space Adventures Ltd, a booking company that arranged several tours to the International space station on the Russian Soyuz spacecraft. Commercial preparations for a space tourism industry have gained momentum since UK tycoon Sir Richard Branson launched Virgin Galactic in 2001. Recently, he previewed the first commercial spaceport in Las Cruces, New Mexico, set to open in 18 months. The tax subsidized venue cost $198 million to build with

tickets selling for $200,000.00. Kenneth Chang, "Boeing Plans to Fly Tourists to Space," *The New York Times*, September 15, 2010, 1; Richard Gray, "Opening of Spaceport's First Runway Brings Space Tourism," *The Telegraph*, October 23, 2010; Larry Greenemeier, "Space Cadets, Grab Your Sunscreen: Space Tourism Set to Liftoff," *Scientific American,* March 27, 2008.

4. The company is owned by Elon Musk, cofounder of PayPal Inc. and founder of the electronic-car company Tesla Motors. Alan Ohnsman, "Elon Musk Anticipates Third IPO in Three Years," *Bloomsburg Business Week*, February 25, 2012. <http://www.spacex.com/dragon.php>.

5. The Land Ordinance of 1875 initiated the survey of public lands in the West. The Army Corps of Topographical Engineers was established as a separate branch of the military in 1838 until the Civil War. William H. Goetzmann, *Army Exploration in the American West, 1803–1863* (New Haven: Yale University Press, 1959), 3–21.

6. Turner associated the Northeast with European, or Old World heritage. He argued that the advancing course of the Frontier decreased dependence on England. He locates the composite, regional formation of social and economic development along the frontier an indigenous representation. Frederick Jackson Turner, "The Significance of the Frontier in American History," in *The Frontier in American History* (New York: Henry Holt, 1958), 3, 22–24.

7. Ibid., 2–3.

8. Hurbet Damisch, "The Scene of the Life of the Future," in *Skyline: The Narcissistic City*, trans. John Goodman (Stanford: University of Stanford Press, 2001), 72–99.

9. "Operation Enduring Freedom" is the official US Government mission name given to the War in Afghanistan in 2001 under former President George W. Bush's War on Terrorism.

10. Turner, "The Significance of the Frontier in American History," 3.

11. See Edward P. Alexander and Mary Alexander, *Museums in Motion: An Introduction to the History and Functions of Museums*, Second ed. (Lanham, MD: AltaMira, 2008).

12. Tony Bennett, *The Birth of the Museum: History, Theory, Politics*, 1995 (London: Routledge, 2009), 63, 67, 69.

13. The law was met with protests. A defense of the law was issued by Gaillard Hunt, head of the Bureau of Citizenship in the Department of State. Calls for reforms date back to the nineteenth century. Immigration and Naturalization were tied to voting fraud by political operatives of candidates. "The New Citizenship Law," *The North American Review*, July 5, 1907, 530; "The Naturalization Law," *The Albany Law Journal: A Weekly Record of the Law and Lawyers*, July 1907, 217; H. B. Bradbury, "The Naturalization Problem," *The North American Review*, November 1892, 638.

14. For an incisive treatment of the labor relations in the progressive era and the Americanization movement, see Frank Van Nuys, *Americanizing the West:*

Race, Immigration and Citizenship, 1890–1930 (Lawrence: University of Kansas, 2002).

15. Louis Jacques Mandé Daguerre's, *An Historical and Descriptive Account of the Various Processes of the Daguerreotype and Diorama*, 1939 (New York: Winter House, 1971).

16. Mary Zeiss Strange, "Women & Hunting in the West," *Montana: The Magazine of Western History* 55.3 (Autumn 2005): 19.

17. Warren latched onto the educational impact of enacting cultural models with live ethnic groups after visiting the 1889 Paris Exposition, which made extensive use of living habitats that included African villages and a Tonkinese temple. Along with his associate at the National Museum in Washington, DC, George Brown Goode, Warren worked with director of the Peabody Museum at Harvard Frederick Ward Putnman, who was head of the Department of Ethnology and Anthropology during the Chicago exhibition. Curtis M. Hinsley, "The World as Marketplace: Commodification of the Exotic at the World's Columbian Exposition, Chicago, 1893," in *Exhibiting Culture: The Poetics and Politics of Museum Display*, eds. Ivan Karp and Steven D. Levine (Washington, DC: Smithsonian Institution Press, 1991), 344–365.

18. Rebecca Schneider, *Performing Remains: Art and War in Times of Historical Reenactment* (London: Routledge, 2011), 41–42.

19. Lee Clark Mitchell, *Witness to a Vanishing America: The Nineteenth-Century Response* (Princeton: Princeton University Press, 1981), 6–10.

20. Other nations he met near North Dakota and Montana were Cheyenne, Crow, Assiniboine, and Blackfeet, and in Texas the Comanches. He compiled his paintings and collection of artifacts in an Indian Gallery that he toured with. A 2-volume edition of his travels was published in 1903, *Manners, Customs, and Conditions of the North American Indians* (New York: Penguin Classics, 2004); *Caitlin and His Indian Gallery*, Renwick Gallery, Smithsonian American Art Museum (Washington, DC: W. W. Norton, 2002).

21. John C. Freemuth, *Islands Under Siege: National Parks and the Politics of External Threats* (Lawrence: University Press of Kansas, 1991), 9.

22. See Louis S. Warren, *Buffalo Bill's America: William Cody and the Wild West Show* (New York: Vintage, 2005).

23. In 1843. Freemuth, *Islands Under Siege*, 55.

24. Marlene Deahl Merrill, ed., *Yellowstone and the Great West: Journals, Letters, and Images from the 1871 Hayden Expedition* (Lincoln: University of Nebraska, 1999), 9.

25. Hornaday cites 85 head of bison remaining in the wild. W. T. Hornaday, "The Extermination of Wild Animals," *The Chautauquan*, December 1889, 304.

26. Ibid.

27. Eric Ames's critical study of Hagenbeck's business enterprises and methods aligns his zoo complexes with development of theme parks. Hagenbeck brought his animal spectacles to Madison Square Garden, New York, in the

late 1890s. *Carl Hagenbeck: Empire of Entertainments* (Seattle: University of Washington Press, 2010), 63–102; "Hagenbeck Trained Animals," *The New York Times*, October 7, 1894, 12; "Mr. Hammerstein's Complaint," *New York Tribune,* October 7, 1894, 8.

28. "Hagenbeck Trained Animals," 12.

29. Olmstead chaired a California State Commission to study the state lands after Congress withdrew them from public sale. His report to Congress was suppressed. From Olmstead "The Yosemite Valley and the Mariposa Big Trees: A Preliminary Report," 1865, quoted in Mitchell, *Witness to a Vanishing America*, 50.

30. His first article on glaciers appeared in December 1871 in Horace Greeley's *New York Tribune* with the aid of Congressman Clinton L. Merriam. In addition to the *Tribune*, his geological studies on glacier evolution appeared in the literary magazine *Overland Monthly* and scholarly scientific publications such as the *American Journal of Science*. Stephen Fox, *John Muir and His Legacy: The American Conservation Movement* (Boston: Little, Brown, 1981), 22–23.

31. Ibid., 24, 86–99.

32. Quoted in Fox, *John Muir and His Legacy*, 59.

33. Ibid., 104–182.

34. Mitchell, *Witness to a Vanishing America*, 62.

35. Notably, mountaineers formed the California Alpine Club (1892), in Oregon, the Mazamas (1894), and the Colorado Mountain Club (1912). John C. Miles, *Guardians of the Parks: A History of the National Parks and Conservation* Association (Washington, DC: Taylor& Francis, 1995), 8; Fox, *John Muir and His Legacy*, 106–107.

36. Fox, *John Muir and His Legacy*, 107.

37. These land surveys spanned Cherokee borders along Arkansas Territory, the Northern border of Missouri along "Indian Territory," and the Eastern and Southern boundaries of Seneca Lands. "Country for Indians West of the Mississippi," House of Representatives, 22nd Congress, First session, No. 172, March 16, 1832, Letter from the Secretary of War, 14, Library of Congress.

38. The report cautioned that if all the Indians east of the Rocky Mountains were relocated within a proposed area 600 miles long and 200 miles wide, "they would be crowded to their inconvenience." Among effected tribes were Cherokee, Creek, Osage, Shawnees, Delaware, Quapaws, Pawnees, and Kanzas. Ibid.

39. Rev. Jedidiah Morse, *Report to Secretary of War of the United States on Indian Affairs, Comprising a Narrative Tour Performed in the Summer of 1820, Under a Commission from the President of the United States, for the Purpose of Ascertaining, for the Use of the Government, the Actual State of the Indian Tribes in the Country* (New Haven: S. Converse, 1822), 12.

40. "Home Department," House of Representatives, 13th Congress, Second session, No. 66, February 12, 1849, Library of Congress.

41. Merrill, *Yellowstone and the Great West*, 7.

42. Ten years later, March 3, 1879, the United States Geographical Survey was established.

43. "Geographical and Geological Surveys West of the Mississippi," House of Representatives, 43rd Congress, First session, No. 240, 1874, Message from the President of the United States, Library of Congress.

44. A useful resource containing listings of annual reports and publications of each survey is L. F. Schmeckebier, *Catalogue and Index of the Publications of the Hayden, King, Powell, and Wheeler Surveys* (Washington, DC: Government Printing Office, 1904).

45. For a history of the surveys, see *The United States Geological Survey: Its Origin, Development, and Operations* (Washington, DC: Government Printing Office, 1904).

46. Survey data from Ibid., 9–10.

47. Hayden returned in 1871 and 1872 to carry out topographical and geographical mapping. Between 1873 and 1876 he continued to survey areas of Colorado, Utah, Arizona, and New Mexico. "Geographical and Geographical Surveys," House of Representatives, 45th Congress, Second session, No. 81, 1878, Letter from the Secretary of the Interior, 2–5, Library of Congress.

48. Merrill, *Yellowstone and the Great West*, 12.

49. The construction and route of the Northern Pacific Railroad was delayed by the Panic of 1873. Ibid., 12, 210.

50. "Colorado and the Cañon: Prof. Albert S. Bickmore's Lecture at the American Museum of Natural History," *The New York Times*, January 30, 1898, 13.

51. Photographers William Bell and Andrew Russell were part of the Powell and Wheeler expeditions. Arizona's Canyon De Chelly was designated a National Monument in 1931. Timothy H. O' Sullivan, *Head of Cañon de Chelle* (1873), Prints and Photographs Division, Library of Congress. See Toby Jurovics, et al., *Framing the West: The Survey Photographs of Timothy H. O'Sullivan* (New Haven: Yale University Press, 2010).

52. The glass plates measured up to 18 × 22 inches. *Beauties of the Rockies* (Denver: H. H. Tammen Curio, 1890a). *New Mexico* (Denver: W. H. Jackson, 1890b); A narrative and pictorial account of Jackson's Western travels was issued in collaboration with Howard R. Driggs, *Pioneer Photographer: Rocky Mountain Adventures with a Camera* (New York: World Book, 1929); Jackson, *With Moran in the Yellowstone: A Story of Exploration, Photography and Art* (Brattleboro, Vermont: Appalachian Mountain Club, 1936), first published in *Appalachia* 82 (December 1936): 149–158.

53. William Welling, *Photography in America: The Formative Years, 1839–1900* (New York: Thomas Y. Crowell, 1978), 219–222.

54. Ibid., 222.

55. Mitchell, *Witness to a Vanishing America*, 52. Among the standard attractions in Yellowstone were Gardiners River Hot Springs, The Great Blue Spring of the Lower Geyser Basin, the Castle Geyser and Upper Geyser Basin, the Lower Yellowstone Range, Yellowstone Lake, Tower Falls and Sulphur Mountain, the head of the Yellowstone River, the Grand Canyon, Tower Falls, and the Mountain of the Holy Cross. Colorado features included the Mosquito Trail, Rocky Mountains of Colorado, the summit

of the Sierras, and the Great Falls of Snake River. In Southern Utah, the Great Salt Lake was a must see.

56. "The Yellowstone Park," House of Representatives, 42nd Congress, Second session, No. 26, February 27, 1872, 2, Library of Congress.

57. Richard West Sellars, "A Very Large Array: The Early Federal Historic Preservation—The Antiquities Act, Mesa Verde, and the National Park Service Act," *Natural Resources Journal* 47 (Spring 2007): 267–328.

58. John C. Miles, *Guardians of the Parks: A History of the National Parks and Conservation Association* (Washington, DC: Taylor& Francis, 1995), 7.

59. Mitchell provocatively traces transformations of cultural perceptions in the nineteenth century from white ethnocentric hierarchy to cultural relativism. *Witness to a Vanishing America*, 213–251.

60. O. C. Marsh, President of the National Academy of Sciences in a letter presented to the Committee on Appropriations on November 26, 1878. "Surveys of the Territories," 45th Congress, Third session, No. 5, November 26, 1878, Letter from the Acting President of the National Academy of Sciences, 26, Library of Congress.

61. George H. Pepper, "The Ancient Basket Makers of Southeastern Utah," *American Museum of Natural History: Supplement to American Museum Journal* 2.4 (April 1902): 6–7.

62. Edna Muldrow, "Who Was the First American," *North American Review* 241.1 (March 1936): 72; E. B. Renaud, "Uncovering the First Americans," *Forum* 75.1 (January 1926): 109; "Pueblos of Cliff Dwellers Yield Bones and Relics," *The New York Times*, October 18, 1925, XX7.

63. Charles Sanders Pierce, "The Order of Nature," in *Selected Philosophical Writings*, Vol. 1, 1867–1893, eds. Nathan Houser and Christian Kloesel (Bloomington: Indiana University Press, 1992): 170–185.

64. Pierce's theory of "logical critic" included methodology to evaluate correct and incorrect reasoning, including the effective use of signs for producing evaluative methods. See Philip Wiener, ed., *Charles S. Pierce: Selected Writings* (New York: Dover, 1966); Robert Burch, "Charles Sanders Peirce," in *The Stanford Encyclopedia of Philosophy*, ed. Edward N. Zalta, Fall 2010 Edition. <http://plato.stanford.edu/archives/fall2010/entries/peirce/>.

65. "Surveys of the Territories," Letter. House of Representatives, 25.

66. Ibid., 25.

67. J. W. Powell, "Exploration of the Colorado River of the West and Its Tributaries," Report (Washington, DC: Government Printing Office, 1875).

68. "Surveys of the Territories," Letter, 25. Scientific research accounted for 8 and one half million dollars annually.

69. "Exploration of the Colorado River," House of Representatives, 41st Congress, Second session, No. 281, 1870, Letter from the Secretary of War, 2, Library of Congress.

70. "A New National Museum: The Building to Be Erected in Washington," *The New York Times*, November 16, 1879, 10.

71. The aesthetic of the industrial landscape taking shape is present in Jackson's *Among the Rockies: Pictures of the Magnificent Scenes in the Rocky Mountains, the Master Works of the World's Greatest Photographic Artist*, with text by Stanley Wood (Boston: H. H. Tammen, 1900).

72. William Henry Jackson, Ruby Canyon; Side Gear Locomotive, Rio Grande Southern, Silverton RR, Shay "Guston" D&RG engines on La Veta Pass, No. 99 & 46 "History of the American West, 1860–1920: Photographs from the Collection of the Denver Public Library," L. C. McClure collection 1890–1935; album III, 154, 153, 144, American Memory, Library of Congress.

73. Useful studies on Peale are Charles Coleman Sellers, *Mr. Peale's Museum: Charles Willson Peale and The First Popular Museum of Natural Science and Art* (New York: W. W. Norton, 1980); Edgar P. Richardson, et al., *Charles Willson Peale and His World* (New York: H. N. Abrams, 1983).

74. See *Ferdinand Vandiveer Hayden and the Founding of Yellowstone*; Merrill, *Yellowstone and the Great West*, 24–25.

75. In Volume 5 of his *Natural History*, Buffon lays out his comparison of quadrupeds. He states America has no animal in size in comparison to the largest quadrupeds of the Old World: among them the elephant, the rhinoceros, the hippopotamus, the buffalo, the camel, the lion, and so on. George Louis Leclerc, Comte de Buffon, *Natural History*, trans. William Smellie (London: A, Strahan and T. Cadell, 1791), 128. See also Jacques Roger, *Buffon: A Life in Natural History*, trans. Sarah Lucille Bonnefoi (Ithaca: Cornell University Press, 1997).

76. Quoted in Sellars, *Mr. Peale's Museum*, 28.

77. Svetlana Alpers, "The Museum as a Way of Seeing," in *Exhibiting Cultures*, 25–32.

78. David L. Browman, "The Peabody Museum, Frederic W. Putnam, and the Rise of U. S. Anthropology, 1866–1903," *American Anthropologist* 104.2 (2002): 508–519.

79. Ivy Lee, "A Horse that Lived a Million Years Ago," *The New York Times*, September 15, 1901, SM 9.

80. Ibid.

81. The extinct species of "American rhinoceros" classified by palaeontologist Henry Fairfield Osborn were prepared for an exhibit in 1904 at the American Museum of Natural History. "Little Rhinoceres [sic] that Once Roamed the Land," *The New York Times*, August 14, 1904, SM5. Barnum Brown, curator of fossils and reptiles of the museum, returned from an expedition in Colorado with evidence of an 8-ton dinosaur footprint and "carload of dinosaur bones." "Dinosaur Tracks Set Up in Museum," *The New York Times*, November 7, 1937; Ivy Lee, "A Horse that Lived a Million Years Ago."

82. P. T. Barnum, *The Life of P.T. Barnum, Written By Himself* (Urbana: University of Illinois Press, 2000), xvi–xvii.

83. See Philip B. Kunhardt Jr., et al, *P.T. Barnum: America's Greatest Showman* (New York: Knopf, 1995).

84. Barbara Kirshenblatt-Gimblett, *Destination Culture: Tourism, Museums and Heritage* (Berkeley: University of California Press, 1998), 54–56.

85. Ibid., 55.

86. Bennett, *The Birth of the Museum*, 51.

87. Ibid., 52.

88. Stephen Christopher Quinn, *Windows on Nature: The Great Habitat Dioramas of the American Museum of Natural History* (New York: Abrams, 2006), 18.

89. Ibid., 10.

90. Opened in 1902, the series of habit groups were completed with the unveiling of the Arctic Cliff group in 1927. Dana Rice, "In the Hall of the North American Birds," *The New York Times*, Sunday Magazine, November 24, 1929, 13.

91. Waldermar Kaempffert, "Vital Museums of the New Era," *The New York Times*, March 20, 1932, SM12; Rice, "In the Hall of the North American Birds," 13.

92. "To Protect the Wild Birds," *The New York Times*, November 12, 1897, 2.

93. Quinn, *Windows on Nature*, 18.

94. See Frederic A. Lucas, "Akeley as a Taxidermist: A Chapter in the History of Museum Methods," *Natural History* 27.2 (March–April 1927): 142–152.

95. See the Peabody Archive biography of diorama artist James Wilson Perry, "1934: Joining the American Museum of Natural History," in *Painting Actuality: Diorama Art of James Wilson Perry*. <http://archive.peabody. yale.edu/james-perry-wilson>.

96. My description is based on visiting the museum. The American Museum of Natural History website <http://www.amnh.org> provides a virtual tour of many of its dioramas, as well as podcasts on their creation, and historical photographs of their fabrication.

97. Quinn, *Windows on Nature*, 11.

98. Ibid.

99. For an account on labor activism, see David Montgomery, *The Fall of the House of Labor: The Workplace, the State, and American Labor Activism* (Cambridge: Cambridge University Press, 1987).

100. "To Speak English Aliens' First Duty," *The New York Times*, August 24, 1915, 4.

101. Hill's recommendations include a centralized government bureau to direct and coordinate work of different agencies, a standard course in citizenship, and special instruction in normal schools. "The Americanization Movement," *The American Journal of Sociology* 24.6 (May 1919): 609–642; Edward George Hartman, *The Movement to Americanize the Immigrant* (New York: Columbia University Press, 1948).

102. Michael R. Olneck, "Americanization and the Education of Immigrants, 1900–1925: An Analysis of Symbolic Action," *American Journal of Education* 97.4 (August 1989): 398–423.

103. Ibid., 399, 400.

104. Studies of note that discuss New Deal administration in relation to radical new infrastructure are Robert D. Leighninger Jr., *Long-Range Public Investment: The Forgotten Legacy of the New Deal* (Columbia: University of South Carolina Press, 2007), 57. Jason Scott Smith, "The New Deal Order," *Enterprise & Society* 9.3 (September 2008): 521–534.

105. For studies on the civil rights movement and labor organization, see Lauren Rebecca Sklaroff, *Black Culture and the New Deal: the Quest for Civil Rights in the Roosevelt Era* (Chapel Hill: University of North Carolina Press, 2009). Alice Kessler-Harris, *In Pursuit of Equity: Women, Men and the Quest for Economic Citizenship in 20th Century America* (Oxford: Oxford University Press, 2001); James J. Lorence, *Organizing the Unemployed: Community and Union Activists in the Industrial Heartland* (Albany: State University of New York Press, 1996). For an examination of how the minority Republican Party shifted right of reform liberalism, see Clyde. P. Weed, *The Nemesis of Reform: The Republican Party During the New Deal* (New York: Columbia University Press, 1994).

106. The addition of new members helped the union. "Scenic Artists Cite Plan," *The New York Times*, November 11, 1937, 31.

107. R. L. Duffus, "The Museum Takes Off Its High Hat," *The North American Review* 242.1 (Autumn 1936): 30.

108. Ibid.

109. Ibid.

110. Kaempffert, "Vital Museums of the New Era," SM12.

111. Ibid.

112. The advisory committee consisted of Dr. H. C. Sherman from the Department of Chemistry of Columbia University, refrigeration engineer, George A. Horne of the Merchants Refrigeration Company, A. E. Albrecht, director of New York State Department of Agriculture and Markets, W. P. Hedden, Chief of the Bureau of Commerce, Port of New York Authority, Clarence Birdseye, General Sea Foods Corporation, and President of Atlantic Coast Fisheries Dr. H. F. Taylor. "Show Opens Today of Food Industries," *The New York Times*, October 11, 1931, N2.

113. "Evolution of Man Shown in Exhibits," *The New York Times*, July 31, 1933, 15.

114. "Block-Long Diorama to Be Built at Fair," *The New York Times*, May 15, 1938, 50; "Consolidated Edison to Tell Utility's Story with Dramatic Exhibit," *Wall Street Journal*, March 31, 1939, 12.

115. Paul Mason Fotsch, "The Building of a Superhighway Future at the New York World's Fair," *Cultural Critique* 48 (Spring 2001): 65–97.

116. Ibid., 65.

117. Ibid., 68–73.

118. "Consolidated Edison to Tell Utility's Story with Dramatic Exhibit."

119. Construction, mining, and manufactured saw the greatest reduction in jobs, as cited in the report. Simon Kuznets, *National Income, 1929–1932* (National Bureau of Economic Research, 1934), 9. <http://www.nber.org/books/kuzn34-1>.

120. "New History Set Ready for Schools," *The New York Times*, August 28, 1938, D4.

121. The Museum of Natural History and the Metropolitan Museum of Art also launched public school initiatives. W. A. MacDonald, "Museum Links Circus to the Ark," *The New York Times*. April 17, 1938, 38.

122. Visual projection techniques included lantern slides. Maps and pictorial illustrations were also standard visual aids. "Federal Show Aids Teachers," *The New York Times*, July 23, 1939, D5.

123. Ibid.

124. For a critical study of the WPA's enactment of New Deal ethos, see Nick Taylor, *American-Made: the Enduring Legacy of the WPA, When FDR Put the Nation to Work* (New York: Bantam Books, 2009).

125. "WPA Funds a Help to Many Museums," *The New York Times*, September 5, 1937, 46.

126. "Dioramas Finished by WPA for Museum," *The New York Times*, July 18, 1937, N3.

127. For an account of New Deal legislation and economic policies modernizing the "American West," see Richard Lowitt, *The New Deal and the West* (Bloomington: Indiana University Press, 1984).

128. LeRoy, R. Hafen, "A Westerner, Born and Bred," *The Western Historical Quarterly* 3.2 (April 1972): 129–135.

129. "WPA Funds a Help to Many Museums," 46.

130. Quoted in "The Colorado Historical Society's Dioramas," Rocky Mountain PBS, October 23, 2009.

131. More than one Federal agency assisted the society. In addition to the WPA, the Civil Works Administration (CWA), the State Relief Administration (SRA), and the Federal Emergency Relief Administration (FERA) contributed yearly funding amounting to $35,000. State funding was $15,000. *Colorado History Now*, May 2005.

132. The FPA funded regional travel guides in 48 states. Susan Schulten, "How to See Colorado: The Federal Writers' Project, American Regionalism, and the 'Old New Western History,'" *The Western Historical Quarterly* 36.1 (Spring 2005): 49–70.

133. The museum has moved many times and undergone numerous revisions. In 1915, it moved from being housed in downtown Denver at the State Capitol to its own building across the street. In 1876, the Museum moved to larger updated quarters as the Colorado History Museum. Ed Sealover, "Colorado History Museum Plans Higher Profile in New Home," *Denver Business Journal*, April 24, 2009, <http://www.bizjournals.com/denver/>.

134. The diorama is now on exhibit in the museum. Mike McPhee, "Museum's Plan to Move Fragile Denver Diorama a Model of Care," *The Denver Post*, November 28, 2009, B1.

135. Tom Noel, "Building a Monument to History," *Denver Post*, May 23, 2010. <http://www.denverpost.com>.

136. Stuart, Banner, *How the Indians Lost Their Land: Law and Power on the Frontier* (Cambridge: Harvard University Press, 2005), 235.

137. "The State's History," *Denver Daily Tribune*, February 11, 1879, 4.

138. The Wetherill's hosted Swedish archaeologist Gustaf Nordenskiöld, who published the first account of the area. He earned the wrath of Coloradans for removing specimens and artifacts. Gustaf Nordenskiöld, *The Cliff Dwellings of the Mesa Verde*, 1893 (reprint, Mesa Verde Museum Association, 1990). Seller, "A Very Large Array," 277.

139. "To Save the Mesa Verde," *The New York Times*, August 25, 1901, SM18.

140. An amendment to the Antiquities Act granted Federal administration to all prehistoric lands within five miles of reservation boundaries. The Interior Department pressured the Ute for a land swap that was signed in 1913 by President Taft. The land was then transferred to the state of Colorado. During these proceedings, the Ute argued forcefully that they had preserved the land by not touching it. Sellers, "A Very Large Array," 298–300.

141. J. A. Jeancon, curator of ethnology and archaeology of the State Museum lectured to raise awareness that the activities of the Historical Society received little private or state funding. Jeancon performed extensive excavations with students from Colorado University. "Jeancon, State Museum Curator Talks to Rotary Club on Cliff Dwellings," *Littleton Independent*, November 3, 1922, 1; "Pueblos of Cliff Dwellers Yield Bones and Relics."

142. Juan Menchaca, "Oral History Interview" Transcript, November 11, 1964, Archives of American Art, Smithsonian Institution.

143. "The Fort Lyon Affair," *Rocky Mountain News*, December 30, 1864, 2; "Official Report of the Battle of Sand Creek," *Rocky Mountain News*, January 3, 1865, 2; "Joint Committee on the Conduct of the War, Massacre of Cheyenne Indians," 38th Congress, Second session (Washington, DC: United States Government Printing Office, 1865). The dense history of the conflict is covered in Stan Hoig's *The Sand Creek Massacre* (Norman: University of Oklahoma Press, 1973). For a legislative context, see Banner, *How the Indians Lost Their Land*, 237–239.

144. Euchee born Negiel Bigpond was one of the speakers appearing at the 2005 Congressional Hearing on a joint resolution offering official apology and acknowledgment of Native American contributions to the country. Mr. Bigpond was adopted by the Creek Nation in Oklahoma. In his remarks, he held up for the record a long history of deprivation and violence among which was reference to the eyewitness testimonies of "Christian soldiers" on the day of the massacre. "Acknowledgment and Apology," S.J. Res. 15, 109th Congress, First session, May 25, 2005 (Washington, DC: United States Government Printing Office, 2005), 22.

145. Amendments to the treaty with Mexico moved the boundary line between the two nations so that the port of San Diego extended to the middle of the Rio Gila, where it met with the Colorado River. "U.S. Report of the Secretary of the Interior," 21st Congress, First Session, February 28, 1850, No. 34, Library of Congress.

146. Following the Ludlow massacre, CEO Jesse Floyd Weborn implemented an employee board, called the Industrial Representation Plan. Van Nuys, *Americanizing the West*, 79–80, 96–99.

147. John Collier, Commissioner of Indian Affairs under Ickes, began restoration of self-governing rights in consultation with Indian tribal leaders. He led legislative measures that resulted in the 1934 (Wheeler-Howard) Indian Reorganization Act. 25 U.S.C. 461, June 18, 1934.

148. Ickes notoriously combative public image is the subject of Graham J. White's, *Harold Ickes of the New Deal: His Private Life and Public Career* (Cambridge: University of Harvard Press, 1985). Jeanne Nienbaber Clarke examines Ickes' role as liberal reformer in *Roosevelt's Warrior: Harold Ickes and the New Deal* (Baltimore: Johns Hopkins University Press, 1996).

149. "Program Mapped to Draw Tourists," *The New York Times*, December 13, 1937, 57.

150. Ibid.

151. Ibid.

152. Ralph Lewis, "Dioramas," Transcript, US Department of the Interior Museum, n.d.

153. The thorny issue came to public attention in 1935 over the building of a major highway into King Canyons, California. The area is Southeast of Yosemite. Miles, *Guardians of the Park,* 115–121; Fox, *John Muir and His Legacy,* 212–217; The fraught tensions over land use and legislative actions are given in-depth examination in Lloyd C. Irland's *Wilderness and Economic Policy* (Lexington, MA: Lexington Books, 1979), 19–30.

154. "Roosevelt Lauds Conservation Aid," *The New York Times*, February 24, 1937, 5.

155. One of the dioramas was a window-size, "true to scale" relief model of a present day Grand Canyon. Tom White, "Our Parks in Diorama," *The New York Times*, June 18, 1939, 140.

156. "Conservation Exhibit Ready in Washington," *The New York Times*, March 9, 1938, 2.

157. J. Paul Hudson, "The Interior Department Museum," US Department of the Interior Museum, n.d.

158. The staff included 12 fabricators, 3 per diem carpenters; 3 per diem helpers; field curator John C. Ewers, equipment engineer A. B. Russell, and clerk Maxwell S. Fulcher. Artists Herman Van Cott and Lee Warthen joined the staff later, along with model makers Rudolf W. Bauss and Frank G. Urban. Lewis, "Dioramas."

159. For the first year the Museum was operated by the National Park Service. Ned Burns, *Field Manual for Museums* (Washington, DC: United States Printing Office, 1941).

160. These dioramas are not on display, along with an Alaska railroad loop and the Triboro Bridge. In Ralph Lewis's notes, he mentions that over time some of the dioramas no longer held relevance. Workshop records include a list of up to 20 dioramas, some of which may have been for park museums. Lewis, "Dioramas."

161. Ibid., 1.

162. For highlights of the collection, see Anne James, "Native Art Gems: Department of the Interior," *Native People's Magazine* 18.2 (March–April 2005): 66–70.

163. Burns, *Field Manual*, 70.

164. Robert V. Hine and John Mack Faraghar, *Frontiers: A Short History of the American* West (New Haven: Yale University Press, 2007), 176–190.

165. The New Deal Reconstruction Finance Corporation funded San Francisco's Bank of America .The bank financed contracts, one of which was granted to Henry J. Kaiser, who erected the structure of Grand Coulee Dam on the Columbia River. Ibid., 188–189.

166. Burns, *Field Manual*, 2.

167. Inspirational portraits of government employees falls together with one the DOI's civilian programs. The Civilian Conservation Corps (CCC) sponsored youth camps and enlisted help with conservation and preservation projects in the National Parks.

168. Burns, *Field Manual*, 12.

Epilogue: Visionary Spaces

1. Diana Taylor, *The Archive and the Repertoire: Performing Cultural Memory in the Americas* (Durham: Duke University Press, 2003), 16–52.

2. Ibid., 20.

3. Angela Ndalianis, *Neo-Baroque Aesthetics and Contemporary Entertainment* (Cambridge: MIT Press, 2004), 157–207.

4. Christopher Kent, "Spectacular History as an Ocular Discipline," *Wide Angle* 18.3 (1996): 2.

5. Dan DiCristoforo, "HCC's Design Honors the Past, Embraces the Future," *Design Matters* 66.2 (February 2010): 42; Ray Mark Rindal, "Colorado History Museum Learns from Its Own Past," *Denver Post*, April 22, 2012, <http:www.denverpost.com>.

6. "I wanted to make work where the viewer wouldn't walk away," Walker remarks about her shadowy representations of America's dark conscience, where "he would giggle nervously, get pulled into history, into fiction, into something totally demeaning and possibly very beautiful." Christian Viveros-Fauné," Kara Walker's Thrilling Whitney Retrospective: Riding the Racial High-Wire," *Village Voice*, October 16, 2007.

7. The exhibition was seen at the Walker Art Center in 2007 and at the Whitney Museum of American Art from 2007 to 2008. Kara Elizabeth Walker, *Walker: My Complement, My Enemy, My Oppressor, My Love* (Minneapolis: Walker Art Center, 2007).

8. See Olafur Eliasson, et al., *Take Your Time: Olafur Eliasson* (San Francisco: San Francisco Museum of Art, 2007); Olafur Eliasson and Peter Weibel, *Olafur Eliasson: Surroundings Surrounded: Essays on Space and Science* (Graz, Austria: Neue Galerie am Landesmuseum Joanneum, 2001).

9. Holland Cotter, "Stand Still a Spectacle Will Happen," *The New York Times*, April 18, 2008, E29.

10. Jeffrey T. Schnapp, "The Mass Panorama," *Modernism/modernity* 9.2 (April 2002): 243–281.

11. Jim Yardley, "China Tightens Security on Tibet Monks After Protest," *The New York Times*, March 24, 2008, A3; "China Before the Olympics" *The Economist*, Briefing, June 1, 2008; David Barboza, "660 Held in Tibetan

Uprising, China Says," *The New York Times*, March 27, 2008a, A14; "Pressed on Tibet, China Berates Foreign Media" *The New York Times*, March 25, 2008d, A7.

12. Jim Yardley and David Barboza, "Games in Beijing Open with a Lavish Ceremony," *The New York Times*, August 9, 2008. <http://www.nytimes. com>.

13. Ibid.

14. Released in the wake of the Tiananmen Square massacre of 1989, *Ju Dou*, one of his first internationally successful films, was immediately banned in his home country. His 1991 *Raise the Red Lantern* tells the story of life in a rich family compound in the 1920s against a backdrop of social change. Nervous Communist officials initially stopped screenings in China. John Bingham, "Beijing Olympics: Zhang Yimou the Director Behind the Opening Ceremony," *The Telegraph*, August 8, 2008, <http://telegraph. com>.

15. David Barboza, "Gritty Renegade Now Directs China's Close-Up," *The New York Times*, August 7, 2008c, A1.

16. 840 Million Chinese viewers tuned in to CCTV. In the United States, NBC reported a prime-time viewing audience of 29 million. David Barboza, "Chinese TV Hits Jackpot with Games: The Hometown Olympics are Drawing Gigantic Audiences and Revenue," *The New York Times*, August 22, 2008b, C1.

17. Mark Magnier, "Chinese Singer was a Ringer Over Looks," *Pittsburgh Post*, August 13, 2008, A4.

18. Big-budget historical dramas, multimillion-dollar art auctions, government-backed opera and dance extravaganzas, and bold new state-financed entertainment venues suggest further melding of art, culture, power, and national pride. Cameron Mackintosh, the British producer of a host of Broadway and West End hits, said Beijing that China could look forward to Chinese versions of "Les Misérables," "Mamma Mia!," "Phantom of the Opera," "Miss Saigon," "My Fair Lady," and "The Lion King," Reuters reported. In a joint venture with China's biggest performing arts agency, China Arts and Entertainment Group, which is affiliated to the Ministry of Culture, the first production would be "Les Misérables," Mackintosh announced. Featuring a Chinese cast, the musical opened at the new National Grand Theater in Beijing in November 2008. Mackintosh added, "It could be no more appropriate that the musical about revolution and the survival of the human spirit, 'Les Misérables' by Victor Hugo, is the opening show in China." Assistant minister of culture Deng Wei stated, "in 5 to 10 years, I hope Beijing and Shanghai will be the third or fourth musical market after New York and London." Barboza, "Gritty Renegade Now Directs China's Close-Up"; "Hit Broadway Musicals to Be Exported to China," *The New York Times*, September 18, 2007, E2.

19. A section of the performance featured 56 "minority" children representing China's ethnic groups. It came to light that they were actually child performers associated with the Galaxy Children's Art Troup, composed

largely from the dominant Han ethnic group. Richard Spencer, "Beijing Olympics: Faking Scandal Over Girl Who 'Sang' in Opening Ceremony," *The Telegraph*, August 12, 2008; Lisa de Moraes, "Something Else at the Olympics Rings False," *The Washington Post*, August 16, 2009, C7.

20. Magnier, "China Abuzz over Lip-syncing Singer."
21. Its initial performance was in a "workshop" version in Newcastle, Great Britain in 2007. The following year it was presented at the Barbicon. Since then *Lipsynch* has toured globally.
22. Ex Machina. <http://www.epidemic.net>.
23. Helen Shaw, "Images at the Speed of Sound," *Time Out New York*, October 1–7, 2009, 31.
24. Sherry Simon, "Robert Lepage and the Language of Spectacle," in *Theatre Sans Frontieres: Essays on the Dramatic Universe of Robert Lepage*, eds, Joseph I. Donohoe Jr. and Jane M. Koustas (East Lansing: Michigan State University Press, 2009), 229.

Bibliography

On-Site and Digital Research Collections

Billy Rose Theatre Collection, New York Library for the Performing Arts.
British Library, Rare Books and Manuscripts, London, UK.
US Department of the Interior Museum and Library, Washington, DC.
Library of Congress, Washington, DC.
Museum of London, UK.

Books and Journals

Abbott, John Stevens Cabott. *The History of Napoleon III, Emperor of the French*. Boston: B. B. Russell, 1869.

Adorno, Theodor. *The Culture Industry, Selected Essays on Mass Culture*. London: Routledge, 1991.

———. *Aesthetic Theory*. Trans. Robert Hullot-Kentor. Minneapolis: University of Minnesota Press, 1997.

Ahrens, Kent. "Nineteenth-Century History Painting and the United States Capitol." *Records of the Columbia Historical Society* 50 (1980): 191–222.

Alexander, Edward P. and Mary Alexander. *Museums in Motion: An Introduction to the History and Functions of Museums*. Second Ed. Lanham, MD: AltiMira Press, 2008.

Allaman, John Lee. "Policing in Mormon Nauvoo." *Illinois Historical Journal* 89.2 (Summer 1996): 85–98.

Alles, Alfred. *Exhibitions: Universal Marketing Tools*. New York: John Wiley & Sons, 1973.

Altick, Richard D. *The Shows of London*. Cambridge: Harvard University Press, 1978.

Ames, Eric. *Carl Hagenbeck's Empire of Entertainments*. Seattle: University of Washington Press, 2008.

America on the Move. National Museum of American History. 2011. Exhibition. http://americanhistory.si.edu/onthemove/exhibition/.

Anderson, Benedict. *Imagined Communities: Reflections on the Origin and Spread of Nationalism*. London: Verso, 1991.

Andress, David. *Massacre at the Champ De Mars: Popular Dissent and Political Culture in the French Revolution*. Suffolk: Boydell Press, 2000.

Andrews, Malcolm. *Landscape and Western Art*. Oxford: Oxford University Press, 1999.

Appadurai, Arjun. *Modernity at Large: Cultural Dimensions of Globalization*. Minneapolis: University of Minnesota Press, 1996.

Appleton, Jay. *The Experience of Landscape*. Second Ed. London: Wiley, 1996.

———. *The Symbolism of Habitat: An Interpretation of Landscape in Art*. Seattle: University of Washington Press, 2008.

Aristotle. *Poetics*. Loeb Classical Library, Cambridge: Harvard University Press, 1995.

Arrington, Joseph Earl. "The Story of Stockwell's Panorama." *Minnesota History* 33.7 (Autumn 1953): 284–290.

———. "William Burr's Moving Panorama of the Great Lakes, the Niagara, St. Lawrence, and Saguenay Rivers." *Ontario History* 51 (Summer 1959): 141–162.

———. "Skirving's Moving Panorama: Colonel Fremont's Western Expeditions." *Oregon Historical Quarterly* 65.2 (June 1964): 133–172.

———. "Henry Lewis's Moving Panorama of the Mississippi River." *Louisiana History: The Journal of the Louisiana Historical Association* 6.3 (Summer 1965): 239–272.

———. "Godfrey N. Frankenstein's Moving Panorama of Niagara Falls." *New York History* 49 (April 1968): 169–199.

———. "Panorama Paintings of the Mormon Temple in Nauvoo." *BYU Studies* (1982): 1–13.

The Art Journal Illustrated Catalogue: The Industry of All Nations 1851. London: George Virtue, 1851.

Austin Allan D. "More Black Panoramas: An Addendum." *The Massachusetts Review* 37.4 (Winter 1996): 636–639.

Avery, Kevin J. "Whaling Voyage Round the World: Russell and Purrington's Moving Panorama and Herman Melville's 'Mighty Book.'" *American Art Journal* 22 (1990): 50–78.

Avery, Kevin J. and Peter L. Fedora. Eds. *John Vanderlyn's Panoramic View of the Palace and Gardens of Versailles*. New York: Metropolitan Museum of Art, 1988.

Ball, James Presley. *Splendid Mammoth Pictorial Tour of the United States: Comprising Views of the African Slave Trade of Northern and Southern Cities; of Cotton and Sugar Plantations; of the Mississippi, Ohio and Susquehanna Rivers, Niagara Falls, etc.* Cincinnati: Achilles Pugh, 1855.

Bank, Rosemarie K. *Antebellum Stagings: Theatre Culture in the United States, 1825–1860*. New York: Cambridge University Press, 1997.

———. "Representing History: Performing the Columbian Exposition." *Theatre Journal* 54.4 (December 2002): 589–606.

————. "'Staging the Native': Making History in American Theatre Culture, 1828–1838." *Theatre Journal* 45.4 (December 1993): 461–486.

Banner, Stuart. *How the Indians Lost Their Land: Law and Power on the Frontier.* Cambridge: Harvard University Press, 2005.

Banvard, John. *Description of Banvard's Panorama of the Mississippi River Painted on Three Miles of Canvas Exhibiting a View of the Country 1,200 Miles in Length Extending from the Mouth of the Missouri River to the City of New Orleans; Being by far the Largest Picture Ever Executed by Man.* Boston: John Putnam, 1847.

Barker, Barbara. "Imre Kiralfy's Patriotic Spectacles: *Columbus and the Discovery of America* (1892–1893) and *America* (1893)." *Dance Chronicle* 17.2 (1994): 149–178.

Barnum, Phineas Taylor. *The Life of P.T. Barnum, Written By Himself.* Urbana: University of Illinois Press, 2000.

Barry, John D. *The City of Domes: A Walk with an Architect about the Courts and Palaces of the Panama-Pacific International Exposition, with a Discussion of its Arch.* San Francisco: John J. Newbegin, 1915.

Barthes, Roland. *Image, Music, Text.* Trans. Stephen Heath. New York: Hill and Wang, 1977.

Beacham, Richard C. *Spectacle Entertainments of Early Imperial Rome.* New Haven: Yale University Press, 1999.

Bell, John. "The Sioux War Panorama and American Mythic History." *Theatre Journal* 48.3 (October 1996): 279–299.

Benjamin, Walter. *The Arcades Project.* Trans. Howard Eiland and Kevin McLaughlin. Cambridge, MA: Belknap Press, 2002.

————. *Charles Baudelaire: A Lyric Poet in the Era of High Capitalism.* New York: Verso, 1997.

Bennett, Tony. *The Birth of the Museum: History, Theory, Politics.* London: Routledge, 2009.

Berkowitz, Joel. *Shakespeare on the American Yiddish Stage.* Iowa City: University of Iowa Press, 2002.

Bernier, Celeste-Marie. *African American Visual Arts: From Slavery to the Present.* Edinburgh: University of Edinburgh Press, 2008.

Billington, Ray Allen. *Westward Expansion: A History of the American Frontier.* Third Ed. London: Macmillan, 1967.

Bishop, Clair. *Artificial Hells: Participatory Art and the Politics of Spectatorship.* London: Verso, 2012.

Bird, S. Elizabeth. Ed. *Dressing in Feathers: The Construction of the Indian in American Popular Culture.* Boulder, Colorado: Westview Press, 1996.

Blaisdell, Bob. Ed. *Great Speeches by Native Americans.* New York: Dover, 2000.

The Blue Book: A Comprehensive Official Souvenir View Book of the Panama-Pacific International Exposition at San Francisco, 1915. San Francisco: Robert A. Reid, 1915.

Boime, Albert. *The Magisterial Gaze: Manifest Destiny and American Landscape Painting, 1830–1865.* Washington, DC: Smithsonian Institution Press, 1991.

Bolossy, Kiralfy. *Creator of Great Musical Spectacles: An Autobiography*. Ed. Barbara M. Barker. Ann Arbor, Michigan: UMI Research Press, 1988.

Bolotin, Norman and Christine Laing. *The World's Columbia Exposition: The Chicago World's Fair of 1893*. Urbana: University of Chicago Press, 2002.

Booth, Michael. *English Melodrama*. London: Herbert Jenkins, 1965.

———. *Victorian Spectacular Theatre, 1850–1910*. Boston: Routledge and Kegan Paul, 1981.

Bourbon, Fabio. *The Lost Cities of the Mayas: The Life, Art and Discoveries of Frederick Catherwood*. Shrewsbury: Swan Hill, 1999.

Brewster, Ben and Lea Jacobs. *Theatre to Cinema: Stage Pictorialism and the Early Feature Film*. Oxford: Oxford University Press, 1997.

Brooks, Daphne A. *Bodies in Dissent: Spectacular Performances of Race and Freedom, 1850–1910*. Durham: Duke University Press, 2006.

Browman, David L. "The Peabody Museum, Frederic W. Putnam, and the Rise of U. S. Anthropology, 1866–1903." *American Anthropologist* 104.2 (2002): 508–519.

Brown, Richard Maxwell. *Strain of Violence: Historical Studies of American Violence and Vigilantism*. New York: Oxford University Press, 1975.

Brownell, Susan. Ed. *The 1904 Anthropology Days and Olympic Games: Sport, Race, and American Imperialism*. Lincoln: University of Nebraska Press, 2008.

Buchanan, Thomas C. *Black Life on the Mississippi: Slaves, Free Blacks, and the Western Steamboat World*. Chapel Hill: University of North Carolina Press, 2004.

Burch, Robert. "Charles Sanders Peirce." In *The Stanford Encyclopedia of Philosophy*. Ed. Edward N. Zalta, Fall 2010 Edition. http://plato.stanford.edu/archives/fall2010/entries/peirce/.

Burford, Robert. "Description of a View of the Falls of Niagara, now exhibiting at the Panorama, Leicester Square." London: T. Brettell, 1833.

———. *Description of a View of the Falls of Niagara*. Boston: Perkins and Marvin, 1837.

Burke, Edmund. *A Philosophical Inquiry into the Origins of Our Idea of the Sublime and Beautiful*. Oxford: Oxford University Press, 1990.

Burnet, Mary Q. "Barton Hays." In *Art and Artists of Indiana*. New York: The Century, 1921.

Burns, Ned. *Field Manual for Museums*. Washington DC: U.S. Government Printing Office, 1941.

Burten, David H. Ed. *The Collected Works of William Howard Taft*. Vol. 3. Athens: Ohio University Press, 2002.

Catlin, George. *Catlin and His Indian Gallery*. Renwick Gallery. Smithsonian American Art Museum. Washington, DC: W. W. Norton, 2002.

———. *Illustrations of the Manners, Customs, and Conditions of the North American Indians*. 1841. New York: Penguin Classics, 2004.

Carstensen, Georg J. B. *New York Crystal Palace*. New York: Rikker, Thorne & Co. 1854.

Clarke, Jeanne Nienbaber. *Roosevelt's Warrior: Harold Ickes and the New Deal*. Baltimore: Johns Hopkins University Press, 1996.

Clark, Kenneth. *Landscape into Art*. New York: Harper & Row, 1976.

Cole, Thomas. "Essay on American Scenery." In *The Collected Essays and Prose Sketches*. Ed. Marshall Tymn. St. Paul: Minnesota: John Colet Press, 1980.

Comment, Bernard. *The Panorama*. London: Reaktion, 1999.

Condensed Facts Concerning the Panama-Pacific Exposition, San Francisco 1915. San Francisco: Panama-Pacific International Exposition, 1914.

Cook, John Graham. "Artist Henry Lewis: The Case of the Falsified Résumé." *Minnesota History* 57.5 (Spring 2001): 238–243.

Cooper, Helen. *The Hand and the Spirit of the Panther*. New Haven: Yale University Press, 1982.

Cosdon, Mark. *The Hanlon Brothers: From Daredevil Acrobatics to Spectacle Pantomime, 1833–1931*. Carbondale: Southern Illinois University Press, 2009.

Cosgrove, Denis E. *Social Formation and Symbolic Landscape*. Madison: University of Wisconsin Press, 1999.

Costola, Sergio. "William Wells Brown's Panoramic Views." *Journal of American Drama and Theatre* 24.2 (Spring 2012): 13–31.

Cowdin, Elliot C. *The Paris Universal Exhibition of 1867*. New York: Baker & Godwin, 1866.

Crary, Jonathan. "Géricault, the Panorama, and Sites of Reality in the Early Nineteenth Century." *Grey Room* 9 (Autumn 2002): 5–25.

———. *Suspensions of Perspective: Attention, Spectacle, and Modern Culture*. Cambridge: Cambridge University Press, 1997.

———. *Techniques of the Observer: On Vision and Modernity in the 19th Century*. Cambridge: MIT Press, 1990.

Curti, Merle. "America at the World Fairs, 1851–1893." *The American Historical Review* 55.4 (July 1950): 833–856.

Cyclorama of Gettysburg of the Battle of Gettysburg by Paul Philippoteaux. Boston: M. J. Kiley, 1886.

Dahl, Curtis. "Mark Twain and the Moving Panoramas." *American Quarterly* 13.1 (Spring 1961): 20–32.

Daguerre, Louis Jacques Mandé. *An Historical and Descriptive Account of the Various Processes of the Daguerreotype and Diorama*. 1939. New York: Winter House, 1971.

Damish, Hurbert. *The Origin of Perspective*. Trans. John Goodman. Cambridge, MA: MIT Press, 1995.

———. *Skyline: The Narcissistic City*. Trans. John Goodman. Stanford: Stanford University Press, 2001.

Davis, Lance E., et al.. *In Pursuit of Leviathan: Technology, Institutions, Productivity, and Products in American Whaling, 1816–1906*. Chicago: University of Chicago Press, 1997.

Day, Nicholas. "Blood on the Tracks: Sensation Drama, the Railway, and the Dark Face of Modernity." *Victorian Studies* 42.1 (October 1998): 47–76.

Debord, Guy. *Comments on the Society of the Spectacle*. Trans. Malcolm Imrie. London: Verso, 1998.

———. *The Society of the Spectacle.* Trans. Donald Nicholson-Smith. New York: Zone Books, 1995.

DeLuxe, Rachel Ziady and James Elkins. Eds. *Landscape Theory.* New York: Routledge, 2008.

Demastes, William W. and Irish Smith Fischer. *Interrogating America through Theatre and Performance.* New York: Palgrave Macmillan, 2009.

Densmore, Christopher. *Red Jacket: Iroquois Diplomat and Orator.* New York: Syracuse University Press, 1999.

Denson, Andrew. "Muskogee's Indian International Fairs: Tribal Autonomy and the Indian Image in the Late Nineteenth Century." *The Western Historical Quarterly* 34.3 (Autumn 2003): 325–345.

The Department of *Commerce.* Washington, DC: Government Printing Office, 1915.

Dickie, George. *The Century of Taste.* Oxford: Oxford University Press, 1996.

DiCristoforo, Dan. "HCC's Design Honors the Past, Embraces the Future." *Design Matters* 66.2 (February 2010): 42.

Dictionary of Canadian Biography Online. "Wiman Erastus." Library and Archives Canada. http://www.collectionscanada.ca.

Documentary History of the Construction and Development of the United States Capitol Building and Grounds. Washington, DC: Government Printing Office, 1904.

Domosh, Mona. "Selling Civilization: Toward a Cultural Analysis of America's Economic Empire in the Late Nineteenth and Early Twentieth Centuries." *Transactions of the Institute of British Geographers* 29.4 (December 2004): 453–467.

Donohoe, Joseph I. Jr and Jane M. Koustas. Eds. *Theatre sans Frontieres: Essays on the Dramatic Universe of Robert Lepage.* East Lansing: Michigan State University Press, 2009.

Dormon, James H. *Theater in the Antebellum South, 1815–1861.* Chapel Hill: University of North Carolina Press, 1967.

Dryfhout, John H. *Augustus Saint-Gaudens: American Sculptor of the Gilded Age.* Washington, DC: Trust for Museum Exhibitions, 2003.

Duffus, R. L. "The Museum Takes Off Its High Hat." *The North American Review* 242.1 (Autumn 1936): 30.

Dunlap, William. *A History of the American Theatre from Its Origins to 1832.* Chicago: University of Illinois Press, 2005.

———. *History of the Rise and Progress of the Arts of Design in the United States.* Ed. Alexander Wyckoff. 2 Vols. 1965. Revised; New York: Benjamin Blom, 1834.

Eagleton, Terry. *The Ideology of the Aesthetic.* Oxford: Blackwell, 1990.

Eisenstadt, Shmuel N. *Comparative Civilizations and Multiple Modernities.* Leidon and Boston: Brill, 2003.

———. Ed., *Multiple Modernities.* New Brunswick: Transaction Publishers, 2002.

———. *Paradoxes of Democracy, Fragility, Continuity, and Change.* Baltimore: Johns Hopkins University Press, 1999.

Elam, Henry and David Krasner. Eds. *African American Performance and Theatre History: A Critical Reader.* New York: Oxford University Press, 2001.

Eliasson, Olafur and Peter Weibel. 2001. *Olafur Eliasson: Surroundings Surrounded: Essays on Space and Science.* Graz, Austria: Neue Galerie am Landesmuseum Joanneum, 2001.

Eliasson, Olafur, et al. *Take Your Time: Olafur Eliasson.* San Francisco: San Francisco Museum of Modern Art, 2007.

Ellis Robert. *Official Descriptive and Illustrated Catalogue of the Great Exhibition of the Works of Industry of All Nations.* 4 Vols. London: Spicer Brothers, 1851.

Emerson, Ralph Waldo. *The Early Lectures of Ralph Waldo Emerson.* Vol. 2: 1836–1838. Eds. Stephen E. Whicher, et al. Cambridge, MA: Belknap Press, 1964.

———. *The Collected Works of Ralph Waldo Emerson.* Ed. Alfred R. Ferguson. Cambridge, MA: Belknap Press, 1971.

Enders, Jody. *The Medieval Theater of Cruelty: Rhetoric, Memory, Violence.* Ithaca: University of Cornell Press, 1999.

Ernest, John. "Outside the Box: Henry Box Brown and the Politics of Antislavery Agency." *Arizona Quarterly* 63.4 (Winter 2007): 1–24.

Fairall, Herbert S. *The World's Industrial and Cotton Centennial Exposition, New Orleans, 1884–85.* Iowa City: Republican Publishing Co, 1885.

Faust, Drew Gilpin. *The Republic of Suffering: Death and the American Civil War.* New York: Vintage, 2008.

Ferdinand Vandiveer Hayden and the Founding of Yellowstone National Park. Washington, DC: U.S. Government Printing Office, 1941.

Fernandez-Bravo, Alvaro. "Ambivalent Argentina: Nationalism, Exoticism, and Latin Americanism at the 1889 Paris Universal Exposition." *Nepanlta: Views from South* 2.1 (2001): 115–139.

Findling, John E. and Kimberly D. Pelle. Eds. *Encyclopedia of World's Fairs and Expositions.* Jefferson, North Carolina: McFarland & Company, 2008.

Flad, Harvey K. "The Parlor in the Wilderness: Domesticating an Iconic American Landscape." *Geographical Review* 99.3 (July 2009): 356–376.

Fotsch, Paul Mason. "The Building of a Superhighway Future at the New York World's Fair." *Cultural Critique* 48 (Spring 2001): 65–97.

Foucault, Michel. *Discipline and Punish: The Birth of the Prison.* Trans. Alan Sheridan. New York: Vintage, 1979.

Foust, Clement Edgar. *The Life and Dramatic Works of Robert Montgomery Bird.* New York: B. Franklin, 1971.

Fox, Stephen. *John Muir and His Legacy: The American Conservation Movement.* Boston: Little, Brown and Company, 1981.

Franko, Mark. *The Work of Dance: Labor, Movement, and Identity in the 1930s.* Middletown: Wesleyan University Press, 2002.

"Frederic Edwin Church." In *Corcoran Gallery of Art, American Paintings to 1945.* Ed. Sarah Cash. Washington, DC: Corcoran Gallery of Art, 2011.

Freemuth, John C. *Islands Under Siege: National Parks and the Politics of External Threats.* Lawrence: University Press of Kansas, 1991.

Fremling, Calvin R. *Immortal River: The Upper Mississippi in Ancient and Modern Times*. Madison: University of Wisconsin Press, 1990.

Frick, John W. *Theatre, Culture, and Temperance Reform in Nineteenth-Century America*. Cambridge: Cambridge University Press, 2003.

Friedberg, Anne. *The Virtual Window: from Alberti to Microsoft*. Cambridge, MA: MIT Press, 2008.

Fruitema, Evelyn J. and Paul A. Zoetmulder. Eds. *The Panorama Phenomenon: Mesdag Panorama 1881–1981*. The Hague: Foundation for the Preservation of the Centenarian Mesdag Panorama, 1981.

Fryd, Vivien Green. *Art and Empire: The Politics of Ethnicity in the United States Capitol, 1815–1860*. New Haven: Yale University Press, 1992.

Fuchs, Elinor and Una Chauduri. Eds. *Land/scape/theater*. Ann Arbor: University of Michigan Press, 2002.

Ganter, Granville. Ed. *The Collected Speeches of Sagoyewatha, or Red Jacket*. Syracuse: Syracuse University Press, 2006.

———. "Red Jacket and the Decolonization of Republican Virtue." *Indian Quarterly* 31.4 (Fall 2007): 559–581.

Gardner, Hamilton, et al. "The Nauvoo Legion, 1840–1845: A Unique Military Organization." *Journal of the Illinois State Historical Society* 54.2 (Summer 1961): 181–197.

Gaspey, William. *Tallis's Illustrated London: In Commemoration of the Great Exhibition of 1851. Forming a Complete Guide to the British Metropolis and Its Environ*. 5 Vols. London: John Tallis, 1851.

Gebauer, Gunter and Christoph Wulf. *Mimesis: Culture, Art, Society*. Trans. Don Reneau. Berkeley: University of California Press, 1992.

"General Electric at the Panama-Pacific Exposition." Pamphlet. General Electric Company, 1915.

Geppert, Alexander C. T. *Fleeting Cities: Imperial Expositions in Fin-de-Siècle Europe*. London: Palgrave Macmillan, 2010.

Gerould, Daniel. Ed. *American Melodrama*. New York: PAJ, 1983.

"Getting Ready to Celebrate the Completion of the Panama Canal." *Current Opinion* 4.4 (October 1913): 229.

Gibbs-Smith, C. H. *The Great Exhibition of 1851*. London: Victoria and Albert Museum, 1981

Gibson, Campbell and Emily Lennon. "Historical Census Statistics on the Foreign-born Population of the United States: 1850–1990." Population Division Working Paper No. 29 (February 1999). US Census Bureau. Population Division. http://www.census.gov.

Gilfoyle, Timothy J. "White Cities, Linguistic Turns, and Disneylands: The New Paradigms of Urban History." *Reviews of American History* 26.1 (1998): 175–204.

Gillespie, Elizabeth Duane. *A Book of Remembrance*. Second Ed. Philadelphia: B. Lippincott, 1901.

Glassberg, David. *American Historical Pageantry: The Uses of Tradition in the Early Twentieth Century*. Chapel Hill: University of North Carolina Press, 1990.

Gluck, Carol. *Japan's Modern Myths: Ideology in the Late Meiji Period.* Princeton: Princeton University Press, 1985.

Goetzmann, William H. *Army Exploration in the American West, 1803–1863.* New Haven: Yale University Press, 1959.

Gotham, Kevin Fox. *Authentic New Orleans: Tourism, Culture, and Race in the Big Easy.* New York: New York University Press, 2007.

Gould, Lewis L. *The William Howard Taft Presidency.* Lawrence, Kansas: University of Kansas Press, 2009.

Grau, Oliver. *Virtual Art: From Illusion to Immersion.* Cambridge, MA: MIT Press, 2003.

Gregory, Brendan Edward. "The Spectacle Plays and Exhibitions of Imre Kiralfy, 1887–1914." Dissertation. University of Manchester, 1988.

Griffiths, Alison. *Shivers Down Your Spine: Cinema, Museums, and the Immersive View.* New York: Columbia University Press, 2008.

Gross, Linda P. and Theresa R. Snyder. *Philadelphia's 1876 Centennial Exhibition.* Arcadia Publishing, 2005.

Hafen, LeRoy, R. "A Westerner, Born and Bred." *The Western Historical Quarterly* 3.2 (April 1972): 129–135.

Hanners, John. "'Vicissitude and Woe': The Theatrical Misadventures of John Banvard." *Theatre Survey* 23.2 (November 1952): 177–187.

———. "The Adventures of an Artist: John Banvard (1815–1891) and His Mississippi Panorama." Dissertation. Michigan State University, 1979. Reprint; UMI, 2001.

Harrison, Helen. *Dawn of a New Day.* New York: New York University Press, 1980.

Hartman, Edward George. *The Movement to Americanize the Immigrant.* New York: Columbia University Press, 1948.

Hayden, Ferdinand V. *The Yellowstone National Park, and the Mountain Regions of Portions of Idaho, Nevada, Colorado and Utah.* Boston: L. Prang and Company, 1876.

Hays, Michael and Anastasia Nikolopoulou. Eds. *Melodrama: The Cultural Emergence of a Genre.* New York: St. Martin's Press, 1996.

Hedgbeth, Llewellyn Hubbard. "Extant American Panoramas: Moving Entertainments of the Nineteenth Century." Dissertation. New York University. Ann Arbor: UMI, 1977.

Heilbron, Bertha L. "Documentary Panorama." *Minnesota History* 30.1 (March 1949): 14–23.

———. "Lewis' 'Mississippithal' in English." *Minnesota History* 32.4 (December 1951): 202–213.

———. "Making a Motion Picture in 1848: Henry Lewis on the Upper Mississippi." *Minnesota History* 17.2 (June 1936): 131–156.

———. "A Mississippi Panorama." *Minnesota History* 23.4 (December 1942): 349–354.

Henderson, Mary C. *The City and the Theatre: New York Playhouses from Bowling Green to Times Square.* Clifton, NJ: James T. White, 1973.

Hewitt, Barnard. *Theatre U.S.A. 1665–1957.* New York: McGraw Hill, 1959.

Hill, Errol G. and James V. Hatch. *A History of African American Theatre*. Cambridge: Cambridge University Press, 2003.

Hill, Howard. "The Americanization Movement." *The American Journal of Sociology* 24.6 (May 1919): 609–642.

Hine, Robert V. and John Mack Faragher. *Frontiers: A Short History of the American West*. New Haven: Yale University Press, 2007.

Historical Dictionary of World's Fairs and Expositions, 1851–1988. Ed. John Findling. Westport, CT: Westwood Press, 1990.

Hodge, Francis. *The Yankee Theatre: The Image of America on Stage*. Austin: University of Texas Press, 1964.

Hoig, Stan. *The Sand Creek Massacre*. Norman: University of Oklahoma Press, 1973.

Howe, Daniel Walker. *What Hath God Wrought: The Transformation of America, 1815–1848*. Oxford: Oxford University Press, 2007.

Hughes, Glenn. *A History of American Theatre, 1750–1950*. New York: Samuel French, 1951.

Hughes, Jim. *The Birth of a Century: Early Color Photographs of America*. London: Taurus Parke Books, 1994.

Hunt, Lynn Avery. *Politics, Culture, Class in the French Revolution*. Berkeley: University of California Press, 2004.

Huntington, David C. "Frederic Church's Niagara: Nature and the Nation's Type." *Texas Studies in Literature and Language* 25.1 (Spring 1983): 100–138.

Hyde, Ralph. *Panoramania! The Art and Entertainment of the "All Embracing View."* London: Trefoil, 1988.

The Illustrated History of the Centennial Exhibition. 1876. Reprint; Philadelphia: National Publishing Company, 1975.

International Exhibition 1876: Main Building. United States Centennial Commission: Centennial Catalogue Company, 1876.

Ingraham, Joseph Wentworth. *A Manuel for the Use of Visitors to the Falls of Niagara*. Buffalo: Charles Faxon, 1834.

Ingram, John M. *Biographical Dictionary of American Business Leaders*. Vol. 2. Westport, CT: Greenwood Press, 1983.

"Industrial and Financial Effects of the War." *Lippincott's Magazine of Literature, Science, and Education* 7 (January 1871): 81–92.

Irland, Lloyd C. *Wilderness Economics and Policy*. Lexington, MA: Lexington Books, 1972.

Jackson, Andrew. Inaugural Address, March 4, 1833. American Presidency Project. http//www.presidency.ucsb.edu.

Jackson, J. B. *Discovering the Vernacular Landscape*. New Haven: Yale University Press, 1984.

Jackson, William Henry. *Among the Rockies: Pictures of the Magnificent Scenes in the Rocky Mountains, the Master Works of the World's Greatest Photographic Artist*. Boston: H. H. Tammen, 1900.

———. *Beauties of the Rockies*. Denver: H. H. Tammen Curio, 1890a.

———. *New Mexico*. Denver: W. H. Jackson, 1890b.

———. *Photographs from the Geological Survey of the Territories for the Years 1869–1873*. Washington, DC: Government Printing Office, 1873a.

————. *Photographs of the Yellowstone National Parks, and Views in Montana and Wyoming.* Washington, DC: Government Printing Office, 1873b.

————. *Time Exposure: The Autobiography of William Henry Jackson.* Tucson, Arizona: Patrice Press, 1994.

————. *Yellowstone National Park, and the Mountain Regions of Portions of Idaho, Nevada, Colorado and Utah.* Boston: L. Prang, 1876.

————. *With Moran in the Yellowstone: A Story of Exploration, Photography and Art.* Brattleboro, Vermont: Appalachian Mountain Club, 1936.

Jackson, William Henry and Howard R. Driggs. *Pioneer Photographer: Rocky Mountain Adventures with a Camera.* New York: World Book, 1929.

James, Anne. "Native Art Gems: Department of the Interior." *Native People's Magazine* 18.2 (March–April 2005): 66–70.

Jameson, Frederic. *A Singular Modernity: Essay on the Ontology of the Present.* London: Verso, 2002.

Jurovics, Toby, et al. *Framing the West: The Survey Photographs of Timothy H. O'Sullivan.* New Haven: Yale University Press, 2010.

Kant, Immanuel. *The Critique of Judgment.* Trans. James Creed Meredith. Oxford: Clarendon, 1952.

Karp, Ivan and Steven Levine. *Exhibiting Cultures: The Poetics and Politics of Museum Display.* Washington, DC: Smithsonian Institution Press, 1991.

Kasson, Jack F. *Amusing the Million: Coney Island at the Turn of the Century.* New York: Hill and Wang, 1978.

Katz, Wendy Jean. *Regionalism and Reform: Art and Class Formation in Antebellum Cincinnati.* Ohio: Ohio State University, 2002.

Kieley, James F. Ed. *A Brief History of the National Park Services.* 1940. United States Department of the Interior. http://www.nps.gov.

Kellner, Douglas. *Media Spectacle.* London: Routledge, 2012.

Kellner, Douglas and Steven Best. "Debord, Cybersituations, and the Interactive Spectacle." *SubStance* 28.3 (1999): 129–156.

Kelly, Franklin. *Frederic Edwin Church.* New Haven: Yale University Press, 2005.

Kent, Christopher. "Spectacular History as an Ocular Discipline." *Wide Angle* 18.3 (1996): 1–21.

Kessler-Harris, Alice. *In Pursuit of Equity: Women, Men and the Quest for Economic Citizenship in 20th Century America.* Oxford: Oxford University Press, 2001.

Ketner II, Joseph D. *The Emergence of the African American Artist: Robert S. Duncanson, 1821–1872.* Columbia, MS: University of Missouri Press, 1992.

Keynes, John Maynard. *The General Theory of Employment, Interest and Money.* 1936. Palgrave Macmillan, 2007.

Kiralfy, Imre. "My Reminiscences." *The Strand* 37.222 (June 1909): 646–648.

Kirshenblatt-Gimblett, Barbara. *Destination Culture: Tourism, Museums, and Culture.* Berkeley: University of California Press, 1998.

Kirstein, Lincoln. *Dance, A Short History of Classical Dancing.* New York: Dance Horizons, 1969.

Klingender, Francis Donald. *Art and the Industrial Revolution.* Ed. Arthur Elton. New York: Schocken Books, 1968.

Knight, Donald. *The Exhibitions: Great White City Shepherd's Bush London.* 1978. Hertfordshire: Print Mania, 2008.

Kruger, Loren. "'White Cities, 'Diamond Zulus,' and the 'African Contribution to Human Advancement' African Modernities and the World's Fairs." *TDR* 51.3 (Fall 2007): 19–45.

Kunhardt Jr, Philip B., et al. *P. T. Barnum: America's Greatest Showman.* New York: Knopf, 1995.

Kuznets, Simon. *National Income, 1929–1932.* National Bureau of Economic Research, 1934.

Leach, William. *Land of Desire: Merchants, Power, and the Rise of a New American Culture.* New York: Pantheon, 1993.

Leclerc, George Louis. *Natural History.* Trans. William Smellie. London: A, Strahan and T. Cadell, 1791.

Leighninger Jr., Robert D. *Long-Range Public Investment: The Forgotten Legacy of the New Deal.* Columbia: University of South Carolina Press, 2007.

Leoni, Frieda. *Catherin de Medici.* London: Phoenix, 2005.

Leslie, Frank. *Illustrated Historical Register of the Centennial Exposition, 1876.* New York: Paddington Press, 1974.

Londré, Felicia Hardison. *Stage: Kansas City at the Crossroads of American Theatre, 1830–1930.* Columbia: University of Missouri Press, 2007.

Lorence, James J. *Organizing the Unemployed: Community and Union Activists in the Industrial Heartland.* Albany: State University of New York Press, 1996.

Lowery, William R. *Repairing Paradise: The Restoration of Nature in America's National Parks.* Washington, DC: Brookings Institution, 2009.

Lowitt, Richard. *The New Deal and the West.* Bloomington: Indiana University Press, 1984.

Lucas, Federic A. "Akeley as a Taxidermist: A Chapter in the History of Museum Methods." *Natural History* 27.2 (March–April 1927): 142–152.

Lyons, Lisa. "Panorama of the Monumental Grandeur of the Mississippi Valley." *Design Quarterly* 101/102 (1976): 32–34.

Macomber, Ben. *The Jewel City: Its Planning and Achievement; Its Architecture, Sculpture, Symbolism, and Music; Its Gardens, Palaces, and Exhibits.* San Francisco: John H. Williams, 1915.

Mackaye, Percy. *Epoch: The Life of Steele Mackaye, Genius of the Theatre, in Relation to His Times and Contemporaries.* Vol. 2. New York: Boni and Liverlight, 1927.

Magelssen, Scott. *Living History Museums: Undoing History through Performance.* Lanham, MD: Scarecrow Press, 2007.

Magelssen, Scott and Rhona Justice-Malloy. Eds. *Enacting History.* Tuscaloosa: University of Alabama Press, 2011.

Malamud, Margaret. "The Imperial Metropolis: Ancient Rome and Turn-of-the-Century New York." *Arion* 7.3 (Winter 2000): 64–108.

———. "Roman Entertainments for the Masses in Turn-of-the-Century New York." *The Classical World* 95.1 (Autumn 2001): 49–57.

Marks, Edward B. *They All Had Glamour: From the Swedish Nightingale to the Naked Lady*. New York: J. Messner, 1944.

Mattie, Eric. *World's Fairs*. Princeton: Princeton Architectural Press, 1998.

Mayer, David. *Stage Struck Filmmaker: D. W. Griffith and the American Theatre*. Iowa: University of Iowa Press, 2009.

McAllister, Marvin Edward. *"White People Do Not Know How To Behave at Entertainments Designed for Ladies and Gentleman of Colour": A History of New York's African and American Theatre*. Chapel Hill: University of North Carolina Press, 2003.

McConachie, Bruce. *Melodramatic Formations: American Theatre and Society, 1820–1870*. Iowa City: University of Iowa Press, 1992.

McCoubrey, John W. Ed. *American Art 1700–1960: Sources and Documents*. Englewood Cliffs, NJ: Prentice-Hall, 1965.

McDermott, John Francis. *The Lost Panoramas of the Mississippi*. Chicago: University of Chicago Press, 1958.

McDougall, Walter A. *Throes of Democracy: The American Civil War Era, 1829–1877*. New York: Harper Collins, 2008.

McGreevy, Patrick. *Imaging Niagara: The Meaning and Making of Niagara Falls*. Amherst: University of Massachusetts Press, 1994.

McKenzie, John M. *Orientalism: History, Theory and the Arts*. Manchester and New York: Manchester University Press, 1995.

McLanathan, Richard. *The American Tradition in the Arts*. New York: Harcourt, Brace & World, 1968.

McNamara, Brooks. *The New York Concert Saloon: the Devil's Own Nights*. Cambridge: Cambridge University Press, 2002.

McKnight, Natalie. "Dickens, Niagara Falls and the Watery Sublime." *Dickens Quarterly* 26.2 (June 2009): 69–78.

Meisel, Martin. *Realizations: Narrative, Pictorial, and Theatrical Arts in Nineteenth-Century England*. Princeton: Princeton University Press, 1983.

Menchaca, Juan. "Oral History Interview." Transcript. Smithsonian Institution. November 11, 1964.

Merrill, Lisa. *When Romeo Was a Woman: Charlotte Cushman and Her Circle of Female Spectators*. Ann Arbor: University of Michigan Press, 2000.

Merrill, Marlene Deahl. Ed. *Yellowstone and the Great West: Journals, Letters, and Images from the 1871 Hayden Expedition*. Lincoln: University of Nebraska, 1999.

Miles, Edwin A. "The Mississippi Slave Insurrection Scare of 1835." *The Journal of Negro History* 42.1 (January 1957): 48–60.

Miles, John C. *Guardians of the Parks: A History of the National Parks and Conservation Association*. Washington, DC: Taylor & Francis, 1995.

Miller, Angela. *The Empire of the Eye: Landscape Representation and American Cultural Politics, 1825–1875*. Ithaca, NY: Cornell University Press, 1993.

———. "The Panorama, the Cinema and the Emergence of the Spectacular." *Wide Angle* 18.2 (April 1996): 35–69.

Mitchell, Lee Clark. *Witness to a Vanishing America: The Nineteenth-Century Response*. Princeton: Princeton University Press, 1981.

Mitchell, W. J. T. Ed. *Landscape and Power*. Chicago: University of Chicago Press, 1994.

Monaghan, Frank. *Official Guide Book of the New York World's Fair 1939*. New York: Exhibition Publications, 1939.

Montise Moses and John Mason Brown. Eds. *The American Theatre as Seen by its Critics, 1752–1834*. New York: Cooper Square, 1967.

Montgomery, David. *The Fall of the House of Labor: The Workplace, the State, and American Labor Activism*. Cambridge: Cambridge University Press, 1987.

Moody, Richard. *Drama from the American Theatre, 1762–1909*. New York: World Publishing, 1966.

———. *Edwin Forrest: First Star of the American Stage*. New York: Alfred A. Knopf, 1960.

Morris, Christopher. "An Event in Community Organization: The Mississippi Slave Insurrection Scare of 1835." *Journal of Social History* 22.1 (Autumn 1988): 93–111.

Morse, Jedidiah. *Report to Secretary of War of the United States on Indian Affairs, Comprising a Narrative Tour Performed in the Summer of 1820, Under a Commission from the President of the United States, for the Purpose of Ascertaining, for the Use of the Government, the Actual State of the Indian Tribes in the Country*. New Haven: S Converse, 1822.

Moy, James S. "Imre Kiralfy's 1890 Boston Production of *The Fall of Babylon*." *Theatre History Studies* 1 (1981): 20–28.

Muldrow, Edna. "Who Was the First American." *North American Review* 241.1 (March 1936): 72.

Mullgradt, Louis Christian. *The Architecture and Landscape Gardening of the Exposition: A Pictorial Survey of the Most Beautiful of the Architectural Compositions of the Panama-Pacific International Exposition*. Second Ed. San Francisco: Paul Elder and Co., 1915.

Murdock, Myrtle Cheney. *Constantino Brumidi: Michaelangelo of the United States Capitol*. Washington, DC: Monumental Press, 1950.

Nathans, Heather S. *Slavery and Sentiment on the American Stage, 1787–1861: Lifting the Veil of Black*. Cambridge: Cambridge University Press, 2009.

Neville, Amelia. "World's Fairs of the Past." *Overland Monthly and Out West Magazine* 58.2 (August 1911): 19–21.

Nichols, Roger L. *Black Hawk and the Warrior's Path*. Illinois: Harlan Davidson, 1992.

Nordenskiöld, Gustaf. *The Cliff Dwellings of the Mesa Verde*. 1893. Reprint; Mesa Verde Museum Association, 1990.

North, Douglass C. *Understanding the Process of Economic Change*. Princeton: Princeton University Press, 2005.

Novak, Barbara. *Nature and Culture: American Landscape Painting, 1825–1875*. New York: Oxford University Press, 1980.

Nyong'o, Tavia. *The Amalgamation Waltz: Race, Performance, and the Ruses of Memory*. Minneapolis: University of Minnesota Press, 2009.

O'Brien, Michael. *Intellectual Life and the American South, 1810–1860*. Chapel Hill: University of North Carolina Press, 2010.

O'Connor, Ralph. *The Earth on Show: Fossils and the Poetics of Popular Science, 1802–1856.* Chicago: University of Chicago Press, 2008.

Oettermann, Stephan. *The Panorama: History of a Mass Medium.* Trans. Deborah Lucas Schneider. New York: Zone Books, 1997.

Official Catalogue of the World's Industrial and Cotton Centennial Exposition: Held under the Joint Auspices: the United States of America, the National Cotton Planter's Association, and the City of New Orleans, During the Period from the 16th of December to the 31st of May 1885. New Orleans: J. S. Rivers, 1885.

Official Descriptive and Illustrated Catalogue of the Great Exhibition of the Works of Industry of All Nations. 4 Vols. London: Spicer Brothers, 1851.

Oleksijczuk, Denise Blake. *The First Panoramas: Visions of British Imperialism.* Minneapolis: University of Minnesota Press, 2011.

Olneck, Michael R. "Americanization and the Education of Immigrants, 1900–1925: An Analysis of Symbolic Action." *American Journal of Education* 97.4 (August 1989): 398–423.

O'Sullivan, John. "The Great Nation of Futurity." *The United States Democratic Review* 6.23 (1839): 426–430.

Panama-Pacific International Exposition. San Francisco: Panama-Pacific International Exposition Publications, 1915.

Panama-Pacific International Exposition: Popular Information. San Francisco: Panama Pacific International Exposition Publications, 1913.

"Panama-Pacific International Exposition, San Francisco 1915." *Brooklyn Eagle Almanac* 30 (1915): 370.

Parke, A. C. *Red Jacket, Last of the Seneca.* New York: McGraw Hill, 1952.

Pearson, Mike and Michael Shanks. *Theatre Archaeology: Disciplinary Dialogues.* New York: Routledge, 2001.

Pendle, Karen and Stephen Wilkins. "Paradise Found: The Salle le Peletier and French Grand Opera." In *Opera in Context, Essays on the Historical Staging from the Late Renaissance to the Time of Puccini.* Ed. Mark A. Radice. Portland, Oregon: Amadeus Press, 1998.

Pepper, George H. "The Ancient Basket Makers of Southeastern Utah." *American Museum of Natural History: Supplement to American Museum Journal* 2.4 (April 1902): 6–7.

Perry, Ellwood. *The Image of the Indian and Black Man in American Art 1590–1900.* New York: George Braziller, 1974.

Perry, James Wilson. "1934: Joining the American Museum of Natural History." *Painting Actuality: Diorama Art of James Wilson Perry.* Peabody Archive. Yale University.

Peterson, William J. *Mississippi River Panorama: The Henry Lewis Great National Work.* Iowa City: Clio Press, 1979.

Pfening, Fred D. Jr. "Spec-ology of the Circus, Part 1." *The Bandwagon* 47.6 (November–December 2003): 4–20.

Pierce, Charles Sanders. *Charles S. Pierce: Selected Writings.* Ed. Philip Wiener. New York: Dover, 1966.

———. *Selected Philosophical Writings.* Vol. 1, 1867–1893. Eds. Nathan Houser and Christian Kloesel. Bloomington: Indiana University Press, 1992.

Pierce, Franklin, *Franklin Pierce, 1804–1869: Chronology, Documents, Bibliographical Aids*. Ed. Irving J. Sloan. New York: Oceana Publications, 1968.

Piott, Steven L. *American Reformers, 1870–1920: Progressives in Word and Deed*. Lanham, MD: Rowman & Littlefield, 2006.

Pizor, Faith K. "Preparations for the Centennial Exhibition of 1876." *The Pennsylvania Magazine of History and Biography* 94.2 (April 1970): 213–232.

Post, Robert C. "Reflections of American Science and Technology at the New York Crystal Palace Exhibition of 1853." *Journal of American Studies* 17.3 (December 1983): 337–356.

Potter, Elisabeth Walton and Beth M. Boland. *Guidelines for Evaluating and Registering Cemeteries and Burial Places*. National Register Bulletin 41. Department of the Interior: Washington, DC, 1992.

Powell, J. W. "Exploration of the Colorado River of the West and Its Tributaries." Report. Washington, DC: Government Printing Office, 1875.

Proceedings of the First Meeting of the National Board of Trade Held in Philadelphia, June 1868. Boston: J. H. Eastburn, 1868.

Prof. Risley's and Mr. J.R. Smith's Original Gigantic Moving Panorama of the Mississippi River, extending from the Falls of St. Anthony to the Gulf of Mexico. London: John K. Chapman, 1849.

Quinn, Stephen Christopher. *Windows on Nature: The Great Habitat Dioramas of the American Museum of Natural History*. New York: Abrams, 2006.

Qureshi, Sadiah. *People's on Parade: Exhibitions, Empire, and Anthropology in Nineteenth Century Britain*. Chicago: University of Chicago Press, 2011.

Rahill, Frank. *The World of Melodrama*. University Park, PA: Pennsylvania State University Press, 1967.

Reed, Peter. *Rogue Performances: Staging the Underclasses in Early American Theatre Culture*. New York: Palgrave Macmillan, 2009.

Renaud, E. B. "Uncovering the First Americans." *Forum* 75.1 (January 1926): 109.

Richards, Jeffrey H. *Drama, Theatre, and Identity in the American New Republic*. Cambridge, MA: Cambridge University Press, 2005.

Richardson, Gary A. *American Drama from the Colonial Period through World War I: A Critical History*. New York: Twayne, 1993.

Rimmel, Eugene. *Recollections of the Paris Exposition of 1867*. London: Chapman and Hall, 1868.

Ripley, C. Peter. Ed. *The Black Abolitionists, I: The British Isles, 1830–1865*. Chapel Hill: University of North Carolina Press, 1985.

Robinson, David. *From Peep Show to Palace: The Birth of American Film*. New York: Columbia University Press, 1996.

Roger, Jacques. *Buffon: A Life in Natural History*. Trans. Sarah Lucille Bonnefoi. Ithaca: Cornell University Press, 1997.

Rogoff, Irit. *Terra Firma: Geography's Visual Culture*. London: Routledge, 2000.

Rosenberger, Homer T. "Thomas Ustick and the Completion of the United States Capitol." *Records of the Columbia Historical Society* 50 (1948/1950): 273–322.

Rourke, Constance. *Roots of American Culture, and Other Essays*. New York: Harcourt, Brace, and World, 1942.

Rydell, Robert W. *All the World's a Fair: Visions of Empire at American International Expositions*. Chicago: University of Chicago Press, 1984.

———. *World of Fairs: The Century of Progress Exhibitions*. Chicago: University of Chicago Press, 1993.

———. Ed. *The Reason Why the Colored American Is Not in the World's Columbian Exposition*. Chicago: University of Chicago Press, 1999.

Saxon, Arthur H. *P. T. Barnum: The Legend and the Man*. New York: Columbia University Press, 1989.

Schivelbusch, Wolfgang. *The Railway Journey: The Industrialization of Time and Space in the Nineteenth 19th Century*. Berkeley: University of California Press, 1986.

Schmeckebier, L. F. *Catalogue and Index of the Publications of the Hayden, King, Powell, and Wheeler Surveys*. Washington, DC: Government Printing Office, 1904.

Schnapp, Jeffrey T. "The Mass Panorama." *Modernism/modernity* 9.2 (April 2002): 243–281.

Schneider, Rebecca. *Performing Remains: Art and War in Times of Historical Reenactment*. London: Routledge, 2011.

Schulten, Susan. "How to See Colorado: The Federal Writers' Project, American Regionalism, and the 'Old New Western History.'" *The Western Historical Quarterly* 36.1 (Spring 2005): 49–70.

Seller, Maxine Schwartz. Ed. *Ethnic Theatre in the United States*. Westport, CT: Greenwood Press, 1983.

Sellers, Charles. *The Market Revolution: Jacksonian America, 1815–1846*. New York: Oxford University Press, 1991.

Sellers, Charles Coleman. *Mr. Peale's Museum: Charles Willson Peale and the First Popular Museum of Natural Science and Art*. New York: W. W. Norton, 1980.

Sellars, Richard West. "A Very Large Array: The Early Federal Historic Preservation—The Antiquities Act, Mesa Verde, and the National Park Service Act." *Natural Resources Journal* 47 (Spring 2007): 267–328.

Sentiller, Renée M. *Performing Menken: Adah Isaacs Menken and the Birth of Celebrity*. Cambridge: Cambridge University Press, 2003.

Severance, Frank H. *Old Trails on the Niagara Frontier*. Buffalo, 1899.

Shepard, Samuel C. "A Glimmer of Hope: The World's Industrial and Cotton Centennial Exposition, New Orleans, 1884–1885." *Louisiana History* 26 (1985): 275–290.

Simmel, Georg. *The Metropolis and Mental life*. Trans. Kurt Wolff. New York: Free Press, 1950.

Sklaroff, Lauren Rebecca. *Black Culture and the New Deal: The Quest for Civil Rights in the Roosevelt Era*. Chapel Hill: University of North Carolina Press, 2009.

Slap, Andrew L. *The Doom of Reconstruction: The Liberal Republicans in the Civil War Era*. New York: Fordham University Press, 2008.

Smalley, Eugene V. "The Centennial Exposition." *Manufacturer and Builder* 8.8 (August 1876): 172–174.

———. "The New Orleans Exhibition." *The Century Illustrated Magazine* 30.1 (June 1885a): 3–14.

———. "The New Orleans Exhibition." *The Century Illustrated Magazine* 30.2 (June 1885b): 185–199.

Smith, Adam. *An Inquiry into the Nature and Causes of the Wealth of Nations.* Ed. Edwin Cannan. 1904. Library of Economics and Liberty. http://www.econlib.org/library/Smith/smWN12.html.

Smith, Andrew. *The National Cookery Book: Compiled from Original Receipt for the Women's Centennial Committees of the International Exhibition of 1876.* Ed. Deborah Jean Warner. Reprint; Bedford, MA: Applewood Books, 1976.

Smith, J. R. *Synopsis of J. R. Smith's Perspective Lectures, or Copy of the Note Book by Which He Gives Perspective Illustrations.* Boston: J. H. Eastburn, 1826.

Smith, Jason Scott. "The New Deal Order." *Enterprise & Society* 9.3 (September 2008): 521–534.

Smith, Jean Edward. *Grant.* New York: Simon & Schuster, 2001.

Sokalski, J. A. "The Madison Square Theatre: Stage Practice and Technology in Transition." *Theatre Survey* 21 (2001): 105–131.

Statistical Abstract of the United States, 1915. Department of Commerce. Washington, DC: Government Printing Office, 1916.

Stewart, Virgil A. "A History of the Detection, Conviction, Life and Designs of John A. Murrell, The Great Western Land Pirate; Together with his System of Villainy and Plan of Exciting a Negro Rebellion, and a Catalogue of the Names of Four Hundred and Forty Five of His Mystic Clan Fellows and Followers and Their Efforts for the Destruction of Mr. Virgil A. Stewart, The Young Man Who Detected Him, to Which is Added Biographical Sketch of Mr. Virgil A. Stewart." 1835.

Stokes, Melvyn and Stephen Conway, Eds. *The Market Revolution in America: Social, Political, and Religious Expressions 1820–1880.* Charlottesville: University Press of Virginia, 1996.

"The Story of a Great Achievement-Telephone Communication from Coast to Coast." Pamphlet. American Telephone and Telegraph Co, 1915.

Strange, Mary Zeiss. "Women & Hunting in the West." *Montana: The Magazine of Western History* 55.3 (Autumn 2005): 14–21.

Strong, Roy. *Splendor at Court: Renaissance Spectacle and the Theater of Power.* Boston: Houghton Mifflin, 1973.

Sugden, John. *Tecumseh: A Life.* New York: Holt, 1997.

Taft, William Howard. *The Collected Works of William Howard Taft.* Vol. 3. Ed. David H. Burton. Athens: University of Ohio Press, 2004.

Taylor, Diana. *The Archive and the Repertoire: Performing Cultural Memory in the Americas.* Durham: Duke University Press, 2003.

Taylor, Nick. *American-Made: The Enduring Legacy of the WPA, When FDR Put the Nation to Work.* New York: Bantam Books, 2009.

Tenorio-Trillo, Mauricio. *Mexico at the World's Fair: Crafting a Modern Nation.* Berkeley: University of California Press, 1996.

Thompson, George F. Ed. *Landscape in America.* Austin: University of Texas Press, 1995.

Todd, Frank Morton. *The Story of the Exposition: Being the Official History of the International Celebration Held in San Francisco in 1915 to Commemorate the Discovery of the Pacific Ocean and the Construction of the Panama Canal.* New York: Knickerbocker Press, 1921.

Toll, Robert C. *Blacking Up: The Minstrel Show in Nineteenth-Century America.* New York: Oxford University Press, 1974.

Trachtenberg, Alan. *The Incorporation of America: Culture and Society in the Gilded Age.* New York: Hill and Wang, 1982.

Transactions of the Engineering Congress. San Francisco: Neal Publishing Company, 1916.

"Tricks of the Stage." *Current Literature* 16.4 (October 1894): 362-363.

Turner, Frederick Jackson. *The Frontier in American History.* New York: Henry Holt, 1958.

Upton, Dell. *Architecture in the United States.* Oxford: Oxford University Press, 1998.

US Congress. "Joint Committee on the Conduct of the War: Massacre of Cheyenne Indians." 38th Congress, Second session. Washington, DC: United States Printing Office, 1865.

——. "Acknowledgment and Apology." S. J. Res. 15. 109th Congress, 1st session. May 25, 2005. Washington, DC: United States Government Printing Office, 2005.

Van Nuys, Frank. *Americanizing the West: Race, Immigrants, and Citizenship, 1890–1930.* Lawrence, Kansas: University Press of Kansas, 2002.

Vardac, Nicholas A. *Stage to Screen: Theatrical Origins of Early Film. From David Garrick to D. W. Griffith.* Cambridge, MA: Harvard University Press, 1949.

Virilio, Paul. *Negative Horizon: An Essay in Dromoscopy.* Trans. Michael Degener. New York: Continuum, 2005.

——. *Open Sky.* Trans. Julie Rose. London: Verso, 2008.

Voskuil, Lynn. M. "Feeling Public: Sensation Theater, Commodity Culture, and the Victorian Public Sphere." *Victorian Studies* 44.2 (Winter 2002): 245–274.

Walker, Kara Elizabeth. *Walker: My Complement, My Enemy, My Oppressor, My Love.* Minneapolis: Walker Art Center, 2007. Exhibition.

Walker, Ronald W., et al. *Massacre at Mountain Meadows: An American Tragedy.* Oxford: Oxford University Press, 2008.

Wallner, Peter A. *Franklin Pierce, New Hampshire's Favorite Son.* Concord: Plaidswede 2004.

Waltz, Gwendolyn. "Filmed Scenery on the Live Stage." *Theatre Journal* 58.4 (2006): 547–573.

Warren, Louis S. *Buffalo Bill's America: William Cody and the Wild West Show.* New York: Vintage, 2005.

Wechsler, Judith. *Daumier Drawings.* New York: Harry N. Abrams, 1993.

Weed, Clyde P. *The Nemesis of Reform: The Republican Party during the New Deal.* New York: Columbia University Press, 1994.

Wehner, William. *The Battles of Chattanooga.* Chicago: W. J. Jefferson, 1886.

Weigley, Russel F. "Captain Meigs and the Artists of the Capitol: Federal Patronage of Art in the 1850s." *Records of the Columbia Historical Society* 69/70 (1969/1970): 285–305.

Weisman, Winston. "Commercial Palaces of New York: 1845–1875." *The Art Bulletin* 36.4 (December 1954): 285–302.

Wells, David. "Contraband of War." *The American Law Review* 5.2 (January 1871a): 247–261.

———. "Industrial and Financial Effects of the War." *Lippincott's Magazine of Literature, Science, and Education* 7 (January 1871b), 81–92.

Welling, William. *Photography in America: the Formative Years, 1839–1900.* New York: Thomas Y. Cromwell, 1978.

West, Peter. "Trying the Dark, Mammoth Cave and the Racial Imagination." *Southern Spaces.* February 9, 2010. http://www.southernspaces.org.

Whitman, Walt. *Leaves of Grass.* 1855. Reprint. New York: Dover, 1855.

White's, Graham J. *Harold Ickes of the New Deal: His Private Life and Public Career.* Cambridge: University of Harvard Press, 1985.

Wickstrom, Maurya. *Performing Consumers: Global Capital and Its Theatrical Seductions.* New York: Routledge, 2006.

Willis, Deborah. *J. P. Ball: Daguerrean and Studio Photographer.* New York: Garland, 1994.

Wilmeth, Don B. "Tentative Checklist of Indian Plays." *The Journal of American Drama and Theatre* (Fall 1989): 34–54.

Witham, Barry B. Ed. *Theatre in the United States: A Documentary History. Vol. 1: 1750–1915, Theatre in the Colonies and United States.* Cambridge: Cambridge University Press, 1996.

Witkowski, Ed. *The Lost History of the 1853 New York Crystal Palace.* New York: Vox Pop, 2008.

Wolanin, Barbara A. *Constantino Brumidi: Artist of the Capitol.* Washington: U. S. G.P.O., 1998.

Wolff, Cynthia Griffin. "Passing beyond the Middle Passage: Henry Box Brown's Translations of Slavery." *The Massachusetts Review* 37.1 (Spring 1996): 23–44.

Wolter, Jürgen C. Ed. *The Dawning of American Drama: American Dramatic Criticism, 1746–1915.* Westport, CT: Greenwood Press, 1993.

Wurts, Richard. *The New York World's Fair 1939/1940.* New York: Dover, 1977.

Young, Harvey. "The Black Body as Souvenir in American Lynching." *Theatre Journal* 57.4 (December 2005): 639–657.

Articles

The Albion, A Journal of News, Politics and Literature, November 29, 1828.

"America Buying Freely of Dry Goods and Textiles." *Wall Street Journal*, April 26, 1909.

"Ancient Babylon's Fall." *The New York Times*, June 12, 1887.

"The Anglo-Japanese Exhibition of 1910." *Outlook 93.1* (1893–1924), September 4, 1909.

"Another Theatrical Combine." *The New York Times*, September 9, 1897.

"Arch Street Theatre." *Saturday Evening Post*, November 15, 1828.

"Architectural Exhibition at the Centennial." *Architect and Building News*, June 24, 1876.

"Art and Artists." *The New York Times*, November 7, 1896.

"Art at Philadelphia." *The New York Times*, May, 17, 1876.

"Art at the Exhibition." *Appleton's Journal of Literature, Science and Art*, June 3, 1876.

Aktinson, Edward. *New York Herald*, August 1880.

"Babylon's Fall." *The New York Times*, June 26, 1887.

"The Ballet Girls Struck." *The New York Times*, June 18, 1890.

"Banvard's Great Painting." *Trumpet and Universalist Magazine*, January 9, 1847.

"Banvard's Mammoth Panorama." *Liberator*, January 15, 1847.

"Banvard's Panorama." *Scientific American* 4.13 (December 16, 1848).

Barboza, David. "Hit Broadway Musicals to Be Exported to China." *New York Times*, September 18, 2007.

———. "660 Held in Tibetan Uprising, China Says." *The New York Times*, March 27, 2008a.

———. "Chinese TV Hits Jackpot with Games: The Hometown Olympics are Drawing Gigantic Audiences and Revenue." *The New York Times*, August 22, 2008b.

———. "Gritty Renegade Now Directs China's Close-Up." *The New York Times*, August 7, 2008c.

———. "Pressed on Tibet, China Berates Foreign Media." *The New York Times*, March 25, 2008d.

Bingham, John. "Beijing Olympics: Zhang Yimou, The Director Behind the Opening Ceremony." *The Telegraph*, August 8, 2008.

"Block-Long Diorama to Be Built at Fair." *The New York Times*, May 15, 1938.

"Boer War Spectacle, Coney Island's Newest Show." *The New York Times*, May 21, 1905.

"Bolossy Tells His Side." *The New York Times*, August 22, 1888.

"Books and Authors." *Christian Union*, June 25, 1892.

Borenstein, Seth. "Panel: NASA Nasa Should Skip Moon, Fly Elsewhere." *U.S. News & World Report*, October 22, 2009.

Brooklyn Eagle, August 19, 1883.

"Buffalo Bill's Good-bye." *The New York Times*, April 1, 1887.

"Burford's Panorama of Jerusalem." *Museum of Foreign Literature, Science, and Art*, August 1835.

"Catherwood's Panoramas." *The Albion, A Journal of News, Politics and Literature*, May 30, 1840.

"The Centennial." *The New York Times*, February 22, 1872.

"Centennial Anniversary." *The New York Times*, April 23, 1873.

"Centennial Anniversary Building Plan." *The New York Times*, October 25, 1873.

"The Centennial Exposition." *The New York Times*, December 5, 1873.

"Centennial Exposition Memoranda." *Potter's American Monthly*, May 1876.

"The Centennial Fair." *New York Tribune*, May 17, 1876.

Chang, Kenneth. "Boeing Plans to Fly Tourists to Space." *The New York Times*, September 15, 2010.

———. "Private Rocket's First Flight Is a Success." *The New York Times*, June 5, 2009a.

———. "Signs of Plentiful Water are Found Below Moon's Stony Face." *The New York Times*, May 27, 2011.

———. "Satellite Found Water on Moon, Researchers Say." *The New York Times*, November 14, 2009b.

———. "Two Bull's-Eyes in Test of Water on the Moon." *The New York Times*, October 10, 2009c.

Charleston Daily Courier. January 3, 1859.

"Chicago's Summer Spectacle." *The New York Times*, June 3, 1892.

"The Chilean Exposition." *New York Tribune*, April 15, 1876.

"China." *New York Times*, June 6, 1868.

"The Chinese Problem." *Zion's Herald*, April 20, 1876.

"Church's Niagara." *New York Daily Times*, May 21, 1857.

"Church Painting." *The Catholic Telegraph*, February 18, 1836.

"The Cincinnati Festival." *The New York Times*, September 7, 1883.

"City and Suburban News." *The New York Times*, April 3, 1888.

"Colorado and the Cañon: Prof. Albert S. Bickmore's Lecture at the American Museum of Natural History." *The New York Times*, January 30, 1898.

"Commercial Relations." *The New York Times*, August 23, 1875.

"Conservation Exhibit Ready in Washington." *The New York Times*, March 9, 1938.

"Consolidated Edison to Tell Utility's Story with Dramatic Exhibit." *Wall Street Journal*, March 31, 1939.

"The Copper Union." *Harper's Weekly*, March 30, 1861.

"Correspondence." *Literary World*, October 20, 1849.

Cotter, Holland. "Stand Still a Spectacle Will Happen." *The New York Times*, April 18, 2008.

"The Cotton Centennial Exhibition at New Orleans." *The American Architect and Building News*, April 11, 1885.

"The Crescent City's World's Fair." *New York Tribune*, December 16, 1884.

Dickens, Charles. "Some Account of an Extraordinary Traveller." *Household Words*, April 20, 1850.

"Dinosaur Tracks Set Up in Museum." *The New York Times*, November 7, 1937.

"Dioramas Finished by WPA for Museum." *The New York Times*, July 18, 1937.

"Effect of the War in Europe on American Exports." *The New York Times*, December 23, 1870.

"Elliot C. Cowdin Dead." *The New York Times,* April 13, 1880.

"Emperor's Speech." *Harper's Weekly,* March 2, 1861.

"England Wants Nero." *The New York Times,* July 1, 1888.

"English Comments on the Centennial." *Christian Union,* June 7, 1876.

"Evolution of Man Shown in Exhibits." *The New York Times,* July 31, 1933.

"Fairmount Park." *The New York Times,* June 14, 1872.

"Fall of Babylon." *The New York Times,* June 17, 1887.

"The Fall of Babylon." *New York Evangelist,* July 21, 1887.

"The Fall of Rome." *The New York Times,* April 9, 1890.

"Farmer's Department." *New York Evangelist,* November 20, 1884.

"Father of the Waters." *The Youth's Companion,* December 14, 1849.

"Federal Show Aids Teachers." *New York Times,* July 23, 1939.

"The Fine Arts." *New York Mirror, or a Weekly Gazette of Literature and the Fine Arts,* August 23, 1834.

"The Fort Lyon Affair." *Rocky Mountain News,* December 30, 1864.

"Forty-Second Congress." *The New York Times,* February 23, 1873.

"From Our Special Correspondent." *Spirit of the Times,* May 11, 1850.

"Funds for the Centennial." *The New York Times,* August 28, 1873.

"General Intelligence." *Christian Advocate and Journal,* August 16, 1849.

———. *Christian Register,* November 2, 1850.

"Gettysburg Again on View." *The New York Times,* December 24, 1887.

"Government and the Centennial." *The New York Times,* August 2, 1873.

Gray, Richard. "Opening of Spaceport's First Runway Brings Space Tourism." *The Telegraph,* October 23, 2010.

"The Great Centennial Exhibition." *Arthur's Home Magazine,* August 1876.

"The Great Exhibition." *Gody's Arm-Chair,* June 1876a.

———. *The Independent,* May 18, 1876b.

———. *The New York Times,* June 4, 1876c.

Greenemeier, Larry. "Space Cadets, Grab Your Sunscreen: Space Tourism Set to Liftoff." *Scientific American,* March 27, 2008.

"Hagenbeck Trained Animals." *The New York Times,* October 7, 1894.

"Hit Broadway Musicals to Be Exported to China." *The New York Times,* September 18, 2007.

Hornaday, W. T. "The Extermination of Wild Animals," *The Chautauquan,* December 1889.

"Hudson's Panorama." *Christian Secretary,* July 28, 1848.

"Imre Kiralfy Sued." *The New York Times,* September 25, 1888.

"Imre Kiralfy's Work." *Dallas Morning News,* June 15, 1919.

"Jeancon, State Museum Curator Talks to Rotary Club on Cliff Dwellings." *Littleton Independent,* November 3, 1922.

"John Banvard, the American Artist." *The Eclectic Magazine of Foreign Literature,* December 1847.

"John Banvard's Great Picture: Life on the Mississippi." *Littell's Living Age,* December 11, 1847.

Kaempffert, Waldermar. "Vital Museums of the New Era." *The New York Times,* March 20, 1932.

"Kiralfy's Big Spectacle." *The New York Times,* June 24, 1888.

"Kiralfy Show for Panama Exposition." *The New York Times*, October 13, 1912.

"Large Territorial Acquisition." *The New York Times*, March 31, 1867.

Lee, Ivy. "A Horse that Lived a Million Years Ago." *The New York Times*, September 15, 1901.

"Lewis Panorama of the Mississippi River." *Western Journal of Agriculture, Manufacturers, Mechanics, Arts*, October 1849.

The Liberator. Letter to the Editor. November 16, 1855.

Life, September 20, 1888.

———. December 21, 1893.

"Little Rhinoceres [sic] that Once Roamed the Land." *The New York Times*, August 14, 1904.

"Machinery Put in Motion." *The New York Times,* July 5, 1988.

MacDonald, W. A. "Museum Links Circus to the Ark." *The New York Times*, April 17, 1938.

"The Magazine." *New York Daily Times*, July 30, 1853.

Magnier, Mark. "Chinese Sing was a Ringer Over Looks," *Pittsburgh Post*, August 13, 2008,.

Main Farmer, October 26, 1848.

"Making Great Preparations." *The New York Times*, June 23, 1887.

"Mammoth Cave of Kentucky." *Friends' Weekly Intelligencer*, September 1, 1849.

"Masks and Faces." *The National Police Gazette*, March 2, 1889.

"Matters in Chicago." *The New York Times*, January 21, 1894.

"May Finish Frieze of 'Michael Angelo of the Capitol.'" *The Sun*, March 22, 1914.

McPhee, Mike. "Museum's Plan to Move Fragile Denver Diorama a Model of Care." *The Denver Post*, November 28, 2009.

"Merchant's Banquet." *The New York Times,* May 2, 1873.

"Mexico." *The New York Times*, September 8, 1873.

"Mr. Gilmore's Plans," *The New York Times*, April 10, 1887.

"Mr. Hammerstein's Complaint." *The New York Tribune,* October 7, 1894.

Napoleon III. "Opening Day Speech," July 1, 1867.

"The National Centennial." *The New York Times*, July 5, 1873.

"The Naturalization Law." *The Albany Law Journal: A Weekly Record of the Law and Lawyers*, July 1907.

"The Naturalization Problem." *The North American Review*, November 1892.

"Nero." *London Evening News and Post*, November 12, 1889.

"New Chinese Treaty with the United States." *The Albion, A Journal of News, Politics and Literature*, August 1, 1868.

"The New Citizenship Law." *The North American Review*, July 5, 1907.

"New History Set Ready for Schools." *The New York Times*, August 28, 1938.

"New Jersey Items." *New York Daily Tribune*, November 20, 1850.

"A New National Museum: The Building to Be Erected in Washington." *The New York Times*, November 16, 1879.

"The New Orleans Centennial Exposition, No. II. *Friends' Weekly Intelligencer*, June 17, 1885.

"New Orleans Exhibition Building." *Southern Planter*, August 1884.

"New Orleans or San Francisco." *New York Times*, July 26, 1911.

"A New Route to Philadelphia." *The Independent*, May 4, 1876.

"The New World's Fair." *New York Tribune*, May 10, 1876.

"Niagara." *The Albion, A Journal of News, Politics and Literature*, October 7, 1826.

Noel, Tom. "Building a Monument to History." *Denver Post*, May 23, 2010.

"No Nonsense Tolerated at Nero." *The New York Times*, August 22, 1888.

"North China Trade." *Merchants' Magazine and Commercial Review*, August 1, 1867.

"Official Report of the Battle of Sand Creek." *Rocky Mountain News*, January 3, 1865.

Ohnsman, Alan. "Elon Musk Anticipates Third IPO in Three Years." *Bloomsburg Business Week*, February 25, 2012.

"Opening the Chambers, The Domestic and Foreign Policy of the Empire." *The New York Times*, February 20, 1860.

Overbye, Dennis. "Offering Funds, U. S. Agency Dreams of Sending Humans to Stars." *The New York Times*, August 18, 2011.

"The Pacific Slope." *New York Tribune*, March 27, 1910.

"A Painting Three Miles Long." *Dwights American Magazine*, October 16, 1847a.

"A Painting Three Miles Long." *Littell's Living Age*, September 25, 1847b.

"The Panorama," *Parley's Magazine,* January 1, 1838.

"Panorama." *The Time Piece and Literary Companion*, November 29, 1797.

"Panorama of Athens." *Christian Register*, 1821.

"Panorama of Mexico." *Atkinson's Saturday Evening Post*, June 15, 1833.

"Panorama of the Mississippi." *Christian Watchman*, December 25, 1846.

"Panorama of Slavery." *The Independent*, June 20, 1850.

"Panorama of Slavery." *Liberator*, August 5, 1853.

"Panorama of Versailles," *Boston Centinel*, April 18, 1827a.

"Panorama of Versailles." *Zion's Herald*, August, 8 1827b.

Paulding, James K. "The Mississippi." *Graham's Magazine*, April 1843.

"Pennsylvania." *New York Times*, June 9, 1873.

Picayune, December 7, 1848.

"Picture of Niagara in Europe-Art in America." *The New York Times*, August 22, 1857.

"Pleased with their Success."*The New York Times*, February 14, 1889.

"Program Mapped to Draw Tourists." *The New York Times*, December 13, 1937.

"Pueblos of Cliff Dwellers Yield Bones and Relics." *The New York Times,* October 18, 1925.

Rice, Dana. "In the Hall of the North American Birds." Sunday Magazine. *New York Times,* November 24, 1929.

Rindal, Ray Mark. "Colorado History Museum Learns from Its Own Past." *Denver Post* April 22, 2012.

"Rome Upon Rails." *The New York Times*, June 8, 1888.

"Roosevelt Lauds Conservation Aid." *The New York Times*, February 24, 1937.

Sealover, Ed. "Colorado History Museum Plans Higher Profile in New Home." *Denver Business Journal*, April 24, 2009.

"Scenic Artists Cite Plan." *The New York Times*, November 11, 1937.

Scientific American March 28, 1863.

Shaw, Helen. "Images at the Speed of Sound." *Time Out New York*, October 1–7, 2009.

Sherwood, E. W. "Frederic E. Church: Studio Gathers Thirty Years Ago." *The New York Times*, April 21, 1900.

"Show Opens Today of Food Industries." *The New York Times*, October 11, 1931.

"The Significance of the Visit of Japanese Business Men." *The Wall Street Journal*, October 9, 1909.

Smith, Eli. "Panorama of Jerusalem." *The New York Observer and Chronicle*, May 9, 1840.

Spencer, Richard. "Beijing Olympics: Faking Scandal Over Girl Who 'Sang' in Opening Ceremony." *The Telegraph*, August 12, 2008.

"Staten Island Attractions." *The New York Times*, April 24, 1887.

"The State's History." *Denver Daily Tribune*, February 11, 1879.

"Stockwell's Panorama." *Spirit of the Times*, January 7, 1849a.

"Stockwell's Panorama." *Spirit of the Times*, June 19, 1849b.

"Sufferings of Col. Fremont and Party among the Rocky Mountains." *Friends' Weekly Intelligencer*, May 19, 1849.

"Summer at St. George." *The New York Times*, April 25, 1888.

"Taking the Mississippi." *The Huntress*, December 16, 1848a.

"Taking the Mississippi." *Spirit of the Times*, October 7, 1848b.

"Taking the Mississippi." *Weekly Reveille*, November 4, 1848c.

"TheTariff Debate in the House." *The New York Times*, May 29, 1892.

"Theatrical Gossip." *The New York Times*, March 10, 1887.

"Theatrical Gossip." *The New York Times*, July 9, 1888.

"Theatrical Gossip." *The New York Times*, September 8, 1894.

"Things Theatrical." *Spirit of the Times*, June 10, 1848.

"Three Cities Want the Panama Fair." *The New York Times*, May 8, 1910.

Tighe, Josephine Gillenwater. "Brumidi, the Michael Angelo of the Capitol." *The Washington Herald*, September 4, 1910.

"To Protect the Wild Birds." *The New York Times*, November 12, 1897.

"To Speak English Aliens' First Duty." *The New York Times*, August 24, 1915.

"To Save the Mesa Verde." *The New York Times*, August 25, 1901.

"A Trip to Niagara." *The New York Mirror, or a Weekly Gazette of Literature and the Fine Arts*, November 22, 1828a.

"A Trip to Niagara." *The New York Mirror, or a Weekly Gazette of Literature and the Fine Arts*, December 20, 1828b.

Viveros-Fauné, Christian. "Kara Walker's Thrilling Whitney Retrospective: Riding the Racial High-Wire." *Village Voice*, October 16, 2007.

Walz, Jay. "Unfreezing a Frieze: A Capitol Eyesore May Presently Be Beautified." *The New York Times*, November 5, 1950.

"Washington." *The New York Times*, January 28, 1873.

"Washington." *The New York Times*, July 4, 1876.

"Watching Babylon Fall." *The New York Times*, June 19, 1887.

Weekly Museum, 1797.

Weekly Reveille, October 15, 1849.

Wendte, Charles W. "The Chinese Problem." *The Unitarian Review and Religious Magazine*, May 1876.

"Whaling Panorama." *Boston Atlas*, January 23, 1849.

White, Tom. "Our Parks in Diorama." *The New York Times*, June 18, 1939.

"Woman Suffrage." *The New York Times*, October 14, 1873.

"The Women's Auxiliary Centennial Commission." *New York Tribune*, August 8, 1873.

"Women's Centennial Union." *The New York Times*, February 23, 1876.

"A Wonderful Spectacle." *The New York Times*, July 17, 1887.

"The World's Exposition: The Attendance Yesterday Greater Than for Some Time Past." *New Orleans Times-Democrat*, January 19, 1885.

"WPA Funds a Help to Many Museums." *The New York Times*, September 5, 1937.

Yardley, Jim. "China Tightens Security on Tibet Monks After Protest." *The New York Times*, March 24, 2008.

Yardley, Jim and David Barboza. "Games in Beijing Open with a Lavish Ceremony," *The New York Times*, August, 9 2008.

Video

Burns, Ken. *The National Parks: America's Best Idea*. DVD. PBS Home Video. 2009.

"The Colorado Historical Society's Dioramas." Rocky Mountain PBS. October 23, 2009.

Eliasson, Olafur. *Space is Process*. Documentary. DVD. 2009

Walker, Kara Elizabeth. *Art21: Art in the 21st Century*. DVD. PBS Home Video. 2003.

Index

Printed in the United States of America